THE SLAPSTICK QUEENS

THE SLAPSTICK QUEENS

by

JAMES ROBERT PARISH

Editor:
T. Allan Taylor

Research Associates:
John Robert Cocchi, Florence Solomon

SOUTH BRUNSWICK AND NEW YORK: A. S. BARNES AND COMPANY
LONDON: THOMAS YOSELOFF LTD

A. S. Barnes and Co., Inc.
Cranbury, New Jersey 08512

Thomas Yoseloff Ltd
108 New Bond Street
London W1Y OQX, England

Library of Congress Cataloging in Publication Data

Parish, James Robert.
  The slapstick queens.

  Includes lists of films.
  1. Actresses, American—Biography. 2. Comedy films.
I. Title.
PN1998.A2P4   790.2′092′2   71-37815
ISBN 0-498-01007-4

Printed in the United States of America

To
Kate Smith
The First Lady of Song

Kate Smith

CONTENTS

PREFACE

Why this book? Simply because these five multi-talented screen personalities have been too long taken for granted by critics, the public, and by entertainment historians. Their expansive contributions to the cinema and other media are enormous and worthy of recital and appraisal.

James Robert Parish
New York City, January 2, 1972

ACKNOWLEDGMENTS

Gene Andrewski
DeWitt Bodeen
Bruco Enterprises
Cinemabilia Book Shop (Ernest Burns)
Jane Danziger
Howard Davis
Film Fan Monthly (Leonard Maltin)
Ray Gain
Richard M. Hudson
Ken D. Jones
Kenneth G. Lawrence Movie Memorabilia
Doug McClelland
Albert B. Manski

Alvin H. Marill
Peter Miglierini
Norman Miller
Movie Poster Service (Bob Smith)
Saturday Review (Hollis Alpert)
Screen Facts (Alan G. Barbour)
Mrs. Peter Smith
Variety
The Village Voice
Special thanks to Paul Myers and the staff of the Theatre Collection, Lincoln Center Library for the Performing Arts.

ABOUT THE CONTRIBUTORS

T. ALLAN TAYLOR, the godson of the late Margaret Mitchell, was born in Greenwich Village, attended Wesleyan University, and is currently production manager at Engineering Index. He has functioned as manuscript editor on *The Fox Girls,* and the forthcoming *The Paramount Pretties,* and *Good Dames.* Mr. Taylor is also critique contributor on classical music to various record journals.

Since the age of five, thirty-two year old Brooklynite, JOHN ROBERT COCCHI has been viewing and collating data on motion pictures and is now regarded as one of the most energetic film researchers in the United States. Professionally he is the chief film reviewer for Boxoffice magazine. He was research associate on *The American Movies Reference Book, The Fox Girls, The Cinema Of Edward G. Robinson* and many other volumes, as well as having written cinema history articles for such journals as *Film Fan Monthly* and *Screen Facts.*

T. Allan Taylor

John Robert Cocchi

New York-born FLORENCE SOLOMON attended Hunter College and then joined Ligon Johnson's copyright research office. Later she was appointed director for research at Entertainment Copyright Research Co., Inc. and is currently a reference supervisor at A.S.-C.A.P. Index Division. Miss Solomon has collaborated on such works as *The American Movies Reference Book, TV Movies,* and *The Great Movie Series.* She is the niece of the noted late sculptor Sir Jacob Epstein.

Florence Solomon

THE SLAPSTICK QUEENS

MARJORIE MAIN

5'5"
145 pounds
Blue eyes
Brown hair
Birth Sign: Pisces

Marjorie Main is most closely associated with her ripsnorting screen characterization of lovable Ma Kettle —the bumpkin farm wife with fifteen unruly kids and one pathetically lazy husband. In her *Kettle* antics, she combined the hilarious crudeness of hillbilly gaucheries with the sensitivities of a well-meaning mother and a concerned citizen. Like Marie Dressler before her, she made you laugh one moment and be on the verge of tears the next. If stuck with a threadbare old slapstick routine, she gave it new life with her galvanized-iron cracking voice, bouncing walk, and he-man strength. When pathos was required, she would subtly lift an eyebrow or briefly pause in her non-stop flow of chatter. It is at this time one becomes aware of the intense humanness of this gruff diamond in the ruff.

In twenty-seven years of filmmaking, Marjorie created a gallery of many other distinct personalities. She took stereotyped roles thrust at her and instilled them with individuality, giving her prison matron, Dead End mother, bristling domestic or Wallace Beery girlfriend parts added dimension and believability. Watching Marjorie was viewing a slice of life.

One of the key ingredients to Marjorie's cinema success was her ability to capture the essence of middle America womanhood. Her rugged appearance blended into any genre of story or any century portrayed on the big screen. More so than fellow character stars Anne Revere, Beulah Bondi, Agnes Moorehead, or Spring Byington, Marjorie represented the core of American life. Audiences recognized this and accepted her as such.

It is to be regretted that Marjorie chose to retire in 1957 after making eighty-five films. She has left a gap in the entertainment world still unfilled—that of the mother figure able to stand on her own and show everybody a thing or two about the real values of life.

Marjorie Main (nee: Mary Tomlinson) was born February 24, 1890, near Acton, Indiana, the daughter of Reverend Samuel Joseph Tomlinson and Mary (McGaughey) Tomlinson.

Reverend Tomlinson was pastor of the First Christian Church and saw to it that his daughter had a strict upbringing. He was very fond of Charles Dickens and would indulge himself on occasion by reading aloud to the family from the author's works. These rare moments of demonstrative behavior deeply impressed Marjorie. Mrs. Tomlinson frequently told her daughter: "I hope some of Mr. Dickens' characters are in heaven. Else Father will never be happy there."

Marjorie carried the art of recitation one step further. At home, she would often burst forth with a brief bit of dynamic oratory, much to the surprise of any visitors at hand, and the deep chagrin of her ultra-conservative father. Once, when Reverend Tomlinson imported "The Jubilee Singers" choristers for the benefit of his congregation, Marjorie was so taken with the performance that she informed her father: "Don't try to stop me, pop. I'm a Hoosier too."

About those days, Marjorie recalls: "I got my first dramatic training under the guise of elocution, a term which covered a multitude of so-called sinful things in my youth." It was at her grammar school commencement that she made her first public appearance, reciting "The Light From Over The Range." It was, remembers Marjorie, ". . . a blood-and-thunder cowboy piece that ended with a fanfare of organ music and dissolved the audience into buckets of tears." It was midst the excitement of projecting this oratory that Marjorie happened upon the gravelly, piercing voice which later became her trademark. "I got it accidentally. . . . My voice stepped up several gears. The effect was startling, even to me. . . . The audience grew tenser, mouths opened. I had them and the voice had me! It screeched on and on, with virtually no effort on my part. I couldn't have let the darn thing back down to a normal tone; that would have made my recitation suddenly ridiculous. So, I let 'er go, right on to the end, with all I had, and sat down to thunderous applause. I had discovered what they called here in Hollywood 'socko.' "

Later on, when Marjorie won first prize in an oratory contest, the practical-minded girl tried to sell the $15 gold watch for the $5 gold piece, the second prize.

Marjorie attended Franklin College, Franklin, Indiana (she later would receive an honorary degree from the institution). By now, Marjorie was more than intrigued by the theatre, although her father had never permitted her to attend any professional performances. He did allow her to attend Hamilton School of Dramatic Expression at Lexington, Kentucky, a church-endowed institution. Said Marjorie: "I did not know what I wanted to achieve by going there, but thought it would help me find a way to express myself." It was at Hamilton that Marjorie first got a taste of social life, and started attending parties. As she recalls: ". . . the girls (there) taught me that a gal has to have 'something' to get along with the boys."

After completing the three-year course in 1909, Marjorie obtained a position at Bourbon College in Paris, Kentucky, as a dramatics instructor. She got the job on the strength of her photograph, which she had sent on to the administrator. She later reminisced: "There were three applicants and my picture won. If that doesn't show there's such a thing as fate, then what could? You've seen my picture, of course." She was fired at the end of the first year when she demanded a salary raise.

After further studies of dramatic art in Chicago and New York, Marjorie landed a position with the Chautauqua lecture circuit, giving short readings from Dickens and Shakespeare. She was paid $18 weekly. After a year, she was being paid $25 weekly, and performing in assorted playlets presented by the company.

She next joined a stock company in Fargo, North

Dakota, where she remained for more than five months. Then she graduated to the vaudeville circuit. About this time, she changed her name: "I didn't want to use my family's name on the stage because I knew they disapproved. The name I chose was my idea of a name easy to remember."

Marjorie appeared in the road company of *Cheating Cheaters* in 1916, which starred John Barrymore. By 1918, she was featured in "Yes Or No" on Broadway at the 48th Street Theatre, having replaced leading lady Adrienne Morrison.

Back in vaudeville, she linked up with W. C. Fields in a popular skit entitled *The Family Ford* which played the Palace Theatre several times in the late teens.

Then Marjorie met Dr. Stanley LeFeire Krebs, 57, a lecturer and psychologist. He had earlier set up the curriculum at American University in Washington, D.C., and taught there from 1907–1911. He was noted for his academic courses in personality development and the art of good salesmanship. Marjorie and Krebs, a widower with a grown daughter, married November 2, 1921. During the next four years, Marjorie virtually abandoned the theatre to tour with Krebs, assisting him by making booking arrangements on the road, and by answering his hefty correspondence. She regards this period of her life as the most fruitful and happiest. Marjorie has said: "Doctor was a creative man, always writing. We didn't need anyone else. We had each other." About his wisdom: "I learned a great deal about people from my husband. An understanding of people is essential to any actor worth his salt."

Whenever their tours ended, they would return to New York. Marjorie would seek work in the theatre, as in *House Divided,* which opened at the Punch and Judy Theatre, November 11, 1923. It lasted one performance. In the late 1920s, the Krebs's moved back to Manhattan permanently, and Marjorie devoted herself to the stage full time. She played Mae West's burlesque queen mother in "The Wicked Age," which opened at Daly's 63rd Street Theatre, November 4, 1927. The saucy play by West dealt with a beauty contest winner who is living the easy life, making huge sums of money for her endorsement of assorted products. Said one reviewer of Marjorie's colorful role as Mrs. Martha Carson: ". . . (she) fills her tights well." The show only lasted twenty-seven performances. Then Marjorie had a character role in "Salvation" which opened at the Empire Theatre, January 31, 1928. The Sidney Howard–Charles MacArthur play starred Pauline Lord as a meddlesome soul saver.

When the road company of the Broadway success

Burlesque was formed in 1929, Marjorie went on the tour with Barbara Stanwyck and Hal Skelly.

Marjorie made her inauspicious film debut in the screen version of *A House Divided,* which was released by Universal on December 5, 1931. Directed by William Wyler (her favorite director), the movie starred Walter Huston in a *They Knew What They Wanted* type story, set on a gloomy New England island. Marjorie had a bit as a local townswoman. Douglass Montgomery essayed Huston's son, who also loves the new hired girl Helen Chandler. In Paramount's *Hot Saturday* (1932), a story of how small-town gossip almost ruins the life of Nancy Carroll, Marjorie was briefly spotted as a loquacious gossip. Each was just a quick bit that paid a few bills and gave her a brief introduction to movie making.

Back on Broadway, Marjorie had an effective minor role as the servant Anna in the Jerome Kerns–Oscar Hammerstein II musical, *Music in the Air,* which debuted at the Alvin Theatre, November 8, 1932. Walter Slezak, Al Shean and Tullio Carminati were starred. The show was very popular, and ran for well over a year.

Marjorie, meanwhile, continued her film career with two made-in-New York productions. *Take a Chance* (1933), based on the 1932 Broadway musical, starred Jimmy Dunn, Charles ("Buddy") Rogers, Lillian Roth and June Knight. Roth, in the role Ethel Merman had played on stage, sang "Eadie Was A Lady." The rather limp film concerned a trio of small-time crooks attempting to go straight by working in Greenwich Village. Marjorie had a brief screen moment as a woman in the crowd. The musical was shot at Eastern Service Studio at Long Island City. Nobody took much notice of the film when it was released.

Crime Without Passion (1933) was the inspired effort of Charles MacArthur and Ben Hecht, concerning a hotshot criminal lawyer (Claude Rains) whose unbounding ego and jealousy leads him into committing the "perfect crime." Filmed at the Astoria Studios on Long Island, Marjorie had an unbilled bit; she appeared in a few crowd scenes. This drama has long been a favorite with film societies, and is constantly revived for study.

Then Marjorie was signed by Fox to re-create her stage role in *Music in the Air,* which marked another of Gloria Swanson's seasonal movie comebacks. While waiting for production to start, she did a small bit in Paramount's two reel short subject *New Deal Rhythm.* Subtitled "A Musical Novelty Illustrating the Spirit of Today," it had delegates from all over the United States convene, and sing the title song. Marjorie was the Arizona delegate, and joined in vocalizing a few stanzas. Others in the cast were: Charles ("Buddy") Rogers and tiny tot Shirley Temple.

Music in the Air premiered at Radio City Music Hall, December 13, 1934, and was far from the success of its original. The filmed operetta had lost much of the whimsy so needed to smooth out the retelling of the love tale between prima donna Swanson employed in Munich and her blasé actor boyfriend, John Boles. Most of Marjorie's role as the domestic ended up on the cutting room floor. This film is remembered, if at all, for historical value: it kept Swanson off the screen again for seven years.

She returned to New York in early 1935 to be with her husband, then ailing. They resided at the Hotel Langwell, 123 West 44th Street. She accepted work in *Jackson White,* which had a brief run at the Provincetown Playhouse. It was a story of "elemental passion" by David Balch. Said Brooks Atkinson in *The New York Times:* "Marjorie Main, Frank McCormack, and John Galedon could not do much more with the parts they have."

Dr. Krebs, 71, died September 27, 1935, of cancer at St. Luke's Hospital. Besides Marjorie, he was survived by his daughter, Mrs. Annabelle Colderwell of New York. At the time of this last illness, he had been researching a new book on sexual psychology. His death, Marjorie recalls: ". . . was the low point of my life. I was broken-hearted and desperately needed work as much to occupy my mind as to make a living."

To take her mind off her sorrow, Marjorie auditioned for and obtained the role of Mrs. Martin in Sidney Kingsley's *Dead End.* She was the contemptuous mother of the despicable gangster, Joseph Downing. Percy Hammond in the *New York Herald-Tribune* praised her: "In a scene remarkably played by Miss Marjorie Main, as the mother, she curses him (Downing) with quiet vehemence and strikes him in the face." Robert Garland in the *New York World Telegram* noted: "But none rise to quite the smoldering intensity of Marjorie Main's Mrs. Martin, the mother of a gunman and a soul in torment."

Marjorie recalls: "When he (Krebs) died, I used to pour my sorrow on the audience night after night as the mother in *Dead End* here on Broadway." Marjorie kept to herself most of the time.

After playing her part for 460 performances, Marjorie left this show to appear in Claire Luce's chic *The Women,* which debuted at the Ethel Barrymore Theatre on December 26, 1936. It toplined Ilka Chase, Margalo Gillmore, and Betty Lawford in a sharp account of bitchy rich women seeking amusement and fulfillment, with and without spouses; Marjorie played Lucy, the cynical Reno hotel keeper. She made her brief appearance in one act count, building her characterization with a loping gait, strident voice, and a breezy stage comedy personality.

Then Samuel Goldwyn signed Marjorie to appear in his film version of *Dead End*. When she arrived on the coast, the production was not quite ready for shooting, so she advised her agent to get her employment, of any kind, in any type of picture (a policy she would follow in the next few years). She appeared at Universal in *Love In A Bungalow* (1937). Leads Nan Grey and Kent Taylor pose as newlyweds to win a radio contest prize, and eventually agree to marry. Marjorie had a quick comedy moment as Miss Emma Bisbee, doing a shout and deaf routine with Margaret McWade, who played her sister. The *New York Times* noted: ". . . and the two pixillated Bisbee spinsters are played in grand style. . . ."

Dead End premiered at the Rivoli Theatre, August 24, 1937; it garnered exceptionally fine reviews. The screen version made few concessions to the raw drama of tenement life and its assortment of harried people. It featured Sylvia Sidney, Joel McCrea, and Wendy Barrie, with Humphrey Bogart as Baby Face Martin, the punk gangster returning home after ten years at large. Most critics agreed with the *New York Times* that: "Marjorie Main's flat-voiced hate as Martin's mother . . . [was] memorable." Humphrey Bogart later joked about the rehearsals of the mother–son scene, in which Marjorie yells "ya dirty yellow dog" as she slaps her killer son. He recalled that she could only do the scene, if done realistically; and before it was perfected, she "had slugged me raw-faced." The film also marked the first teaming of Marjorie and the Dead End Kids.

In *Stella Dallas* (1937), also for Goldwyn, Marjorie was sixth-billed as Mrs. Martin, wife of Edmund Elton, and mother of Barbara Stanwyck in this tale of Stanwyck's maternal sacrifices. Marjorie appeared briefly in the opening sequences.

Her fourth of six 1937 film releases was *The Man Who Cried Wolf* at Universal. Lewis Stone starred as a distinguished actor who continually confesses to murders, so that the police will ignore him when he actually kills a long-intended victim. His prey is Jameson Thomas, the man who years before ran off with his wife and son. Marjorie's role as Amelia Bradley, sister of the murdered man, was noted by *Variety:* ". . . [she] is a new and striking type with an interesting screen voice."

Her next effort was a programmer for Republic Pictures, *The Wrong Road,* which debuted on a double bill at the Fox Brooklyn on November 5, 1937. She was seventh-billed as Mrs. Foster, playing another thankless mother's role. The slight yarn, which received a two-and-one-half star *New York Daily News* review, was directed by James Cruze. It featured Richard Cromwell and Helen Mack as bank robbers who hide their loot, go to jail, and plan to live on easy street once released. But, of course they do not. The censors demanded crime could not be rewarded.

Marjorie's last 1937 production was in Columbia Pictures' *The Shadow*. Rita Hayworth was toplined in this quickie murder mystery dealing with a girl who inherits a trouble-plagued circus, haunted by a cloaked figure who murders too freely at will. Marjorie was Hayworth's well-wishing aunt, Hannah Gillespie.

In 1938, Marjorie had a rash of assignments at various studio lots. Her output of thirteen films, albeit mostly in small roles, gave her plenty of screen exposure and experience.

Ever since *Dead End,* Hollywood had been trying to repeat the success of its formula, with or without the use of the original Dead End Kids, and Marjorie was considered by producers to be a necessary adjunct to the well-being of such tales. Marjorie said not long ago: "I got so tired of playing a slum mother to one or another of the Dead End Kids."

Boy of the Streets, opening January 1, 1938 at New York's Globe Theatre, was a surprisingly good variation of the typical theme, especially when considered that it was produced by the ultra low-budget studio, Monogram Pictures. Marjorie was Mary Brennan, the mother-drudge of Jackie Cooper in this tale which had the "authentic flavor of alleyways." Cooper was the leader of a gang of thugs on the lower east side, who eventually straightens himself out and enlists in the Navy. The film was publicized as "Dead End in working clothes: Dead End without any make-up . . ." *The New York Post's* Archer Winsten penned: "Jackie [Cooper]'s parents are beautifully realized in the performances of Guy Usher and Marjorie Main."

City Girl (1938) found Marjorie as the bedraggled mother of Phyllis Brooks. The story was a hastily contrived melodrama in which Brooks tangles with a hoodlum, commits manslaughter, and is eventually killed. It played the bottom half of a double bill at the Palace Theatre with *Tovarich*. *Penitentiary* (1938) was a poor remake of *The Criminal Code* (1931). Marjorie was Katie Matthews, wife of District Attorney Walter Connolly, now warden of the state prison, and mother of Jean Parker. In *King of the Newsboys* (1938) she was Mrs. Stephens, wife of Oscar O'Shea in a slum tale of poor boy Lew Ayres, who rises to become a big city power.

Marjorie was then cast in a prestige production,

Test Pilot (1938), at MGM, and turned in a seasoned performance. The glossy movie starred Clark Gable as a test pilot who crash lands in a Kansas wheatfield while on a transcontinental plane race, and meets college graduate Myrna Loy. The two fall in love, marry, and she has a child. Spencer Tracy enacted Gable's flight pal, who is killed in a crash. Marjorie's characterization was a good change of pace; she was a quizzical landlady who is a spectator to the on-again, off-again romance of Gable and Loy. The well-mounted film received additional publicity when the widow of pilot Jimmy Collins sued the studio over its use of the film's title, claiming it was the same name that was used for her husband's prior book of flight reminiscences. The case was settled out of court.

Prison Farm (1938) at Paramount saw Marjorie adapt to another soon-to-be typical role for her. She was matron Brand, the stern custodian, in the story of naive Shirley Ross, who is tricked by her boyfriend, Lloyd Nolan, into assisting on a criminal caper. They both are caught and sent to a prison farm, where she falls in love with doctor John Howard. Veteran silent film stars Anna Q. Nilsson and Mae Busch took the bulk of acting honors in this superficially written melodrama.

Romance of the Limberlost (1938), another screen adaptation of Gene Stratton Porter's *Girl of the Limberlost,* had Marjorie third-billed as Nora. She is the cantankerous old aunt of Jean Parker, the orphaned swampland girl. Marjorie's role calls for her to demand that Parker marry villainous Edward Paley. When the latter is accidentally killed, Parker falls in love with Eric Linden, the attorney defending the innocent defendant, Hollis Jewel. The film was publicized as "Not just characters from a famous story . . . but real people who live!" In her three-star review for the *New York Daily News,* Dorothy Masters wrote: "Marjorie Main, nothing short of superb in a difficult, unsympathetic role. . . ." The *New York Journal-American* penned, ". . . acting honors going to Marjorie Main." Years later, Marjorie remarked to an interviewer that another cast member had advised her to play the courtroom scene for all it was worth. She did so; but later realized it would have been more effective if she had listened to her intuition and handled it more subdued.

Marjorie was Mrs. Boylan, the nagging mother of Billy Halop, in *Little Tough Guy* (1938), another rubber stamp copy of *Crime School* and *Dead End.* She enacted the lazy, prodding wife who instigates husband Edward Pawley's downfall by pushing him to become a strike breaker. This sets into motion the family's run of bad luck. *Variety* observed: "Marjorie Main contributes her familiar acid mother characterization."

In *Under the Big Top* (1938) at Monogram, Marjorie had the colorful role of Sara, the weather-beaten owner of the seedy Post Circus, which is facing hard times. When she takes in Anne Nagel and has her taught to be a great aerialist, a love triangle develops between the girl and brothers Jack LaRue and Grant Richards. Marguerite Tazelaar in the *New York Herald-Tribune* complimented: "The acting is of one piece, in its similarity to that of most melodramas, with the exception of Marjorie Main, who gives an unusual personality to the dominative circus owner. . . ." Since the story covered a span of years, it offered Marjorie the opportunity to age on screen, and to present a contrasting characterization.

Too Hot to Handle (1938) returned Marjorie to MGM and another role in a Clark Gable "A" film. Gable and Walter Pidgeon play rival newsreel cameramen, both in love with aviatrix Myrna Loy. There were excellent vignettes by supporting players Leo Carrillo as Gable's cameraman assistant and Walter Connolly as the newsreel company boss. *Variety* noted: ". . . Marjorie Main is agreeably acid as Connolly's philosophical secretary (Miss Wayne)."

Girls' School (1938), a B picture quickie, offered Marjorie as Miss Armstrong, a prim faculty member at Magnolia Hall, where poor girl Anne Shirley has matriculated on a scholarship. Before the finale, Shirley proves she is worthy of her upper crust classmates, who have been snubbing her all along.

United Artists' *There Goes My Heart* (1938) was a piece of fluff starring Virginia Bruce as an heiress on the run from her grandfather. She is romanced by reporter Frederic March, and befriended by salesgirl Patsy Kelly, who gets her a department store job. Marjorie received good notices for her "delightful sequence" with Bruce, in which she appears as an exasperated customer who eventually demonstrates the virtues of a pressure cooker to inexperienced employee Bruce. The movie received added publicity, when a citizen's chiropractic committee sued producer-director Hal Roach *et al.* for $100,000 damages, claiming that the screenplay was casting aspersions on their profession.

MGM's polished *Three Comrades* (1938), based on Erich Remarque's novel of pre-World War II Germany, featured Margaret Sullavan as the dying daughter of a once well-to-do family who marries Robert Taylor. In this piece of expensive sentimental propaganda, Marjorie was briefly seen as an old woman in the town.

Midst her filming schedule, Marjorie continued her radio work, and was a frequent featured player on *Fred Allen, Rudy Vallee, Edgar Bergen and Charlie McCarthy,* and other variety shows. Back in New York, she had had a semi-regular assignment on *The Gold-*

bergs, starring Gertrude Berg. She always enjoyed this medium, and deeply regretted its decline in later decades.

By 1939, Marjorie was a firm fixture in Hollywood's entourage of leading featured players. She was a very familiar face to filmgoers; her name was becoming associated with that raucous, plain-featured, raspy-voiced middle America woman seen in a variety of screen roles. Her agent was able to pick lusher assignments for her in more lavish productions.

Marjorie's initial appearance that year was in MGM's *Lucky Night* (1939), in which penniless Robert Taylor marries skittish heiress Myrna Loy and is eventually cowered into taking a job to support his loving wife. Marjorie portrayed the rental agent who assists the newlyweds in finding an apartment. The *New York Herald-Tribune* thought she and the other character performers ". . . contribute[d] realism to a production which could have stood for a lot more."

They Shall Have Music (1939) was noteworthy for Jascha Heifitz's screen debut, although the Samuel Goldwyn production lacked a strong enough storyline to properly back up the violinist's virtuoso playing. The plot attempted to weave together a noble story of slum kids taking music lessons at Professor Walter Brennan's school, and the inevitable staging of the big charity show. As Mrs. Miller, wife of Arthur Hohl, Marjorie was one of the slum mothers who band together to keep the police from interrupting the vital youth concert. One of the musically-talented girls in the cast was young Dolly Loehr, later known as Diana Lynn.

Marjorie was signed by Warner Brothers to appear as slum-dweller Bernard Punsley's mother, Mrs. Arkelian, in *Angels Wash Their Faces* (1939), in which the Dead End Kids—now the Termite Boys Club of Beale Street—expose an arsonist when they take over City Hall during youth week. Her small role was notable for being her last assignment in this stereotyped part.

Marjorie joined MGM's luminous cast of *The Women* (1939), re-creating her no-nonsense role of realistic Lucy, the Reno hotel proprietor, who makes her living playing nursemaid to the scads of wealthy women awaiting their Nevada divorces. Marjorie said: "It was a fine part and I enjoyed playing Lucy for the screen as much as I had on the stage."

In *Another Thin Man* (1939), which continued the madcap adventures of amateur sleuths Nick and Nora Charles (William Powell and Myrna Loy), Marjorie brightened up her scenes as Mrs. Dolley who runs a frankly unrespectable boarding house. The *New York Times*'s Frank Nugent termed her ". . . our favorite biddy. . . ."

At RKO, Marjorie was in the low-budget *Two Thoroughbreds* (1939), as the unsympathetic, overly practical Aunt Hildegarde. Set in Arizona, the film told the story of sixteen-year-old orphan boy Jimmy Lydon, who comes to love a runaway prize horse. He discovers that his neighbors are not ogres after all, especially young Joan Leslie, the girl he soon loves.

I Take This Woman (1940) had been filmed in 1939, but Louis B. Mayer ordered most of it re-shot, changing the cast and plotline somewhat. Marjorie was in both versions. The critics thought the pain and expense poured into the production was wasted; the public accepted it as just another piece of tinsel coming off the MGM mass production line. Spencer Tracy enacted an over-earnest doctor who saves Hedy Lamarr from suicide in Yucatan; they marry, but she still nurses a love for philandering ex-boyfriend, Kent Taylor. Tracy is induced to leave his Lower East Side medical clinic to inaugurate a wealthy practice, hoping to reestablish his floundering marriage. Marjorie had a brief role as Gertie, a clinic nurse. The *New York Herald-Tribune* remarked: "Veree Teasdale, Louis Calhern and Marjorie Main take the show in their stride, as good character actors have a way of doing."

Marjorie reverted to familiar type in *Women Without Names* (1940), a minor Paramount film. She was prison matron Mrs. Lowry. Kate Cameron in her two and one-half star *New York Daily News* critique commented on: "Louise Beavers, Esther Dale and Marjorie Main [who] stand out in their minor roles."

Then Marjorie jumped over to Republic to fill out the cast of *Dark Command* (1940), which was that studio's lavish western epic for the year. It proved to be a well executed and expansive depiction of the career of Kansas marauder William Quantrill (Walter Pidgeon) on the loose at the time of the Civil War. Marjorie was his embittered mother, with John Wayne as the heroic marshal of Lawrence, Kansas, Claire Trevor was the daughter of the town banker who marries Pidgeon to spite Wayne, Roy Rogers was Trevor's brother who gets in a jam, and Gabby Hayes was the itinerant barker-dentist. Majorie had a memorable deathbed scene, which in a less fertile year might have netted her an Oscar nomination. Howard Barnes of the *New York Herald Tribune* thought Marjorie and the other character performers were ". . . fine in reproducing a vanished era in terms of human drama."

In her continual change of pace, Marjorie next appeared in the wacky *Turnabout* (1940) made for Hal Roach from Thorne Smith's popular story. Marjorie initiated another role stereotype that would recur throughout her career, that of a cook. Herein, she was the sourpuss kitchen domestic in the bizarre household of John Hubbard and Carole Landis. When the married couple have a tiff, each assumes the other's bodily form, retaining their own personality and voice. As always, Marjorie had the knack of interacting well with the other players: in this case, with Donald Meek, the butler. Roach was much impressed by her performance and would have offered her a long-term contract had not MGM grabbed up her services beforehand.

MGM's prestigious *Susan and God* (1940) derived from the stage hit, had Joan Crawford emoting in the Gertrude Lawrence role of a selfish Long Island socialite returning from Europe with a philosophy of "new thought" (do-goodism). Crawford nearly makes a shambles of everyone's life, including her husband Frederic March and her daughter Rita Quigley. George Cukor directed the chic drama. Marjorie in her small role as the gardener's wife was said by the *New York Times* ". . . [to] stand out in a competent cast. . . ."

The Captain Is a Lady (1940) was a minor MGM film, but a delightfully cast story of old sea captain Charles Coburn who sneaks into a ladies' retirement home to live with his wife, Beulah Bondi. By salvaging a floundering fishing schooner, he becomes a hero at the finale. As the cook-housekeeper, Marjorie made her presence well felt, probing new avenues to her stereotype as a domestic.

By now, Marjorie had her own legion of admirers across the country. One noted fan was Damon Runyon, who wrote about Marjorie in his syndicated column: "It is difficult to reconcile the name Marjorie with Marjorie Main's appearance, and her manner. She has a dead pan, square shoulders, a stocky build, a voice like a file, and an uncurried aspect. She has a stride like a section boss. She has bright, squinty eyes. She generally starts off looking as if she never smiled in her life, then suddenly she smiles from her eyes out."

Her last 1940 release, *Wyoming,* proved to be a very important venture in her continuing screen career. Set in the post-Civil War days, the western had Marjorie cast as Mehitabel, the rowdy village blacksmith who sets her cap on badman Wallace Beery. He has already plundered Missouri and is moving westward, one step ahead of the law. Both reviewers and audiences were highly enthusiastic of her boisterous portrayal.

Wanda Hale's three-star *New York Daily News* piece asserted: "Beery takes advantage of a lot of footage but he isn't the whole show, not when Marjorie Main is around. There's one thing Damon Runyon and I have in common—admiration for Miss Main. To me, she is the first picture stealer and the greatest picture saver in Hollywood. Here, she is as tough as a Cornell linesman. I've been waiting all these years

to see her whack Beery in the seat of the pants with a shovel." Robert W. Dane in the *New York Herald Tribune* was less enthusiastic: ". . . with a man's tongue and a stiff backbone . . . [she was] Beery's most effective foil, but even her performance has a tendency of getting out of joint now and then."

The scenes between Beery and Marjorie worked well, whether she was jibing the outlaw into a more honest mode of living or joshing him into romancing her. The two of them sitting in a haystack, hiding out from the authorities at the finale, with Beery blowing away on his harmonica, is capped in sentimental nostalgia when Marjorie wistfully proclaims: "There's a home in Wyoming." Leo Carrillo, Beery's outlaw cohort, provided an amusing bouncing board straight man for the shenanigans of the two courters. To fill out the action, there were Indian raids, a few shootouts, and the mawkishness of Beery's repeating his good-natured slob characterization first created for *The Champ* (1931). This time he is forced to show affection for the children of ranchers who are orphaned in the gun battle he started.

Louis B. Mayer and MGM were sure they had found a successor to the popular Beery-Marie Dressler comedy team of the early 1930s. Marjorie was quickly put under a seven-year contract. Marjorie recalls Mayer telling her: "I like everything about you except your name." She remembers that "we huddled but we both agreed it was too late to do anything about it." She was grateful that prestigious MGM had pulled her from the ranks of freelance players. Marjorie remarked in the early 1950s: "Guess I'd still be doing *Dead Ends* out in Hollywood if MGM hadn't been looking for a new gal friend for Wally Beery." At age fifty, Marjorie had arrived!

And Marjorie was ready to tell the press her theories on life: "Nobody can sharpen a knife on a smooth emery wheel. I'm better for the rough days." On preparing for a new role: "I never read the whole script. It would spoil the preview for me." On acting: "Character actors are best, I believe, when they portray characters that give them a chance to draw on their own experiences, backgrounds and observations. Imagine me trying to play a 'society woman!' " (she would). When queried about her striding walk that went along with her gravel-throated voice and confetti-like windblown hair, she stated: "I got it (the walk) from aggressive rural type women as a child in the Middle West. My dramatics teacher trained it out of me in college, but I put it right back when I got into pictures."

MGM kept their new character actress star busy in 1941. Marjorie appeared in six major films, in rather sizeable, meaty roles.

In *Wild Man of Borneo* (1941), based on an out-dated, trite 1920s play, Marjorie again appeared as an aggressive, no-nonsense cook in Billie Burke's civilized Manhattan boarding house. Frank Morgan was the ex-medicine show spieler who comes to New York to share in his daughter's supposed inheritance. He is forced to fabricate wild tales of being a renowned actor and world traveler to keep from paying rent or finding work. The *New York Daily News* pointed out: "Miss Main (as Irma) is the film's spice but even she isn't as funny as she usually is."

The Trial of Mary Dugan (1941) was a far less prestigious retelling of the studio's 1929 courtroom melodrama. Laraine Day had the title role of a re-formatory escapee who moves to Los Angeles to make a fresh start, falls in love with attorney Robert Young, and is later accused of murdering her lecherous boss, Tom Conway. As an anti-police landlady, Marjorie created another gem of a performance from a poten-tially standard role. In one courtroom scene, she is called upon to show the jury the position the corpse was in when she found it. Without batting an eyelash, she plunks herself down on the floor and assumes the pose of the dead body. Howard Barnes in the *New York Herald Tribune* praised: "The best impersona-tion in the show is that of a raucous landlady by Mar-jorie Main. It contributes touches of vitality to a show which might much better not have been resurrected." Her role here is one of Marjorie's all-time favorites.

Again working with director George Cukor and super star Joan Crawford, Marjorie was featured in the highly lauded *A Woman's Face* (1941). She was housekeeper Emma Kristiansdotter, renowned as the terror of Barring Hall, the Swedish estate owned by elderly Albert Basserman. Wearing a drab, black outfit, hair brushed back severely, and a scowl on her be-spectacled face, she was one of the menacing witnesses testifying in the homicide case involving ex-underworld figure Crawford. (Plastic surgeon Melvyn Douglas had repaired her fire-scarred face, but she was still tangled up in a murder plot with villain Conrad Veidt.)

Marjorie exerted intense concentration for this role. Her austere manner gave added dimension to her char-acterization as a domestic who recoils at seeing thirty-two years of unquestioned household authority usurped by the new governess (Crawford). Only briefly during her testimony scene does Marjorie lose her Germanic inflection, and let slip her midwestern accent. At the film's finale, she realizes that her meddling to protect her employer from Crawford has almost caused ir-reparable damage. She informs Crawford "I'm a silly old fool" and sadly marches from the courtroom, shaken loose from her lifetime of strict values.

Barnacle Bill (1941) continued the teaming of Mar-jorie and Beery. It was Beery's first waterfront picture since *Min and Bill* (1932) and was obviously pro-duced to re-create the flavor of that box-office champion. Donald Meek was Pop Cavendish, the San Pedro fish harbor storekeeper, whose forty-year-old daughter, Martha (Marjorie), takes a renewed fancy to Beery, the bankrupt owner of a small fishing boat, the *Monte-rey*. He had paid court to her eight years before, but skipped out after running up a huge bill in the family store. Now he is shining up to the spinster, hoping to wheedle money out of her for a new schooner. Connie Gilchrist (a veteran character actress who often por-trayed Marjorie's nemesis) was Marge of the local saloon, who also hankered after Beery. Virginia Weid-ler (who inherited the role originally planned for Shirley Temple) was Beery's daughter, who suddenly appears on the scene.

Marjorie and the girl join forces to reform no-good Beery, who has wangled the price of the new boat from her. Besides prodding him into marriage, Beery is coaxed—as always—to give up his excessive drinking and swearing and to assume his share of mature re-sponsibility. Alternately mean and sweet, Marjorie made the most of her role as a blowsy, seaside business woman. Once again, she had to contend with Beery's salty pal Leo Carrillo.

The critics were full of good words for Marjorie. The *New York Times* exclaimed: "Wallace Beery has found the perfect foil in Marjorie Main, all right. And, perhaps more than either he or his Metro bosses bar-gained for, as competition who comes close to stealing some of his best scenes. . . . It's a nip-and-tuck contest most of the way, and Mister Beery manages to dom-inate the screen, principally because he's the one around whom this trite tale about a lazy, albeit likeable, old soak revolves." Irene Thirer of the *New York Post* offered: "Miss Main who's really an attractive woman in spite of her slovenly get up, makes a vigorous foil for the bluff Beery." Another Manhattan film reviewer noted: "In her most vigorous moments, Miss Main is excellent, but she should force the scenarist who made her simper and be coy to walk the plank."

One of *Barnacle Bill*'s highlights occurs when Mar-jorie, Weidler and Beery attend church services, and Marjorie unabashedly raises her cracked voice in sing-ing the hymnal. More astute filmgoers noted that the schooner used in this film was the same *We're Here* utilized in the studio's *Captains Courageous* (1937) and that some of the squall sea storm scenes were lifted from the earlier MGM classic. MGM promoted *Barn-acle Bill* as "Ahoy! They're together again. . . . The Min and Bill of 1941."

For her full-bodied role, Marjorie's costuming consisted of two cotton housedresses, blue jeans, checkered shirts, and heavy boots. About her hog calling, buzz-saw voice, she informed reporters on the set of *Barnacle Bill:* "Of course, with this voice of mine, there's never any danger of having to worry about my looks. Glamor and this voice just won't work together."

According to Robert S. Dana in *The New York Herald Tribune:* "Apparently Metro has little intention of keeping the association (of the two leads) in other pictures, although Richard Thorpe the director is said to have lamented the fact that Bud and Marge get married in *Barnacle Bill.* It is our belief that a series of this kind wouldn't be very successful as Mr. Beery's type of role is so familiar that he gets all he can out of it in the first round, leaving nothing further to exploit."

It was not all peaches and cream being professionally linked with the erratic Beery. "Working with Wally [Beery] wasn't always easy" Marjorie told *Films in Review* writer W. Franklyn Moshier in 1966. "He'd never rehearse his lines or bits of 'business,' but he'd want me to rehearse mine. I've always been extremely conscientious in my work and his behavior sometimes unnerved me." Marjorie once asked Beery's co-worker and good friend Leo Carrillo how she should handle the situation. Said Carrillo: "You'll never get the same cues. Just look at him, and listen to him, and when he stops talking, say your line. That's as near as you'll ever come to getting a cue." It worked.

Marjorie was more serious than not when she told one interviewer that for working with Beery and Carrillo she thought MGM should provide ". . . one salary for the actin', the other for workin' with those two. I deserve it every time I come out alive."

As would prove true with her later series co-star Percy Kilbride, Marjorie never socialized with Beery off the lot. She much preferred spending her time puttering about her small house near the studio. Far from being status-struck, she usually took the bus to work each day, enjoying the chance to mingle with the working people types she portrayed on the screen. During the filming of *Barnacle Bill* she learned to drive and bought her first car, but still remained much to herself. She rarely attended parties or took part in the social functions revolving around the movie colony.

On loanout to Paramount, Marjorie appeared in her first color feature film, *The Shepherd of the Hill* (1941). It was an elaborately mounted remake of the Ozarks tale of backwoods moonshiners. Marjorie gave a finely modulated performance as blind Granny Becky, whose sight is eventually restored after a delicate operation. For many, the scene of the bandages being removed from her eyes was a touching piece of drama,

although *The New York Times* thought it ". . . was more a production number than a moving episode." Given back her sight, it is Marjorie who identifies stranger Harry Carey as John Wayne's father who had run away years ago. Other good performances were given by Betty Field as a simple mountain girl, Marc Lawrence as the mute simpleton, James Barton as the head moonshiner, and Beulah Bondi as a nasty type. (It was an interesting change of casting that saw 49-year-old Bondi, usually the sympathetic mother, cast as a minor heavy; while Marjorie softened her voice to incorporate a drawl and play a kindly soul.)

Back at MGM, Marjorie was sixth-billed as Reverend Mrs. Varner in the silky western *Honky Tonk* (1941), which teamed Clark Gable and Lana Turner for the first time. Marjorie was the boarding-house owner who has visions of moral rejuvenations among the townfolk. Gable played the footloose gambler who brings out the worst element in everybody, with Turner as the Boston-bred daughter of drunken old judge Frank Morgan. Marjorie's role called for her to be crusading to build a church to "help the Lord beat the devil to the draw." Upon accepting a $1500 donation from Gable, Marjorie tells an onlooker about his easy-going charm: "I'm young enough to like it, and too old to believe it." She wistfully concedes there should be more ladies' men like Gable. When she finds the gambler pulling too tightly on the reins of the town, she turns against him.

Once again, Marjorie demonstrated her worth with a potentially flat part. Seemingly without effort, she stole most of her scenes away from the stars.

For her final 1941 release, Marjorie again took second billing to Beery in *The Bugle Sounds.* She was self-sufficient Susie, who ran an army post beanery. For nineteen years she had been chasing after an old cavalry sergeant, following him from post to post. When Beery's favorite horse is destroyed by a burning army tank, he goes berserk and is discharged from the service. Through Marjorie's persuasion with commanding officer Lewis Stone (in which she has a long weeping scene) and Beery's round-up of a fifth column sabotage ring headed by George Bancroft, he is reinstated.

Location filming at Fort Knox, Lewis and Ord did not save this lesser vehicle. Nor did the secondary love scenes of Donna Reed and William Lundigan. *New York Herald Tribune's* Howard Burnes recognized: ". . . (she) plays his middle-aged inamorata with her usual acidity, but she rarely succeeds in saving the alleged romantic interludes."

Nevertheless, owing to the block booking system still prevalent in the 1940s—as well as to America's hunger for folksy, safe escape entertainment—this entry of the middle-aged love team did sufficiently well at the box office to insure future Marjorie-Beery productions.

We Were Dancing (1942) highlighted Norma Shearer in her next-to-last screen role. It was a pseudo-sophisticated comedy taken from Noel Coward's *Tonight At Eight*. Shearer appeared as the Polish countess whom professional guest Melvyn Douglas marries; once wed the couple (now lodged in South Carolina) become disenchanted with the surface allure of the other, and divorce. Marjorie, in another change of on-screen professions, portrayed the lecherous, happy-go-lucky Judge Sidney Hawkes who presides like a tyrant at the divorce hearing. She makes no bones about enjoying each bit of information about the domestic unbliss of the swank couple. *Variety* found that Marjorie ". . . earns the only genuine laughs with her mugging."

The Affairs of Martha (1942) proved to be a bubbly programmer that accidentally passed quickly from sight. It had a lively premise: a newspaper item appears stating that the maid of one of the prominent families in Rocky Bay (Long Island) is writing an exposé on the family she works for. The action focuses on the Sommerfield family, headed by Spring Byington and Melville Cooper. There Marjorie is the domineering jack-of-all-trades cook and Marsha Hunt the domestic. The family's headstrong son, Richard Carlson, was once married to Hunt, but he is now dating socialite Frances Drake. Before the finale, it is revealed Hunt was the girl in question, and she and Carlson are reunited: simple, unaffected, but very effective. An interesting contrast of acting style is offered by 49-year-old screen veteran Spring Byington as the flibberty-gibbit mother, and Marjorie as the 1940s answer to women's liberation.

In a press interview at this time, Marjorie discussed her theories about imparting authenticity to her screen portrayals of culinary wizards: "It always seems to me that real fodder on a movie table makes the picture more life-like. The folk look more natural eating a baked spud than hacking at a hunk of gutta percha. Take Wallace. You can see the pleasure in his eyes when he wraps around a meal."

Jackass Mail, which opened at the Criterion Theatre in New York on July 1, 1942, found Marjorie as Tiny Tucker, proprietress of the Gold Camp gambling saloon in a small town of the old west. There she can be seen leading the chorus line of can can dancers (wearing tights) and singing harsh songs at the evening shows. When horse thief and mail robber Wallace Beery cannot succeed in hijacking her mail line—she is also the town's postmistress—he decides that marrying her is the only way to obtain her business.

With wedding bells in the offing, Marjorie turns blue

nose, and agrees to become his wife, if he will reform into an honest, non-drinking man. To get her way, she is not above hitting him over the head with the nearest utensil at hand. Her favorite threat to blustering Beery is "Git goin' before I blast the daylights outta ya!" With the wild gleam in her eyes, it was more than convincing that she would, if she had to. It is ever-suspicious Marjorie who constantly queries her "partner": "Ye ain't sparkin' me, air ye Baggott?"

To wangle in the by-now obligatory youngster in a Beery vehicle, the outlaw is shown taking reluctant responsibility for ingratiating young Darryl Hickman, when Beery shoots the kid's father. J. Carroll Naish was cast as Beery's Mexican-Irish pal. Before the wrapup, Marjorie and Beery wed, and the story ropes in the 1850s railroad expansion across the continent to California. In contrast to its prototype, *Wyoming,* this production suffers. It has too little action, too few fist fights, and everyone tries too hard to recapture the magic of before. As a plot gimmick, *Jackass Mail* opens with a scene of present day Baggott City and the town square with its statues of founders Marjorie and Beery. The rest of the tale is an extended flashback.

Bosley Crowther in *The New York Times* reported about *Jackass Mail:* "There is certainly nothing novel in this latest Beery-Main bout, nor is there any deviation from the familiar in the performance of the two principals. . . . This time, at least, they are repeating their variation on the Min-and-Bill routine among companions whose resemblance to burlesque is just as unabashed as their own and that is the film's one modest virtue; it doesn't pretend to be anything but a lark."

Tish (1942) proved to be an unlikely piece of wimsy, very loosely adapted from the Mary Roberts Rinehart stories. Marjorie, Aline MacMahon, and ZaSu Pitts were billed over the title, starring as three eccentric old maids who enjoy meddling in others' affairs. As Letitia Carberry, Marjorie would just as soon go roller skating, fishing, or bow and arrow shooting, as sit home. She might use slang, but anyone who swore in her presence had to contribute to her swear box. Her life long enemy is Judge Guy Kibbee.

In the intricate plot, Marjorie fails to induce her nephew Lee Bowman to marry Susan Peters, rather than Kibbee's daughter Virginia Grey. It develops that Peters is already married to Richard Quine. He is drafted and dies in combat, she dies giving birth to her baby (which Marjorie later retrieves on a trip to Canada). Eventually Kibbee has Marjorie committed to a mental institution, but her sanity is proved. Typical of the "gentle" humor in the film is having the trio of women on an outing scared off by a dancing bear on the loose.

Wanda Hale in her two-star *New York Daily News* review complained: "Miss Main, a great comedienne and quite capable of doing any reasonable role splendidly, has to run the gamut of emotions in this musty, silly, old comedy-drama. She is called upon to be undignified, dignified, high-tempered and long-suffering in unnecessary persecution. The new star does the best she can in the unreasonable role and she should be relieved of the blame for the film's failure to entertain. *The New York Times* thought *Tish* had "about as much point and humor as a cheap radio 'soap opera.'"

Marjorie was exceedingly unhappy over her role in this lace-frilled production.

Her sixth and final 1942 release was the historically-pretentious *Tennessee Johnson,* a piece of overzealous propaganda, tracing the "humble" career of United States president Andrew Johnson (Van Heflin) from his days as an illiterate tailor to his White House confrontation with Thaddeus Stevens (Lionel Barrymore) who maneuvers to have him impeached. Marjorie was fourth-billed as Mrs. Fisher, a high-spirited pioneer woman, who is on the scene when, in early manhood, Heflin escapes from jail and has the blacksmith knock the shackles from his chains. She is part of the town's committee to restore a more just set of virtues to the county.

Meanwhile, Marjorie was living a quiet life in Hollywood. As she later recalled about these World War II years: "The one consolation I got from the last war is that I could do all my own gardening and wear old clothes. People attributed it to patriotism."

She only made two films in 1943; both were on loanouts to other studios and both were fairly atypical roles for her. At Twentieth Century-Fox, she was cast in Ernest Lubitsch's lush technicolor period comedy *Heaven Can Wait* (1943). She was Mrs. Strabel, wife of Kansas City beef tycoon Eugene Pallette and mother of genteel Gene Tierney, who eventually weds wealthy Don Ameche. Marjorie was bedecked in elaborate gowns and accessories for the first time on the screen and looked quite at ease.

A running gag for her role involved Marjorie and her obese, crude husband fighting over the newspaper comics. One morning at breakfast, she is so furious with her childish spouse, that she punishes him by deliberately telling all the best highlights of the day's comics to the properly disinterested butler Clarence Muse. Pointing up Pallette's gross *nouveau riche* taste is the huge statue of pet cow Mabel, perched on the front lawn. Bosley Crowther wrote in the *New York Times*: "Marjorie Main and Eugene Pallette play a pair of Kansas in-laws screamingly, and through them Mr. Lubitsch and Mr. Raphaelson satirize wealth in a lusty vein . . . [they are] performers who make the Lubitsch burlesque flicker with amusement."

For James Cagney's new producing company, which released its product through United Artists, Marjorie appeared in *Johnny Come Lately* (1943). The film provided Marjorie with one of her favorite roles. Based on a Louis Bromfield novel, the film marked the screen debut of stage star Grace George, who in an overly genteel manner played the owner of a small midwestern town newspaper of the early 1900s. Her fight against corruption and criminal boss Edward McNamara is taken up by wandering vagrant James Cagney, who is hired on by her newspaper. Marjorie was rambunctious Gashouse Mary McGovern, proprietress of a strictly legitimate dance hall. She is quickly won over by Cagney's brash honesty and informs him about what really is happening in Plattsville. When Marjorie reveals that she has been paying off to McNamara's phony orphans' fund, Cagney now has a peg upon which to expose the crooks. Later, Cagney visits Marjorie's old beau, Robert Barrat, now a state senator. He offers a glowing account of his courtship days with Marjorie, which adds a new depth to the Gashouse Mary characterization. Virtue eventually triumphs in *Johnny Come Lately.*

A high point of this film occurs when Marjorie and the other townswomen storm the local jail to free Cagney. After exerting a bundle of energy in physical effort and loud shouting, Marjorie is nonplussed to discover that a simple turn of the handle opens the unlocked jailhouse door. In several scenes, Marjorie again had the opportunity to be gussied up in elaborate evening gowns. She looked the tough grand dame at all times.

About *Johnny Come Lately,* Bosley Crowther in *The New York Times* offered: ". . . [she] plays a madam in the style of noisy, incredible farce." Another New York film critic observed: "Gashouse Mary is raucous and not particularly convincing, but then none of the characters have much of a semblance of reality." (E.g. Hattie McDaniels as Grace George's stereotyped maid, Margaret Hamilton as the sourpussed bookkeeper, George Cleveland as a drunken old reporter.)

Offscreen, Marjorie did not even own an evening gown. When she was invited to attend a formal dance given by her college sorority, Delta Delta Delta; she borrowed a gown from the MGM costume department. Not until she returned home after the ball did she discover why the gown had rustled so loudly all evening. She had forgotten to remove the weights from the dress!

Back at MGM in 1944, she was reteamed with Wallace Beery in *Rationing,* their first contemporary story. She was Iris Tuttle, postmistress and sole ration board official of Tuttleton. Beery appeared as the local meat market operator, harassed by wartime meat shortages and the red tape of rationing. When everything becomes too much for the browbeaten Beery, he trudges off to Washington, determined to enlist in the military service. Instead, he is advised to return home as meat selling is a vital industry. He is also asked to assist on the ration board. Expectedly, the dominating Marjorie and gruff Beery (the story pegs them as having dated years ago) come to loggerheads, aggravated by the fact that her daughter Dorothy Morris and Beery's adopted son Tommy Batten are in love. Since he will be drafted into the army soon, the youths want to marry now, but Marjorie feels they should wait till after the war is over.

As in *Barnacle Bill,* Connie Gilchrist functions as Marjorie's competition for Beery's affection; here she is the town's lady barber with her romantic eye on the butcher. To get a nice bankroll for his son's wedding, Beery sells a half interest in his store to Howard Freeman, who turns out to be a stooge for a local black market ring. Before the fadeout, Beery cracks open the conspiracy and in a slugfest reduces the opposition to shambles. And Marjorie buys out Freeman's share, informing the baffled Beery that it would be far simpler for him to marry her than to set about dissolving the new partnership. A running gag in the film had a billy goat munching on ration books.

Marjorie, whose real-life grandmother was one of the organizers of the W.C.T.U. in Indianapolis years before, had always been firmly against the drinking of liquor. She had insisted upon the insertion of a clause in her MGM contract to the effect that she would not be required to drink hard beverages in any of her film scenes. Marjorie reasoned: "Why, after seeing a movie in which everybody's drinkin' all the time, even I feel like going out on a bender." However, in *Rationing* she took her first screen drink, in a quaint scene in which she has a bad toothache and sips some liquor for strictly medicinal purposes. Marjorie recalls: "It was such a delightful bit of 'business," I consented."

Gentle Annie (1944) topcast Marjorie as the mother of two train robbers (Paul Langton and Henry Morgan) in 1901 Oklahoma. Affectionately known as "Muddy," Marjorie is certainly not above breaking the law to keep her ranch out of debt and to earn sufficient money to return to her old southern homestead. U.S. marshal James Craig arrives in town to solve the rash of train robberies. Teaming up with saloon waitress Donna Reed, the new duo adopt aliases and take jobs at Marjorie's ranch, hoping she will lead them to the wanted criminals. Before the wrapup, Marjorie is killed by corrupt sheriff Barton MacLane, Langton is shot

dead, and Morgan is caught and sent to trial, leaving Craig and Reed to seek happiness together. As the cantankerous but lovable, wrong-side-of-the-law mother, Marjorie easily stole the programmer's limelight, but the film was quickly passed off as a lesser product from the busy MGM production line.

In her first musical in a decade, *Meet Me in St. Louis* (1944), Marjorie appeared as Katie the maid in the color tribute to turn-of-the-century America. The nostalgic confection focused on the Smith family in St. Louis at the time of the World's Fair of 1903. The wholesome household consisted of grandpa Harry Davenport, parents Mary Astor and Leon Ames, son Hank Daniels, daughters Lucille Bremer, Judy Garland, Joan Carroll, and Margaret O'Brien, as well as the family cat. Whether she was deciding if the brewing ketchup is too sweet or sour, hurrying the family through dinner, sympathizing with injured O'Brien, or taking sides in the domestic crisis about moving to New York, Marjorie made her barrelhouse presence felt. Striding about the house authoritatively, she mugged and tossed out acerbic remarks like the seasoned trouper she was. Since the musical is so often revived theatrically and shown so frequently on television, it is one of Marjorie's best remembered cinema outings.

Her other 1945 release, *Murder He Says,* was done on loan-out to Paramount and has become a minor film classic. It was a wacky murder comedy, in which Fred MacMurray is investigating the disappearance of a fellow poll taker in the backwoods area of Kallikaw City. He stumbles upon the bizarre Jukes-type Fleagle family, presided over by Mamie Johnson (Marjorie), matriarch of the fruity clan. (The rest of the family consists of the highly educated, mealy-mouthed husband, Porter Hall, who builds coffins in the cellar, the idiot twin sons, the daughter, Jean Heather, who sings in baby talk and entwines flowers in her hair, and aging granny Mabel Paige.) When not shouting orders to her crazy brood, Marjorie is picking flies off the walls with a deadly effective bullwhip, or whopping one of her idiot sons on the back to repair a crick gone astray. The mad plot gets underway when the Fleagles poison Granny with phosphorescent ingredients, hoping she will tell where a bank robbing granddaughter hid $70,000 that the family covets.

In one of the movie's highlights, Marjorie sits the family down to a dinner loaded with phosphorescent poison, which glows brightly when the lights are dimmed. Everyone at the dinner table desperately tries to pass the poisoned food on to the next person, as the circular food tray whirs around at the table. Eventually, Hall seemingly dies and his glowing body is laid out in a bedroom upstairs.

MacMurray and Helen Walker, who has arrived on the scene, search through the house and eventually uncover the secret panel which leads them to the treasure. The mysterious lurking figure in the house turns out to be Hall, not dead after all. In a neat finale, the Fleagle family are in the barn involved in hay-stacking. At the climax, each member is shown tidily bound in a bundle of hay.

Murder He Says did fine enough in general release, with Marjorie receiving solid notices for being "incredibly ferocious." In the movie's advertisement, Marjorie was billed as "Maw has bats in the belfry—and coffins in the cellar!"

Throughout World War II, Marjorie had contributed to the morale-boosting effort by touring army camps, and in late 1945 she received a most singular honor. The 96th Infantry Division, stationed in the Philippines, held a contest to decide who would be the "Occupation Girl" for the Division. Early on in the contest, movie queens Joan Leslie, Vivian Blaine, and Olivia de Havilland were popular choices. Then someone suggested that rugged pistol-packing Marjorie Main would be a more appropriate selection. She won the voting, with the slogan: "a rough gal for a rough division." General J. L. Bradley, Division Commander, wrote Marjorie: "With a shotgun in one hand and a horsewhip in the other, you are truly the epitome of all that the 96th Division has accomplished." He promised to name a street after her in the first town they occupied. When Division members came back to San Francisco on a troop ship in January 1946, Marjorie, dressed as a cowgirl and flashing a pistol in each hand, was on the deck of a large ship stationed there, smiling a greeting to her war hero fans.

In 1946, Marjorie again appeared with Judy Garland in the highly successful color musical *The Harvey Girls,* in which she was Sonora Cassidy, in charge of instructing new waitresses in the art of running the chain of restaurants growing up along the Santa Fe train route in the West of the 1870s. The bulk of the action occurred in Sandrock, New Mexico, where Marjorie shepherds a group of new recruits, including Virginia O'Brien. And stranded Garland in need of a job. The town is run by a crook, Preston Foster, with Angela Lansbury presiding at the Alhambra Bar and Dance Hall. John Hodiak appeared as Lansbury's beau, who develops a yen for Garland; Kenny Baker was the saloon pianist, and Ray Bolger was an itinerant dancer. Marjorie even got to join in some of the lilting group musical numbers written by Johnny Mercer and Harry Warren, including "On the Atchison, Topeka and the Santa Fe."

For the first time since she had teamed with Wallace Beery, Marjorie was dropped down in the cast billing by MGM moppet star Margaret O'Brien in *Bad Bascomb* (1946). Marjorie was Abey Hanks, the overbearing grandmother of orphan O'Brien. They are part of the Morman wagon train trekking to Utah. Beery is an outlaw on the lam who seeks refuge with the pioneers, hoping to throw the federal troops off his trail. As they roll westward, Beery's partner in crime, J. Carrol Naish, tries to convince him to help in stealing the folks' gold shipment, which will be used to finance a Morman hospital in Utah. Instead, Beery remains to help ward off an Indian attack and assist the wagons in crossing a swollen river (when Marjorie's wagon overturns and O'Brien is carried downstream, Beery saves the moppet). At the finish, Beery brings the cavalry from the fort to save the settlers and quietly goes off to pay for his crimes. *The New York Times* complimented the "loving but acid harangues of . . . Marjorie Main."

Marjorie was scheduled for Clark Gable's *Lucky Baldwin* at MGM in 1946, but the project did not materialize. When female impersonator Arthur Blake was performing a Marjorie Main routine at the Hollywood Trocadero Club that year, Marjorie made her first nightclub foray. She confided: "If people laugh as much as I laughed at his impersonatin' me, I must be funnier than I thought I was!"

Her next release was the overblown melodrama *Undercurrent* (1946), in which Katharine Hepburn, daughter of a famed scientist, marries war-profiteering industrialist Robert Taylor, whose brother, Robert Mitchum, is supposedly missing. Hepburn falls in love with Mitchum sight unseen, and it remains for him to rescue her when crazed Taylor attempts to murder his wife. Marjorie was Lucy the domestic, who heartily and vocally disapproves of the peculiar goings-on at home. Howard Barnes in *The New York Herald Tribune* remarked: ". . . Miss Main gets humor out of sequences that are sorely in need of them." Marjorie told *Films in Review* writer W. Frankyn Moshier: "I was ill throughout most of the shooting and don't remember my part. But I remember the kindness of director [Vincente] Minnelli."

Marjorie's last 1946 appearance on the screen was a version of George Kelly's Broadway play *The Show-Off,* converted into a Red Skelton comedy vehicle. Marjorie was third-billed as Mrs. Fisher, the practical-minded wife of George Cleveland, and mother of Marshall Thompson and Marilyn Maxwell. Big talker Skelton marries Maxwell, much to her parents' disapproval. The unwelcome windbag is still a verbose fool at the close-out, kidding no one but himself. He has succeeded in wrecking a friend's car while recklessly driving without a license, and has in the process crippled a policeman, botched Thompson's business deal, run up big debts, and been evicted from his apartment. The movie was not particularly successful. *The New York Herald Tribune* tossed Marjorie a brief compliment: ". . . [she] has chances to make a point here and there." When *The Show Off* was made into a mid-1950s television special, the decade's "new" Marie Dressler, Thelma Ritter played Marjorie's role.

Marjorie had now reached the peak of her salary escalations at MGM, receiving $1,000 weekly, which was about $750 less weekly than the top character stars (such as Angela Lansbury, Agnes Moorehead) earned from the studio, but $250 more than such featured players as Leon Ames were paid under their long-term MGM contracts. Marjorie was definitely not in the same league with frequent co-star Wallace Beery, who because of his long-standing popularity earned $15,000 weekly (based on a thirteen weeks per year salary, since studio mogul Louis B. Mayer could not tolerate the frequently crude performer on the lot any longer than absolutely necessary to turn out his profitable, stock characterizations). Marjorie did have her own dressing room trailer on the lot, not so much as a tribute to her drawing power, but as an accommodation for her physical infirmity (she had a bad kidney condition, which necessitated frequently trips to the bathroom).

Marjorie showed up in a Columbia Screen Snapshot short subject in 1947, in which she performs a quick change from being a windblown frump to a well-dressed matron. She began her second seven-year MGM term contract on loan out to Universal for *The Egg and I* (1947), which changed her screen career as fortuitously as had her first teaming with Wallace Beery seven years before.

Universal paid $100,000 for Betty MacDonald's best selling novel, *The Egg and I,* and starred Claudette Colbert and Fred MacMurray as the newlyweds who move to a chicken farm in the Pacific northwest. Marjorie and Percy Kilbride were teamed for the first time as the weatherbeaten Ma and Pa Kettle, the boisterous neighbors of the green farmers, whose run-down farm and brood of thirteen screaming children offer no fit example of what the future can hold for the former city dwellers.

The Kettle house is a model of chaos: screenless screen doors, jam-packed closets, bulging and sagging floors, and with everything that could possibly be in disarray and disrepair in precisely that condition. Ma and Pa are true sights to behold: her well-worn house dresses and bird's nest hairdo are matched by Pa's baggy trousers, torn shirts, moth-eaten sweater, and derby hat. Their constant bickering hits a new high in domestic untranquility. Then there is the amazing contrast of Ma's strutting and screaming masculine ways, compared to Pa's carefully executed laziness.

When Pa's barn catches on fire and creates a forest fire, MacMurray's ranch is ruined. To end the film happily, he buys out ranch widow Louise Albritton's modernistic spread, and he is reunited with his disillusioned wife Colbert.

As she had done in *Dead End,* Marjorie designed her own wardrobe for Ma Kettle. "I have a feeling for costumes. I read a script, confer with the producer or director about what kind of woman it is, and then usually ask for the right to work out my own wardrobe. On the majority of my films I've done my own costumes, and for the Kettle series my motto was 'If it's wrong, it's right.' "

The Egg and I grossed $5.5 million in United States and Canadian film rental, making a tidy profit for the studio.

Variety stated: "Percy Kilbride and Marjorie Main, as the Kettles, the tobacco-road-like neighbors of Miss Colbert and MacMurray are literally tops as character players, accounting by their feeling and understanding of their roles, for high points in the film every time they're on the screen." Bosley Crowther in *The New York Times* was more critical and less in keeping with audience reaction: "To be sure, these pattern-minded authors have got into their film the Jeeter Lesterish Kettles who were so amusing in Mrs. MacDonald's book, and as played by Percy Kilbride and Marjorie Main as Pa and Ma and by a slue of smudge-faced children, they do contribute some bits of rustic spoof. But, mostly, they and the other rural characters which have been rung in are used for nothing more original than old-time bumpkin burlesque." Noted writer James Agee penned in *The Nation:* "Marjorie Main, in an occasional fit of fine, wild comedy, picks the show up and brandishes it as if she were wringing its neck. I wish to God she had."

For her role as Ma Kettle, Marjorie received her only Academy award nomination. However, Celeste Holm won the best supporting actress Oscar for her role in *Gentleman's Agreement* (1947).

Marjorie was just as homey offscreen as on. In her bungalow trailer on the lot, she had a built-in kitchen, where she would spend most of her non-acting time, whipping up lunches and snacks for fellow cast members. Usually she was experimenting with new variations of health food recipes and sipping her kevo substitute coffee brew.

With the Ma Kettle role enlarging Marjorie's popularity, MGM found it quite lucrative to loan her out to other producers. The difference between the high price they got for her services and her contractual salary went into the studio's coffers.

Marjorie also did *The Wistful Widow of Wagon Gap* for Universal in 1947, playing second fiddle to that studio's waning comedy team of Bud Abbott and Lou Costello (as did slapstick queens Joan Davis and Martha Raye in the early 1940s). Set in nineteenth-century Montana, *The Wistful Widow* has Marjorie cast as Mrs. Hawkins, with a brood of seven young kids. When Costello accidentally kills her husband, local custom demands he become guardian of the victim's family. Thus he works on her farm in the day, and at night he is employed in the town's saloon to pay off the dead man's debts. The town toughies avoid getting in fat Costello's way for fear of being saddled with Marjorie and her flock. He is made sheriff of the town. Eventually circumstances free him of his obligations, the duo go off to California, and Marjorie gets to marry judge George Cleveland.

Marjorie was billed in the advertisements for *The Wistful Widow* as: "Marjorie 'Calamity' Main, the pistol packin' 'Ma Kettle.'" Otis L. Guernsey Jr. said in the *New York Herald Tribune:* "Miss Main, in the title role, is not quite as believably acid as in her past roles. . . ."

Marjorie's only 1948 release was Universal's *Feudin' Fussin' and A Fightin',* in which she was Maribel Matthews, mayor of Rimrock. When fast-talking, fleet-footed patent medicine salesman Donald O'Connor comes to town, she keeps him there to help win the annual foot race against Big Bend. The humor was very obvious, and a scattering of mediocre songs did not enliven the thin production. Percy Kilbride played Marjorie's political assistant, and Joe Besser was the not-so-bright local sheriff.

With the boxoffice bonanza of *The Egg and I,* and most audience reaction being very high for the Kettles, Universal decided to continue the series. Marjorie was at first against doing a series, but MGM, her contract holder, insisted she do it. The success of the Kettle films (which earned more than $35 million) is credited with saving Universal from bankruptcy at the time. Each Kettle film cost less than $500,000 to produce, with Betty MacDonald being paid $10,000 per entry for permission to use the characters, which incidentally were much watered-down from the original book. Each series entry was shot in less than thirty days, usually filmed entirely on Universal's expansive but unimaginative back lot.

In *Ma and Pa Kettle* (1949) the farm family is about to be evicted from their dilapidated abode, when the kingsized brood (now fifteen children strong) is saved by Pa's prizewinning slogan in a tobacco company contest. Characteristically, he only entered the contest be-cause he wanted to win a new pouch. The family moves to a super duper new home, Ma carries Pa over the threshhold, and much of the film is taken up with their amazement and confusion with the new fangled gadgets filling the house. Town busybody Esther Dale insists that the Kettles cheated to win the contest, and it is only through the help of magazine writer Meg Randall that Pa's honesty is proven. Ma, meanwhile, has been holding off the sheriff with a shotgun. Randall marries the elder Kettle son, Richard Long. At the finale, Pa has won another contest.

This entry established the mode for future installments. Marjorie played her role of the "hard-working crusty helpmate" broadly for the expected amusing results (she registers great surprise but equal nonchalance when she sets about making pancakes in which Pa has accidentally spilled unpopped corn). She constantly confuses the names of her brood. If something gets in her way, she virtually destroys it; if people bother her, she ignores them and goes on her way. In her own way, she respects her no-good husband and is continually berating her children to show proper reverence for the nominal head of the household. When Pa does manage to do a few chores, it is in his own un-ruffled, unhurried way; such as milking the cows to the strains of the "Blue Danube Waltz." Also living nearby the ranch are the perennial Indian squatters, Crowbar and Geoduck, the stereotype of shiftless savages who are smart enough to do nothing.

Besides selecting her mail order-style wardrobe and overseeing her own makeup, Marjorie rewrote much of her own dialogue for the Kettle series. She recalls: "I was ready on the set for a take thirty minutes after arriving at the studio." And being a health and sanitation addict, she firmly insisted that the huge sound-stage doors be opened to air out the set each morning. When one of her directors on the series had a cold, she demanded that he wear a surgical mask while at work. Always one to stand up loudly for her rights as a performer, she felt cheated at not having shared in the huge profits being made by Universal, and to a lesser extent MGM. But she began to enjoy doing the series, reasoning: "Good for a lot of laughs, and I would rather make people laugh than anything else."

In reviewing *Ma and Pa Kettle,* A. H. Weiler in *The New York Times* thought: "Marjorie Main's Ma Kettle is a warm and natural character whose willingness to defend her new home with the aid of her trusted shotgun and numerous progeny, is completely understandable."

Her first MGM picture in three years and her last with Wallace Beery was *Big Jack* (1949), directed by Richard Thorpe who had so successfully helmed *Wy-*

oming. Beery is the scourge of Maryland and Virginia in the 1890s. He saves Dr. Richard Conte from the gallows when the latter is convicted for grave robbing—he is practicing new surgery methods and needs bodies to experiment on. Marjorie was the rough hewn Flapjake Kate, the pipe-smoking, gun-totting woman who marries her "precious" Beery. It was a sad finale to the screen teaming, for Beery was ill throughout production. He died of a heart attack shortly after completing the movie. The best the critics could say was that "Marjorie Main tags along as usual."

Starting off the new decade, Marjorie appeared in another Kettle episode, *Ma and Pa Kettle Go to Town* (1950). When Pa wins another slogan contest, the duo travel to New York, having left their brood in the charge of Charles McGraw, who is really a gangster on the loose. Pa is entrusted en route with a suitcase of stolen money destined for the mobster's big city pals, but he loses the valise. The crooks are eventually captured at a swank evening party, and when the Kettles return to the farm, McGraw is glad to surrender after enduring the rigors of dealing with a house full of wild kids.

The film was filled with the sight gags to be expected from the stock situation of the befuddled country couple gawking at the sights and habits of Gotham. One particularly bright episode had Marjorie undergoing a complete beauty treatment. She emerges from the salon, elegant as any matronly lady, and sporting all the la-di-da mannerisms. Marjorie and Kilbride went on location to New York for this picture, and did a great many publicity appearances in the city. She was named honorary screen mother of the year by American Mothers' Committee for the State of New York.

In *Summer Stock* (1950), her third MGM color musical with Judy Garland, Marjorie was Esme, the housekeeper at Garland's Connecticut farm. When Garland's younger sister, Gloria De Haven, brings home a troupe of actors, the barn is converted into a rehearsal and show place, to present the Broadway-bound musical *Fall in Love*. Naturally, Garland assumes the lead role in the show. Marjorie's stock part called for her to be overly suspicious of the actors' morality, feeling it her duty to chaperone their barn domitory by sleeping there each night, shotgun in hand. When not feeding the crew of hungry actors, Marjorie is around to give harassed Judy a rubdown on the opening night of the show. *Variety* argued that Marjorie was ". . . wasted in a short spot." Bosley Crowther in *The New York Times* noted: ". . . [she] now and then kicks up a ruckus as a wary and skeptical farm maid." *Summer Stock* proved quite popular and did very nicely at the box office.

Then in the hopes of getting "some of the Kettle gravy" MGM teamed Marjorie with contract player James Whitmore in a projected series, the first being *Mrs. O'Malley and Mr. Malone* (1950). Marjorie played a Proudfoot, Montana, housewife who has won the Treasure Ship radio contest by properly identifying the phantom tune. She is heading east to collect her big prize. At the Chicago stopover, criminal lawyer James Whitmore boards the train, hoping to track down some criminals who know the whereabouts of hidden money. Also on board are Fred Clark, the District Attorney office investigator; Douglas Fowley, just released from prison and out to find the missing money; Ann Dvorak, Fowley's alimony hunting ex-wife; Don Porter, Fowley's slippery ex-boss; Phyllis Kirk, a super secretary; and Dorothy Malone, Porter's girlfriend. Since Marjorie is also an avid mystery story reader, she and Whitmore get along famously. Before the train reaches New York, Malone and Porter are murdered, and amateur detectives Marjorie and Whitmore have been accused of the crime and are handcuffed together. The caper is eventually solved, and Marjorie and her lawyer pal are cleared. In the course of the train junket, Marjorie sings "Possum Up a Gum Stump."

MGM plugged the movie as: "They'll tickle the nation's funny bone . . . MGM's new screen team." But, says Marjorie: "It wasn't given the advertising and exploitation needed to launch such a project." *The New York Times* thought Marjorie's performance was ". . . a sanitized Ma Kettle. . . ." The short 69-minute programmer quickly passed through the distribution mill.

In October 1950 MGM had purchased *Cherchez La Frame,* another detective story by Craig Rice and Stuart Palmer, who had authored the tale used in *Mrs. O'Malley and Mr. Malone.* But the failure of the initial entry to do sufficiently well at the box office caused the studio to axe the series plan.

Universal's 1951 Kettle entry—they determined the market would only support one such film per year—was *Ma and Pa Kettle Back on the Farm.* Ma and Pa are still in their modern dream house and are just about to become grandparents, when their snobbish Boston in-laws arrive on the scene, and make life most unpleasant for their rural relations. The child is born and Ma's resistance to hygienic baby raising is given the full treatment. Then there is a supposed uranium discovery on the Kettle's farm, which proves to have been triggered only from Pa's war surplus overalls. Before the Boston contingent is converted to the Kettle's happy if unconventional life mode, there is a rousing car chase with the Kettles seeking to reconcile their son and daughter-in-law. Much is made of Ma being

". . . a woman who shoulders her husband from the rigors of work." One projected scene for this feature called for a billy goat to chase a nanny goat over the hill, with one definite object in mind. Marjorie vetoed the sequence and it never appeared in the release print.

In February 1951, Albert Bishop and his six sons and two daughters, and Raymond H. Johnson (a quarter-blood Indian and the model for the Indian Crowbar) sued Betty MacDonald, Universal Pictures, et al for $975,000 in the Seattle courts, claiming the Kettle films satirized them in a most unfavorable light. The studio won the case.

By 1951, Marjorie had purchased a new home, selected by one of her few Hollywood friends, a far-out local character called Peter the Hermit. An interviewer visiting her at the new abode noted: "Marjorie is always in motion. She is a very nervous person; as she talks she leaps up frequently to attend to some small, forgotten business, seated again, she squints and frequently brushes her hand across her pale-blue eyes. (She's short-sighted, but hates glasses.) Occasionally she pushes up her graying hair, which slips down continually, much in the manner of Ma Kettle's. A reporter who interviewed her in her back yard not long ago had to shoot his questions between rounds of a three cornered fight involving a belligerent mockingbird, a cat with murder in his eye, and Marjorie, bent on preserving the peace."

Although she had purchased a spanking new convertible in 1950 with all the trimming, and owned another smaller car (she regarded drivers who went more than fifteen miles per hour as speed demons), Marjorie most often could be seen riding her bicycle to the local grocery store, wearing shorts and a halter. If she ate out, she most often preferred dining in cafeterias, chatting with passers-by. She would be usually found wearing long white gloves there.

The Law And The Lady (1951) was a limp remake of *The Last Of Mrs. Cheyney* (1937). It dealt in superficial manner with two genteel criminals (Greer Garson and Michael Wilding), who after a career of jewel robbing on the continent and in the far east, come to turn-of-the-century San Francisco. Wilding poses as a butler at liberty and Garson claims to be a snooty marchioness, thus gaining entrance to the household of Mrs. Wortin (Marjorie), a *nouveau riche* snob, said to be the richest woman in the world. ("you may not like the way I got it, but I have it"). The crooks are after her fortune—her fabled necklace in particular—which is all locked in the safe behind the portrait of her late husband. Before the close, the thieves are exposed— along with the sordid pasts of Marjorie's house guests— and Garson and Wilding go off to jail to serve their time, planning to marry when they are released. Marjorie, bedecked in fine clothing, plays an unpolished gem, who admits at the finale: "I haven't had so much fun since the fleet came back from Manila." (Her favorite charity is a home for fallen sailors—("I'm crazy about the navy. Come see my boys.") The *New York Herald Tribune* pointed out: ". . .[Marjorie] is called upon for little else but to talk with an exaggerated western accent." Marjorie admits she was badly miscast for the part, and had felt no rapport with the type of character she had to portray. Her uneasiness was quite obvious in the final, drawn-out scenes, in which she had little to do but stand by and show assorted forced reactions while Garson makes her protracted decision whether she loves Wilding or Fernando Lamas, a local impoverished aristocrat.

Her final 1951 release was a medium-budgeted Lana Turner musical, *Mr. Imperium,* a showcase for opera singer Ezio Pinza, whom MGM was trying to push into film stardom. Turner essayed a Cinderella-like Hollywood film star, who is reunited with her former Italian lover, now a European king without a country to rule. They rendezvous in Palm Springs at a home owned by Mrs. Cabot (Marjorie) and her niece, Debbie Reynolds. Marjorie enjoyed this comedy role, although her screen time was much shortened when the final print was released.

MGM's new studio head, Dore Schary, had long felt impelled to make a strong patriotic message picture. *It's a Big Country* (1952) was his eight-episode paeon to America. In one of the lesser segments, *Letter From A Soldier,* Marjorie was Mrs. Wrenley, a Protestant mother who is brought news of her son's death in Korea by Jewish soldier Keefe Brasselle. *The Christian Science Monitor* thought: "For the quiet sincerity of its playing, this is one of the more noteworthy of the eight episodes."

The Belle of New York (1952) was a dreary color musical featuring Fred Astaire as a turn-of-the-century Manhattan playboy who romances Bowery mission worker Vera-Ellen. Marjorie rambled about as Mrs. Phineas Hill, Astaire's rich hearty aunt. *Time* magazine noted: "This pretty period piece is punctuated with a few chuckles provided by Marjorie Main as a Park Avenue dowager. . . ."

Ma and Pa Kettle at the Fair (1952) has Ma and Pa financing daughter Lori Nelson's college education by entering some prize money contests at the annual fair. Pa parcels out to his creditors fifty percent interests in Ma's potential fair winnings for the jam-making and bread-baking events, in exchange for an old nag. Ma does win the jam contest, but is disqualified. She is number one in the baking contest, but all the money goes to the creditors. Then she enters their new horse in the race, with Pa riding the silks. Pa's Indian friends, Crowbar and Geoduck, feed Ma's bread to the competing horses. (Since Pa had stored cement in her flour tins, she unknowingly made cement bread.) When Ma learns all the townfolk have bet on the other horses, she insists that Pa slow down their entry. For the bread episode, Pa is jailed, but released when their neighbors learn how Ma really helped them in the race. *Variety* said: "Miss Main and Kilbride breeze through the familiar characters easily."

Ma and Pa Kettle on Vacation (1953) find the lovable old couple departing Cape Flattery for their "improbable but well deserved" vacation, as traveling companions to their in-laws. Once again it is Ma who supplies the money for the trip, through a modest family inheritance. A spy on the plane induces them to take a bundle of what proves to be intelligence secrets and deliver it in Paris to another spy contact. The U.S. secret service persuades Pa to help them corral enemy agents Sig Ruman and Bodil Miller. At the finale, when Pa, via a wild car chase, brings the cops to the gang's hideout, Ma has already knocked the villains out cold.

Expectedly, Pa oogles at the saucier sights of Parisian life; and at a nightclub, Ma becomes involved in a wild apache dance, when she brashly informs the male dancing partner: "that's no way to treat a lady." Before Ma is through with the luckless performer, he has ended up in a spaghetti pot in the kitchen. Pa meets his match when a waiter brings on flaming *crêpes suzette*. *Variety* predicted good grosses for the film (which it obtained), finding that Marjorie and Kilbride "spark chuckles" as always.

For the March 28, 1953, issue of *The Saturday Review,* critic Hollis Alpert composed a lengthy appreciation about the Kettles, the new national institution:

"Hey Paw!" Ma Kettle yells and thus we introduce the theory of the American matriarchy with the Kettles representing the true, if unconscious, state of affairs here. The male has become devitalized and inadequate, the female is in the ascendant, if not really dominant. Well, take a look, Pa Kettle's primary role seems to be that of breeder, for he has indeed been the progenitor of fifteen children. On the other hand, he is just plain lousy at providing for them and he wears the abstracted air of the artist or the handy-man. He didn't even provide the wonderful house for that was won in a radio contest. There's never enough money, and it's Ma who generally comes through to save the day, though sometimes it's the relatives, or a friend. . . . Ma runs the house in a frowsy, slapdash way, makes the best crabapple jelly in town, as well as the best bread. . . . Ma puts up with Pa's little schemes and protects him from the slurs of the children who sometimes wonder if he isn't really a little inadequate.

Marjorie really threw herself into the Ma Kettle role and all its demands. When Marjorie and Kilbride went on one of their personal appearance tours, they stopped in Wichita, Kansas, where the movie stars were queried about soil cultivation by the gathered local 4-H club people. Kilbride was silenced by the query, but Marjorie quickly filled in the gap by retorting: "First, I would like to know something. As a farm child, I was told that more chicks were produced from brown eggs than white ones. Is that true?" The non-plussed audience was too busy debating the issue to get back to the original question.

Whenever reporters inquired how Kilbride found Marjorie as a co-worker, he would typically reply in his nasal, drawn-out speech: "Marjorie's too busy for temperament, her gusto and versatility are fascinating." For her part, Marjorie considered: ". . . Percy the best deadpan actor in the business, and a complete gentleman." Ironically, the two members of the screen team envied each other: Marjorie was hurt that Kilbride's Universal contract gave him modest luxuries denied her; and Kilbride wished he had not become so type-cast and could get non-Kettle roles as Marjorie did.

Fast Company (1953) was an inexpensive programmer, with Marjorie top-billed as Ma Parkson, owner of a small horse stable. Polly Bergen inherits a race horse and decides to race it, eventually assisted by race track tout Howard Keel who has fallen in love with her. With television pulling away theatrical audience attendance, this low budget entry disappeared quietly and quickly.

Marjorie had been suffering from bad sinuses for years, and eventually was forced to have her sinus membranes removed. Thus she had to drop out of the cast of Esther Williams's *Dangerous When Wet* (1953), as one necessary film sequence would require her to take a long dip in the ocean. Her doctors strongly advised against her accepting the role. Appearing so robust and hearty on screen, it was difficult for Marjorie and her employers to reconcile themselves to the reality of her weak physical condition. Eventually, Marjorie bought another home in the desert area of Palm Springs, and moved there permanently when her sinus condition became further aggravated in the mid-1950s.

During a bad bout in 1954, Marjorie was hospitalized at the Good Samaritan Hospital. She was so grateful for the fine medical treatment she received there, that she willed her entire estate to the institution.

In the Lucille Ball-Dezi Arnaz starrer, *The Long Long Trailer* (1954), Marjorie had only a small featured role as Mrs. Hittaway, an overly neighborly resident of the trailer park where Ball and Arnaz end up after their wild cross country trek in the title vehicle. In the frenzied trailer camp party sequence, Marjorie is among the gypsies involved in a hilarious bit of annoyance.

MGM's third version of *Rose Marie* (1954), in color and Cinemascope, featured Howard Keel and Ann Blyth as the lovesmitten leads. Marjorie portrayed Lady Jane Dunstock, Maple Rock's leading citizen. Her vis-a-vis was Canadian mountie Bert Lahr. Much of their comic interacting was cut from the final release print. Bosley Crowther in *The New York Times* wrote: "The dialogue is long, the plot is ponderous and the occasional intrusion of Bert Lahr and Marjorie Main as comic relief (in small doses) are disappointingly brief." It was Marjorie's last picture under her fourteen-year MGM contract. A tepid finale to her years of service there.

Her third 1954 release was *Ma and Pa Kettle at Home*. When the Kettle's eldest son, Brett Halsey, and the neighbor's daughter tie in a magazine essay contest about "My Life on a Typical American Farm," judges Alan Mowbray and Ross Elliott pay each contestant a visit to determine who will win the prize—a scholarship to the agricultural college. Ma and Pa do their level best to spruce up the old farm, with a fake modern barn, a little whitewash and a lot of hope. Much of the film's humor revolves around pompous Mowbray's stay with the Kettles, and his shocked disbelief at the rural people and their unreal homestead. To impress Mowbray, Pa even organizes a fake Indian raid, hoping he will seem brave and good. The truth of the situation is soon discovered, when a rainstorm washes away the phony front at the farm. However, Mowbray is eventually warmed by the folksy goodness of the Kettles, so he awards two, two-year scholarships to the youths.

When asked by reporters what had created the huge success of the Kettle films, Marjorie ruminated: "I've wondered about that. They're cheaply made, many of them done by inexperienced writers. They do seem to have this general appeal, though. . . . Ma is real to me, the kind of woman you feel you could go and visit in the country. And no hayseed. They tried to get that in, but I'd always say no." About her role: "You absorb certain things when you're a child. I've always believed an actor should use the things you store away subconsciously. About co-star Kilbride: "He's a fine man too. I can't think of anyone I respect more than my partner."

In the spring of 1954, Marjorie stopped over in New York for personal appearances and to prepare for her first European trip. She told one interviewer: "I was in the Easter Parade on Fifth Avenue on Sunday, just walkin' along mindin' my own business, and suddenly my hat blew off. Well, you know the kind of hair I have. I never can do anything with it—and that's when everybody started recognizing me."

About traveling abroad she confessed: "I don't speak any foreign languages, but I don't expect to starve. A friend's going with me—a socialite. If we find ourselves at some high-toned place, say, like Buckingham Palace, I'll just push her in ahead of me."

When Marjorie returned from Europe some time later, the movie star was pleased to repeat a favorite anecdote to the press: "Father was a big Charles Dickens fan, so I went to the Poet's Corner in Westminster Abbey. I asked the guard where Dickens was: He replied: 'You're standing on him, ma'am.' Sure enough I was. I looked down and there was my big feet on Dickens' plaque." About Paris and the famed Lido, she evaluated: "Uninspiring. The girls look tired and their skin is leathery. They eat too much spaghetti and noodles."

Ricochet Romance (1954) was Universal's uninspired attempt to pair Marjorie and Chill Wills as a new screen team, since Kilbride had stated that after one more Kettle film he was through with the series. Marjorie was Pansy Jones, the new cook at the Flying W Guest Ranch. Besides whipping together the daily vittles, Marjorie could not resist butting into everyone's business, from matchmaking to dude ranch running. Chill Wills was the happy go lucky owner of the spread whose overwhelming desire to practice the conjuring arts almost cost him the ranch. Despite the gusto of Marjorie's playing, the film was only a passable programmer. As *The British Monthly Film Bulletin* advised: "Marjorie Main's vigorous playing is unable to bring much life to an insipid though good-humored domestic comedy, embellished with a good deal of simple slapstick."

Marjorie had long ago developed the habit of moving right onto the Universal lot for the duration of her Kettle filmmaking, setting up headquarters in her dressing room bungalow. "I used to have Deanna Durbin's swank cottage," she chuckled, "but they made it into offices, so now I shack up right next to the studio fire department. Makes it pretty nice too, because in the evenings I play a bit of nickle-dime poker with the boys on duty."

Ma and Pa Kettle at Waikiki was Marjorie's sole 1955 release, and the final Kettle production costarring Kilbride. In this entry, Pa has been bragging to his cousin in Honolulu about his great business abilities. When the cousin is taken ill, Pa is asked to supervise the pineapple plant. Ma and daughter Lori Nelson tag along. Pa causes pandemonium at the plant, by accidentally speeding up the production assembly line to causing a huge explosion. Meanwhile, Ma is invited into the island's top social circles where her rustic ways are not appreciated. To get Pa out of the way, a competitor of the cousin tricks Pa into traipsing off to another island, on the pretext that hidden treasure is buried there. Pa encounters a Hawaiian family which is a direct counterpart to the Kettles (i.e. lazy father, hard-working mother, a big brood of kids). Pa feels right at home. Ma shows up, turns the tables, and even captures the villains. It develops that Pa's explosion has accidentally created a new preservative formula, and Pa is a hero. However, Ma and Pa decide to return home.

Kilbride, age 66, by now had had more than enough of the stereotyped Kettle assignment and refused to extend his Universal contract for the Kettle series. He also turned down a five-year $1 million contract to appear in a television version of the Kettles, with or without Marjorie. He then went into retirement, living as quietly as always. On December 11, 1964, at age 76, he died while undergoing brain surgery, as the result of being hit by a car while crossing the street.

Universal, convinced there was more voltage left in the Kettle series, allowed Marjorie to carry the box office load herself in *The Kettles in the Ozarks* (1956). Marjorie was now under direct contractual arrangements with Universal. However, since the series had passed its peak, her bargaining position was not great. In this entry, Ma and her kids traipse off to Arkansas to visit Pa's brother, Arthur Hunnicutt. Upon arrival, Ma discovers he is a chip off the old block, and just as lazy as her husband. She serves as matchmaker, prodding Hunnicutt to marry his longtime girlfriend, Una Merkel. The usual slapstick occurs on the new farm setting. Marjorie told interviewers at the time: "If this goes over, Arthur [Hunnicutt] and I will do some more. I like the series. We have the same crew, same director. You can relax. Sometimes the stories are corny, but I'd stand on my head to make people laugh. That's all I have to live for. I don't want to retire."

However, whatever magic had existed between Marjorie and Kilbride failed to come alive with Hunnicutt.

Friendly Persuasion (1956) was Marjorie's last major film assignment in an A picture to date. In this big money making version of Jessamyn West's novel of Indiana Quakers during the Civil War, Marjorie was the robust Widow Hudspeth who has three burly, marriageable daughters she wants wed—and soon. In her mannish, exuberant way, Marjorie gave a bigger than life characterization to her scenes with Gary Cooper and his son Anthony Perkins, who come to bargain for a horse, and narrowly escape having Perkins married off to one (any one) of the girls. *Variety* penned: ". . . [she] tops an extremely broad comedy episode involving Cooper's yen for a faster horse so he can

beat a friend (Robert Middleton) to church each Sunday, and three out-sized daughters who go on the make for Cooper's unworldly son, Anthony Perkins."

Marjorie's final film to date is *The Kettles on Old MacDonald's Farm* (1957) which introduced Parker Fennelly (famed for his "Titus Moody" on radio's *Allen's Alley* and Pepperidge Farm television commercials) as the new Pa Kettle. He proved quite satisfactory in his different interpretation of the role. In this installment, the Kettles have purchased another farm, not far from their old place. Their former homestead is used by poor lumberjack John Smith and rich, spoiled Gloria Talbot. Ma and Pa decide to chaperone the young people, who have yet to marry, waiting to see if they can first make a honest go from tilling the soil. The Kettles create more confusion in trying to set an example of what farmers and married folk should be. *Variety* observed: "Marjorie Main's Ma creation handles most of the laugh lode."

By now, second features of the Kettle type were fast disappearing from the scene. Television had taken over this genre, incorporating them into series entries such as *The Real McCoys* and more recently *The Beverly Hillbillies, Green Acres,* and *Petticoat Junction.* Thus Universal decided to call it quits with their once-profitable bucolic property.

Marjorie tried her hand at television, guesting on Spring Byington's *December Bride* in 1957. Along with Linda Darnell and Margaret O'Brien, she appeared on "The Sacramento Story" episode (June 25, 1958) of *Wagon Train* on NBC-TV. However, Marjorie did not enjoy working in the newer medium, finding the rapid production schedule too hectic.

After that, she dropped completely out of Hollywood life, residing in her desert-situated home, doing her own cooking and housecleaning. She often watches her old films on television. She told Vernon Scott, United Press International reporter, recently: "I see so many old friends (on television) that have passed on. . . . It's like renewing old acquaintances. Otherwise, I don't spend much time with television except to watch the news shows or a very good special.

"I've lived alone for such a long time I can't get used to the idea of having a maid move in with me. So I do my own shopping at health food stores and I enjoy cooking. If you asked me how I filled the hours during the day I probably couldn't tell you. But I manage to keep busy—and I rest quite a bit."

When asked if she would ever return to picture making, Marjorie replied: "I'd like to work with the oldtimers again. But they aren't making pictures. And I don't think I'd fit in with this new young set. I wouldn't be at ease with them." About choosing the right roles:

"We are often cornered into parts we can get away with or even successfully play, but we always know whether or not the role is right. I hit my stride in the Wally Beery films and the Ma Kettle roles because I felt close to the women I played and could work in little bits of 'business' I knew instinctively were true to the parts. I was fortunate in being allowed to create personally many of the things I've done best."

About the path of her professional career, she admits to having no regrets: "If I had any of it to do over I think I'd be a bit more assertive in going after the choice roles. There were a few along the way I wanted—and could have done well."

For some years, Marjorie was active in the Los Angeles Friday Morning Club, which sponsored lectures and luncheons. She is a firm believer that the Moral Re-Armament movement is "the one hope for the world." She still participates in the annual Santa Claus Lane Parade, riding in the procession, and waving to the crowds.

Marjorie only wishes: ". . . I'd had some children. They would be good company for me and give me a little something more to do around the house. As you know, I had plenty of kids as Ma Kettle."

FILMOGRAPHY: MARJORIE MAIN

Feature Films

A HOUSE DIVIDED (Univ. '31) 71 M.
Director, William Wyler; based on story *Heart And Hand* by Olive Edens; screenplay, John B. Clymer, Oale Van Every; dialogue, John Huston; camera, Charles Stumar.

Walter Huston (Seth); Douglass Montgomery (Matt); Helen Chandler (Ruth); Mary Fay (Mary); Frank Hagney (Bill Bill); Lloyd Ingraham (Doctor); Charles Middleton (Minister); Vivian Oakland, Marjorie Main (Women).

HOT SATURDAY (Par. '32) 73 M.
Director, William Seiter; based on the novel by Harvey Fergusson; adaptation, Josephine Lovett, Joseph M. March; screenplay, Seiter; camera, Arthur L. Todd.

Nancy Carroll (Ruth Brock); Cary Grant (Romer Sheffield); Randolph Scott (Bill Fadden); Edward Woods (Connie Billop); Lillian Bond (Eva Randolph); William Collier Sr. (Harry Brock); Jane Darwell (Ida Brock); Rita La Roy (Camille Renault); Rose Coughlin II (Annie Brock); Oscar Apfel (Ed. W. Randolph); Jessie Arnold (Aunt Minnie); Grady Sutton (Archie); Stanley Smith (Joe); Dave O'Brien (Guest); Marjorie Main, Nora Cecil (Gossips).

TAKE A CHANCE (Par. '33) 82 M.
Director, Lawrence Schwab, Monte Brice; based on a musical comedy by B. G. DeSylva, Sid Silvers, Nacio Brown, Schwab, Richard Whiting, Vincent Youman; screenplay, Schwab, DeSylva, Brice; songs, DeSylva, Whiting and Brown; DeSylva and Youmans; Billy Rose, E. Y. Harburg and Harold Arlen; Arthur Swanstrom and Louis Alter; Herman Hupfeld; camera, William Steiner.

James Dunn (Duke Stanley); Cliff Edwards (Louie Webb); June Knight (Toni Ray); Lillian Roth (Wanda Hill); Charles 'Buddy' Rogers (Kenneth Raleigh); Lillian Bond (Thelma Green); Charles Richmond (Andrew Raleigh); Dorothy Lee (Consuelo Raleigh); Robert Gleckler (Mike Caruso); Lona Andre (Miss Miami Beach); Harry Shannon (Bartender); George McKay (Steve); Mildred Webb (Chorus Girl); Marjorie Main (Woman).

CRIME WITHOUT PASSION (Par. '34) 72 M.
Director-story-screenplay, Ben Hecht, Charles MacArthur; camera, Lee Garmes; special effects, Slavko Vorkapich.

Claude Rains (Lee Gentry); Margo (Carmen Brown); Whitney Bourne (Katy Costello); Stanley Ridges (Eddie White); Paula Trueman (Buster Malloy); Leslie Adams (O'Brien); Greta Granstedt (Della); Esther Dale (Miss Keeley); Charles Kennedy (Lt. Norton); Fuller Mellish (Judge); Ben Hecht (Reporter); Helen Hayes (Woman In Hotel Lobby); Fanny Brice (Woman Sitting In Lobby); Marjorie Main (Woman).

MUSIC IN THE AIR (Fox, '34) 85 M.
Director, Joe May; based on the play by Oscar Hammerstein II and Jerome Kern; screenplay, Howard Young, Billie Wilder; songs, Hammerstein, Kern; music director, Louis de Francesco; choreography, Jack Donahue; camera, Ernest Palmer.

Gloria Swanson (Frieda Hertefeld); John Boles (Bruno Mahler); Douglass Montgomery (Karl Roder); June Lang (Seiglinda Lessing); Al Shean (Dr. Walter Lessing); Reginald Owen (Ernst Weber); Joseph Cawthorn (Hans Uppman); Sara Haden (Martha); Hobart Bosworth (Cornelius); Jed Prouty (Kirschner); Roger Imhof (Burgomeister); George Chandler (Assistant Stage Manager); Marjorie Main (Anna the Maid); Ferdinand Munier (Innkeeper); Grace Hayle (Innkeeper's Wife); Otto Fries (Butcher); Torben Meyer (Pharmacist); Otis Harlan (Baker); Herbert Heywood (Fire Captain); Lee Kohlmar (Priest); Christian Rub (Zipfelhuber); Fuzzy Knight (Nick); Adolph Dorr (Bearded Peasant); Perry Ivins (Radio Engineer); Ann Howard (Elsa); Betty Jane Graham (Marguerita); Dave O'Brien (Roder's Voice Double); Betty Heistand (Lessing's Voice Double).

LOVE IN A BUNGALOW (Univ. '37) 67 M.

Associate producer, E. M. Asher; director, Raymond B. McCarey; story, Eleanore Griffin, William Rankin; screenplay, Austin Parker, Karen DeWolf, James Mulhauser; music director, Charles Previn; art director, John Harkrider; camera, Milton Krasner; editor, Bernard Burton, Irving Burnbaum.

Nan Grey (Mary); Kent Taylor (Jeff); Louise Beavers (Millie); Jack Smart (Babcock); Minerva Urecal (Mrs. Kester); Hobart Cavanaugh (Mr. Kester); Richard Carlo (Bisbee); Marjorie Main (Emma); Margaret McWade (Lydia); Robert Spencer (Tracy); Arthur Hoyt (Man); Florence Lake (Woman); Armand "Curley" Wright (Janitor); Dell Henderson (Manager); Otto Fries (Policeman); William Benedict (Telegraph Boy); Sherry Hall, Edward Earle, Art Yeoman, James T. Mack, John Iven, Burr Carruth (Clerks In Bisbee's Office); Bobby Watson (Barker); Henry Roquemore (James); Stanley Blystone (Policeman); Betty Mack (Girl).

DEAD END (UA '37) 93 M.

Producer, Samuel Goldwyn; associate producer, Marritt Hulbrud; director, William Wyler; based on the play by Sidney Kingsley; screenplay, Lilian Hellman; art director, Richard Day; music director, Alfred Newman; camera, Gregg Toland; editor, Daniel Mandell.

Joel McCrea (Dave); Sylvia Sidney (Drina); Humphrey Bogart (Baby Face Martin); Allen Jenkins (Hunk); Wendy Barrie (Kay); Claire Trevor (Francey); Gabriel Dell (T.B.); Billy Halop (Tommy); Huntz Hall (Dippy); Bobby Jordan (Angel); Leo B. Gorcey (Spit); Bernard Punsley (Milty); Charles Peck (Philip Griswold); Minor Watson (Mr. Griswold); Marjorie Main (Mrs. Martin); James Burke (Mulligan); Marcelle Corday (Governess); Ward Bond (Doorman); George Humbert (Pascagli); Esther Dale (Mrs. Fenner); Elizabeth Risdon (Mrs. Connell); Bob Womans (Cop); Bill Pagwell (Drunk); Gertrude Valerie (Old Lady); Tom Rickets (Old Man); Charlotte Treadway, Maude Lambert (Women With Poodle); Bud Geary (Kay's Chauffeur); Sidney Kilbrick, Larry Harris, Norman Salling (Boys); Esther Howard (Woman With Coarse Voice); Donald Barry (Interne); Charles Halton (Whitey); Earl Askam (Griswold's Chauffeur).

STELLA DALLAS (UA '37) 104 M.

Producer, Samuel Goldwyn; associate producer, Merritt Hulbrud; director, King Vidor, based on the novel by Olive Higgins Prouty and the drama by Harry Wagstaff Kribble; screenplay, Victor Heerman, Sara Y. Mason; art director, Richard Day; music director, Alfred Newman; camera, Rudolph Mate; editor, Sherman Todd.

Barbara Stanwyck (Stella Martin Dallas); John Boles (Stephen Dallas); Anne Shirley (Laurel Dallas); Barbara O'Neil (Helen); Alan Hale (Ed Munn); Marjorie Main (Mrs. Martin); Edmund Elton (Mr. Martin); George Walcott (Charlie Martin); Gertrude Short (Carrie Jenkins); Tim Holt (Richard); Nella Walker (Mrs. Grosvenor); Dickie Jones (John); Ann Shoemaker (Miss Phillibrown); Jack Egger (Lee); Bruce Satterlee (Con); Jimmy Butler (Con-Grown Up).

THE MAN WHO CRIED WOLF (Univ. '37) 66 M.

Associate producer, E. Masher; director, Lewis R. Foster; based on the story *Too Clever To Live* by Arthur Rolhsfel; screenplay, Charles Grayson, Cy Bartlett; camera, George Robinson; editor, Frank Gross.

Lewis Stone (Lawrence Fontaine); Tom Brown (Tommy Bradley); Barbara Read (Nan); Marjorie Main (Amelia Bradley); Robert Spencer (Reporter); Robert Gleckler (Captain Walter Reid); Forrester Harvey (Jocko); Billy Wayne (Halligan); Jameson Thomas (George Bradley); Pierre Watkin (Governor); Russell Hicks (Prosecuting Attorney); Selmer Jackson (Defence Attorney); Howard Hickman (Doctor On Stage); Stanley Andrews, John Hamilton (Judges); Matt McHugh (Reporter); Fredrik Vogeding (Resident Doctor); Ben Taggart (Plain Clothes Officer); Anne O'Neal (Landlady); Reverend Neal Dodd (Priest); Sherry Hall (Ballistic Expert); Jack Daley (Policeman); Jason Robards Sr. (Doctor); Walter Miller (Killer); William Castle, Hal Cooke (Customers at Box Office); Eddie Fetherston (Box Office Cashier); Ernie Adams (Reporter); Russ Clark (Prison Guard); Charles Bennett (Taxi Manager); James Blaine (Doorman); Wilson Benge (Butler); Arthur Yeoman (Court Clerk); Gertrude Astor (Landlady); Harry Boman (Lodger).

THE WRONG ROAD (Rep. '37) 62 M.

Associate producer, Colbert Clark; director, James Cruze; story, Gordon Rigby; screenplay, Rigby, Eric Taylor; music director, Alberto Colombo; camera, Ernest Miller; editor, Murray Seldeen, Wlliam Morgan.

Richard Cromwell (Jimmy Caldwell); Helen Mack (Ruth Holden); Lionel Atwill (Mike Roberts); Horace MacMahon (Blackie Clayton); Russ Powell (Chief Ira Foster); Billy Bevan (McLean); Marjorie Main (Martha Foster); Rex Evans (Victor J. Holbrook); Joseph Crehan (District Attorney); Arthur Hoyt (Beamish, The Banker); Syd Saylor (Big Hobo); Selmer Jackson (Judge); Chester Clute (Dan O'Fearna); Gordon Hart (Headwaiter); Sidney Bracey (Waiter); Gladden James (Bank Official); Harry Wilson (Convict); Forbes Murray (Chairman of Parole Board); James Marcus (Parole Board Member); Jack Perrin (Policeman); Ferris Taylor (Bidder); Frank O'Connor, Larry Steers (Men at Auction).

THE SHADOW (Col. '37) 59 M.

Director, Charles C. Coleman; story, Milton Riason; screenplay, Arthur T. Horman; camera, Lucien Ballard; editor, Byron Robinson.

Rita Hayworth (Mary Gillespie); Charles Quigley (Jim Quinn); Marc Lawrence (Kid Crow); Arthur Loft (Sheriff Jackson); Dick Curtis (Carlos); Vernon Dent (Dutch Schultz); Marjorie Main (Hannah Gillespie); Donald Kirke (Senor Martinet); Dwight Frye (Vindecco); Bess Flowers (Marianne); Bill Irving (Mac); Eddie Fetherston (Woody); Sally St. Clair (Dolores); Sue St. Clair (Rosa); John Tyrrell (Mr. Moreno); Beatrice Curtis (Mrs. Moreno); Ann Dora (Miss Shaw); Harry Strang, Bud Jamison (Ticker Sellers); Ernie Adams (Roustabout); Mr. and Mrs. Clemens (Knife Throwing Act).

BOY OF THE STREETS (Mon. '38)

Producer, George Kahn; director, William Nigh; story, Rowland Brown; screenplay, Gilson Brown, Scott Darling; camera, Gilbert Warrenton; editor, Russel Schoengarth.

Jackie Cooper (Chuck Brennan); Maureen O'Connor (Norah); Kathleen Burke (Julie); Robert Emmett O'Connor (Rourke); Matty Fain (Blackie); George Cleveland (Tim); Marjorie Main (Mrs. Brennan); Gordon Elliott (Dr. Alben); Gush Usher (Foghorn Brennan); Don Latorre (Tony); Paul White (Spike).

CITY GIRL (20th, '38) 60 M.

Producer, Sol M. Wurtzel; director, Alfred Werker; screenplay, Frances Hyland, Robin Harris, Lester Ziffren; music director, Samuel Kaylin; camera, Harry Jackson; editor, Norman Colbert.

Phyllis Brooks (Ellen Ward); Ricardo Cortez (Charles Blake); Robert Wilcox (Donald Sanford); Douglas Fowley (Ritchie); Chick Chandler (Mike Harrison); Esther Muir (Flo Nichols); Adrianne Ames (Vivian Ross); George Lynn (Steve); Charles Lane (Dr. Abbott); Paul Stanton (Ralph Chaney); Norman Willie (Leader); Richard Terry, Lon Chaney Jr. (Gangsters); Lee Phelps (Sargeant Farrell); Ralph Dunn (Mac, The Policeman); Marjorie Main (Mrs. Ward); Charles Trowbridge (Pierson); Robert Lowery (Greenleaf); Heinie Conklin (Cook); Gloria Roy (Girl in Cafe); Edward Marr (Gangster, Wearing Derby); Edgar Dearing (Detective Lieutenant); Lee Shumway (Policeman); Eddie Hart, Jack Gargen, King Mojave (Bookies); Ben Welden (Blake's Valet); Lynn Bari (Waitress); Harold Goodwin (Chaney's Aide); Cyril Ring (Cigar Stand Proprietor); George Magrill (Plainclothesman); George Reed (Elevator Operator); Irving Bacon (Porter); Wade Boteler (Police Radio Announcer); Emmett Vogan (Policeman in Phone Booth); Milton Kibbee (Doctor's Assistant); Harry Worth (Gangster in Phone Booth); Carroll Nye (Radio Commentator); William Newell (Gas Station Attendant); Brooks Benedict (Pete); Chick Collins (Customer).

PENITENTIARY (Col. '38) 74 M.

Associate producer, Robert North; director, John Brahm; story, Martin Flavin; screenplay, Seton I. Miller, Fred Niblo Jr.; camera, Lucien Ballard; editor, Viola Lawrence.

Walter Connolly (Thomas Mathews); John Howard (William Jordan); Jean Parker (Elizabeth Mathews); Robert Barrat (Captain Grady); Marc Lawrence (Jack Hawkins); Arthur Hohl (Finch); Dick Curtis (Tex); Paul Fix (Punch); Marjorie Main (Katie Mathews); John Gallaudet (State's Attorney); Edward Van Sloan (Dr. Reinewulf); Ann Doran (Blanche Williams); Dick Elliott (McNaulty); Charles Halton (Leonard Nettleford); Ward Bond (Prison Barber); James Flavin (Doran); Stanley Andrews (Captain Dorn); Robert Allen (Doctor); Jack Dougherty, Ethan Laidlaw, Frank Mayo, Harry Hellingsworth, Frank Meredith (Cops); Lee Shumway (Guard); Lester Dorr (Reporter); Thurston Hall (Judge); Louise Stanley, Bess Flowers (Women); Perry Ivins (Lou); Billy Arnold (Finger Print Man); Eric Wilton (Butler); Lee Prather (Sergeant).

KING OF THE NEWSBOYS (Rep. '38) 65 M.

Producer-director, Bernard Vorhaus; story, Samuel Ornitz, Horace McCoy; screenplay, Louis Weitzenkorn; music, Alberto Columbo; camera, Jack Marta; editor, Ernest Nims.

Lew Ayres (Jerry Flynn); Helen Mack (Mary Ellen Stephens); Alison Skipworth (Nora); Victor Varconi (Wire Arno); Sheila Bromley (Connie Madison); Alice White (Dolly); Horace MacMahon (Lockjaw); William Benedict (Squimpy); Victor Ray Cooke (Pussy); Jack Pennick (Lefty); Mary Kormman (Peggy); Gloria Rich (Maizie); Oscar O'Shea (Mr. Stephens); Marjorie Main (Mrs. Stephens); Tony Warde (Henchman); Ralph Dunn (Guard); Byron Foulger (Gazette Owner); Emmett Vogan (Newsman); Ferris Taylor (John Sampson); Ethan Laidlaw (Hood); Dale Van Sickel (Escort); Howard Hickman (Judge); John Baird (Henchman); Inez Palange (Neighbor); Allan Cavan (Mr. Madison); Alphonse Martel (Head Waiter); Horace Carpenter (Fisherman); Ben Taggart (Lawyer); Paul Stanton (Jeweler); Joe Cunningham (Gazette Managing Editor); Harry Semels (Grocer); Frances Morris (Mabel); Jack Chefe (Waiter); Harry Wilson (Coachman); Charlie Sullivan (Bookie); Bob Livingston (Passerby).

TEST PILOT (MGM '38) 118 M.

Producer, Louis D. Lighton; director, Victor Fleming; story, Frank Wead; screenplay, Vincent Lawrence, Waldemar Young; camera, Ray June; editor, Tom Held.

Clark Gable (Jim Lane); Myrna Loy (Ann Barton); Spencer Tracy (Gunner Sloane); Lionel Barrymore (Howard B. Drake); Samuel S. Hinds (General Ross); Arthur Aylesworth (Frank Barton); Claudia Coleman (Mrs. Barton); Gloria Holden (Mrs. Benson); Louis Jean Heydt (Benson); Ted Pearson (Joe); Marjorie Main (Landlady); Gregory Gaye (Grant); Virginia Grey (Sarah); Priscilla Lawson (Mabel); Dudley Clements (Mr. Brown); Henry Roquemore (Fat Man); Byron Foulger (Designer); Frank Jaquet (Motor Expert); Roger Converse (Advertising Man); Phillip Terry (Photographer); Robert Fiske (Attendant); Garry Owen (Pilot); Dorothy Vaughan (Fat Woman); Billy Engle (Little Man); Brent Sargent (Movie Leading Man); Mary Howard (Movie Leading Woman); Gladden James (Interne); Douglas McPhail (Singing Pilot in Cafe); Forbes Murray, Richard Tucker, Don Douglas, James Flavin, Hooper Atchley, Dick Winslow, Ray Walker, Frank Sully (Pilots in Cafe); Fay Holden (Saleslady); Tom O'Grady (Bartender); Syd Saylor (Boss Leader).

PRISON FARM (Par. '38) 67 M.

Associate producer, Stuart Walker; director, Louis King; story, Edwin V. Westrate; screenplay, Eddie Welch, Robert Yost, Stuart Anthony; art director, Hans Dreier, Earle Hedwick; music director, Boris Morros; camera, Harry Fischbeck; editor, Edward Dmytryk.

Shirley Ross (Jean Forest); Lloyd Nolan (Larry); John Howard (Dr. Roi Conrad); J. Carrol Naish (Noel Haskins); Porter Hall (Chiston R. Bradby); Esther Dale (Cora Waxley); May Boley ("Shifty" Sue); Marjorie Main

(Matron Brand); Anna Q. Nilsson (Matron Ames); John Hart ("Texas" Jack); Diana R. Wood (Dolly); Howard Mitchell, Carl Harbaugh, Jack Hubbard (Guards); Mae Busch (Trixie); Ruth Warren (Josie); Robert Brister (Joe Easy); Virginia Debney (Maizie); Phillip Warren (Injured Prisoner); Blanche Rose (Woman Trusty); Betty Mack (Meg); Jimmy Conlin (Dave, The Clerk); Dick Elliott (Judge); Ethel May Halls, Cecil Weston (Matrons); Bosy Roth (Waitress); Archie Twitchell (Telegraph Operator); Pat West (Station Agent); Edwin J. Carlie (Mailman); Charles C. Wilson (Reardon).

ROMANCE OF THE LIMBERLOST (Mon. '38) 75 M.

Director, William Nigh; based on the novel *Girl of the Limberlost* by Gene Stratton Porter; screenplay, Marion Orth; camera, Gilbert Warrenton; editor, Russell Schoengarth.

Jean Parker (Laurie); Eric Linden (Wayne); Hollis Jewell (Chris); Marjorie Main (Nora); Edward Pawley (Corson); Betty Blythe (Mrs. Parker); George Cleveland (Nathan); Sarah Padden (Sarah); Guy Usher (Judge); Jack Kennedy (Abner); Jean O'Neill (Ruth); Harry Harvey (Jones).

LITTLE TOUGH GUY (Univ. '38) 85 M.

Associate producer, Ken Goldsmith; director, Harold Young; story, Brenda Weisberg; screenplay, Gilson Brown, Weisberg; art editor, Jack Ottorson; music director, Charles Previn; camera, Elwood Brodell; editor, Philip Kahn.

Robert Wilcox (Paul Wilson); Helen Parrish (Helen Boylan); Billy Halop (Johnny); Gabriel Dell (Pig); Bernard Punsley (Ape); David Gorcey (String); Huntz Hall (Dopey); Hally Chester (Sniper); Marjorie Main (Mrs. Boylan); Jack Searl (Cyril Gerrard); Peggy Steward (Rita Belle); Edward Cehman (Carl); Eleanor Hanson (Cashier); Edward Pawley (Jim Boylan); Olin Howland (Baxter); Charles Trowbridge (Judge); Selmer Jackson (Judge); Buster Phelps, George Billings (Kids); Ben Taggart, William Ruhl (Detectives); Hooper Atchley (Mr. Randall); Clara Mackin Blore (Mrs. Daniels); Jason Robards Sr. (Supervisor); John Fitzgerald (Eddie); Richard Selzer (Bud); Monte Montague (Policeman); Frank Bischell (Band Leader); Johnny Green (Usher).

UNDER THE BIG TOP (Mon. '38) 63 M.

Producer, Charles J. Bigelow; director, Karl Brown; screenplay, Marion Orth; camera, Gilbert Warrenton; editor, Russell Schoengarth.

Anne Nagel (Penny); Marjorie Main (Sara); Jack LaRue (Ricardo); Grant Richards (Pablo); George Cleveland (Joe); Herbert Rawlinson (Herman); Rolfe Sedan (Pierre); Betty Compson (Marie); Snowflake (Juba); Harry Harvey (McCarthy); Charlene Wyatt (Penny—As a Child); Speed Hansen (Marty).

TOO HOT TO HANDLE (MGM '38) 105 M.

Producer, Lawrence Weingarten; director, Jack Conway; story, Len Hammond; screenplay, Laurence Stallings, John Lee Mahin; camera, Harold Rosson; editor, Frank Sullivan.

Clark Gable (Chris Hunter); Myrna Loy (Alma Harding); Walter Pidgeon (Bill Dennis); Walter Connolly (Gabby MacArthur); Leo Carillo (Joselito); Virginia Weidler (Hulda Harding); Henry Kolker (Pearly Todd); Marjorie Main (Miss Wayne); Robert Emmett Keane (Foreign Editor); Johnny Hines (Parsons); Betty Ross Clarke (Mrs. Harding); Gregory Gaye (Popoff); Aileen Pringle (Mrs. MacArthur); Richard Loo (Charlie); Willie Fung (Willie); Josephine Whittell (Fake Mrs. Harding); Patsy O'Connor (Fake Hulda Harding); Al Shean (Gumpel); Walter Miller (Flyer); James Flavin (Young Reporter); Lane Chandler (Cameraman); Edwin Parker (Coast Guard Attendant); Frank Faylen (Assistant Dubber); Nell Craig (Todd's Secretary); Cyril Ring (Cameraman).

GIRLS' SCHOOL (Col. '38) 71 M.

Associate producer, Samuel Marx; director, John Brahm; story, Tess Slesinger; screenplay, Slesinger, Richard Sherman; art director, Stephen Goosson; music director, Morris Stoloff; music, Gregory Stone; assistant director, Art Black; camera, Frank Planer; editor, Otto Mayer.

Anne Shirley (Natalie Freeman); Nan Grey (Linda Simpson); Ralph Bellamy (Michael Hendragin); Dorothy Moore (Betty Fleet); Gloria Holden (Miss Laurel); Marjorie Main (Miss Armstrong); Margaret Tallichet (Gwennie); Peggy Moran (Myra); Kenneth Howell (Edgar); Cecil Cunningham (Miss Brewster); Pierre Watkins (Mr. Simpson); Doris Kenyon (Mrs. Simpson).

THERE GOES MY HEART (UA '38) 81 M.

Producer, Hal Roach; director, Norman Z. McLeod; story, Ed Sullivan; screenplay, Eddie Moran, Jack Jevone; art director, Charles D. Hall; music director, Marvin Hatley; camera, Norbert Brodine; special effects, Roy Seawright; editor, William Terhune.

Fredric March (Bill Spencer); Virginia Bruce (Joan Butterfield); Patsy Kelly (Peggy O'Brien); Alan Mowbray (Pennypepper); Nancy Carroll (Dorothy Moore); Eugene Pallette (Mr. Stevens); Claude Gillingswater (Cyrus Butterfield); Etienne Girardot (Hinckley); Arthur Lake (Flash Fisher); Robert Armstrong (Detective O'Brien); Irving Bacon (Mr. Dobbs); Irving Pichel (Mr. Gorman); Syd Saylor (Robinson); J. Farrell MacDonald (Officer); Marjorie Main (Irate Customer).

THREE COMRADES (MGM '38) 100 M.

Producer, Joseph L. Mankiewicz; director, Frank Borzage, based on the novel by Erich Maria Remarque; screenplay, F. Scott Fitzgerald, Edward E. Paramore; art director, Cedric Gibbons; songs, Chet Forrest, Bob Wright and Franz Waxman; camera, Joseph Ruttenberg; editor, Frank Sullivan.

Robert Taylor (Erich Lohkamp); Margaret Sullavan (Pat Hollmann); Franchot Tone (Otto Koster); Robert Young (Gottfried Lenz); Guy Kibbee (Alfons); Lionel Atwill (Franz Breuer); Henry Hull (Dr. Heinrich Becker); George Zucco (Dr. Plauten); Charley Grapewin (Local Doctor); Monty Woolley (Dr. Jaffe); Spencer Charters (Herr Schultz); Sarah Padden (Frau Schultz); Ferdinand

Munier (Burgomaster); Morgan Wallace (Owner of Wrecked Car); Priscilla Lawson (Frau Brunner); Esther Muir (Frau Schmidt); Walter Bonn (Adjutant); Edward McWade (Major Domo); Henry Brandon (Man with Patch); George Chandler, Ralph Bushman, Donald Haines (Comics); Claire McDowell (Frau Zalewska); Marjorie Main (Old Woman); Mitchell Lewis (Boris); E. Alyn Warren (Bookstore Owner); Ricca Allen (Housekeeper); Roger Converse (Becker's Assistant); Jessie Arnold (Nurse); Barbara Bedford (Rita); Alva Kellogg (Singer); Norman Willis, William Haade (Vogt Men); Leonard Penn (Tony).

LUCKY NIGHT (MGM '39) 90 M.

Producer, Louis D. Lighton; director, Norman Taurog; story, Oliver Claxton; screenplay, Vincent Lawrence, Grover Jones; camera, Ray June; editor, Elmo Vernon.

Robert Taylor (Bill Overton); Myrna Loy (Cora Jordan); Joseph Allen Jr. (Joe Hilton); Henry O'Neill (Calvin Jordan); Douglas Fowley (George); Charles Lane (Carpenter); Bernadene Hayes (Blondie); Gladys Blake (Blackie); Bernard Nedell (Dusty Cormack); Lillian Rich (Secretary); Carl Stockdale (Clerk); Jessie Arnold (Forelady); Charles Dorety, George Cooper, Jack Daley (Passersby); Edward Gargan (Cop in Park); Hal Price (Waiter); Donald Kerr (Seller in Arcade); Frank Faylen (Announcer); Oscar O'Shea (Lt. Murphy); Garry Owen (Bandit); Howard Mitchell (Cop); Irving Bacon (Bus Conductor); Bobby Watson (Orchestra Leader); Raymond Kelly (Bellboy); Henry Roquemore (Mr. Applewaite); Fern Emmett (Mrs. Applewaite); Marjorie Main (Mrs. Briggs); Barbara Norton (Mrs. Briggs' Servant); Josephine Whittell (Lady in Paint Store); Frank Coghlan Jr. (Boy in Paint Store); Harold Schlickenmayer (Cab Driver); Baldy Cook (Waiter in George's); Al Thompson (Bum); C .L. Sherwood (Tramp).

THEY SHALL HAVE MUSIC (UA '39) 105 M.

Producer, Samuel Goldwyn; associate producer, Robert Riskin; story, Irmgard von Cube; screenplay, John Howard Lawson; camera, Gregg Toland; editor, Sherman Todd.

Jascha Heifetz (Himself); Joel McCrea (Peter); Walter Brennan (Professor Lawson); Andrea Leeds (Ann Lawson); Gene Reynolds (Frankie); Terry Kilburn (Dominick); Tommy Kelly (Willie); Chuck Stubbs (Fever Jones); Walter Tatley (Rocks Mulligan); Jacqueline Nash (Betty); Mary Ruth (Susie); Arthur Hohl (Ed Miller); Marjorie Main (Jane Miller); Porter Hall (Mr. Flower); Paul Harvey (Heifetz's Manager); John St. Polis (Menken); Alex Schonberg (Davis); Frank Jaquet (Mr. Morgan); Perry Ivins (Mr. Wallace); Dorothy Christie (Young Woman); Paul Stanton (Inspector Johnson); Charles Coleman (Heifetz's Butler); Arthur Aylesworth, John Hamilton (Detectives); Virginia Brissac (Willie's Mother); James Flavin (Police Sergeant); Wade Boteler (Police Lieutenant); J. Farrell Macdonald (Police Chief); Roger Imhof, Louis Mason (Deputies); Marjorie Wood (Mother); Emmett Vogan (Police Chief's Aide); Lee Phelps (Policeman in Auditorium); Jessie Arnold (Woman in Alley); Mrs. Willard Louis, Dulce Daye (Women in Line); Bryant Washburn Jr. (Usher); Diana Lynn (Girl at Piano).

ANGELS WASH THEIR FACES (WB '39) 76 M.

Director, Ray Enright; story, Jonathan Finn; screenplay, Michael Fessier, Niven Busch, Robert Buchner; camera, Arthur L. Todd; editor, James Gibbon.

Ann Sheridan (Joy Ryan); Ronald Reagan (Pat Remson); Billy Halop (Billy Shafter); Bonita Granville (Peggy Finnegan); Frankie Thomas (Gabe Ryan); Bobby Jordan (Bernie); Bernard Punsley (Sleepy Arkelian); Leo Gorcey (Leo Finnegan); Huntz Hall (Huntz); Gabriel Dell Luigi); Henry O'Neill (Remson Sr.); Eduardo Ciannelli (Martino); Burton Churchill (Mayor Dooley); Minor Watson (Maloney); Margaret Hamilton (Miss Hannaberry); Jackie Searle (Alfred Goonplatz); Bernard Nedell (Kramer); Cy Kendell (Hynes); Dick Rich (Shuffle); Grady Sutton (Gildersleeve); Aldrich Bowker (Turnkey); Marjorie Main (Mrs. Arkelian); Robert Strange (Simpkins); Egon Brecher (Mr. Smith); Sibyl Harris (Mrs. Smith); Frank Coghlan Jr. (Boy); Lee Phelps (Guard); Eddy Chandler, Jack Clifford, Tom Wilson (Cops); Ed Keane (Defense Attorney); Howard Hickman (Judge); William Hopper (Photographer); John Ridgeley, John Harron, Max Hoffman Jr. (Reporters); John Hamilton (Marton—assistant Chief of Police); Wen Niles (Announcer), Harry Strang (Assistant Turnkey); Elliott Sullivan (Prisoner).

THE WOMEN (MGM '39) 132 M.

Producer, Hunt Stromberg; director, George Cukor; based on the play by Clare Boothe; screenplay, Anita Loos, Jane Murfin; art director, Cedric Gibbons; music, Edward Ward, David Snell; song, Chet Forrest, Bob Wright, and Ward; camera, Oliver T. Marsh, Joseph Ruttenberg; editor, Robert J. Kerns.

Norma Shearer (Mary Haines); Joan Crawford (Chrystal Allen); Rosalind Russell (Sylvia Fowler); Mary Boland (Countess Delave); Paulette Goddard (Miriam Aarons); Joan Fontaine (Peggy Day); Lucile Watson (Mrs. Moorehead); Phyllis Povah (Edith Potter); Florence Nash (Nancy Blake); Virginia Weidler (Little Mary); Ruth Hussey (Miss Watts); Muriel Hutchison (Jane); Margaret Dumont (Mrs. Wagstaff); Dennie Moore (Olga); Mary Cecil (Maggie); Marjorie Main (Lucy); Esther Dale (Ingrid); Hedda Hopper (Dolly Dupuyster); Mildred Shay (French Maid); Priscilla Lawson, Estelle Etterre (Hairdressers); Ann Morriss (Exercise Instructress); Mary Beth Hughes (Miss Trimmerback); Marjorie Wood (Old Maid in Powder Room); Virginia Grey (Pat); Cora Witherspoon (Mrs. Van Adams); Theresa Harris (Olive); Virginia Howell, Vera Vague (Receptionists); Aileen Pringle (Saleslady); Judith Allen (Model); Mariska Aldrich (Singing Teacher).

ANOTHER THIN MAN (MGM '39) 102 M.

Producer, Hunt Stromberg; director, W. S. Van Dyke; story, Dashiell Hammett; screenplay, Frances Goodrich, Albert Hackett; art director, Cedric Gibbons; music, Edward Ward; camera, Oliver T. Marsh, Willian Daniels; editor, Frederick Y. Smith.

William Powell (Nick Charles); Myrna Loy (Nora Charles); Virginia Grey (Lois MacFay); Otto Kruger (Assistant District Attorney Van Slack); C. Aubrey Smith (Colonel MacKay); Ruth Hussey (Dorothy Waters/Linda Mills); Nat Pendleton (Lt. Guild); Patric Knowles (Dudley Horn); Tom Neal (Freddie Coleman); Phyllis Gordon (Mrs. Bellam); Sheldon Leonard (Phil Church); Don Costello (Diamond Back Vogel); Harry Bellaver (Creeps Binder); William A. Poulsen (Nicky Charles Jr.); Muriel Hutchinson (Smitty); Abner Biberman (Dum Dum); Marjorie Main (Mrs. Dolley); Asta (Himself); Ralph Dunn (Expressman); Horace MacMahon (Chauffeur); Doodles Weaver (Gatekeeper); George Guhl, Paul Newlan, Joe Devlin (Bodyguards); Paul E. Burns (Ticket Agent); Milton Parsons (Coroner); Milton Kibbee, Dick Elliott, Thomas Jackson, Edward Gargan (Detectives); William Tannen (State Trooper); Joe Downing, Matty Fain (Hoods); Martin Garralaga (Informant); Alphonse Martel, Alberto Marin (Waiters); Nestor Paiva (Headwaiter); Frank Sully, John Kelly, Murray Alper (Fathers); Shemp Howard (Wacky); Edward Hearn (Detective); Alex D'Arcy (Gigolo).

TWO THOROUGHBREDS (RKO '39) 62 M.
Producer, Cliff Reid; director, Jack Hively; story, Joseph A. Fields; screenplay, Joseph A. Fields, Jerry Cady; music, Roy Webb; camera, Frank L. Redman; editor, Theron Warth.

Jimmy Lydon (David Carey); Joan Leslie (Wendy Conway); Arthur Hohl (Thaddeus Carey); J. M. Kerrigan (Jack Lenihan); Marjorie Main (Hildegarde Carey); Selmer Jackson (Bill Conway); Spencer Charters (Doc Purdy); Paul Fix (Stablemaster); Bob Perry (Henchman); Al Ferguson (Rancer); Frank Darien (Beal, the Mailman); Crystal Jack (Horse); Rex (Dog).

I TAKE THIS WOMAN (MGM '40) 97 M.
Director, W. S. Van Dyke; story, Charles MacArthur; screenplay, James Kevin McGrunness; art director, Cedric Gibbons; music, Bronislau Kaper, Arthur Guttman; camera, Harold Rosson; editor, George Boemler.

Spencer Tracy (Karl Decker); Hedy Lamarr (Georgi Gregor); Verree Teasdale; Kent Taylor (Phil Mayberry); Mona Barrie (Sandra Mayberry); Paul Cavanagh (Bill Rodgers); Jack Carson (Joe); Louis Calhern (Dr. Duveen); Laraine Day (Linda Rodgers); Reed Hadley (Bob Hampton); Frances Drake (Lola Estermonte); Marjorie Main (Gertie); George E. Stone (Katz); Willie Best (Sambo); Leon Belasco (Pancho); Don Castle (Ted Fenton); Charles Trowbridge (Dr. Morris); Charles D. Brown (Lt. of Police); Gayne Whitman (Dr. Phelps); John Shelton, Tom Collins (Internes); Florence Shirley (Mrs. Bettincourt); Rafael Storm (Raoul Cedro); Natalie Moorhead (Saleslady); Syd Saylor (Taxi Driver); David Clyde (Steward); Nell Craig (Nurse on Boat); Lee Phelps (Policeman); Matt McHugh, Polly Bailey, George Humbert, Rosina Galli, Esther Michelson (People at Clinic); Peggy Leon (Georgi's Maid); Edward Keane (Dr. Harrison); Jack Chefe (Waiter); Jean De Briac (Headwaiter); Flor-

ence Wix (Mrs. Winterhalter); Jimmie Lucas (Taxi Driver); Charles Sherlock (Steward); William Cartledge (Newsboy).

WOMEN WITHOUT NAMES (Par. '40) 62 M.
Associate producer, Eugene Zukor; director, Robert Florey; based on the play by Ernest Booth; screenplay, William R. Lipman, Horace McCoy; art director, Hans Dreier, William Flannery; assistant director, Joseph Lefert; camera, Charles Lang; editor, Anne Bauchens.

Ellen Drew (Joyce King); Robert Paige (Fred MacNeil); Judith Barratt (Peggy Athens); John Miljan (Assistant District Attorney John Marlin); Fay Helm (Millie); John McGuire (Walter Ferris); Louise Beavers (Ivory); James Seay (O'Grane); Esther Dale (Head Matron Inglis); Marjorie Main (Mrs. Lowry); Audrey Maynard (Maggie); Kitty Kelly (Countess); Virginia Dabney (Ruffles); Helen Lynch (Susie); Mae Busch (Rose); Thomas E. Jackson (Detective Sergeant Reardon); Joseph Sawyer (Principal Keeper Grimley); Eddie Saint (Priest); Wilfred Lucas, Dick Elliott, Ruth Warren (Roomers); Harry Worth (Trailer Salesman); Lillian Elliott (Mrs. Anthony); George Anderson, Henry Roquemore, John Harmon, Arthur Aylsworth, Leila McIntyre, Helen MacKellar, Mary Gordon (Jurors); Eddie Fetherston, Allen Fox, Ralph McCullough, Allen Conner, Jack Egan, Paul Kruger (Reporters); Blanche Rose (Jail Matron); Douglas Kennedy (Secretary); James Flavin (Guard).

DARK COMMAND (Rep. '40) 94 M.
Associate producer, Sol C. Siegel; director, Raoul Walsh; based on the novel by W. R. Burnett; screenplay, Grover Jones, Lionel Houser, F. Hugh Herbert; camera, Jack Marta; editor, Murray Seldeen.

John Wayne (Bob Seton); Claire Trevor (Mary McCloud); Walter Pidgeon (William Cantrell); Roy Rogers (Fletch McCloud); George "Gabby" Hayes (Grunch); Porter Hall (Angus McCloud); Marjorie Main (Mrs. Cantrell); Raymond Walburn (Buckner); Joseph Sawyer (Bushropp); Helen MacKellar (Mrs. Hale); J. Farrell MacDonald (Dave); Trevor Bardette (Hale); Alan Bridges (Bandit Leader); Ferris Taylor (Banker); Ernie S. Adams (Wiry Man); Harry Cording (Killer); Edward Hearn, Edmund Cobb (Jurymen); Glenn Strange (Tough); Mildred Gover (Ellie the Maid).

TURNABOUT (UA '40) 83 M.
Producer-director, Hal Roach; based on the novel by Thorne Smith; screenplay, Mickell Novak, Berne Giler, John McClain; art director, Nicholai Remisoff; music, Arthur Morton; assistant director, Bernard Carr; camera, Norbert Brodine; special effects, Roy Seawright; editor, Bert Jordan.

Adolphe Menjou (Phil Manning); Carole Landis (Sally Willows); John Hubbard (Tim Willows); William Gargan (Joel Clare); Verree Teasdale (Laura Bannister); Mary Astor (Marion Manning); Donald Meek (Henry); Joyce Compton (Irene Clare); Inez Courtney (Miss Edwards); Franklin Pangborn (Mr. Pingboom); Marjorie Main (Nora); Polly Ann Young (Miss Twill); Berton

Churchill (Julian Marlowe); Margaret Roach (Dixie Gale); Ray Turner (Moss); Norman Budd (Jimmy).

SUSAN AND GOD (MGM '40) 115 M.

Producer, Hunt Stromberg; director, George Cukor; based on the play by Rachel Crothers; screenplay, Anita Loos; music, Herbert Stothart; art director, Cedric Gibbons; camera, Robert Planck; editor, William Terhune.

Joan Crawford (Susan Trexel); Fredric March (Harry Trexel); Ruth Hussey (Charlotte); John Carroll (Clyde Rochester); Rita Hayworth (Leonora Stubbs); Nigel Bruce (Hutchins Stubbs); Bruce Cabot (Michael O'Hara); Rose Hobart (Irene Burrows); Rita Quigley (Blossom Trexel); Norma Mitchell (Paige); Romaine Callender (Oliver Leeds); Marjorie Main (Mary); Aldrich Bowker (Patrick); Constance Collier (Lady Wiggam); Herbert Evans (Bronson); Coco Broadhurst (Cowboy Joe); Richard D. Crane (Bob); Don Castle (Attendant); Henryette Yate (Fifi); Oscar O'Shea (Sam, the Bartender); Claude King (J.F.); Dan Dailey Jr. (Homer); Sam Harris (Amos); Bobby Hale (Tom); Joan Leslie, Susan Peters, William Lechner, David Tillotson (Guests); Gloria De Haven (Enid); David Oliver (Man at Bar); Edward Gargan (Cab Driver).

THE CAPTAIN IS A LADY (MGM '40) 63 M.

Producer, Frederick Stephani; director, Robert B. Sinclair; based on the play *Old Lady 31* by Rachel Crothers, and novel by Louise Forssluard; screenplay, Harry Clark; camera, Leonard Smith; editor, Frank Hull.

Charles Coburn (Abe Peabody); Beula Bondi (Angie Peabody); Billie Burke (Blossy Stort); Helen Broderick (Nancy Crocker); Virginia Grey (Mary); Marjorie Main (Sarah May Willett); Dan Dailey Jr. (Perth Nickerson); Helen Westley (Abigail Morrow); Cecil Cunningham (Mrs. Hamans); Clem Bevans (Samuel Darby); Francis Pierlot (Roger Bartlett); Robert Middlemass (Peterson); Tom Fadden (Pucey Kintner); Ralph Byrd (Randy); Harry Tyler (Lem); Earl Hodgins (Man); Helen Dickson, Dorothea Wolbert, Vangie Beilby, Barbar Norton, Helen Bertram (Old Ladies); Joe Bernard, Henry Sylvester, Milton Kibbee (Men in Store); Ed. J. Brady, Murdock MacQuarrie, Frank Hammond, Carl Stockdale, George Guhl (Seamen); Robert Homans (Clem).

WYOMING (MGM '40) 89 M.

Producer, Milton Bren; Director, Richard Thorpe; story, Jack Jevne; screenplay, Jevne, Hugo Butler; camera, Clyde DeVinna; editor, Robert J. Kern.

Wallace Beery (Reb Harkness); Leo Carrillo (Pete); Ann Rutherford (Lucy Kincaid); Lee Bowman (Sgt. Connolly); Joseph Calleia (Buckley); Bobs Watson (Jimmy Kincaid); Marjorie Main (Mehitabel); Henry Travers (Sheriff); Paul Kelly (General Custer); Stanley Fields (Curley); William Tannen (Reynolds); Chill Wills (Lafe); Donald MacBride (Bart); Clem Bevans (Pa McKinley); Russell Simpson (Bronson); Addison Richards (Kincaid); Dick Curtis (Corky); Dick Alexander (Gus); Chief Thundercloud (Lightfoot); Ethel Wales (Mrs. Bronson); Dick Botiller (Rusty); Glenn Lucas (Smokey); Francis McDonald (Dawson); Edgar Dearing (Officer); Archie Butler,

Harley Chambers (Cavalrymen); Glenn Strange (Bill Smalley); Lee Phebs (Man); Ted Adams (Brother); Betty Jean Nichols (Child); Howard Mitchell (Conductor).

WILD MAN OF BORNEO (MGM '41) 78 M.

Director, Robert B. Sinclair, based on the play by Marc Connelly, Herman J. Mankiewicz; screenplay, Waldo Scott, John McClain; music, David Snell; art director, Cedric Gibbons; camera, Oliver T. Marsh; editor, Frank Sullivan.

Frank Morgan (J. Daniel Thompson); Mary Howard (Mary Thompson); Dan Dailey Jr. (Ed LeMotte); Billie Burke (Bernice Marshall); Donald Meek (Prof. Charles Birde); Bonita Granville (Francine Diamond); Marjorie Main (Irma); Connie Gilchrist (Mrs. Diamond); Walter Catlett ("Doc" Skelby); Andrew Tombes ("Doc" Dumbar); Joseph J. Greene (Mr. Ferderber); Joe Yule (Jerry); Phil Silvers (Murdock); Henry Roquemore (Sheriff); Tom Conway (Actor in Film Scene); Karen Verne (Actress in Film Scene); Matt McHugh, Irving Bacon (Cabbies).

THE TRIAL OF MARY DUGAN (MGM '41) 87 M.

Producer, Edwin Knopf; director, Norman Z. McLeod; based on the play by Bayard Z. Veiller; camera, George Folsey; editor, George Boemler.

Laraine Day (Mary Dugan); Robert Young (Jimmy Blake); Tom Conway (Edgar Wayne); Frieda Inescort (Mrs. Wayne); Henry O'Neill (Galway); John Litel (Mr. West); Marsha Hunt (Agatha Hall); Sara Haden (Miss Matthews); Marjorie Main (Mrs. Collins); Alma Kruger (Dr. Saunders); Pierre Watkin (Judge Nash); Addison Richards (Captain Price); Francis Pieriot (John Masters); George Watts (Inspector Hunt); Ian Wolfe (Dr. Winston); Cliff Danielson (Robert, the Chauffeur); Cliff Clark (John Dugan); Milton Kibbee (Court Clerk); Nora Perry (Sally); Minerva Urecal (Landlady); Paul Porcasi (Ship's Captain); Larry Wehat (Court Stenographer); Walter Lawrence (Newsboy); Matt Moore (Bailiff); Anna Q. Nilsson (Juror); Wiliam Tannen (Driver); Kay Sutton (Secretary); Joe Yule (Sign Painter); Joan Barclay, Betty Farrington (Spectators).

A WOMAN'S FACE (MGM, '41) 105 M.

Producer, Victor Saville; director, George Cukor; based on the play *Il Etait Une Fois* by Francis de Croisset; screenplay, Donald Ogden Stewart; art director, Cedric Gibbons; music, Bronislau Kaper; camera, Robert Planck; editor, Frank Sullivan.

Joan Crawford (Anna Holm); Melvyn Douglas (Dr. Segert); Conrad Veidt (Torsten Barring); Reginald Owen (Bernard Dalvik); Albert Basserman (Consul Barring); Marjorie Main (Emma); Donald Meek (Herman); Connie Gilchrist (Christina Lalvik); Richard Nichols (Lars Erik); Osa Massen (Vera Segert); Charles Quigley (Eric); Henry Kolker (Judge); George Zucco (Defense Attorney); Henry Daniell (Public Prosecutor); Robert Warwick, Gilbert Emery (Associate Judges); William Farnum (Notary); Sarah Padden (Police Matron); Gwili Andre (Gusta); Manart Kippen (Olaf); Lionel Pape (Einer); Doris Day, Mary Ellen Popel (Girls at Party); Lilian Kemble-Cooper, Vede Buckland (Nurses).

BARNACLE BILL (MGM '41) 90 M.

Producer, Milton Bren; director, Richard Thorpe; story, Jack Jerve; screenplay, Jerve, Hugo Butler; camera, Clyde De Vinna; editor, Frank E. Hull.

Wallace Beery ("Biff" Johansen); Marjorie Main (Marge Cavendish); Leo Carrillo (Pico Rodriquez); Virginia Weidler (Virginia Johansen); Donald Meek (Pop Cavendish); Barton MacLane (John Kelly); Connie Gilchrist (Mamie); Sara Haden (Aunt Letty); William Edmunds (Joe Petillo); Don Terry (Dixon); Alec Craig (MacDonald); Montoe Montague (Dolan); Irving Bacon (Deckhand); Harry Fleischmann (Detective); Francis Pierlot (Minister); Harry Semels (Tony); George Guhl (Harry); Charles Lane (Auctioneer); Art Miles (Driver); Marie Genardi (Mrs. Petillo); William Forrest (Naval Officer); James Millican (Sailor); Milton Kibbee, Frank Yaconelli (Fishermen).

THE SHEPHERD OF THE HILLS (Par. '41) 98M.

Producer, Jack Moss; director, Henry Hathaway; based on the novel by Harold Bell Wright; screenplay, Grover Jones, Stuart Anthony; assistant director, Dink Templeton; camera, Charles Lang Jr., W. Howard Greene; editor, Ellsworth Hoagland.

John Wayne (Young Matt Matthews); Betty Field (Sammy Lane); Harry Carey (Daniel Howitt/The Shepherd); Beulah Bondi (Aunt Mollie Matthews); James Barton (Old Matt Matthews); Samuel S. Hinds (Andy Beeler); Marjorie Main (Granny Becky); Ward Bond (Wash Gibbs); March Lawrence (Pete Matthews); John Qualen (Coot Royal); Fuzzy Knight (Mr. Palestrom); Tom Fadden (Jim Lane); Olin Howland (Corky); Dorothy Adams (Elvy Royal); Virita Campbell (Baby); Fern Emmett (Mrs. Palestrum); John Harmon (Charlie); Selmer Jackson (Doctor); Charles Middleton (Blacksmith); Bort Kortman (Hand); Hank Bell (Man with Mustache).

HONKY TONK (MGM '41) 104 M.

Producer, Pandro S. Berman; director, Jack Conway; screenplay, Marguerite Roberts, John Sandford; music, Franz Waxman; art director, Cedric Gibbons; songs, Jack Yellen, Milton Ager; camera, Harold Rosson; editor, Blanche Sewell.

Clark Gable (Candy Brown); Lana Turner (Elizabeth Cotton); Frank Morgan (Judge Cotton); Claire Trevor ("Gold Dust" Nelson); Marjorie Main (Reverend Mrs. Varner); Albert Dekker (Brazos Hearn); Chill Wills (The Sniper); Henry O'Neill (Daniel Wells); John Maxwell (Kendall); Morgan Wallace (Adams); Douglas Wood (Governor Wilson); Betty Blythe (Mrs. Wilson); Hooper Atchley (Senator Ford); Harry Worth (Harry Gates); Veda Ann Borg (Eleanore); Dorothy Granger (Pearl); Sheila Darcy (Louise); Cy Kendall (Man with Tar); Erville Alderson (Man with Rail); John Farrell (Man with Feathers); Don Barclay (Man with Gun); Ray Teal (Poker Player); Esther Muir (Prostitute); Francis X. Bushman Jr. (Ralph Bushman); Art Miles (Dealer); Anne O'Neal (Nurse); Russell Hicks (Dr. Otis); Henry Roquemore (Butcher); Lew Harvey (Blackie); John "Jack" Carr (Brazos' Henchman); Demetrius Alexis (Tug).

THE BUGLE SOUNDS (MGM '41) 101 M.

Producer, J. Walter Ruben; director, S. Sylvan Simon; story, Cyril Hume, Lawrence Kimble; screenplay, Hume; music, Lennie Hayton; camera, Clyde DeVinna; special effects, Arnold Gillespie; editor, Ben Lewis.

Wallace Beery ("Hap" Doan); Marjorie Main (Susie); Lewis Stone (Colonel Lawton); George Bancroft (Russell); William Lundigan (Joe Hanson); Henry O'Neill (Lt. Colonel Seton); Donna Reed (Sally Hanson); Chill Wills (Dillon); Roman Bohnen (Leech); Jerome Cowan (Nichols); Tom Dugan (Strong); Guinn Williams (Krim); Ernest Whitman (Cartaret); Arthur Space (Hank); Jonathan Hale (Brigadier General); Lane Chandler, Ray Teal, Ed Parker, Harry Strang, Alexander Lockwood, Lee Phelps (Sergeants); Walter Sande (Headquarters Sergeant); Cliff Danielson, James Spencer, Hal LeSueur, William Edwards, James Millican, Dick Winslow, Allan Nixon, Jon Dawson (Recruits); Stanley Andrews (Vet); Don Douglas (Clye, F.B.I. Man); Reed Hadley (T.J.A.); Kane Richmond (Captain); Jack Luden, Bradley Page (Adjutants).

WE WERE DANCING (MGM '42) 93 M.

Producer, Robert L. Leonard, Orville Dull; director, Leonard; based in part on the play *Tonight at 8:30* by Noel Coward; screenplay, Cleaudine West, Hans Rameau, George Froeschel; art director, Cedric Gibbons; camera, Robert Planck; editor, George Boemler.

Norma Shearer (Vicki Wilomarsky); Melvyn Douglas (Nicki Prax); Gail Patrick (Linda Wayne); Lee Bowman (Hubert Tyler); Marjorie Main (Judge Sidney Hawkes); Reginald Owen (Major Tyler-Blane); Alan Mowbray (Grand Duke Basil); Florence Bates (Mrs. Vanderlip); Sig Rumann (Baron Prax); Dennis Hoey (Prince Wilomirsky); Heather Thatcher (Mrs. Tyler-Blane); Connie Gilchrist (Olive Ransome); Florence Shirley (Mrs. Chartoris); Paul Porcasi (Manager); Philip Ahn (Chinaman); Mary Forbes (Mrs. Sandys); Thurston Hall (Senator Quimby); Alan Napier (Captain Blacktone); Martin Turner (Red Cap); Bryant Washburn Sr. (Mr. Lambert); Pierre Watkin (Mr. Bentley); Dorothy Morris (Claire Bentley); Duncan Renaldo (Sam Estrella); Russell Hicks (Bryce-Carew); Dick Alexander (Moving Man); Ian Wolfe (Reggie); Emmett Vogan (Bailiff); Harry Hayden (Clerk); Tim Ryan (Traffic Cop).

THE AFFAIRS OF MARTHA (MGM '42) 66 M.

Producer, Irving Starr; director, Jules Dassin; screenplay, Isobel Lennart, Lee Gold; music, Bronislau Kaper; art director, Cedric Gibbons; camera, Charles Lawton; editor, Ralph Winters.

Marsha Hunt (Martha Lindstrom); Richard Carlson (Jeff Sommerfield); Marjorie Main (Mrs. McKissick); Virginia Weidler (Miranda Sommerfield); Spring Byington (Mrs. Sophie Sommerfield); Allyn Joslyn (Joel Archer); Barry Nelson (Dannie O'Brien); Melville Cooper (Dr. Clarence Sommerfield); Frances Drake (Sylvia Norwood); Ernest Truex (Llewellyn Castle); Cecil Cunningham (Mrs. Castle); William B. Davidson (Homer Jacell); Inez Cooper (Mrs. Jacell); Aubrey Mather (Justin Peacock); Sara Haden (Mrs. Peacock); Grady Sutton (Junio Peacock); Jody Gilbert (Hadwig); Margaret Hamilton (Guinevere); Robin Raymond (Juanita); Gloria Gaye, Mae Roberts, Virginia Tallent (Castle's Daughters); Raymond Hatton (Guard); Buddy Messinger (Butcher Boy); Ralph Volkie (Garbage Man); Ralph McCullough (Postman).

JACKASS MAIL (MGM '42) 80 M.

Producer, John W. Considine Jr.; director, Norman Z. McLeod; story, C. Gardner Sullivan; screenplay, Lawrence Hazard; music, David Snell, Earl Brent; camera, Clyde De Vinna; editor, Gene Ruggiero.

Wallace Beery ("Just" Baggott); Marjorie Main (Clementine "Tiny" Tucker); J. Carroll Naish (O'Sullivan); Darryl Hickman (Tommie Gargan); William Haade ("Red" Gargan); Hobart Cavanaugh ("Gospel" Jones); Dick Curtis (Jim Swade); Joe Yule (Barky); Harry Fleischmann (Carp); Louis Mason (Slim); George Carleton (Pastor); Bobby Larson (Boy); Mary Currier (Mother); Harry Woods (Ranch Owner); Paul Newlan (Rancher); Murdock MacQuarrie (Hickory Jake); Duke York (Rancher); Esther Howard, Babe London (Dance Hall Girls); Wade Boteler (Doctor); Ruth Warren (Doctor's Wife); LeRoy Mason (Vigilante); Bobb Barker (Storekeeper); Robert Emmet O'Conner (Peter Lawson); Eddie Hart, Al Ferguson, Art Belasco, Robert E. Perry (Miners); Frank Darien (Postmaster); Malcolm Waite (Cocky).

TISH (MGM '42) 84 M.

Producer, Orville O. Dull; director, S. Sylvan Simon; based in part on stories by Mary Roberts Rinehart; adaptation, Annalee Whitmore Jacoby, Thomas Seller; screenplay, Harry Ruskin; camera, Paul Vogel; editor, Robert J. Kerns.

Marjorie Main (Letitia Carberry); Zasu Pitts (Aggie Pilkington); Aline MacMahon (Lizzie Wilkins); Lee Bowman (Charles Sands); Guy Kibbee (Judge Bowser); Susan Peters (Cora Edwards); Richard Quine (Ted Bowser); Virginia Grey (Katherine Bowser); Al Shean (Reverend Ostermaier); Ruby Dandridge (Violet); Gerald Oliver Smith (Butler); Sam Ash, King Baggott (Men on Street); Margaret Bert (Mrs. Phelps); Jessie Arnold (Woman on Street); Jenny Mac, Nora Cecil, Gertrude Hoffmann (Spinsters); Kathryn Sheldon (Aciduous Spinster); George Humbert (Italian); Robert Emmett O'Conner (Game Warden); Arthur Space (Court Clerk); Howard Hickman (Mr. Kelbridge); William Farnum (Gardener); Rudy Wissler (Newsboy); Bryon Shores (Dr. McRegan).

TENNESSEE JOHNSON (MGM '42) 100 M.

Producer, J. Walter Ruben; director, William Dieterle; story, Milton Gunsberg, Alvin Meyers; screenplay, John Balderson, Wells Root; camera, Harold Rosson; special effects, Warren Newcombe; editor, Robert J. Kerns.

Van Heflin (Andrew Johnson); Ruth Hussey (Eliza McCardle); Lionel Barrymore (Thad Stevens); Marjorie Main (Mrs. Fisher); Regis Toomey (McDaniel); Montagu Love (Chief Justice Chase); Porter Hall (The Weasel); Charles Dingle (Senator Jim Waters); J. Edward Bromberg (Coke); Grant Withers (Mordecai Milligan); Alec Craig (Andrews); Morris Ankrum (Jefferson Davis); Sheldon Leonard (Atzerodt); Noah Beery Sr. (Sheriff Cass); Lloyd Corrigan (Mr. Secretary); Charles Trowbridge (Lansbury); Harry Worth (John Wilkes Booth); Robert Warwick (Major Crooks); Dane Clark (Wirts); Robert Emmet O'Connor (Robinson); Lee Phelps (Deputy); Brandon Hurst, Charles Ray, Harlan Briggs, Hugh Sothern, Frederick Burton (Senators); Allen Pomeroy, Duke York (Assassins); Ray Barcroft (Officer on Crutches); Ed O'Neill (Lincoln); Jack Norton (Drunk); Russel Simpson (Kirby); Louise Beavers (Addie); James Davis, William Roberts, Frank Jaquet, Emmett Vogan, Pat O'Malley (Reporters); William Wright (Alderman); William Davidson (Vice President Breckenridge); Russell Hicks (Emissary).

HEAVEN CAN WAIT (20th, '43) 113 M.

Producer-director, Ernest Lubitsch; based on the play Birthday by Lazlo Bush-Fekete; screenplay, Samuel Raphaelson; music, Alfred Newman; art director, James Basevi, Leland Fuller; camera, Edward Cronjager; editor, Dorothy Spencer.

Gene Tierney (Martha); Don Ameche (Henry Van Cleve); Charles Coburn (Hugo Van Cleve); Marjorie Main (Mrs. Strabel); Laird Cregar (His Excellency); Spring Byington (Bertha Van Cleve); Allyn Joslyn (Albert Van Cleve); Eugene Pallette (Mr. Strabel); Signe Hasso (Mademoiselle); Louis Calhern (Randolph Van Cleve); Helen Reynolds (Peggy Nash); Aubrey Mather (James); Tod Andrews (Jack Van Cleve); Leonard Carey (Flogdell); Clarence Muse (Jaspe); Dickie Moore (Henry—Age 15); Dickie Jones (Albert—Age 15); Trudy Marshall (Jane); Florence Bates (Mrs. Craig); Clara Blandick (Grandmother); Anita Bolster (Mrs. Cooper-Cooper); Alfred Hall (Albert's Father); Grayce Hampton Smith (Grace's Mother); Nino Pipitone Jr. (Jack as a Child); Claire DuBrey (Miss Ralston); Charles Halton (Clerk in Britano's); James Flavin (Policeman); Michael McLean (Henry—Age 15 Months); Scotty Beckett (Henry—Age 9); Doris Merrick (Nurse); Marlene Mains (Mary); Edwin Maxwell (Doctor).

JOHNNY COME LATELY (UA '43) 97 M.

Producer, William Cagney; director, William K. Howard; based on the novel McLeod's Folley by Louis Bromfield; screenplay, John Van Druten; camera, Theodore Sparkuhl; editor, George Arthur.

James Cagney (Tom Richards); Grace George (Vinne McLeod); Marjorie Main (Gashouse Mary); Marjorie Lord (Jane); Hattie McDaniel (Aida); Ed McNamara (W. M. Dougherty); Bill Henry (Pete Dougherty); Robert Barrat (Bill Swain); George Cleveland (Willie Ferguson); Margaret Hamilton (Myrtle Ferguson); Norman Willis (Hirsh); John Miller, Arthur Hunnicutt. Victor Kilian (Tramps), and Henry Hall.

RATIONING (MGM '44) 93 M.

Producer, Orville O. Dull; director, Willis Goldbeck; screenplay, William R. Lipman, Grant Garrett, Harry Ruskin; art director, Cedric Gibbons; music, David Snell; camera, Sidney Wagner; editor, Ferris Webster.

Wallace Beery (Ben Barton); Marjorie Main (Iris Tuttle); Donald Meek (Wilfred Ball); Dorothy Morris (Dorothy Tuttle); Howard Freeman (Cash Ridule); Connie Gilchrist (Mrs. Porter); Tommy Batten (Lance Barton); Gloria Dickson (Miss McCue); Henry O'Neill (Senator Edward A. White); Richard Hall (Teddy); Charles Halton (Ezra Weeks); Morris Ankrum (Mr. Morgan); Douglas Fowley (Dixie Samson); Chester Clute (Roberts); Chill Wills (Bus Driver); Carol Ann Beery (Carol Ann); Arthur Space (Leafy); Milton Parsons (Hank); Suzanne Kaaren, Kathleen Williams, Natalie Draper, Hazel Brooks, Kay Medford (Information Girls); Robert Emmett O'Connor (Sheriff McGuinness); Ed Kilroy (Minister); Erville Alderson (Gil); Eddy Waller (Smith).

GENTLE ANNIE (MGM '44) 80 M.

Producer, Robert Sish; director, Andrew Martin; based on the novel by MacKinlay Kantor; screenplay, Lawrence Hazard; music, David Snell; art director, Cedric Gibbons, Leonid Vasian; camera, Charles Salerno, Jr.; editor, Chester W. Schaeffer.

Marjorie Main (Annie Goss); James Craig (Lloyd Richland); Henry Morgan (Cottonwood Goss); Paul Langton (Violet Goss); Donna Reed (Mary Lingen); Barton MacLane (Sheriff Tatum); John Philliber (Barrow); Morris Ankrum (Gansby); Arthur Space (Barker); Frank Darien (Jake); Noah Beery Sr. (Hansen); Norman Willis (Cowboy); Lee Phelps, Ray Teal (Expressmen); Lee Shumway (Fireman); Art Miles, Jim Farley (Conductors); John Merton (Engineer); Charlie Williams (Candy Butcher); Jack Clifford, Wade Crosby (Brakemen).

MEET ME IN ST. LOUIS (MGM '44) 113 M.

Producer, Arthur Freed; director, Vincente Minnelli; based on the stories and novel by Sally Benson; screenplay, Irving Brecher, Fred F. Finklehoffe; music director, Georgie Stoll; orchestrations, Conrad Salinger; songs, Andrew B. Sterling and Kerry Mills; Hugo Martin and Ralph Blaine; choreography, Paul Jones; dance director, Charles Walters; art director, Cedric Gibbons, Lemuel Ayers; camera, George Folsey; editor, Albert Akst.

Judy Garland (Esther Smith); Margaret O'Brien ("Tootie" Smith); Mary Astor (Mrs. Anne Smith); Lucille Bremer (Rose Smith); June Lockhart (Lucille Ballard); Tom Drake (John Truett); Marjorie Main (Katie); Harry Davenport (Grandpa); Leon Ames (Mr. Alonzo Smith); Hank Daniels (Lon Smith Jr.); Joan Carroll (Agnes Smith); Hugh Marlowe (Colonel Darly); Robert Sully (Warren Sheffield); Chill Wills (Mr. Neely); Donald Curtis (Doctor Terry); Mary Jo Ellis (Ida Boothby); Ken Wilson (Quentin); Robert Emmett O'Connor (Motorman); Darryl Hickman (Johnny Tevis); Leonard Walker (Conductor); Victor Kilian (Baggage Man); John Phipps (Mailman); Major Sam Harris (Mr. March); Mayo Newhall (Mr. Braukoff); Belle Mitchell (Mrs. Braukoff); Sidney Barnes (Hugo Borvis); Myron Tobias (George); Victor Cox (Driver); Kenneth Donner, Buddy Gorman, Joe Cobbs (Clinton Badgers); Helen Gilbert (Girl on Trolley).

MURDER HE SAYS (Par. '45) 91 M.

Associate producer, E. D. Leshin; director, George Mar-

shall; story, Sack Moffitt; screenplay, Lou Breslow; art director, Hans Dreier, William Flannery; song, Lew Porter and Teepee Mitchell; special effects, Gordon Jennings, Paul Lerpae; camera, Theodor Sparkuhl; editor, LeRoy Stone.

Fred MacMurray (Pete Marshall); Helen Walker (Claire Mathews); Marjorie Main (Mamie Johnson); Jean Heather (Elany Fleagle); Porter Hall (Mr. Johnson); Peter Whitney (Mert Fleagle); Mabel Paige (Grandma Fleagle); Barbara Pepper (Bonnie Fleagle); Peter Whitney (Bert Fleagle); Walter Baldwin (Vic Hardy); James Flavin (Police Officer); Francis Ford (Lee); Si Jenks (80 Year Old); Milton Parsons, Syd Saylor, Ralph Peters (Townsmen); Tom Fadden (Sheriff Murdock); George McKay (Storekeeper); Joel Friedkin (Little Man).

THE HARVEY GIRLS (MGM '46) 104 M.

Producer, Arthur Freed; associate producer, Roger Edens; director, George Sidney; based on the novel by Samuel Hopkins Adams; story, Eleanore Griffin, William Rankin; screenplay, Edmund Beloin, Nathaniel Curtis; music director, Lennie Hayton; art director, Cedric Gibbons, William Ferrari; songs, Johnny Mercer and Harry Warren; special effects, Warren Newcombe; camera, George Golsey; editor, Albert Akst.

Judy Garland (Susan Bradley); John Hodiak (Ned Trent); Ray Bolger (Chris Maule); Preston Foster (Judge Sam Purvis); Virginia O'Brien (Alma); Angela Lansbury (Em); Marjorie Main (Sonora Cassidy); Chill Wills (H. H. Hartsey); Kenny Baker (Terry O'Halloran); Selena Royle (Miss Bliss); Cyd Charisse (Deborah); Ruth Brady (Ethel); Catherine McLeod (Louise); Jack Lambert (Marty Peters); Edward Earle (Jed Admas); Virginia Hunter (Jane); William ("Bill") Phillips, Norman Leavitt (Cowboys); Morris Ankrum (Reverend Claggett); Ben Carter (John Henry); Mitchell Lewis (Sandy); Stephen McNally (Goldust McClean); Bill Hall (Big Joe); Ray Teal, Robert Emmett O'Connor (Conductors); Vernon Dent (Engineer); Jim Toney (Mule Skinner).

BAD BASCOMB (MGM '46) 112 M.

Producer, Orville O. Dull; director, S. Sylvan Simon; story, D. A. Loxley; screenplay, William Lipman, Grant Carrett; special effects, Warren Newcombe; camera, Charles Schoenbraum; editor, Ben Lewis.

Wallace Beery (Zeb Bascomb); Margaret O'Brien (Emmy); Marjorie Main (Abbey Hanks); J. Carroll Naish (Bart Yancy); Frances Rafferty (Dora); Marshall Thompson (Jimmy Holden); Russell Simpson (Elijah Walker); Warner Anderson (Luther Mason); Donald Curtis (John Felton); Connie Gilchrist (Annie Freemont); Sara Haden (Tillie Lovejoy); Renio Riano (Lucy Lovejoy); Wally Cassell (Curley); Jane Green (Hanna); Henry O'Neill (Governor Winter); Frank Darien (Elder McCabe); Joseph Crehan (Governor Ames); Clyde Fillmore (Governor Clark); Arthur Space (Sheriff); Eddie Acuff (Corporal); Stanley Andrews (Colonel Cartright).

UNDERCURRENT (MGM '46) 114 M.

Producer, Pandro S. Berman; director, Vincente Minnelli; story, Thelma Strabel; screenplay, Edward Chodorov; music, Herbert Strothart; art director, Cedric Gibbons, Randall Duell; camera, Karl Freund; editor, Ferris Webster.

Katharine Hepburn (Ann Hamilton); Robert Taylor (Alan Garroway); Robert Mitchum (Michael Garroway); Edmund Gwenn (Professor "Dink" Hamilton); Marjorie Main (Lucy); Jayne Meadows (Sylvia Burton); Clinton Sundberg (Mr. Warmsley); Dan Tobin (Professor Herbert Bangs); Kathryn Card (Mrs. Foster); Leigh Whipper (George); Charles Trowbridge (Justice Putnam); James Westerfield (Henry Gilson); Billy McLain (Uncle Ben); Milton Kibbee (Minister); Forbes Murray (Senator Edwards); Jean Andren (Mrs. Davenport); Robert Emmett O'Connor (Station master); Sarah Edwards (Manager); Ellen Ross (Gwen); Betty Blythe (Saleslady); Helen Eby-Rock (Fitter).

THE SHOW-OFF (MGM '46) 83 M.

Producer, Albert Lewis; director, Harry Beaumont; based on the play by George Kelly; screenplay, George Wells; art director, Cedric Gibbons, Preston Ames; music, David Snell; camera, Robert Planck; editor, Douglas Biggs.

Red Skelton (Aubrey Piper); Marilyn Maxwell (Amy); Marjorie Main (Mrs. Fisher); Virginia O'Brien (Hortense); Eddie "Rochester" Anderson (Rochester); George Cleveland (Pop Fisher); Leon Ames (Frank Hyland), Marshall Thompson (Joe Fisher); Jacqueline White (Clara Hyland); Wilson Wood (Horace Adams); Lila Leeds (Flo); Emory Parnell (Appleton); Charles Lane (Quiz Master); Grady Sutton (Mr. Hotchkiss); Frank Orth (Kopec); Francis Pierlot (Judge Ederman); Russell Hicks (Thorbison); Ida Moore (Mrs. Ascot); Pat McVey, Robert Williams (Officers); Byron Foulger (Jenkins); Kitty Murray (Rochester's Girl Friend); John Tyers (Producer), Jody Gilbert (Woman); Tim Hawkins (Little Boy); Robert Emmett O'Connor (Motorman).

THE EGG AND I (Univ. '47) 108 M.

Producer, Fred F. Finklehoffe, Leonard Goldstein, Chester Erskine; director, Erskine; based on the novel by Betty MacDonald; screenplay, Erskine, Finklehoffe; music, Frank Skinner; camera, Milton Krasner; editor, Russell Schoengarth.

Claudette Colbert (Betty MacDonald); Fred MacMurray (Bob MacDonald); Marjorie Main (Ma Kettle); Louise Albritton (Harriet Putnam); Percy Kilbride (Pa Kettle); Richard Long (Tom Kettle); Billy House (Billy Reed); Ida Moore (Old Lady); Donald MacBride (Mr. Henty); Samuel S. Hinds (Sheriff); Esther Dale (Mrs. Hicks); Elisabeth Risdon (Betty's Mother); John Berkes (Geoduck); Vic Potel (Crowbar); Fuzzy Knight (Cab Driver); Kisabel O'Madigan (Mrs. Hicks's Mother); Dorothy Vaughan (Maid); Sam McDaniel (Waiter); Jesse Graves (Porter); Jack Baxley (Judge); Howard Mitchell (Announcer); Lou Mason (Bergheimer); Judith Bryant, Gloria Moore, Eugene Persson, Diane Florentine, George McDonald, Colleen Alpaugh, Teddy Infuhr, Robert Winans, Diana Graeff, Kathleen Mackey, Robert

Beyers (Kettle Children); Beatrice Boerts (Nurse); Ralph Littlefield (Photographer).

THE WISTFUL WIDOW OF WAGON GAP (Univ. '47) 78 M.

Producer, Robert Arthur; director, Charles T. Barton; story, D. D. Beauchamp, William Bowers; screenplay, Robert Lees, Frederic I. Renaldo, John Grant; music, Walter Shumann; camera, Charles Van Enger; editor, Frank Gross.

Bud Abbott (Duke Eagan); Lou Costello (Chester Wooley); Marjorie Main (Widow Hawkins); Audrey Young (Juanita Hawkins); George Cleveland (Judge Benbow); Gordon Jones (Jake Frame); William Ching (Jim Simpson); Peter Thompson (Phil); Olin Howlin (Undertaker); Bill Clauson (Matt Hawkins); Pamela Wells (Sarah Hawkins); Billy O'Leary (Billy Hawkins); Paul Dunn (Lincoln Hawkins); Diane Florentine (Sally Hawkins); Jimmie Bates (Jefferson Hawkins); Rex Lease (Hank); Glenn Strange (Lefty); Edmund Cobb (Lem); Dewey Robinson (Miner); Emmet Lynn (Old Codger); Iris Adrian (Dance Hall Hostess); Charles King (Gunman); Ed Peil (Townsman); Lee Lasses White (Shot Gun Rider); Gilda Feldrais (Hostess); Billy Engle (Undertaker's Helper); Dave Sharpe (Man thrown by Window); Frank Hagney (Barfly); Harry Evans (Card Dealer); Frank Marlo, Ethan Laidlaw, Jerry Jerome (Cowboys).

FEUDIN', FUSSIN' AND A-FIGHTIN' (Univ. '48) 78 M

Producer, Leonard Goldstein; director, George Sherman; screenplay, D. D. Beauchamp; art director, Bernard Herzbrun, Frank A. Richards; music, Leith Stevens; camera, Irving Glassberg; editor, Edward Curtiss.

Donald O'Connor (Wilbur McMurty); Marjorie Main (Maribel Matthews); Percy Kilbride (Billy Caswell); Penny Edwards (Libby Matthews); Joe Besser (Sharkey Dolan); Harry Shannon (Chauncey); Fred Kohler Jr. (Emory Tuttle); Howland Chamberlin (Doc Overholt); Edmund Cobb (Stage Driver); Joel Friedkin (Stage Passenger); I. Stanford Jolley (Guard); Louis DaPron (Specialty); Charles Middleton (Citizen); Kenneth MacDonald, Herbert Heywood (Judges); Harry Brown (Man in Tree); Arthur Miles, Gene Stutenroth (Big Men); Roy Butler, Bill Sundholm, Monte Montague (Men in Cafe); Francis Ford, Tommy Coats (Checkers); Francis Williams (Citizen at Dance).

MA AND PA KETTLE (Univ. '49) 75 M.

Producer, Leonard Goldstein; director, Charles Lamont; based on characters from *The Egg and I* by Betty MacDonald; screenplay, Herbert Margolis, Louis Morheim, Al Lewis; art director, Bernard Herzbrun, Emrich Nicholson; music, Milton Schwarzwald; camera, Maury Gertsman; editor, Russell Schoengarth.

Marjorie Main (Ma Kettle); Percy Kilbride (Pa Kettle); Richard Long (Tom Kettle); Meg Randall (Kim Parker); Patricia Alphin (Secretary); Esther Dale (Mrs. Birdie Hicks); Barry Kelley (Mayor Swiggins); Isabel O'Madigan (Mrs. Hicks's Mother); Ida Moore (Emily); Emory

Parnell (Billy Reed); Boyd Davis (Mr. Simpson); O. Z. Whitehead (Mr. Billings); Ray Bennett (Sam Rogers); Alvin Hammer (Alvin); Lester Allen (Geoduck); Chief Yowlachie (Crowbar); Rex Lease (Sheriff); Dale Belding (Danny Kettle); Teddy Infuhr (George Kettle); George McDonald (Henry Kettle); Robin Winans (Billy Kettle); Gene Persson (Ted Kettle); Paul Dunn (Donny Kettle); Margaret Brown (Ruthie Kettle); Beverly Wook (Eve Kettle); Diane Florentine (Sara Kettle); Gloria Moore (Rosie Kettle); Melinda Plowman (Susie Kettle); Harry Tyler (Ticket Agent); Dewey Robinson (Giant Man); Sam McDaniel (Waiter); Ted Stanhope (Steward); Harry Cheshire (Fletcher); Eddy C. Walter (Mr. Green); John Wald (Dick Palmer); Donna Leary (Salty Kettle); Elena Schreiner (Nancy Kettle); George Arglen (Willie Kettle).

BIG JACK (MGM '49) 85 M.

Producer, Gottfried Reinhardt; director, Richard Thorpe; screenplay, Gene Fowler, Marvin Borowsky, Osso Van Eyss; music, Herbert Stothart; art director, Cedric Gibbons; camera, Robert Surtees; editor, George Boemler.

Wallace Beery (Big Jack Horner); Richard Conte (Dr. Alexander Meade); Marjorie Main (Flapjack Kate); Edward Arnold (Mayor Mahoney); Vanessa Brown (Patricia Mahoney); Clinton Sundberg (C. Petronius Smith); Charles Dingle (Mathias Taylor); Clem Bevans (Saltlick Joe); Jack Lambert (Bud Valentine); Will Wright (Will Fransworth); William "Bill" Phillips (Toddy); Syd Saylor (Pokey); Vince Barnet (Tom Speed); Trevor Bardette (John Oakea); Andy Clyde (Putt Cleghorn); Edith Evanson (Widow Simpson); Tom Fadden (Sheriff Summers); Robert B. Williams (Jed); Eddie Dunn (Coachman); Francis McDonald (Prisoner); Minerva Urecal (Mrs. Summers); Ann Doran (Sarah); Hank Bell (Driver); Dick Alexander, Lynn Farr, Jimmy Martin, Lane Bradford, Casey McGregor, Cactus Mack, Carl Sepulveda, Bill Dix, Bob Filmer, Fred Gilman (Bandits); Jim Pierce (Man in Buggy); Helen Dickson (Woman in Buggy); Carol Henry, Frank McCarroll, Hollis Bane, Frank McGrath (Posse Members).

MA AND PA KETTLE GO TO TOWN (Univ. '50) 79 M.

Producer, Leonard Goldstein; director, Charles Lamont; screenplay, Martin Ragaway, Leonard Stern; camera, Charles Van Enger; editor, Russell Schoengarth.

Marjorie Main (Ma Kettle); Percy Kilbride (Pa Kettle); Richard Long (Tom Kettle); Meg Randall (Kim Kettle); Ray Collins (Jonathan Parker); Barbara Brown (Elizabeth Parker); Esther Dale (Birdie Hicks); Ellen Corby (Emily); Teddy Hart (Crowbar); Oliver Blake (Geoduck); Emory Parnell (Billy Reed); Peter Leeds (Manson); Dale Belding (Danny Kettle); Teddy Infuhr (Benjamin Kettle); Rex Lease (Sheriff); Diane Florentine (Sara Kettle); Paul Dunn (George Kettle); Eugene Persson (Willie Kettle); Margaret Brown (Ruthie Kettle); Donna Leary (Sally Kettle); Lynn Wood Coleman (Billy Kettle); Mary Ann Jackson (Rosie Kettle); Jackie Jackson (Henry Kettle); Sherry Jackson (Susie Kettle); Beverly Mook (Eve Kettle); Elana Schreiner (Nancy Kettle); Joyce Holden (Miss Trent); Ann Pearce (Miss Clyde); Lucille Barkley (Miss

Cooper); Edward Clark (Dr. Bagley); Dee Carroll (Miss Stafford); Edmund Cobb (Engineer); Jack Ingram (State Trooper); Herry Hausner (Burley); Verna Kornman (Mrs. Quinlan); Alice Richey (Mrs. Tullet); Steve Wayne (Mr. Chadwick).

SUMMER STOCK (MGM '50) 108 M.

Producer, Joe Pasternak; director, Charles Walters; story, Sy Gomberg; screenplay, George Wells, Gomberg; choreography, Nick Castle; music director, Johnny Green; songs, Harry Warren, Mack Gordon; camera, Robert Planck; editor, Albert Akst.

Judy Garland (Jane Falbury); Gene Kelly (Joe D. Ross); Eddie Bracken (Orville Wingait); Gloria De Haven (Abigail Falbury); Marjorie Main (Esmen); Phil Silvers (Herb Blake); Ray Collins (Jasper G. Wingait); Carleton Carpenter (Artie); Nita Bieber (Sarah Higgins); Hans Conried (Harrison I. Keath); Paul E. Burns (Frank); Carol Haney, Dorothy Tuttle, Arthur Loew Jr., Dick Humphreys, Jimmy Thomspon, Bridget Carr, Joanne Tree, Jean Coyne, Jean Adcock, Joanne Tree, Rena Lenart, Joan Dale, Betty Hannon, Elynne Ray, Marilyn Reiss, Carol West, Eugene Freedley, Don Powell, Joe Roach, Albert Ruiz (Members of Stock Company); Roy Butler, Henry Sylvester, George Bunny, Frank Pharr (Townsmen); Cameron Grant, Jack Daley, Reginald Simpson (Producers); Michael Chapin, Teddy Infuh (Boys); Almira Sessions (Constance Fliggerton); Kathryn Sheldon (Amy Fliggerton); Jack Gargan (Clerk); Eddie Dunn (Sheriff); Erville Alderson (Zeb).

MRS. O'MALLEY AND MR. MALONE (MGM, '50) 69 M.

Producer, William H. Wright; director, Norman Taurog; based on the story by Craig Rice, Stuart Palmer; screenplay, William Bowers; art director, Cedric Gibbons, Daniel B. Cathcart; music, Adolph Deutsch; camera, Ray June; editor, Gene Ruggiero.

Marjorie Main (Hattie O'Malley); James Whitmore (John J. Malone); Ann Dvorak (Connie Kepplar); Phyllis Kirk (Kay); Fred Clark (Tim Marino); Dorothy Malone (Lola Gillway); Clinton Sundberg (Donald); Douglas Fowley (Steve Kepplar); Willard Waterman (Mr. Ogle); Don Porter (Myron Brynk); Jack Bailey (Announcer); Nancy Saunders (Joanie); Basil Tellou (The Greek); James Burke (Conductor); Eddie Walter (Rigger); Regis Toomey, Herbert Vigran (Reporters); Fred Brady (Orchestra Leader); Henry Corden (Sascha); Edward Earle (Mr. Fillion); Elizabeth Flournoy (Mrs. Fillion); Noreen Mortensen (Margie); Mae Clarke, Thelma Rigdon, Stanley Blystone, Bette Arlen, Lisa Lowry, Philo McCullough, Jerry Lacoe Jr. (Passengers); Pat Williams (Pirate Girl); Jeffrey Sayre, J. Lewis Smith (Photographers); Diana Norris (Jessie); Donna Norris (Bessie).

MA AND PA KETTLE BACK ON THE FARM (Univ. '51) 81 M.

Producer, Leonard Goldstein; associate producer, Bill Grady, Jr.; director, Edward Sedgwick; story-screenplay, Jack Henley; art director, Bernard Herzbrun, Emrich Nicholson; music director, Joseph Gershenson; camera, Charles Van Enger; editor, Russell Schoengarth.

Marjorie Main (Ma Kettle); Percy Kilbride (Pa Kettle); Richard Long (Tom Kettle); Meg Randall (Kim Kettle); Ray Collins (Jonathan Parker); Barbara Brown (Elizabeth Parker); Emory Parnell (Billy Reed); Peter Leeds (Manson); Teddy Hart (Crowbar); Oliver Blake (Geoduck).

THE LAW AND THE LADY (MGM '51) 104 M.

Producer-director, Edwin H. Knopf; based on the play *The Last of Mrs. Cheney* by Frederick Lonsdale; screenplay, Leonard Spiegelglass, Karl Tunberg; art director, Cedric Gibbons, Daniel Cathcart; music, Carmen Dragon; camera, George J. Folsey; editor, James E. Newcome, William Gulick.

Greer Garson (Jane Hoskins); Michael Wilding (Nigel Duxbury/Lord Minden); Fernando Lamas (Juan Dinas); Marjorie Main (Mrs. Wortin); Hayden Rorke (Tracy Collins); Margalo Gillmore (Cora Caighn); Ralph Dumke (James H. Caighn); Phyllis Stanley (Lady Minden); Rhys Williams (Inspector McGraw); Natalie Schafer (Pamela Femberson); Soledad Jiminez (Princess Margarita); Lalo Rios (Fanchito); Stanley Logan (Sir Roland Epping); Holmes Herbert (English Colonel); John Eldredge (Assistant Manager); Andre Charlot (Maire d'Hotel); Victor Sen Yung (Chinese Manager); Anna Q. Nilsson (Mrs. Scholmm); Bess Flowers (Mrs. Bruno Thayar); Stuart Holmes (Mr. Bruno Thayar); Betty Farrington (Miss Belpayasa); Nikki Juston (Miss Belpayasa); Richard Hale (Sheriff); Spencer Chan (Servant); Matt Moore (Senator Scholmm).

MR. IMPERIUM (MGM '51) 87 M.

Producer, Edwin H. Knopf; director, Don Hartman; based on a play by Knopf; screenplay, Hartman, Knopf; music director, Johnny Green; music, Bronislau Kaper; song, Harold Arlen and Dorothy Fields, Ray Gilbert and Augustin Lara; camera, George J. Folsey; editors, George White, William Gulick.

Lana Turner (Fredda Barlo); Ezio Pinza (Mr. Imperium); Marjorie Main (Mrs. Cabot); Barry Sullivan (Paul Hunter); Sir Cedric Hardwicke (Bernand); Keenan Wynn (Motor Cop); Debbie Reynolds (Gwen); Ann Codee (Anna Pelan); Wilton Graff (Andrew Bolton); Giscomo Spadoni (Giovanni); Chick Chandler (George Hoskins); Joseph Vitale (Bearded Man); Mae Clarke (Secretary); Don Haggerty (Director); Tony Marlo (Lackey); Cliff Clark (Restaurant Proprietor); Matt Moore (Gateman); Mitchell Lewis (Old Watchman); Arthur Walsh, Allan Ray, Wilson Wood, Bobby Troup (Specialties in Band).

IT'S A BIG COUNTRY (MGM '51) 88 M.

Producer, Robert Sisk; directors, Richard Thorpe, John Sturges, Charles Vidor, Don Weis, Clarence Brown, William A. Wellman, Don Hartman; screenplay, Dore Schary, William Ludwig, Edgar Brocke, Helen Deutsch, Ray Chordes, Isobel Lennart, Claudea Cranston, Allen Rivkin, Lucile Schlossberg, Dorothy Kingsley, George Wells, Joseph Petracca; camera, John Alton, Ray June, William Mellor, Joseph Ruttenberg; editors, Ben Lewis, Frederich Y. Smith.

Episode Five: LETTER FROM KOREA: Marjorie Main (Mrs. Wrenley); Keefe Brasselle (Sergeant Maxie Klein).

THE BELLE OF NEW YORK (MGM '51) 80 M.

Producer, Arthur Freed; director, Charles Walters; based on the play by Hugh Morten; adaptation, Chester Erskine, Robert O'Brien, Irving Elinson; songs, Harry Warren, Johnny Mercer; music director, Adolph Deutsch; choreography, Robert Alton; camera, Robert Blanck; editor, Albert Akst.

Fred Astaire (Charlie Hill); Vera-Ellen (Angela Collins); Marjorie Main (Mrs. Phineas Hill); Keenan Wynn (Max Ferris); Alice Pearce (Elsie Wilkins); Clinton Sundberg (Gilfred Spivak); Gale Robbins (Dixie McCoy); Henry Slate (Clancy); Tom Dugan, Percy Helton, Dick Wessel (Bowery Bums); Lyn Wilde, Carol Brewster, Meredith Leeds (Frenchie's Girls); Lisa Ferraday (Frenchie); Roger Davis (Judkins); Buddy Roosevelt (Cab Driver); Reginald Simpson (Maitre D'); Oliver Blake (Mr. Currier); Billy Griffith (Mr. Ives); Benny Rubin (Herman).

MA AND PA KETTLE AT THE FAIR (Univ. '52) 78 M.

Producer, Leonard Goldstein; director, Charles Barton; story, Martin Ragaway, Leonard Stein, Jack Hanley; screenplay, Richard Morris, John Grant; camera, Maury Gertsman; editor, Ted. J. Kent.

Marjorie Main (Ma Kettle); Percy Kilbride (Pa Kettle); Lori Nelson (Rosie Kettle); James Best (Marvin Johnson); Esther Dale (Birdie Hicks); Russell Simpson (Clem Johnson); Emory Parnell (Billy Reed); Oliver Blake (Geoduck); Hallene Hill (Mrs. Hicks's Mother); Rex Lease (Sheriff); James Griffith (Medicine Man); Edmund Cobb, Roy Regnier (Men); Teddy Infuhr (Benjamin Kettle); George Arglen (Willie Kettle); Ronald R. Rondell (Danny Kettle); Margaret Brown (Ruth Kettle); Jackie Jackson (Henry Kettle); Billy Clark (George Kettle); Donna Leary (Sally Kettle); Elana Schreiner (Nancy Kettle); Eugene Persson (Teddy Kettle); Jenny Linder (Sara Kettle); Sherry Jackson (Susie Kettle); Gary Lee Jackson (Billy Kettle); Beverly Mook (Eve Kettle); Zachary Charles (Crowbar); Frank Ferguson (Sam, the Jailer); Syd Saylor (Postman); Harry Harvey (Chairman); Harry Cheshire (Preacher); Wheaton Chambers (Injured Man); Harry Cording (Ed); William Gould, Frank McFarland (Judges); Claire Meade (Sarah); James Guilfoyle (Birdie's Trainer); Mel Pogue (Delivery Boy); Doug Carter (Ticket Seller); Bob Donnelly (Clown).

MA AND PA KETTLE ON VACATION (Univ. '53) 75 M.

Producer, Leonard Goldstein; director, Charles Lamont; screenplay, Jack Henley; camera, George Robinson; editor, Leonard Weiner.

Marjorie Main (Ma Kettle); Percy Kilbride (Pa Kettle); Ray Collins (Jonathan Parker); Bodil Miller (Inez Kraft); Sig Ruman (Cyrus Kraft); Barbara Brown (Elizabeth Parker); Ivan Triesault (Henri); Oliver Blake (Geoduck); Teddy Hart (Crowbar); Peter Brocco (Mr. Wade); Jay Novello (Andre); Jean De Briac (Chef Chantilly); Larry Dobkin (Farrell); Harold Goodwin (Harriman); Jack

Kruschen (Jacques); Rosario Imperio, Andre D'Arcy (Apache Team); Ken Terrell (Taxicab Driver); Alice Kelley (Stewardess); Rita Moreno (Soubrette); John Eldredge (Masterson); Zachary Yacconnelli (Maitre D'); Sherry Jackson (Susie Kettle); Gary Lee Jackson (Billy Kettle); Billy Clark (George Kettle); Jackie Jackson (Henry Kettle); Elana Schreiner (Nancy Kettle); Ronnie Rondell (Dannie Kettle); Margaret Brown (Ruthie Kettle); Jon Gardner (Benjamin Kettle); Jenny Linder (Sara Kettle); Beverly Mook (Eve Kettle); Donna Leary (Sally Kettle); Robert Scott (Teddy Kettle); George Arglen (Willie Kettle); Gloria Pall (French Girl); Major Sam Harris (Plane Passenger); Carli Elinor (Orchestra Leader); Eddie Le Baron (Wine Steward).

FAST COMPANY (MGM '53) 67 M.
Producer, Henry Berman; director, John Sturges; based on the story by Eustace Cockrell; adaptation, Don Mankiewicz; screenplay, William Roberts; music director, Alberto Colombo; art director, Cedric Gibbons, Leonid Vasean; camera, Harold Lipstein; editor, Joseph Dervim.

Howard Keel (Rick Grayton); Polly Bergen (Carol Maldon); Marjorie Main (Ma Parkson); Nina Foch (Mercedes Bellway); Robert Burton (Dave Sandring); Carol Nugent (Jigger Parkson); Joaquin Garay (Mauel Morales).

THE LONG, LONG TRAILER (MGM '54) 96 M.
Producer, Pandro S. Berman; director, Vincente Minnelli; based on the novel by Clinton Twiss; screenplay, Albert Hackett, Frances Goodrich; art director, Cedric Gibbons, Edward Carfagno; music, Adolph Deutsch; song, Haven Gillespie, Seymour Simmons, and Richard A. Whiting; camera, Robert Surtees; editor, Ferris Webster.

Lucille Ball (Tracy Collini); Desi Arnaz (Nicky Collini); Marjorie Main (Mrs. Hittaway); Keenan Wynn (Policeman); Gladys Hurlbut (Mrs. Bolton); Moroni Olsen (Mr. Tewitt); Bert Freed (Foreman); Madge Black (Aunt Anastacia); Walter Baldwin (Uncle Edgar); Oliver Blake (Mr. Judlow); Perry Sheehan (Bridesmaid); Charles Herbert (Little Boy); Herb Vigran (Trailer Salesman); Karl Lukas (Inspector); Emmett Vogan (Mr. Bolton); Edgar Dearing (Manager); Geraldine Carr, Sarah Spencer (Girl Friends); Ruth Warren (Mrs. Dudley); Dallas Boyd (Minister); Howard McNear (Mr. Hittaway); Jack Kruschen (Mechanic); Edna Skinner (Mrs. Barrett); Alan Lee (Mr. Elliott); Robert Anderson (Carl Barrett); Phil Rich (Mr. Dudley); John Call (Shorty); Wilson Wood (Garage Owner); Dorothy Neumann (Aunt Ellen); Howard Wright (Uncle Bill); Connie Van (Grace); Dennis Ross (Jody); Christopher Olsen (Tom); Ida Moore (Candy Store Clerk); Emory Parnell (Officer); Fay Roope (Judge); Ruth Lee (Mrs. Tewitt); Dick Alexander (Father); Frank Gerstle (Attendant); Peter Leeds (Garage Manager); Judy Sackett (Bettie); Juney Ellis (Waitress).

MA AND PA KETTLE AT HOME (Univ. '54) 81 M.
Producer, Richard Wilson; director, Charles Lamont; screenplay, Kay Lenard; music director, Joseph Gershenson; camera, Carl Guthrie; editor, Leonard Weiner.

Marjorie Main (Ma Kettle); Percy Kilbride (Pa Kettle); Alan Mowbray (Mannering); Ross Elliott (Pete Crosby); Alice Kelley (Sally Maddocks); Brett Halsey (Elwin Kettle); Mary Wickes (Miss Wetter); Irving Bacon (Mr. Maddocks); Emory Parnell (Bill Reed); Virginia Brissac (Mrs. Maddocks); Stan Ross (Crowbar); Oliver Blake (Geoduck); Guy Wilkerson (Jones); Edmund Cobb (Jefferson); Edgar Dearing (Perkins); Betty McDonough, Helen Gibson (Ranch Wives); Judy Nugent (Betty Kettle); Carol Nugent (Nancy Kettle); Richard Eyer (Billie Kettle); Donald MacDonald (Benjamin Kettle); Coral Hammond (Eve Kettle); Patrick Miller (Teddy Kettle); Nancy Zane (Sara Kettle); Gary Pagett (George Kettle); Donna Cregan Moots (Ruthie Kettle); Whitey Haupt (Henry Kettle); Pat Morrow (Susie Kettle); Tony Epper (Danny Kettle); James Flavin, Robert Nelson (Motorcycle Cops); Rick Vallin, Hank Worden, Ken Terrell (Indians).

RICOCHET ROMANCE (Univ. '54) 80 M.
Producer, Robert Arthur, Richard Wilson; director, Charles Lamont; screenplay, Kay Lennard; music director, Joseph Gershenson; assistant director, William Holland; art director, Alexander Golitzen, Alfred Sweeney; camera, George Robinson; editor, Russell Schoengarth.

Marjorie Main (Pansy Jones); Chill Wills (Tom Williams); Rudy Vallee (Worthington Higgenmacher); Pedro Gonzales-Gonzales (Manuel Gonzales); Alfonso Bedoya (Alfredo Gonzales); Ruth Hampton (Angela Mansfield); Benay Venuta (Claire Renard); Darryl Hickman (Dave King); Lee Aaker (Timmy Williams); Irene Ryan (Miss Clay); Judith Ames (Betsy Williams).

ROSE MARIE (MGM '54) 106 M.
Producer-director, Mervyn LeRoy; based on the story play by Otto A. Harbach and Oscar Hammerstein II; music, Rudolf Frimel, Herbert Stothart; screenplay, Ronald Miller, George Froeschel; art director, Cedric Gibbons, Merrill Pye; assistant director, Arvid Griffin; music director, Georgie Stoll; additional songs, Friml, Stoll, Herbert Baker; new lyrics, Paul Francis Webster; music numbers, Busby Berkeley; special effects, A. Arnold Gillespie, Warren Newcombe; camera, Paul Vogel; editor, Harold F. Kress.

Ann Blyth (Rose Marie Lemaitre); Howard Keel (Mike Malone); Fernando Lamas (James Severn Duval); Bert Lahr (Barney McGorkle); Marjorie Main (Lady Jane Dunstock); Joan Taylor (Wanda); Roy Collins (Inspector Appleby); Chief Yowlachie (Black Eagle); James Logan (Clerk); Thurl Ravenscroft (Indian Medicine Man); Abel Fernandez (Indian Warrior); Billy Dix (Mess Waiter); Al Ferguson, Frank Ragney (Woodsmen); Marshall Reed (Mountie); Sheb Wooley (Corporal); Dabbs Greer (Committeeman); John Pickard, John Damler (Orderlies); Sally Yarnell (Hostess); Gordon Richards (Attorney); Lumsden Hart (Judge); Mickey Simpson (Trapper); Pepi Lanzi (Johnny Lang).

MA AND PA KETTLE AT WAIKIKI (Univ. '55) 79 M.
Producer, Leonard Goldstein; director, Lee Sholem; screenplay, Harry Clark, Elwood Ullman; art director,

Bernard Herzbrun, Erie Urbom; camera, Cliff Stine; editor, Leonard Weiner.

Marjorie Main (Ma Kettle); Percy Kilbride (Pa Kettle); Lori Nelson (Rosie Kettle); Byron Palmer (Bob Baxter); Loring Smith (Rodney Kettle); Lowell Gilmore (Robert Coates); Mabel Albertson (Mrs. Andrews); Fay Roope (Fulton Andrews); Oliver Blake (Geoduck); Teddy Hart (Crowbar); Esther Dale (Birdie Hicks); Russell Johnson (Eddie Nelson); Ben Welden (Shorty Bates); Dick Reeves (Lefty Conway); Myron Healey (Marty); Rick Roman (Chuck Collins); Hilo Hattie (Mama Lotus); Charles Lung (Papa Lotus); Byron Kane (Professor Gilfallen); Sandra Spence (Pa's Secretary); Harold Goodwin (Dr. Barnes); Norman Field (Dr. Fabian); Elana Schreiner (Nancy Kettle); Beverly Mook (Eve Kettle); Jenny Linder (Sara Kettle); Ronnie Rondell (Dannie Kettle); Tim Hawkins (Teddy Kettle); Margaret Brown (Ruthie Kettle); Billy Clark (George Kettle); George Arglen (Willie Kettle); Jon Gardner (Benjamin Kettle); Jackie Jackson (Henry Kettle); Donna Leary (Sally Kettle); Bonnie Kay Eddy (Susie Kettle); Luukiuluana (Masseuse).

THE KETTLES IN THE OZARKS (Univ. '56) 81 M.

Producer, Richard Wilson; director, Charles Lamont; screenplay, Kay Lenard; art director, Alexander Golitzen, Alfred Sweeney; music director, Joseph Gershenson; assistant director, Joseph E. Kenny; camera, George Robinson; editor, Edward Curtiss.

Marjorie Main (Ma Kettle); Arthur Hunnicutt (Sedge Kettle); Una Merkel (Miss Bedelia Baines); Ted de Corsia (Professor); Richard Eyer (Billy); David O'Brien (Conductor); Joe Sawyer (Bancroft Baines); Richard Deacon (Cod Head); Sid Tomack (Benny); Harry Hines (Joe); Jim Hayward (Jack Dexter); Oliver Sturgess (Nancy); George Arglen (Feddie); Eddie Pagett (Sammy); Cheryl Calloway (Susie); Pat Morrow (Sally); Bonnie Franklin (Betty); Louis DePron (Mountaineer); Sarah Padden (Miz Tinware); Roscoe Ates (Man); Kathryn Sheldon (Old Woman); Stuart Holmes (Bald-Headed Man); Elvia Allman (Meek Man's Wife); Paul Wexler (Reverend Martin); Robert Easton (Lafe).

FRIENDLY PERSUASION (AA '56) 139 M.

Producer-director, William Wyler; associate producer, Robert Wyler; based on the book by Jessamyn West; assistant director, Austen Jewell; songs, Paul Francis Webster and Dimitri Tiomkin; music, Tiomkin; camera, Ellsworth Fredericks; editor, Robert Swink, Edward Beery, Jr., Robert Belcher.

Gary Cooper (Jess Birdwell); Dorothy McGuire (Eliza Birdwell); Marjorie Main (Widow Hudspeth); Anthony Perkins (Josh Birdwell); Richard Eyer (Little Jess); Robert Middleton (Sam Jordan); Phyllis Love (Mattie Birdwell); Mark Richman (Gard Jordan); Walter Catlett (Professor Quigley); Richard Hale (Elder Purdy); Joel Fluellen (Enoch); Theodore Newton (Army Major); John Smith (Caleb); Edna Skinner (Opal Hudspeth); Marjorie Durant (Pearl Hudspeth); Frances Farwell (Ruby Hudspeth); Frank Jenks (Shell Game Operator); Russell Simpson, Charles Halton, Everett Glass (Elders); Joe Turkel, James Anderson (Poor Losers); Mary Carr (Emma); Diane Jergens (Quaker Girl); John Craven (Leader); Jean Inness (Mrs. Purdy); Nelson Leigh (Minister); Helen Kleeb (Old Lady); Harry Hines (Barker); Henry Rowland (O'Hara); Ivan Rasputin (Billy Goat); Donald Kerr (Manager); Steve Warren (Haskell); Earle Hodgins (Shooting Gallery Operator); John Pickard (Ex-Sergeant); Richard Garland (Bushwhacker); Norman Leavitt (Clem); Don Kennedy (Buster); Samantha (The Goose).

THE KETTLES ON OLD MACDONALD'S FARM (Univ. '57) 81 M.

Producer, Howard Christie; director, Virgil Vogel; screenplay, William Raynor, Herbert Margolis; art director, Alexander Golitzen, Philip Barber; music director, Joseph Gershenson; camera, Alfred E. Arling; editor, Edward Curtiss.

Marjorie Main (Ma Kettle); Parker Fennelly (Pa Kettle); Gloria Talbott (Sally Flemming); John Smith (Brad Johnson); George Dunn (George); Claude Akins (Pete Logan); Roy Barcroft (J. P. Flemming); Pat Morrow (Bertha); George Arglen (Henry); Ricky Kelman (Elmer); Donald Baker (Abner); Polly Burson (Agnes Logan); Hallene Hill (Granny); Sara Taft (Clarabelle); Harvey B. Dunn (Judge); Don Clark, Boyd Red Morgan, Glenn Thompson (Shivaree Men); Edna Smith, Verna Korman (Shivaree Women); Roger Creed, Frank Hagney, Henry Wills, Clem Fuller (Townsmen); Carl Saxe, George Barrows (Hunters); Eva Novak, Chuck Hamilton, George Hickman (Ad Libs).

With Jack Smart, Richard Carle, Margaret Mc Wade,
Nan Grey, Louise Beavess in *Love in a Bungalow*
(Universal, 1940).

Publicity poses for stage production of *Dead End* (1937).

With Edmund Elton, George Walcott in *Stella Dallas* (UA, 1937).

With Richard Cromwell, Helen Mack in *The Wrong Road* (Republic, 1937).

With Ann Doran, Charles Quigley, Marc Lawrence,
Rita Hayworth (seated), Bess Flowers in *The Shadow*
(Columbia, 1937).

With Shirley Ross, Blanche Rose in *Prison Farm* (Paramount, 1938).

With Anne E. Todd in *Under the Big Top* (Monogram, 1938).

With Walter Connolly, Robert Emmett Keane, Gregory Gay in *Too Hot to Handle* (MGM, 1938).

With Jean Parker in *Romance of the Limberlost* (Monogram, 1938).

With Virginia Bruce in *There Goes My Heart* (UA, 1938).

With Delmar Watson, Phyllis Brooks, George Guhl
in *City Girl* (20th Century-Fox, 1938).

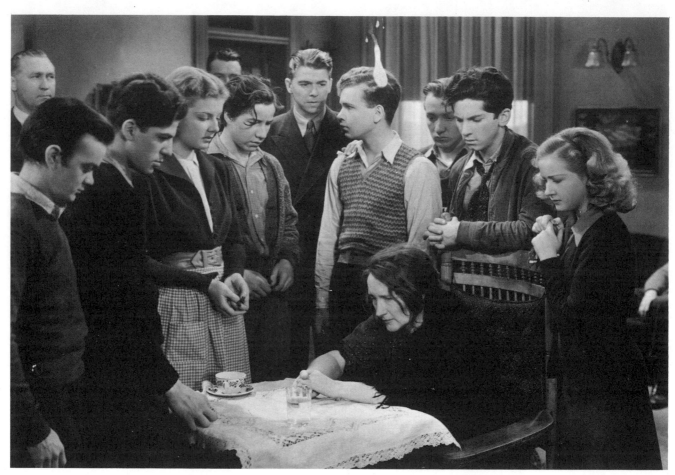

With Leo Gorcey, Billy Halop, Ann Sheridan, Bobby
Jordan, Ronald Reagan, Frankie Thomas, Huntz Hall,
Gabriel Dell, Bonita Granville in *Angels Wash Their
Faces* (WB, 1939).

With Rosalind Russell in *The Women* (MGM, 1939).

With Arthur Hohl in *Two Thoroughbreds* (RKO, 1939).

With Walter Pidgeon in *Dark Command* (Republic, 1940).

With Helen Broderick, Helen Westley, Cecil Cunning-
ham, Billie Burke, Clem Bevans, Beulah Bondi, Charles
Coburn, Virginia Grey, Dan Dailey, Francis Pierlot in
The Captain is a Lady (MGM, 1940).

With Wallace Beery in *Wyoming* (MGM, 1940).

In *Wild Man of Borneo* (MGM, 1941).

With Wallace Beery, Leo Carrillo in *Barnacle Bill* (MGM, 1941).

With Albert Basserman, Richard Nichols, Joan Crawford in *A Woman's Face* (MGM, 1941).

With Clark Gable in *Honky Tonk* (MGM, 1941).

In *The Shepherd of the Hills* (Paramount, 1941).

With Wallace Beery in *The Bugle Sounds* (MGM, 1941).

With Wallace Beery in *The Bugle Sounds*.

With Melvyn Douglas in *We Were Dancing* (MGM, 1942).

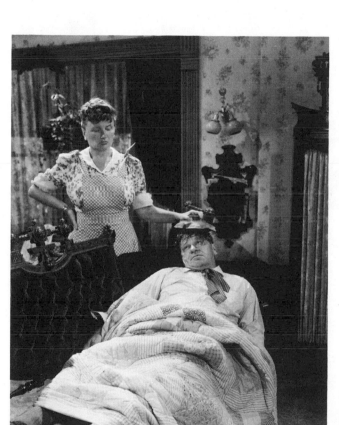

With Wallace Beery in *The Bugle Sounds.*

With Marsha Hunt in *Affairs of Martha* (MGM, 1942).

With Spring Byington, Frances Drake, Richard Carlson, Marsha Hunt in *Affairs of Martha*.

With Wallace Beery (as statues) in *Jackass Mail*
(MGM, 1942).

With ZaSu Pitts, Aline MacMahon, Lee Bowman in *Tish* (MGM, 1942).

With Van Heflin, Regis Toomey, Alec Craig, Grant Withers in *Tennessee Johnson* (MGM, 1942).

Marjorie Main in 1942.

With Eugene Pallette, Gene Tierney in *Heaven Can Wait* (20th Century-Fox, 1943).

With James Cagney, Henry Hall in *Johnny Come Lately* (UA, 1943).

With James Cagney in *Johnny Come Lately*.

Lobby Card for *Rationing*, with Wallace Beery (MGM, 1943).

With Wallace Beery, Dorothy Morris in *Rationing*.

In *Meet Me in St. Louis* (MGM, 1944).

With James Craig, Donna Reed in *Gentle Annie* (MGM, 1944).

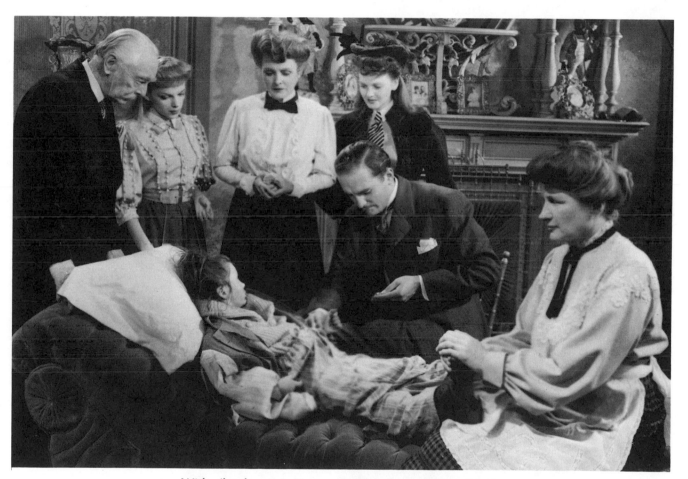

With (back row) Harry Davenport, Judy Garland,
Mary Astor, Lucille Bremer; and (front row) Margaret
O'Brien, Donald Curtis in *Meet Me in St. Louis.*

With Fred MacMurray, Porter Hall in *Murder, He Says* (Paramount, 1945).

With Margaret O'Brien in *Bad Bascomb* (MGM, 1946).

With Chill Wills in *The Harvey Girls* (MGM, 1946).

With Dan Tobin, Katharine Hepburn in *Undercurrent* (MGM, 1946).

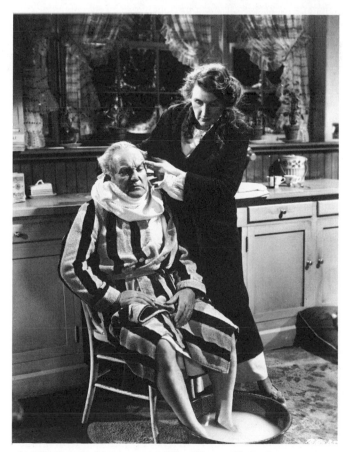

With Frank Morgan in *The Showoff* (MGM, 1946).

With Red Skelton, Marilyn Maxwell in *The Showoff*.

With Claudette Colbert in *The Egg and I* (Universal, 1947).

In *Wistful Widow of Wagon Gap* (Universal, 1947).

With Joe Besser, Percy Kilbride in *Feudin' Fussin' and A-Fightin'* (Universal, 1948).

In *Ma and Pa Kettle* (Universal, 1949).

With Percy Kilbride in *Ma and Pa Kettle*.

With Percy Kilbride in *Ma and Pa Kettle*.

With Wallace Beery in *Big Jack* (MGM, 1949).

With Wallace Beery, Joan Blair, Vanessa Brown (far
right) in *Big Jack*.

With Wallace Beery in *Big Jack*.

With (in foreground) Wallace Beery, Richard Conte, Vanessa Brown in *Big Jack*.

Lobby card for *Ma and Pa Kettle Go to Town* (Universal, 1950).

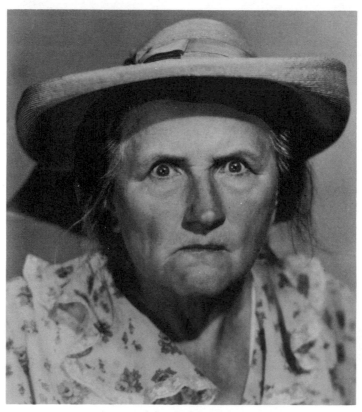

In *Ma and Pa Kettle Go to Town.*

With Judy Garland in *Summer Stock*.

In *Summer Stock*.

With Gloria DeHaven, Gene Kelly, Judy Garland in *Summer Stock* (MGM, 1950).

With James Whitmore in *Mrs. O'Malley and Mr. Malone* (MGM, 1950).

With Basil Tellou, James Whitmore in *Mrs. O'Malley and Mr. Malone.*

With Percy Kilbride, Emory Parnell, Richard Long, Teddy Hart, Oliver Blake in *Ma and Pa Kettle Back on the Farm* (Universal, 1951).

With Michael Wilding, Hayden Rorke, Natalie Schafer, Phyllis Stanley in *The Law and the Lady* (MGM, 1951).

With Michael Wilding in *The Law and the Lady*.

In *The Law and the Lady*.

With Keefe Brasselle in *It's a Big Country* (MGM, 1951).

With Ezio Pinza in *Mr. Imperium* (MGM, 1951).

With Fred Astaire, Vera-Ellen, Alice Pearce in *The Belle of New York* (MGM, 1952).

With Esther Dale in *Ma and Pa Kettle at the Fair* (Universal, 1952).

With Percy Kilbride in *Ma and Pa Kettle on Vacation* (Universal, 1953).

With Jack Kruschen, Bodil Miller (rear), Barbara Brown, Sig Ruman in *Ma and Pa Kettle on Vacation*.

With Polly Bergen, Joaquin Gray in *Fast Company* (MGM, 1953).

With Lucille Ball, Desi Arnaz in *The Long, Long Trailer* (MGM, 1954).

With Bert Lahr in *Rose Marie* (MGM, 1954).

Lobby card for *Ricochet Romance* (Universal, 1954).

With Chill Wills in *Ricochet Romance.*

With Rudy Vallee in *Ricochet Romance.*

With Lori Nelson (left), Percy Kilbride in *Ma and Pa
Kettle at Waikiki* (Universal, 1955).

With Arthur Hunnicutt in *The Kettles in the Ozarks*
(Universal, 1956).

In *Friendly Persuasion* (AA, 1956).

With Gary Cooper, Marjorie Durant, Edna Skinner, Frances Farwell, Anthony Perkins in *Friendly Persuasion.*

With Parker Fennelly in *The Kettles on Old MacDonald's Farm* (Universal, 1957).

MARTHA RAYE

5'4"
110 pounds
Blue eyes
Dark brown hair
Birth sign: Virgo

Faster than a speeding bullet. More powerful than a locomotive. Able to leap tall buildings in a single bound. Look in the sky. It's a bird! It's a plane! No—it's Martha Raye.

Since she was a tiny tot in the late 1910s, Martha has been going like a cyclone—singing, clowning, and churning up a storm of entertainment wherever she performs. She has so successfully projected the bombastic image of the tomboy schnook for so long that few people pay her serious heed. No matter that she is an ever excelling songstress, a fine dramatic actress, and possessed of a superior sense of mimicry. Good old Martha is always able to deliver a laugh—so have her ham it up, be the stooge to another less showy performer. For an extra chuckle she will give an unsuspecting stage partner a sturdy love tap, or take a flying fall on her backside. Thus for decades, Martha has been holding back most of her spectrum of performing ability, concentrating on what always leaves the masses laughing—the lowest form of comedy, the broad slapstick.

When Martha first rose to prominence in the show business world in the early 1930s, her nearest parallel—and quite different at that—was stage comedienne Imogene Coca. Since Martha established her zany powerhouse clown image, other female performers have tried to duplicate her unique combination of roughhouse comedy–expert vocalist style. Nancy Walker and Carol Burnett are the two more famous Martha Raye followers, but neither has succeeded in improving upon the outrageous caricature of the good natured buffoon made so famous by Martha.

Critics have long overlooked one of the essential elements that has endeared Martha to audiences in all media. Beneath the dynamo stage character whose big mouth emits a flow of childish wisecracks and insults lies a lonely heart yearning for affection and attention. It is a prime reason Martha's appeal extends far beyond kiddie audiences, who accept her pratfall and mugging at face value. Obviously, it shines through on a much deeper level to her most loving audience, the soldiers stationed in Vietnam, whom she has been entertaining at the front these past years.

Martha has been in the entertainment spotlight for 53 years to date. For a gal who knows five languages and has learned much about life the hard way (witness her six marriages), she has the wisdom to allow people to think of her as the professional dunce. She merely shrugs her broad, expressive shoulders, opens her famous mouth wider, and lets mayhem run rampant. It keeps folks smiling and content, and that makes her happy. Very happy indeed.

Martha Raye (nee: Margaret Theresa Yvonne Reed) was born August 27, 1916, in Butte, Montana—backstage at the local vaudeville theatre where her parents Pete Reed and Mabelle Hooper were performing. Billed as Reed and Hooper, the Irish immigrant song-dance-comedy troupers were known as "The Girl and the Traveler" on the dilapidated vaudeville circuit they toured. Two days after Martha was born, her mother was back doing her act.

As Martha recalls: "I must have been hypnotized by the spotlight." She joined the family act when she was three—mugging, singing and already making those extravagant clown faces, which her wide, large mouth exaggerated so effectively. The first song she performed on stage was "How I Love To Shimmy Like My Sister Kate." Her brother Bud was born in 1918, and in 1920 Mrs. Reed gave birth to Melodye.

About those years, Martha remembers: "I thought I was having a wonderful life. I never realized I was being culturally deprived, that I was having a lousy upbringing. We were too busy making a living to worry about stuff like that. So I guess I grew up secure, with no home ties. And maybe that's why I'll always be insecure and worried about finding happiness. But I do remember those as happy years, even when we didn't have enough to eat."

Martha obtained a smattering of organized education whenever her parents' act stayed put for any length of time, whether in Montana or in Chicago. Most of her learning, she "got on the fly." For a while she attended the Professional Children's School in New York.

As Martha and Bud developed into seasoned troupers, their talent outshone their parents', and the name of the act was changed to Bud and Margie. They played with the Benny Davis Revue, Ben Blue's company, and others. Their salaries soared to a mighty $400 weekly. Then came a landslide. "We never knew why," Martha later said, "but we began slipping. We were just as good as we'd ever been, but nobody wanted us. Pretty soon we were working one week out of three. Then we were down to club work, one-night stands. We'd drive sixty miles for a $15 date at an Elks Club or a Saturday night binge put on by the machinists union." The family resorted to sleeping in their old car, which also served as the kitchen.

When the family's fortune had reached its lowest ebb, their luck finally turned. Martha, now fifteen, went to see performer Paul Ash, with whom she had played on the midwest circuit. He was now an up and coming bandleader. She auditioned for him, and he hired her as the band vocalist. After working with his group for eleven months in Chicago, she went to New York to be the vocalist with Boris Morros' Orchestra, then playing the showcase Paramount Theatre on Broadway.

At one point, she had an act with other teenagers—Jackie Heller, Sonny O'Day, Hal LeRoy, Buddy and Vilma Ebsen. Later she toured the Loew's vaudeville circuit as a single, and then joined Will Morrisey's act for three seasons.

Back in New York, she was a member of Morrisey's musical comedy The Crooner, which tried out in the summer of 1931 at Asbury Park, New Jersey. Slated for a Broadway bow in April 1932, the show folded out of town. Others in the cast were Jean Malin, Gertrude Niesen, Margaret Padula.

By now, Martha had adopted a new stage name (Martha Raye) picked from the Manhattan telephone directory. Following the lead of such popular Broadway performers as Ethel Merman, Martha adopted a belting vocalizing style, putting all the vibrato she could muster into her socko renditions of popular songs.

Martha made her inauspicious movie debut in Universal's two-reel revue, A Night In A Nightclub, released in 1934. She appeared billed as a singer; others in the musical short included Buck and Bubbles.

Then Martha landed a featured role in Lew Brown's musical revue Calling All Stars, which opened at the Hollywood Theatre in New York on December 13, 1934. The cast included Lou Holtz, Phil Baker, Jack Whiting, Gertrude Niesen, Mitzie Mayfair, Judy Canova and Ella Logan. Out of town newcomer Martha lost most of her song numbers as the show took final shape. However, when Ella Logan proved unsuited for some comedy sequences later added to the revue, Martha inherited these fast-paced repartée skits. Burns Mantle in the New York Daily News unenthusiastically said: ". . . Martha Raye is a shouter of hot songs, and fairly trying in the assignment." (The critics would be the last, if at all, to jump on the Martha bandwagon, once the public had enthusiastically endorsed her special brand of talent in later assignments.) Her best bits in the short-lived production—it ran 36 performances—was a drunk act in the sketch "So This Is Hollywood." She would use this routine over and over in years to come.

Martha was announced in late 1934 to appear in a series of filmed short subjects for MGM, but the project never materialized. Various sources have listed Martha as appearing in Earl Carroll's Vanities of 1934 or his Sketch Book of 1935, but a close study of the playbills and show reviews fail to reveal her role in these revues.

Next Martha was hired as a vocalist at the Riviere and Chez Paree Clubs in Manhattan. One club reviewer in 1936 reported: "She's the hottest, slap-happiest, slam-bangingest singer of pop songs to drop anchor at a local port in a blue moon." Martha was at her best working the club scene, because in that milieu she could sing as she wished with all the emotional stops pulled. Later that year, she was appearing at the Century Club in Hollywood, at $100 weekly. Her engagement there was only moderately successful. When she was forced to accept play dates at smaller clubs at lower salaries, she supplemented her income by working as a nurse's aide at the Cedars of Lebanon Hospital. The latter provided such a satisfying experience that she later became a full fledged nurse.

Following up a practice she had used to good advantage in New York, Martha began singing gratis at such west coast night places as Louis Prima's Famous

Door, the Casanova, and the Clover Club. During her first night singing at the Trocadero Club, she gave a bouncing rendition of "I've Got You Under My Skin," letting loose an impressively loud and wide range of melodic notes. Martha recalls: "When I opened my mouth, they thought it was a cave-in. They could hear me in Santa Barbara."

Studio heads Adolph Zukor and Darryl F. Zanuck and film director Norman Taurog were in the audience that night. Each was interested in signing the novel but obviously talented Martha to a film contract on the spot. Martha accepted Taurog's offer of $1300 weekly for an as-yet-unwritten role in *Rhythm on the Range,* which he had already begun shooting at Paramount. It starred Bing Crosby. Martha commented on her "overnight success": "It's a cinch. All you need is a lot of talent and being able to do without meals for a year or two."

Luckily, Martha crashed onto the Hollywood scene and into Paramount Pictures at just the right time. The studio was running full force with its heavy production schedule of lavish comedy musicals, many of them set on college campuses or wherever it seemed likely or not to tie together a host of songs and a slim plot. Most of all, these structureless vehicles required plenty of variant talent to fill out the proceedings.

Rhythm on the Range (1936) was typical of the creampuff productions Martha would grace during her Paramount tenure. The story ostensibly dealt with Bing Crosby, a hired hand at Lucille Gleason's posh dude ranch. Frances Farmer played Gleason's wealthy niece, newly arrived from the East, whom the local baddies decide to kidnap for some fun and loot. Martha was fourth billed as gauche Emma Mazda, who managed without much difficulty to get in everybody's way. She ran hog wild in the film, and director Taurog allowed her to use every bit she could think of: doing her drunk routine when high on vodka, mugging, performing extended double takes, tripping over every (un)-likely obstacle. In the midst of the movie, which was more musical than western, Martha launched into Sam Coslow's new ditty "Mr. Paganini," a wildly infectious word song that soon became her trademark number. In the finale, she and Crosby dueted "If You Can't Sing It, You'll Have To Swing It." (*Rhythm on the Range* would later be remade as the Dean Martin–Jerry Lewis *Pardners* (1957) with Taurog again directing.)

Trade reviewers, having had an advance peek at *Rhythm on the Range,* were ecstatic over Martha's unique comedy and singing talents. *Variety* penned: "Despite the title, the costumes and the characters, this is no western. There's very little range, but plenty of rhythm, and the latter makes it pleasant entertain-

ment. . . . Both Martha Raye and Bob Burns—and it is something far from customary for Hollywood first-timers—were permitted by Norman Taurog to shoot the works with whatever they know or can do. For Martha Raye it was an exceptional break. She has a perfect (for her) song for her forte department—singing. She gets in her drunk bit and has an opportunity to show off all of her tricks, particularly the mugging and from this performance, Martha Raye and her director can determine what should be dropped from her extensive repertoire for future film work. There are some flaws in Miss Raye's performance, which is to be expected, but at first sight she impresses as a very promising picture comedienne."

Rhythm on the Range opened at the studio's flagship Paramount Theatre in Manhattan, July 30, 1936. The majority of critics were enthusiastic over her raucous, uncontrolled performance. Frank S. Nugent in *The New York Times* described:

Martha Raye is a stridently funny comedienne with a mammoth cave, or early Joe E. Brown, mouth, a dental supply vaguely reminiscent of those frightening uppers and lowers they used to hang over the portals of painless extraction emporia, and a chest which, in moments of burlesque aggressiveness, appears to expand fully ten inches.

It's entirely possible that she had several clever lines of dialogue in the picture; we wouldn't know, because every time she opened her mouth the audience started laughing. There remains then, only the conviction that Hollywood has found a truly remarkable pantomimist, an actress who can glare in several languages, become lovelorn in Esperanto and register beautific delight in facial pothooks and flourishes. She sings, too, swing music in a voice with saxophone overtones and an occasional trace of pure foghorn. Puzzling at first, but you grow accustomed to it.

Only a few reporters carped: "Martha Raye needs toning down and the restraining hand of a severe director, for she is noisy and inclined to grab the camera."

Paramount quickly signed Martha to an exclusive five-year contract, renegotiated in early 1937 at even better terms. Al Jolson hired her as vocalist for his CBS radio show (which changed its name to *The Tuesday Night Party* on March 21, 1939). She accepted nightclub appearances, and soon was endorsing lipstick and other facial products. With her excess of energy and craving to be liked by the public in all media, no task was too much for her.

Variety reviewed her appearance on radio's *Shell Chateau Show* on September 12, 1936: ". . . [it] was mostly a nervous ordeal for the girl. She admitted it. . . . [Her] style is undiluted swing, with closing stanzas to a song sample devoted to repetitious smatterings of sock blasts. When done evenly, it's novel and arresting. Date last week had her on edge. . . . Besides singing, girl develops into comedienne assignments. Pet quips are 'oh boy!' and 'yeah, man!', should be chucked."

In fast succession, Martha was tossed into Paramount vehicles already on the assembly line. She was taking over, in a fashion, where studio contract comics George Burns and Gracie Allen and W. C. Fields were leaving off, filling in the filmic voids in a variety of pictures with her specialty routines.

In *The Big Broadcast of 1937* (1936), Martha was Patsy, secretary to radio station manager Jack Benny. The nonsensical plot had Gracie Allen as a birdbrained manufacturer of Platt's Golf Balls, which sponsored an expensive show on Benny's station. Shirley Ross was a hick radio announcer who had come to the big city under false promises of a new job. Ray Milland appeared as the romantic press agent in love with Ross. Benny Goodman and Band were on hand for musical interludes. In the midst of tumbling down the stairs and playing leap frog with Burns and Allen, Martha sings *Vote for Mr. Rhythm* (when Benny puts her on the air as a substitute for his lead vocalist who failed to appear). *The New York Times* wrote that Martha ". . . keeps her facial gymnastics and her foghorn swing music on tap" and *Variety* thought her "hip-swinging, hoof-shuffling technique . . . is swell entertainment."

The Big Broadcast of 1937 premiered October 21, 1936, at the New York Paramount, and in its first week there 189,000 people saw the movie, breaking a ten-year boxoffice record for the theatre.

By now, Martha's parents had separated, and her brother Bud had formed his own band, which would gain a small amount of prominence.

In *College Holiday,* Mary Boland holds the mortgage on a hotel resort that is losing lots of money. Being interested in eugenics, she persuades band leader Jack Benny to invite the cream of the college crop to this California retreat. Martha was fifth-billed as Daisy Schloggenheimer, a boy-hungry (but shy) collegiate who has never been away from her cornfield home or overpowering mama before. Competing with zany Gracie Allen—herein an eccentric professor's daughter —Martha demonstrated her acrobatic burlesques, including one joyous moment in which she topples a temple stage set with the mere touch of her right arm. As had become her custom, she zonks about the film at a fast clip, perpetually heralding her arrival with her coon-shouting of "oh boy!" and "yeah, man!" Within the film's thin plot, the collegiates present a musical revue, and Martha is allowed a few undistinguished numbers. In the strange wrapup of the film, Benny

comes front and center to advise the movie going audience that everything that has preceded has all been in fun, and he expresses the hope that the audience has enjoyed it. Howard Barnes in *The New York Herald Tribune* complained: "Martha Raye remains for me a young girl with a big mouth and very little aptitude for clowning." If tabulation of audience reaction to Martha is any indication, Barnes was almost alone in his stringent views.

For her initial 1937 cinema release, Martha was top-billed in *Hideaway Girl,* which actually featured Shirley Ross in the title role. Ross, avoiding her suitor, takes refuge on Bob Cummings's yacht. She is thought to be a notorious robber on the lam. She and Cummings fall in love. Martha is the moving spirit among the upper-crust waterfront set, that populate the story's background. She croons, among others, "Beethoven, Mendelssohn and Liszt," which composer Sam Coslow wrote as a follow up to her very popular "Mr. Paganini." Martha belts the tune across in a strong Cab Calloway style. With Ross, she duets "Two Birdies Up a Tree." Kate Cameron in her two-star *New York Daily News* review criticized: "But now Paramount has made the mistake of building a whole production around Miss Raye and her flexible phy(*sique*). . . . [it] impresses one with the fact that a little of this sort of comedy goes a whale of a long way."

The New York Times was more charitable—and closer to the reaction of the enraptured public—when it jokingly remarked: "Some one in our circle has suggested that the explosive Miss Raye has but one opportunity left—to swallow a stick of dynamite and light the fuse, distributing her animated self over a Paramount set." And *The New York Post*'s Irene Thirer pointed out: "Whenever Miss Raye appears— which is in almost every scene—they laugh in anticipation of her antics. The reaction to Martha can only be compared celluloidistically to that of the fluttery Miss ZaSu Pitts. Of course, they're different workers. ZaSu is the timid soul, and Martha, the 1937 Polly Moran— only younger and possessed of a weird and wicked coon-shouting voice."

Waikiki Wedding (1937) again teamed Martha with Bing Crosby, Bob ("Bazooka") Burns (her studio hillbilly male counterpart), and perpetually short-shrifted Shirley Ross. Crosby was the lackadaisical idea man for George Barbier's pineapple company (Grady Sutton played the petulent boss's son) who dreams up the stunt of having a "Miss Pineapple" contest. Ross wins the Hawaiian vacation, and Crosby promises to provide a romantic holiday if she will write a day-by-day account of her adventures. To insure the success of his scheme, Crosby arranges for Ross to be kidnapped.

Leif Erikson was Ross's dentist fiance from back home, who is chasing after her. Martha was barrelhouse Myrtle Finch, Ross's energetic secretary, with Burns as a sailing friend of Crosby. Donning a hula skirt, Martha "of the elastic mouth, the rubbery legs and the amazing holler" put across the catchy tune "Okoleohao" in her own bombastic style. Camping it up, she tumbled off awnings, jumped off verandas and took pratfalls, landing on her stomach with no apparent injury. Despite her healthy public following, critics were going at great lengths in their reviews to warn Paramonut about the inherent dangers of destroying their new prize package: Archer Winsten in *The New York Post* admonished: "Martha came up fast and she'll go down the same way if she doesn't richen her mixture, and I don't mean with more explosive gas." Another more sympathetic critic noted that Martha ". . . every now and again explodes with an understandable impatience with the doings of her fellow players."

Martha was highly touted as the ball of fire in the Hollywood community. Rushing from her daily takes at Paramount, she would scamper to rehearsals for the Al Jolson radio show and other radio guest appearances, make the round of clubs late at night, often taking the floor to toss out a few off-the-cuff tunes. Martha explained: "I sang in them back in the days when a pretzel was a full meal. Why should I stop now?"

As Martha was known for her impromptu bits of business, the cinema capital was not particularly surprised when, after a whirlwind courtship, she and makeup artist Hamilton ("Buddy") Westmore, age 21, eloped to Las Vegas on May 30, 1937 and were married. It did cause industryites to reappraise the quotient of Martha's pulchritude, since Westmore was already known as a sharp womanizer.

Mountain Music, the third of her five 1937 Paramount releases, costarred her with Bob Burns. Martha was cast as folksy Mary Beamish, an Ozark yokel who yearned for the glitter of theatre life and for a man. She knows she is anything but gorgeous, yet figures her total enthusiasm offsets that deficit. Burns's family insist he marry Terry Walker, hoping the wedding will patch up a generations-old feud. Since he knows his brother, John Howard, loves Walker, Burns runs away, landing in the town of Monotony, where he encounters Martha. Burns happens to suffer from a peculiar form of amnesia.When he is under its spell, he thinks Martha is the girl of his dreams, when he has sobered up via a splash of water, he is more realistic. Martha aims to keep him in a state of amnesia, stating "If I can't be a wildflower, I won't be a wallflower." However, she learns that Burns's testimony is required to prove his brother's innocence in a murder trial now underway. To save the day, Martha unleashes an awningfull of rain on top of Burns. As she commits this heroic act, she orates: "Tis a far, far better thing I do than I have done before. . . ." Martha's heartiest musical number was "Good Mornin'," and there is a bit of wildness when she becomes entangled in a chandelier while doing an adagio dance.

Irene Thirer of *The New York Post* thought this production-line film entry: ". . . reveals a softer side to the hot-lipped, jazz swinging Raye of Hollywood sunshine." In contrast, *Variety* was of the opinion: "The big-mouthed comedienne works too hard and is continually forcing her comedy. That's her style; however, she should tone down for a little of it goes a long way."

By the time *Double or Nothing* was released September 1, 1937, Martha had returned from an extensive public appearance tour back east, consolidating her growing popularity. In this new movie, she is one of four strangers made potential heirs to an eccentric's will. Each of the quartet is left $5000; if any of them can double it within thirty days, he or she receives $1 million. Martha appeared as effervescent Liza Lou Lane, who decides to open a rowing boat club in Central Park, with sailorgirls to lure customers; Andy Devine invests in a golf range; William Frawley is swindled in a fake gold mine deal; Bing Crosby, playing a song writer and crooner, opens a nightclub and wins the fat inheritance, as well as the love of the deceased millionaire's niece, Mary Carlisle.

Martha's prime bit of whimsy in this nifty film is that, as a former burlesque performer, she always gets the yen to start stripping whenever she hears the tune "It's On, It's Off." Inevitably, the tune is played, and she performs a wild parody of Gypsy Rose Lee's famed act. Along with Crosby and Frances Faye, Martha takes part in a wild jam session at Crosby's club.

Variety smartly appraised the shape of Martha's career at this critical juncture: "Stage is set for the public to go for Raye in a big way right now, but the studio muffs the chance, as she has little to do beyond an exaggerated and horsey broad comedy part. Her song numbers have been built up with elaborate production backgrounds, but they contain nothing she hasn't done before, and the edge is dulled by repetition." If Paramount executives had read these words to the wise, the onslaught of forthcoming Martha vehicles failed to reveal it.

Martha's last 1937 film was the expensively mounted *Artists and Models,* which extravagantly displayed the studio's penchant for ultra modernistic settings and chorus-girl-filled production numbers that smacked of the ethereal. Jack Benny—in a rare and most effective change of casting—was allowed to be a real male lead, playing a Romeo who chases after (and catches, no less) the leading ladies. He portrayed the head of a large upper echelon New York City advertising agency, whose sole big account is Richard Arlen's Townsend Silverware Company. Arlen orders Benny to locate just the right model to become the tasteful symbol for his product. Professional model Ida Lupino angles for the lucrative job, but Arlen does not think she is high tone enough. Socialite Gail Patrick appears in Benny's office on a charity request and ends up with the modeling assignment and Benny as well. The scene shifts from New York to Miami and back with Martha appearing in a specialty number at the big artists ball finale. Describing her segment, *Variety* warned: "There are a couple of misguided sequences, one of which may react negatively to the future of Martha Raye whom the studio has developed into sizeable box office. It's that 'Public Melody No. 1' sequence done in a frankly Harlem setting, with Louis Armstrong toothing his trumpet against a pseudo musical gangster idea. While Martha Raye is under cork, the intermingling of the races isn't wise, especially as she lets herself go into the extremist manifestations of Harlemasla torso twisting and gyrations. It may hurt her personally."

In a minor way, the trade paper's prediction proved true, for many people for years afterwards assumed Martha was (part) black. When she attempted to lease a Greenwich Village apartment in the late 1930s, her deposit was refused, as it turned out, on racial grounds. Whenever *Artists and Models* is shown on television, her number is among the scenes deleted. Others in the film were Ben Blue, with whom Martha had worked in vaudeville in the 1920s, and Judy Canova, a fellow player from *Calling All Stars* on Broadway.

Starting out 1938, Martha was second billed in *The Big Broadcast of 1938*, in which W. C. Fields perambulated as twin brothers. Martha was the bad luck daughter of master jinxer T. Frothingell Bellows. (Fields) Bellows's brother, S. B. (also Fields) owns the new powerhouse ship S.S. *Gigantic*, which is engaged in a transatlantic race to Cherbourg, France, with the S.S. *Colossal*. T. Frothingell is ordered by his brother to board the *Colossal* and delay its run, but by error he books passage on the *Gigantic* and causes havoc. Others on board are Bob Hope (in his feature film debut) as the radio announcer reporting the day-by-day boat race, and a host of his ex-wives as well as his new girlfriend, Dorothy Lamour. Martha arrives on the scene midway through the story, when in mid Atlantic, an S.O.S. to the *Gigantic* advises that Martha's fifth yacht has just sunk and that she is afloat on a nearby raft. She is picked up, and further chaos is un-

leashed: mirrors crack, cargo goes whirling about the deck, and the crew goes on strike demanding she be thrown overboard. She is tossed over, but clings to the anchor and manages to save herself. The *Gigantic* wins the race, Hope is reunited with ex-wife Shirley Ross, Lamour finds romance with inventor-sailor Leif Erikson. And Fields, all two of him, well. . . .

Martha's highlight here was a rousing rendition of *Mama that Moon Is Here Again,* which saw her being tossed around the ship's deck by the sailor chorus as she warbles her specialty song. Sandwiched in between Field's golf and pool routines are Hope and Ross dueting the enormously popular "Thanks For The Memory," Kirsten Flagstaf's Wagnerian tidbit, and Tito Guizar's "Zuni Zuni." Martha's performance by comparison did "fall a little flat." In prints of *The Big Broadcast of 1938* now shown on television, much of Martha's non-singing slapstick performance has been edited out, leaving reviewers to wonder why she was second-billed.

Her marriage to Bud Westmore quickly went on the skids and by September 1938, Martha had filed for divorce. She charged that they had been happy for about a week after the marriage, whereupon "he began a course of cruel and inhuman treatment." She claimed he had slapped her mouth, and had threatened to "destroy her." Martha confided to the press: "Don't ask me what happened. I don't know. All I know is that I'm sorry it's all over. But it is over, definitely and nothing can be done about it." Years later, Martha would recall: "We were both a couple of kids. We didn't know what marriage was all about. I didn't, anyway. He was my first serious date, and I thought I loved him. He was a very nice, attractive person. We got the divorce in Las Vegas. And right then I decided it was always best never to look back."

College Swing (1938) returned Martha to the movies' mythical college campus scene again, teaming her with Bob Hope, Gracie Allen, and George Burns. In smaller roles were the real-life newlyweds Betty Grable and Jackie Coogan. The storyline had Allen as a descendant of Miss Alden, who failed to graduate from Alden College in 1738. As a result, the college was made the custodian of the Alden fortune until some female Alden did manage to graduate. For a fee, Bob Hope tutors Allen and provides her with a walkie-talkie radio so he can feed her the answers to the big exam. Having graduated, Gracie becomes Dean of Men and institutes some radical faculty changes. Martha is hired as Professor of Applied Romance, with Hope her most ardent pupil. Among Martha's livelier numbers are her duet with Hope: "How D'ja Like To Love Me" and her song with Ben Blue, singing "What A Rumba

Does To Romance." One bit of zaniness had Martha and Hope raiding a refrigerator, and while eating up a storm proceeding to zing out a song and dance fest. The film was a profitable item off the studio assembly line; Martha's fans had certainly not gotten tired of her.

On October 8, 1938, Martha married composer-conductor-arranger David Rose, age 28, who was then her music director at Paramount pictures and for her various radio appearances.

Give Me a Sailor (1938) was a distinct change for Martha, with the studio deciding to rechannel her into a glamor image. In actuality, Martha possessed (and still does) an extremely attractive figure, and her shapely legs were no less beautiful than Paramount's own Marlene Dietrich (as she proved to one doubting producer, who bet her on the fact at the time). Martha and Betty Grable played opposite type sisters; Martha the drudge, and Betty the spunky coquette. Bob Hope and Jack Whiting were brothers, both naval officers and both madly in love with Grable. Martha hankers for Whiting and promises to aid Hope in winning Grable if he will assist her in trapping his brother for her. Thinking she is entering a yum yum food contest, Martha mistakenly enters a photograph of herself in a beautiful legs contest. She wins! Now she is known as "Legs" Larkin, America's girlfriend. She has money, fame, and turns glamorous, easily snaring Whiting. But she decides she loves Hope and marries him. In the early part of the film, clutsy Martha attempts to parade through the household chores, from energetic cleaning to artistically decorating a boat-shaped layer cake. One bright comic moment later on has her applying a mud-pack on her face. She finds she cannot remove it, nor can Hope, who smacks away at her hardened fright mask puss in vain. Her best melody was "Little Kiss At Twilight." *The New York Daily Mirror* noted: "Miss Raye, who was discovered to have a figure long after the fans had applauded her great mouth, her robust voice and her compelling rhythm, employs her shapeliness for the first time in 'Give Me A Sailor.' Fans were not pleased with the "new" Martha, and Paramount quickly returned her to pure slapstick fare. (Ironically, this is the most frequently shown Martha Raye feature film on television.)

Her final 1938 release—her twelfth film in three years—was *Tropic Holiday,* which unreeled at the Paramount Theatre in New York on June 29, 1938. Martha was shoved down to third billing, playing Midge Miller, secretary to screen writer Ray Milland, who was in Mexico to find inspiration for his latest hack film assignment. There he falls in love with local beauty Dorothy Lamour, much to the chagrin of his fiancee, Binnie Barnes. Meanwhile, Bob Burns, Martha's fiance from Oklahoma, follows her south of the border, to pursue the courtship. Highlights of the film include an amusing takeoff on *A Star Is Born* (1937) in which lovelorn Burns plunges into the ocean à la Fredric March to prove his devotion to Martha, and an elongated segment in which Martha becomes a matador and tangles in the ring with a young bull she thought was just an old beast. Throughout, the comedy was broad and the wit scarce. Most critics noted that Martha was more carefully photographed here than she had been before in films. *The New York Mirror* evaluated: "Martha Raye can thank whoever imposed restraint upon her for making her a more polished and attractive comedienne." Howard Barnes in *The New York Herald Tribune* wrote: ". . . the arena scenes have a pace and flavor which are badly wanting in the rest of the offering, and Martha Raye makes the most of her bullfighting burlesque."

Although Paramount and Hollywood were going full blast on their production schedules, Martha's cinema career in 1939 tapered off to two films, neither of them in the same league with her earlier screen efforts. The studio was already undergoing a changeover in its lineup of comic stars. Judy Canova had quickly left Paramount in 1937, W. C. Fields departed the next year, and Gracie Allen (without Burns) would make just one more film at the lot. It would not be until the early 1940s before Paramount restocked its comic-singer roster with a new breed of energetic comedy-song performers, namely Betty Hutton, Cass Daley, and Eddie Bracken. Only Nancy Walker briefly at MGM and on Broadway in the early 1940s and Carol Burnett on television in the 1960s and 1970s would duplicate Martha's unique combination of broad slapstick funster with a good singing voice, but not to the same degree of fan devotion.

Never Say Die (1939), based on a play and a 1924 silent film, top-billed Martha as Mickey Hawkins, the man-hungry ugly-duckling daughter of a wealthy Texas oilman. Bob Hope was a millionaire hypochondriac who comes to an Alpine resort, hoping to escape fortune-hunting widow Gale Sondergaard. By error, Hope is informed by a local physician that he has only thirty days left to live. Martha arrives, pining for her beloved bus driver boyfriend Andy Devine of whom her dad disapproves. Martha and Hope marry for mutual protection. Martha has the only song in the film to sing, "The Tra-La-La And Oom-Pah-Pah." *Variety* criticized: "Both Martha Raye and Bob Tope play too straight and dramatic." The film met with such meagre audience response that Paramount dumped it from its Manhattan flagship theatre after a one-week run, the first time it had done such a thing to its own product.

Her other 1939 release, "$1,000 a Touchdown," was so dismal that Paramount hastily tossed it away at Loew's Criterion, October 4, 1939. In this "painfully written football farce of almost fantastic unoriginality," Martha took a back seat to Joe E. Brown. She played Martha Madison, descendant of the founder of Madison University. At her psychiatrist's office, she is introduced to Brown, scion of a prominent theatrical family, who is girl shy. In a rash moment of desperation, Martha makes him president of the University and head football coach. She allows him to hire a professional football team—anything to save the school from being closed and having the campus converted into a shoe factory. The thesis of the spiritless programmer was, gridiron greats are paid not made. Martha chirped the ditty, "Love With A Capital 'U.'" The potentially amusing concept of teaming two loud-mouthed comedians misfired; Eric Blore in his stock role of the butler-valet came off much better.

Martha's career in other media was progressing far better. In the June 1939 *Radio Guide* Popularity Poll, she was voted #2 swing singer. Bea Wain was #1, Martha Tilton #3, and Judy Garland was #12.

The Farmer's Daughter (1940) proved to be Martha's last Paramount film. On the final day of a rather hectic production schedule, Martha's studio employers slipped a note under her dressing room door, stating her services were no longer required. This ignoble heave-ho from the studio was a great shock to Martha's ego, and took many years for her to conquer.

The Farmer's Daughter proved an unfitting requiem to the first chapter of her cinema career. The tired B film did not have much to offer. She played Patience Bingham, the rural miss to whose farm producer Charlie Ruggles brings his Broadway-bound show to rehearse. As the bucolic bungler, Martha tumbled downstairs, caught her foot in apple cans, stumbled over ladders, *ad infinitum*. When star Gertrude Michael walks out of the musical, Martha takes over her role. William Frawley was the stock press agent, and Richard Denning the leading man. Martha sang snatches of "Jeannie With The Light Brown Hair" and was involved with the Frank Loesser-Frederick Hollander number, "Jungle Jingle." Critics had a field day pointing out that the film had nothing whatsoever to do with the proverbial risque stories about the farmer's daughter. *The New York Herald Tribune*'s eulogy read: ". . . she is emoting in all her glory. Her stock in trade—mugging, tumbling and strutting—is funny at first, but rapidly becomes tiresome because of continuous repetition."

Finding herself at liberty, and with no movie offers coming her way, Martha wisely returned to the vaudeville circuit. *Variety* caught her act and reported: "Miss Raye launches her turn at top speed and is never off the pace. Customers go for the knockdown dragout technique and eat up the adlibbing that figuratively land the lady in their laps. Vocal offerings suit perfectly her brand of warbling. 'Three Little Fishes' sung after the manner of Miss Raye's five year old niece, is tops in this department, but there's nothing wrong with her rendition of 'Want The Waiter' and 'I Can't Dance.'"

Under a freelance contract with Universal Pictures, and at a reduced salary, Martha costarred in the screen version of George Abbott's 1938 stage success, *The Boys from Syracuse* (1940). She was Luce, the raucous serving girl madly in love with one of the twin witless slaves, Dromio, played by Joe Penner. Allan Jones was starred in dual roles as the ancient Greek masters (twin brothers also) in this nicely mounted costumer. Martha warbled *He and She* with Penner, and chirped herself "The Greeks Had No Word For It" and "Sing For Your Supper." She worked in some of her expected comic antics and mugging, which worked well in this pleasant adaptation of Shakespeare's *Comedy of Errors*. *Variety* applauded: ". . . provided with the swell Rodgers and Hart tunes, [she] gets good opportunity to use her pipes as well as exhibit her broad comedy style . . ." The film proved quite popular, but could not be classed as a Martha Raye vehicle.

Then with Al Jolson, who had also found himself washed up in Hollywood, Martha returned to Broadway to co-star in *Hold on to Your Hats*. It had a book by Guy Bolton, Matt Brooks and Eddie Davis, with music by Burton Lane and lyrics by E. Y. Harburg. Jolson's then wife Ruby Keeler was signed for the show too, but she dropped out during the pre-Broadway engagement. The featherweight plot concerned a timorous radio cowboy, the Lone Rider (Jolson), involved in daring doings at a dude ranch plagued by Mexican bandits. Martha was an overhelpful, bumbling ranch lady. Others in the cast were Bert ("Mad Russian") Gordon, Gil Lamb, Jack Whiting, and Jinx Falkenberg. The musical premiered at the Shubert Theatre, September 11, 1940.

In the play, Martha did a rousing song, "Down on the Dude Ranch," with Jolson and Gordon, dueted "Would You Be So Kindly" with Jolson, and performed an energetic specialty dance, "She Came, She Saw, She Can Canned."

Richard Watts Jr. in the *New York Herald Tribune* had very kind words for Martha: "I can say, however, that she [Martha] is a willing and strenuous worker, that she is about three hundred times better on the stage than she was on the screen and that she certainly adds to the zest of 'Hold On To Your Hats.'" George

Freedley in *The New York Morning Telegraph* observed: "Miss Raye's Mamie is a comic creation that only occasionally spills over into the grotesque."

The show would have run much longer than its 158 performances had not Jolson's illness forced a premature closing.

Martha returned to California, only to find that her marriage had collapsed during her absence. Rose had fallen in love with Judy Garland. She and Rose were divorced on May 19, 1941. Twenty-one years later, Martha still felt the scars of this disunion. She said: "I was deeply in love with him. I guess he was really the first great love I had. He taught me a good deal about music, and he taught me calmness. He educated me, and when he left I was battered and hurt. I learned to accept the hurt as part of living. You can't fight love. No one starts out to fall in love. In this racket, you're on the set every day.

"I had hoped so desperately that this marriage would last. I just wanted someone to love me for myself. I had a good job. My career was going fine, I was earning more money than ever before, but I was poor again, poor where it hurts the most; in the heart."

While filming *Navy Blues* on location in Miami, Martha met and married hotel executive Nick Lang on June 25, 1941. The marriage only lasted a few months. Martha later admitted: "I was torching for Dave. I married Neal on the rebound. But honest, I didn't know it at the time."

Navy Blues (1941) was a not-so-bright Warner Brothers musical starring Ann Sheridan as a nightclub singer in Honolulu. The thin plot had Jack Haley and Jack Oakie as two gobs out to earn some money by winning a bet that the U.S.S. *Cleveland*'s crew could win the division's gun target title. To insure their victory, they must keep gunner expert (and hog caller) Herbert Anderson in the Navy. Sheridan is asked to be the bait. Martha, as Lulabelle Bolton, had a rather minor part as the ex-wife of Haley, on his trail to collect back alimony. She performed a few bits of her angular buddy-buddy slapstick, and for one scene was decked out in a hula skirt. Bosley Crowther in *The New York Times* reported: "Miss Raye sticks her face in now and then to open wide and make a lot of noise. . . ." Wrote another critic: "At least she's quit the glamour gal gig and gone back to her clowning."

By now, Martha was known as the jaded expert on mismarriages, and the columnists dug hard to find quotes from her ex-husbands about her. One former spouse told Hedda Hopper: "I loved Maggie. I really did. But she wore me out. She's a bundle of nerves wrapped up in a ball of fire." Martha was quoted as saying: "Maybe if I had more education, I'd be a better judge of people."

Then back at Universal she performed in *Keep 'Em Flying* (1941), functioning as second fiddle to the ultra popular comedy team of Bud Abbott and Lou Costello. This service comedy found the nutty duo in the U.S. Army Air Corps. Martha cavorted through the production as twin sisters Barbara and Gloria Philips, both of whom work at the base canteen. Naturally one sister had a heart of gold and is in love with chunky Costello; the other was a toughie who had little use for the dumpy dummy. Martha sang "Pig Foot Bill" in her own inimitable brassy style. Her best comedy moment occurred at the canteen lunch counter in a snappy if obvious routine with Costello. It involved a slab of layer cake that one twin keeps offering to the hungry fat guy and the other keeps removing in a most menacing manner. Howard Barnes in *The New York Herald Tribune* reflected: "She is as energetic as ever, but she works very hard for few laughs."

Her final release of the year was *Hellzapoppin'* (1941) which opened at Manhattan's Rivoli Theatre Christmas day. Martha was Betty Johnson, playing in support of rugged comedians Olsen and Johnson, who had starred in the mayhem on Broadway. The actual hodgepodge plot is a story within a story, which evolves as Olsen and Johnson sit in at a story conference on a Hollywood soundstage with script writer Elisha Cook Jr. The plotline concerned Robert Paige's effort to produce a charity show on Long Island. A love triangle develops between him, Jane Frazee and her fiance Lewis Howard. Martha essayed a wacky man-hungry girl-child chasing after eccentric count Mischa Auer. Olsen and Johnson and other assorted Universal contractees put in appearances throughout, adding moments of inspired insanity to the melee.

Martha sang several songs, including: "What Kind of Love Is This," "Watch the Birdie," "Conga Beso," and "Robert E. Lee." Despite her frantic zigzagging in and out of the movie, she was definitely a subordinate figure in the madcap happenings.

The following year, on November 11, 1942, Martha married dancer Nick Condos, part of the well-known Condos Brothers act. They had met years before when each was playing the vaudeville circuit. Once again, Martha was too busy to settle down to being just an ordinary housewife. Between radio broadcasts, recording sessions, club dates, etc., she went back to nursing, and embarked on a U.S.O. tour to North Africa with Kay Francis, Mitzie Mayfair, and Carole Landis. A most unlikely quartet brought together for the wartime good!

Martha has often repeated her favorite story about her African tour: " 'I beg your pardon (said a soldier), but are you Martha Raye?' He couldn't tell because I had dark glasses on my mouth. So I said 'Yes, I'm Martha Raye and what can I do for you?' He said: 'Well, gee, I hate to bother you but really things are tough. I haven't had a bite for four days.' So, I bit him."

Martha found her tour so rewarding that she continued it long after the other movie colony gals had returned to California. During her stay, she contracted pernicious anemia, a condition which has recurred over the years.

In 1944, Twentieth Century-Fox filmed *Four Jills in a Jeep* based on the book Carole Landis "prepared" for Random House. It was a glamorized retelling of the quartet's African trek. Martha played herself. Her role called for her to have a romance with Phil Silvers, who portrayed the wisecracking army sergeant assigned to driving the movie stars around the base. Martha did a reprise of her famed "Mr. Paganini." One wry bit had the aggressive Martha arriving at the service mess hall and eagerly inquiring where she was to eat. Replied the officer: "You mess with the men." Martha retorts: "I know that, but where do we eat?" Archer Winsten in *The New York Post* acknowledged: "The winners in this sweepstakes are clearly Martha Raye, whose comedy has never been more raucous, rough and pleasing. . . ."

Her other 1944 release was *Pin-Up Girl,* also made at Twentieth. Martha was third-billed as Marian, a jealous singer at Joe E. Brown's nightclub. She had little to do in this routine musical, which was a pedestrian showcase for studio breadwinner Betty Grable. The Condos Brothers were among the specialty acts in the production.

And then her career finally took a backseat to domestic life, as she gave birth to daughter Melodye in mid 1945.

By early 1946 her professional activities had slowed down to a standstill. Then in a surprise piece of casting, Charles Chaplin signed the comedienne for a featured role in *Monsieur Verdoux.* Martha was overjoyed at this break, and thought her cinema career was surely off to a new start. She purchased a home in Burbank: "It was the first house I could really call home."

Martha was Annabella Bonheur, one of Chaplin's inamoratas in this black comedy. The plot has Henri Verdoux, a French bank teller who loses his job in the depression, evolve a scheme to support his crippled wife and small child. He becomes a professional murderer of wealthy women. The movie focuses on four of Chaplin's victims; Martha essaying the unstable

former prostitute who has made a fortune in the lottery. She believes mysterious Chaplin is a sea captain, and leads him a merry chase as he attempts to subdue and murder his most kittenish victim. The United Artists release opened April 11, 1947, at the Broadway Theatre; despite some favorite reviews it died at the box office. Audiences expected a typical whimsical slapstick comedy, and were not ready for an essentially serious study of a self-inflated, pompous, French Bluebeard. That Chaplin was undergoing adverse press at the time because of tax problems and his alleged communist affiliations did not help the movie at all.

Ironically the film, which put a kiss of death on Martha's movie career, garnered her superior reviews from the critics. Bosley Crowther in the *New York Times* assessed: ". . . those who assist him, especially Martha Raye, are completely up to snuff. Miss Raye's bumptious character is a mammoth of loud vulgarity. . . ." Howard Barnes of *The New York Herald Tribune,* no fan of Martha in the past, admitted: "Miss Raye makes altogether the best foil for the actor's miming at the Broadway. In her rough and tumble scenes with the star something of the gaiety of the early Chaplin masterpieces is recaptured. . . ."

Martha did gain from the erstwhile Little Tramp a piece of invaluable career advice. He told his willing pupil: "Listen, if you're ever going to do any more personal appearances—and you probably will on the new television medium—remember your forte is slapstick comedy. This means that you have to dress beautifully, gown yourself exquisitely, make sure your hair and makeup are perfect—so that when you finally do take a fall, you don't have to take a full pratfall. All you have to do is trip and you're twice as funny as if you did the same thing in plain clothes."

Martha's mother died October 20, 1947, following an operation for a ruptured appendix. However, the comedienne continued to work.

After assorted club dates in the States, Martha made a theatre tour of England, and played the London Palladium for four weeks, opening March 29, 1948. She recalls: "I was afraid my type of comedy might be a bit too boisterous for staid English people. What a relief to find out I was wrong; I mugged all over the place and they came back for more." *The London Daily Herald* applauded her 35-minute turn, co-starred with Danny Kaye. The newspaper praised ". . . her grotesquely mobile mouth and a boisterous sense of broad humor. . . . Her gags were as fertile as they were unexpected."

When Martha returned to America she opened the Five O'Clock Club and other night spots in Miami

Beach, making that Florida resort center her new home base. In the mid-1950s she described to actress-interviewer Faye Emerson the professional hell of the post-*Verdoux* years: "I couldn't even get arrested in Hollywood. Nobody seemed to give a damn whether I made another picture or not, and the only work I could get was club dates. Of course, I had my own spot in Miami Beach, but my career seemed at a standstill until Milton [Berle] literally dragged me into TV, first with guest spots on his show and then browbeating everybody at NBC about giving me my own show. At one time he even suggested tying me in with his contract to make sure I would get a fair deal."

Martha continued to appear in television specials, such as *Anything Goes* (October 2, 1950, NBC), co-starred with John Conte, Betty Lynn, and Fred Waynne. Martha had the Ethel Merman stage role in this capsuled sixty minute version. Her highlight was singing "Blow, Gabriel, Blow." But *Variety* criticized Martha's performance. "Miss Raye too often relied on mugging where artistry could have served the show in better stead, although at times her frantic comedics paid off."

During the 1951–1952 season, Martha appeared on NBC's prestigious *All Star Revue* and increased her appearances to five shows the next year. Critics were generally impressed by her impressive array of talents. *Variety,* reviewing her September 27, 1952, *All Star Revue* appearance, which co-starred Cesar Romero, Rocky Graciano (her beloved "Gumpa" and a frequent mainstay on her early video years), and Rise Stevens, applauded her ". . . native ability. She's a genuinely funny gal and what's more, she can be tops in the field without a single blue line. She's still an actress of ability, an asset that gives greater direction to her comedy."

From the various polls taken, it was obvious that home viewing audiences were bowled over by her roughhouse brand of humor. For generations unfamiliar with the rugged, physical comedy of the old vaudeville and burlesque days, Martha's antics were a revelation. In her exaggerated style, she was doing what every ordinary mortal wanted—thumbing her nose at conventions and class structure. If someone or something got in her way, she would charge at the object-person with a flying tackle and reduce it to shambles. In her outrageous broad comedy, she was outdoing Uncle Miltie Berle on every avenue. What's more, she could sing and was quite a looker besides.

The Martha Raye Show debuted on NBC, December 26, 1953, and appeared once monthly through May 15, 1954, with a similar schedule the next season. For the 1955–1956 season, premiering September 20, 1955, she performed in thirteen hourly shows, with the series concluding May 29, 1956. Martha was seemingly riding in clover under her fifteen year contract with NBC, renegotiated in June 1955. From magazine articles and from her *This Is Your Life* showcase (November 25, 1953) the public was well aware of her trouble-laden past and her desire to be loved and needed.

While doing television, she commuted back and forth between New York and Miami Beach. She played the Latin Quarter club in New York in September 1952. *The New York Journal of Commerce* noted: "Svelte in a change of smart Kathryn Kuhn gowns (white lace and gold), chic in a poodle cut attractively shot with silver, the gal from Butte, Montana, sweeps the house like a whirlwind, a dynamic bundle of slapstick, with a never a concession that even Joe E. Brown could have stretched his mouth further. Backed by a tartan dinner-jacketed pianist, and drummer who accompany her with relish, rhythm, and riot, Martha tees off with 'Got My Love To Keep Me Warm' followed by a calypso swing 'My Feet's Too Big For The Bed.' Then she 'deviates,' as she calls it, skipping clowning to sing 'Old Black Magic' expressively and far more acceptably to my mind, than the mannered interpretation of Billy Daniels. Needling the performers who warble French, regardless of ability, Martha grunts, garbles and double-talks her own 'La Vie En Rose' to destroy that ballad until Piaf restores it."

Martha's marital life was undergoing its usual discord. She and Condos (who was her business manager) divorced June 17, 1953. She claimed that "he beat me and mistreated me terribly." However, he remained as her professional consultant because "we don't fight over money—just everything else."

On April 21, 1954, Martha married Ed Begley, 30, a dancer in the chorus of her television show. He was no relation to the late Academy Award winning character actor.

When queried about her career philosophy, Martha replied: "An important part of my strategy directed toward success in the theatre is not to allow yourself to become diverted by the opinions of any one person. . . . On a number of occasions, I've done better than it was in me to do, because others believed in me, and tutored me."

By 1955, her television success (and at the peak of her career she had been earning $150,000 yearly) began to sour. She rehearsed more (57½) hours for each show, but the magic was gone. Part of her problem was that her chief writer, Nat Hiken, had left to join Phil Silvers's writing squad for the *Sergeant Bilko* success. Said *Time Magazine* on October 1, 1955: "Martha Raye proved that slapstick can be tasteless with an interminable skit that required Douglas Fairbanks, Jr. to pretend that he was madly in love with her (a role often filled last year by Actor Cesar Romero)." Jack Gould wrote in *The New York Times:* "Martha Raye is an exasperating girl. When she is given the right material and is willing to accept guidance, she can be a true mistress of slapstick. But when not afforded every protection, she can exhaust a viewer's patience. . . . But she should learn to keep her guard up against the false friends who sometimes may lack the fortitude to tell her 'no.' "

After her video series expired, Martha guested on assorted television variety shows. She was announced as a star in *Boffalo,* a musical revue for the fall 1956 Broadway season, but the show never materialized.

In the summer of 1956, she returned to Miami, intending to establish residency in order to divorce Begley. She advised the press: "I haven't any other fella in mind, and I'm honestly frightened of getting married ever again. . . . . What the heck, I have enough names now to start a small town of my own."

Inwardly, Martha was far from being a self-sufficient person. In late 1955, when she was still living at her ten room mansion in Westport, Connecticut, she began receiving threatening telephone calls, implying she would be kidnapped and badly disfigured. Already separated from Begley, she hired a battery of private detectives. One of them was local patrolman Bob O'Shea, 28 years old. Martha grew dependent on his presence. On April 1956, his wife, Barbara Ann, filed a suit in court, charging Martha with being a housewrecker, and that while Barbara Ann was in the hospital giving birth to her first child, her husband had been more than a bodyguard at Martha's home. She asked $50,000 in damages. O'Shea denied the charges, as did Martha's attorney. Then in May 1956, when her video season ended, she headed for Miami. She told the press: "I'm never coming back. Three fires (two mysterious explosions and one caused by careless cigarette smoking) in six months are three more than I need. I'm going to Florida to cool off. Down there when the heat's on you know it's just the damn weather."

Martha encountered difficulty in the Florida courts proving her Sunshine State residency. When on the night of August 14, 1956, she attempted suicide with an overdose of sleeping pills, she insured her position as one of the year's top newsmakers. After recovering, she stated: "Life looks different to me now that I know Somebody up there cares. You get religion and a deep

sense of security when you're skipping into the abyss and awaken to find that God touched you. It's a sort of signal from Him to stop being sad and be glad you've got the gift of making other people happy."

Because she had received such good treatment at the Sisters of St. Francis Hospital in Miami, she thereafter would say "good night, Sisters" at the closing of her television programs. To this day, Martha wears a St. Christopher's medal, St. Genesius medal (patron saint for actors) and a Star of David (given her by Sophie Tucker).

On October 6, 1966, Martha got her divorce from Begley.

In 1957, one big television star told a gossip columnist in an "anonymous" interview: "She (Martha) has no peer in the knockabout school of comedy, and she knows it, but you'll never find her bragging about it. Socially she's completely unsure of herself. Ironically enough, she lacks the poise and confidence she fabricates for audiences. She has nothing to talk about outside of her work and herself. She has no interests. She spends hours in front of her television set, and when she does go out it's usually to a nightclub. Once in a while, she makes a trip to Florida where her friends aren't exactly members of the elite. She likes to be with them because she knows she's a little above those people, and that makes her feel a lady." Martha put it more succinctly: "I thought success in show business was the answer to everything. It isn't. I don't know what is. Don't misunderstand me; I'm grateful . . . Few people actually know me, or take me seriously. It's great for my career though, I guess."

Martha settled with Mrs. O'Shea out of court for $20,000, and told the press: "I love Bob and I know he loves me. If people will just give us a chance, I know the marriage will succeed. After two years of legal complications, they were married on November 7, 1958 in Teaneck, New Jersey. Joan Crawford was matron of honor.

Meanwhile, Martha had returned to club work with a vengeance. She was back at the Copacabana Club in New York in October 1957. Gene Knight of *The New York Journal American* reviewed her act: " 'I'm only a clown,' said Martha Raye as she began her act at the Copa last nite. And then, in the next forty minutes, she proved that she was 100% wrong.

"Less nervous, seemingly happier than in years, the tunnel-mouthed comedienne sang, capered, mimed and danced right into the hearts of a near capacity audience at Jules Podell's gay night spot.

"There was some comment following her opening that Martha tended toward material that was shaded deep blue. I'm happy to report the talented gal, who certainly has no need of off-color material to score her comedic points, certainly used none last night. She offered talent—great gobs of it and the Copa patrons loved it."

Martha was scheduled to appear in the City Center revival of *Annie Get Your Gun* (she had done it in Florida in 1952), but she suffered from a ruptured appendix and had to be replaced by Betty Jane Watson before the February 19, 1958 opening.

Since nothing was being done for her by NBC, her contract was settled in 1958, so she would be at liberty to perform on other networks.

Her marriage to O'Shea, who had opened a private detective agency, also went bad. On December 9, 1959, he sued her in a Mineola, New York, court, claiming fraud. He claimed she had promised him $60,000 to induce him to marry her. The marriage was dissolved soon thereafter.

Martha went back to the clubs and to television guest spots. Said Martha "My career is my whole life. I'll always work." When CBS's *Studio One* show planned to do "The Mother Bit," which purportedly was about a Martha Raye-like performer and her daughter, Martha threatened to sue the network for infringing on her privacy. The May 1959 show was dropped from the lineup.

In April 1960, she told the Hollywood press: "These days I only come out here to do a TV show once in a while. And then I rehearse, do the program, and head back to Florida the next day. My daughter and business are there so I don't have any reason to stay in Hollywood."

With summer theatre business burgeoning across America, Martha merrily entered this facet of the theatre on a large scale. She did *The Solid Gold Cadillac* and *Wildcat* in 1960. She would frequently repeat these two shows in subsequent seasons. She became a favorite of the tent circuits, and was not above using a few showbusiness tricks to ensnare her willing audience. She, along with Judy Garland, was a fine practitioner of the art of deliberately flubbing lines to gain audience support, and then ad libbing with planned abandon. It worked every time—almost. In the summer of 1961, when touring with *Calamity Jane,* she had the misfortune to offend Michael Holmberg of the Pittsburgh press. Their rhubarb made quite a stir. Holmberg declared that his bad reviews of the play (and of Martha specifically) had nothing to do with the fact that she had cancelled out on an interview with him at the last minute. Holmberg wrote in a widely reprinted newspaper piece: "One of the difficulties of acting with Martha Raye seems to be that you never

know what she's going to say next. There are not many actresses who can get away with breaking off in the middle of the show to chase a moth offstage; explaining that it hasn't bought a ticket."

Meanwhile, back in films Martha was announced for the motion picture *Celestina* to be filmed in Italy in 1961. She was to play a big hearted madam. The project never came off.

Then in early 1962, producer Joe Pasternak and director Charles Walters had a part built up for Martha in *Billy Rose's Jumbo,* a Doris Day color musical shot at MGM. It was publicized as her comeback film and she received much column space. *Jumbo* opened at Radio City Music Hall, December 1, 1962, and while not a critical success, made a decent profit at the box-office. The featherweight plot had to do with two rival circuses, and the romance of Day with performer Stephen Boyd. Jimmie Durante clowned as Day's father, and the owner of the down-and-out circus, whose star attraction, the elephant Jumbo, was in danger of being sold for debts overdue to Dean Jagger's competing outfit. Durante and fortune teller Lulu (Martha) have been engaged for fourteen years, but she can never get him to the altar. By the finale, Day and Boyd are being wed, so Durante decides to take the matrimonial plunge. When he sees Martha all dressed up in her wedding gown, he exclaims: "All this time I thought she looked like George Washington." Martha and Day dueted "Why Can't I" and she joined in on several other numbers. Paul V. Beckley in *The New York Herald Tribune* observed: "Miss Raye has most of the best lines . . . she can breathe life into it as only fine clowns can, making the grimace add golden weight to the words."

In a widely syndicated interview with Louella Parsons in January 1963, Martha told the gossip wag: "No more nightclubs for me. I'm definitely through competing with noisy drunks and the clatter of crockery. I've bought a home in Bel Air and I'm here to stay—I hope, I hope." And Parsons had a few observations about her interviewee: "Like many great entertainers who thrive on audience reaction, Martha is 'on' at the drop of a cue. At a party she will sing and clown her heart out for hours. She's boisterous, hilarious, loud. But get her alone and you'll find a soft-spoken, serious, thoughtful woman who talks with honesty and simplicity."

Martha's confessions about her life were always grist for the newspaper mills: "Looking back," she said at this time, "I have no regrets about the men I've known or the men I've married. If I've learned anything in this life, I've learned that it's much easier to love than to hate. . . . It's not possible for me to lead a manless life. The greatest thing in a woman's life is a man who truly loves a gal and wants to marry her. . . . People say I'm wacky to ever consider getting married again, but I don't think so. Maybe I'm addicted to marriage. I can't break the habit." (To date, Martha has not remarried, nor has she even been rumored dating any particular man on a steady basis.) About Hollywood: "I feel everybody is much more serious about their work. You don't read any more about people getting tossed into pools at parties. I read they're doing that in Washington now."

Martha was one of the standard television guest stars making the rounds of the networks. Often she appeared with Bob Hope. On his April 14, 1963, special she and Hope did a spoof on *Dr. Kildare* entitled "Calling Miss Nightingale." In December 1963, she made her first appearance on Red Skelton's comedy hour, joined by her daughter Melodye, who had tackled a stage career, after having worked for a spell as a secretary at the William Morris Agency. She also accepted a dramatic cameo appearance on *Burke's Law*.

When the Vietnam trouble escalated in 1964–1965, Martha volunteered her services, as she had during World War II and the Korean War. She did a 3½ month U.S.O. tour of the Far East trouble spot, beginning in October 1965. Garbed in the "Tiger" night camouflage uniform of the Green Beret special forces she staged over 600 performances, traveling from outpost to outpost via helicopter. The delighted troops nicknamed her "Boondock Maggie." She was at the Plei Me outpost in the fall of 1965 when the Viet Cong attacked and she barely escaped alive. The following year, she was at Soc Trang on the Mekong delta, when the latest war casualties were being flown in. Unceremoniously, she pitched in, giving nursing aid day after day. Since then she has made eight trips all told to Vietnam, and has won a host of medals, including citations from General Westmoreland, the Marine Corps League's Dickey Chapelle Memorial Award, U.S.O. Woman Of The Year Award, Amvets Silver Helmet Special Award. She was made an honorary marine colonel (July 18, 1969), and President Lyndon Johnson designated her "the only person outside the elite corps [Berets] who may wear their proud symbol." She was wounded three times in her warfront treks. But she thrives on her usefulness in a time of need.

Then on February 27, 1967, she returned to Broadway in the role of Dolly Levi in *Hello Dolly!*, replacing Ginger Rogers. She proved an instantaneous success. Don Sullivan, writing in *The New York Times,* said: "Someday someone is going to write a great role for Martha Raye. Just as Miss Raye's face at times suggests a haunting combination of the Greek masks of comedy and tragedy, so her force as a performer stems as much from her sense of pathos as from her rowdy, slapstick sense of fun. . . . When Miss Raye's Dolly Gallagher Levi is summoning up the ghost of her late husband to ask his permission to marry again, there is a piteousness in her pleas that is new to the show. . . . The negative aspects can be summed up in the simple statement that Martha and Dolly have almost nothing in common. Martha the hoyden; Dolly the lady. Martha with the elbow in the ribs; Dolly with the hand in the velvet glove. As one of Dolly's songs says—'If You Ain't Got Elegance, You Can Never Carry It Off.' To expect that kind of elegance from Miss Raye was surely a little unrealistic of David Merrick, the producer, since she has never displayed it before. Martha belongs on Broadway, but in a different kind of show than *Hello, Dolly!*"

Martha thoroughly enjoyed her *Dolly stay.* At the end of each performance, she would quip and clown and mug for the audience, thanking them for coming and wishing everyone good health. She was replaced on June 12, 1967, by Betty Grable. Martha took a shortened version of the musical to Vietnam to perform for the troops. More than once, she collapsed during a performance from over-exhaustion and the extreme heat.

Also in 1967, she became a grandmother, when her daughter Melodye gave birth to a son, Nick.

At the 41st Annual Academy Awards ceremony in April 1969, Martha was awarded the Jean Hersholt Humanitarian Award for "her devoted and often dangerous work in entertaining troops in combat areas almost continuously since World War II." In accepting the special Oscar from presenter Bob Hope, a teary-eyed, over-joyed Martha said she would devote the rest of her life "to deserving this."

In the summer of 1969, Martha toured in what was to have been the pre-Broadway engagement of a new musical, *Hello Sucker,* based on the life of 1920s performer, movie star, and nightclub hostess Texas Guinan. With music and lyrics by Wilson Stone, and book by Larry B. Marks and Robert Ennis Tournoff, the show played the Guber-Gross-Ford summer tent circuit on the east coast. Dennis Patrick and Joseph Mascola were the male leads. *Variety's* review of the show said: "With the personal draw of a Martha Raye, it might even go further, but without such a spark plug, it probably would come thru as something of a routine musical. . . . Miss Raye is all over the lot, singing, dancing, emoting and mugging, and she gets a standing ovation for her contribution." The production was disbanded after the summer season.

Martha returned to theatrical filmmaking in 1970 with two pictures. Neither venture was worthy of her talent. In the "undeveloped lentil" *The Phynx,* Martha was one of the horde of "camp" names corraled together to give boxoffice appeal (nostalgia being the name of the game) to a shoddy piece of junk. The picture's premise has Joan Blondell and George Tobias kidnapping a group of one-time movie celebrities to a retreat in Albania. Why, is never explained. A new rock group is formed so that it will be invited to perform behind the Iron Curtain and succeed in freeing these memory-celebrities. Martha, at least, had the chance for a few solo screen moments as double agent Foxy who scampers about pell mell in the nonsense fracus; the other guest stars are only spotted in a short sequence in which they are found seated in hard back metal chairs row after row, each once-name actor looking mighty embarrassed by the whole thing. *The Phynx* played a few engagements in the hinterlands, and then disappeared from sight, when the changeover regime at Warner Brothers-7 Arts decided to bury the mistake. It has long been slated for television disposal, but has yet to show up on the small tube.

Martha's other 1970 picture was the more respectable *Pufnstuf,* produced by Universal. In this fantasy tale set on Living Island, Martha was Boss Witch, one of the few live actors discernable on screen. Most of the characters were stuffed oversized dolls, with people inside. In its review of this novelty film, *Variety* commented: "Martha Raye plays the boss witch at a witches' Convention and is ill used along with [Jack] Wild and Miss [Billie] Hayes." Nevertheless, Martha had a ball playing the outlandish character. Mama Cass Elliott made her movie debut in this under $1 million musical comedy, which did not even come close to the financial take of similar Walt Disney-type movies geared for the kiddie matinee market.

Then in the fall of 1970, she turned up as the star of a Saturday morning NBC television series *The Bugaloos,* a program definitely for the younger set, which is still being produced and televised. Besides four young British performers, the rest of the cast is encased in animal outfits. Martha plays Benita Bizarre, who she says "is a vicious witch but not really. I live in a juke box, wear a turkey-feather boa, and want to make a

record even though I can't sing. What more could a girl ask?" The show is high camp at best, and Martha could not give a hoot that the program obviously lacks artistic merit. In her madcap marathon mugging, she prances about the stage like a true teenager discovering that it can be fun to be an outrageous childish ham. Typical of her seemingly impromptu bits was one episode in which she exerts tremendous effort to learn the secret of youth which the four "Bugaloos" possess. (She finds it difficult to believe that anyone can be so young naturally.) In one frantic moment, Martha rushes up to a wall mirror and pleads: Mirror, mirror, I want the truth, have I regained my flower youth." Preening her devilish locks and contorting her expressive face out of shape, she cannot find any pose that is even vaguely flattering. Shrugging her shoulders, she gives up the quest in disgust.

Obviously, Martha has not lost her youthful sense of fun and vitality. She continues a hectic professional pace, guesting on her favorite television shows like the Red Skelton and Carol Burnett programs and taping new episodes of *The Bugaloos.* (She and Burnett recorded a LP song album—already out of print—entitled *Together Again for the First Time.* Much of Martha's time is spent in Vietnam because: "In Nam I feel loved, I got my whole family there." Mostly Martha performs as a surgical nurse near the battle zone. A registered nurse since 1936, she is now officially Lt. Col. Martha Raye of the Army Nurses Corps Reserve and serves with the Special Forces, the Green Berets. ("What I do isn't from sympathy or pity. It's just trying to help in a small way. Our servicemen give so much and ask for so little.")

When she is back in the States, she lives at her Bel-Air home. Often it is filled with military personnel, invited to rest up at her place. Nick Condos, still her manager, pops in and out constantly, on business matters.

Although it is dubious Martha will risk taking husband number seven, she has said: "Only cowards give up the search for happiness because they're afraid of getting hurt." What is certain, is that "My career is my whole life. I'll always work."

FILMOGRAPHY: MARTHA RAYE

Feature Films

RHYTHM ON THE RANGE (Par. '36) 87 M.
Producer, Benjamin Glazer; director, Norman Taurog; story, Mervin J. Houser; screenplay, John C. Moffett,

Sidney Salkow, Walter DeLeon, Francis Martin; music director, Boris Morros; songs, Leo Robin and Richard Whiting; Johnny Mercer; Robin and Frederick Hollander; Robin and Ralph Rainger; Walter Bullock; Richard Whiting; Whiting and Hollander; Bager Clark and Gertrude Ross; Billy Hill and J. Keirn Brennan; camera, Karl Struss; editor, Ellsworth Hoagland.

Bing Crosby (Jeff Larrabee); Frances Farmer (Doris Halliday); Bob Burns (Buck Burns); Martha Raye (Emma); Samuel S. Hinds (Robert Halliday); Lucille Webster Gleason (Penelope Ryland); Warren Hymer (Big Brain); George E. Stone (Shorty); James Burke (Wabash); Martha Sleeper (Constance); Clem Bevans (Gila Bend); Leonid Kinskey (Mischa); Charles Williams (Gopher); Beau Baldwin (Cuddles); Emmett Vogan (Clerk); Dennis O'Keefe (Heckler); Duke York (Officer); James Blaine (Conductor); Herbert Ashley (Brakeman); James "Slim" Thompson (Porter); Jim Toney (Oil Station Proprietor); Sid Saylor (Gus); Sam McDaniel (Porter); Harry C. Bradley (Minister); Charles E. Arnt (Steward); Oscar Smith (Waiter); Bob McKenzie (Farmer); Heinie Conklin (Driver); Frank Dawson (Butler); Sons Of The Pioneers (Singers).

THE BIG BROADCAST OF '37 (Par. '36) 100 M.

Producer, Lewis E. Gensler; director, Mitchell Leisen; story, Erwin Gelsey, Arthur Kober, Barry Trivers; screenplay, Walter DeLeon, Francis Martin; art director, Hans Dreier, Robert Usher; choreography, LeRoy Prinz; songs, Leo Robin, Ralph Rainger; camera, Theodore Sparkuhl; editor, Stuart Heisler.

Jack Benny (Jack Carson); George Burns and Gracie Allen (Mr. and Mrs. Platt); Bob Burns (Bob Black); Martha Raye (Patsy); Shirley Ross (Gwen Holmes); Ray Milland (Bob Miller); Frank Forest (Frank Rossman); Benny Fields (Himself); Sam Hearn (Schlepperman); Stan Kavanaugh (Kavvy); Benny Goodman and Orchestra (Themselves); Virginia Weidler (Flower Girl); David Holt, Billy Lee (Train Bearers); Leopold Stokowski and Symphony Orchestra (Themselves); Ernest Cossart (The Uncle); Irving Bacon (Property Man); Eleanore Whitney (Specialty); Louis DaPron (Specialty); Larry Adler (Specialty); Bill Bletcher (Property Man); Harry Depps (Assistant Property Man); Don Hulbert (Page Boy); Billie Bellport (Mrs. Peters); Cupid Ainsworth (Penelope); Frank Jenks (Trombone Player); Nora Cecil (Home Economics Woman); Ellen Drew (Telephone Girl); Jack Mulhall (Clerk).

COLLEGE HOLIDAY (Par. '36) 87 M.

Producer, Harlan Thompson; director, Frank Tuttle; screenplay, J. P. McEvoy, Harlan Ware, Jay Gorney, Henry Myers; choreography, LeRoy Prinz; songs, Leo Robin and Ralph Rainger, Ralph Freed and Burton Lane; camera, Theodor Sparkuhl.

Jack Benny (J. Davis Bowster); George Burns (George Hymen); Gracie Allen (Calliope Dove); Mary Boland (Carola Gaye); Martha Raye (Daisy Schloggenheimer); Etienne Girardot (Professor Hercules Dove); Marsha Hunt (Sylvia Smith); Leif Erikson (Dick Winters); Eleanore Whitney (Eleanor Wayne); Johnny Downs (Johnny Jones); Olympe Bradna (Felice L'Hommedieu); Louis DaPron (Barry Taylor); Ben Blue (Stage Hand); Jed Prouty (Sheriff); Richard Carle (Judge Bent); Margaret Beddon (Mrs. Schloggenheimer); Nick Lukats (Wisconsin); Spec O'Donnell (Lafayette); Jack Chapin (Colgate); California Collegians (Themselves); Nora Cecil (Miss Elkins); Ellen Drew (Student); Snowflake Toones (Porter); Charlie Arnt (Clerk); Harry Hayden (Mr. Smith); Howard Mitchell (Deputy); Buddy Messinger

(Minstrel); Joseph Franz, Earl Pingree (Policemen); Ray Hansford (Deputy Sheriff); Marjorie Reynolds, Eddie Foy (Dancers).

HIDEAWAY GIRL (Par. '37) 72 M.

Producer, A. M. Botsford; director, George Archainbaud; story, David Garth; screenplay, Joseph Moncure March; songs, Ralph Freed and Burton Lane; Leo Robin, Ralph Rainger, and Victor Young; Sam Coslow; camera, George Clemens; editor, Arthur Schmidt.

Shirley Ross (Toni Ainsworth); Robert Cummings (Michael Winslow); Martha Raye (Helen Flint); Monroe Owsley (Count de Montaigne); Wilma Francis (Muriel Courtney); Elizabeth Russell (Cellette Martin); Louis DaPron (Tom Flint); Ray Walker (Freddie MacKaye); Robert Middlemann (Captain Dixon); Edward Brophy (Bugs Murphy); James Eagles (Birdie Arnold); Bob Murphy (Captain McArthur); Lee Phelps (Police Sgt. Davis); Kenneth Harlan (Head Steward); Jimmie Dundee (Detective); Chill Wills and the Avalon Boys (Specialty); Martin Lamont, Frank Losee Jr. (Sailors); Pop Byron (Dock Watchman); Chester Gann (Chinese Cook); Harry Jordan (Chauffeur); Allen Pomeroy, James Barton (Motorcycle Cops); Donald Kerr, Bert Moorhouse (Cameramen).

WAIKIKI WEDDING (Par. '37) 89 M.

Producer, Arthur Hornblow Jr.; director, Frank Tuttle; story, Frank Butler, Don Hartman; screenplay, Butler, Hartman, Walter DeLeon, Francis Martin; music director, Boris Morros; orchestrations, Victor Young; choreography, LeRoy Prinz; songs, Harry Owen; Ralph Rainger and Leo Robin; camera, Karl Struss; special effects, Farciot Edouart; editor, Paul Weatherwax.

Bing Crosby (Tony Marvin); Bob Burns (Shad Buggle); Martha Raye (Myrtle Finch); Shirley Ross (Georgia Smith); George Barbier (J. P. Todhunter); Leif Erikson (Dr. Victor Quimby); Grady Sutton (Everett Todhunter); Granville Bates (Uncle Herman); Anthony Quinn (Kimo); Prince Lei Lani (Priest); Mitchell Lewis (Koalani); George Regas (Muamua); Nick Lukats (Assistant Purser); Kuulei De Clercq (Lani); Nalani De Clercq (Maile); Miri Rei (Specialty Dancer); Spencer Charters (Frame); Alexander Leftwich (Harrison); Harry Stubbs (Keith); Augie Goupil (Specialty Dancer); Ralph Remley (Tomlin); Pierre Watkin (John Durkin); Iris Yamaoka (Secretary); Jack Chapin (Photographer); Pedro Regas (Cab Driver); David Newell (Radio Operator); Emma Dunn (Tony's Mother); Robert Emmett O'Connor, Lalo Encinas (Policemen); Sojin Jr. (Bellboy); Ray Kinney (Singer).

MOUNTAIN MUSIC (Par. '37) 76 M.

Producer, Benjamin Glazer; director, Robert Florey; story, MacKinlay Kantor; screenplay, John C. Moffitt, Duke Atteberry, Russell Crouse, Charles Lederer; art director, Hans Dreier, John Goodman; songs, Sam Coslow; camera, Karl Struss; editor, Eda Warren.

Bob Burns (Bob Burnside); Martha Raye (Mary Beamish; John Howard (Ardinger); Terry Walker (Lebelia); Rufe Davis (Ham); George Hayes (Grandpappy); Spencer Charters (Justice Sharody); Charles Timblin (Shep); Jan Duggan (Ma); Olin Howland (Pappy); Fuzzy Knight (Amos); Wally Vernon (Odette Potta); Cliff Clark

(Medicine Show Doctor); Goodee Montgomery (Alice); Rita LaRoy (Mrs. Lovelace); Red Donahue and Mule (Themselves); Arthur Hohl (Prosecuting Attorney); Charlie Arnt (Hotel Manager); Miranda Giles (Aunt Effie); Jimmy Conlin (Medicine Show Shill); Ward Bond, Wally Maher (G-Men); Eddie Tamblyn (Bellboy); Paul Kruger (Attendant); Lew Kelly (Mailman); Ellen Drew (Helen); Robert St. Angelo (Chef); Harvey Parry (Bus Boy); Charles Judela (Orchestra Leader); Louis Hatheaux (Mr. Lovelace).

DOUBLE OR NOTHING (Par. '37) 95 M.

Producer, Benjamin Glazer; director, Theodore Reed; story, M. Coates Webster; screenplay, Charles Lederer, Erwin Gelsey, John C. Moffitt, Duke Atteberry; music director, Boris Morros; choreography, LeRoy Prinz; songs, Al Siegel and Sam Coslow; Johnny Burke and Victor Young; Irving Kahal and Johnny Greene; Burke and Arthur Johnson; Arthur Freed and Burton Lane; camera, Karl Struss; editor, Edward Dmytryk.

Bing Crosby (Lefty Boylan); Matha Raye (Liza Lou Lane); Andy Devine (Half-Pint); Mary Carlisle (Vicki Clark); William Frawley (Peterson); Benny Baker (Sailor); Samuel S. Hinds (Jonathan Clark); William Henry (Egbert); Fay Holden (Martha Sewell Clark); Bert Hanlon (Praxitales); Gilbert Emory (Mr. Mitchell); Walter Kingsford (Mr. Lobson); John Gallaudet (Rutherford); Harry Barris (Orchestra Conductor); Alphonse Berg, Tex Morrissay, Frances Faye, Ames and Arno, Ed Rickard, Steve and Andre Calgary (Specialties); Jimmy Notaro (Dancing Cop); Olaf Hytten (Eustace); Arthur Housman, Charles Irwin (Drunks); Herbert Ashley (Doorman); Rolfe Sedan (Headwaiter); Jack Pennick (Taxi Driver); Stanley Andrews (Police Lt.).

ARTISTS AND MODELS (Par. '37) 97 M.

Producer, Lewis E. Gensler; director, Raoul Walsh; story, Sig Herzig, Gene Thackrey; adaptation, Eve Greene, Harlan Ware; screenplay, Walter De Leon, Francis Martin; music arrangements, Victor Young; songs, Leo Robin and Ralph Rainger; Ted Koehler and Victor Young; Koehler and Burton Lane; Frederick Hollander and Robin; camera, Victor Milner; editor, Ellsworth Hoagland.

Jack Benny (Mac Brewster); Ida Lupino (Paula); Richard Arlen (Alan Townsend); Gail Patrick (Cynthia); Ben Blue (Jupiter Pluvius); Judy Canova (Toots); Cecil Cunningham (Stella); Donald Meek (Dr. Zimmer); Hedda Hopper (Mrs. Townsend); Martha Raye, Andre Kostelanetz And Orchestra, Russell Patterson's Personettos, Louis Armstrong and Orchestra, Judy, Anne and Zeke Canova, The Yacht Club Boys, Connee Boswell (Specialties); Peter Arno, McClelland Barclay, Arthur William Brown, Rube Goldberg, John LaGatta, Russell Patterson (Artists); Sandra Storme (Model); Madelon Grey (Marjorie); Alan Birmingham (Craig Sheldon); Kathryn Kay (Lois); Jerry Bergen (Bartender); Mary Shepherd, Gloria Wheeden (Water Waltzers); Dell Henderson (Lord); Virginia Brissac (Seamstress); Henry and Harry C. Johnson (Jugglers); Jack Stary (Cycling Star); Harvey Poirier (Sharpshooter); David Newell (Romeo); Jane Weir (Miss Gordon); Edward Earle (Flunky); Howard Hickman (Mr. Currie); Pat Moran (Tumbler).

THE BIG BROADCAST OF '38 (Par. '38) 90 M.

Producer, Harlan Thompson; director, Mitchell Leisen; story, Frederick Hazlitt Brennan; screenplay, Walter De Leon; Francis Martin, Ken Englund; music director, Boris Morros; choreography, LeRoy Prinz; songs, Ralph Rainger and Leo Robin, Tito Guizar; camera, Harry Fishbeck; special effects, Gordon Jennings; editor, Eda Warren, Chandler House.

W. C. Fields (T. Fronthingell Bellows/S. B. Bellows); Martha Raye (Martha Bellows); Dorothy Lamour (Dorothy Wyndham); Shirley Ross (Cleo Fielding); Lynne Overman (Scoop McPhail); Bob Hope (Buzz Fielding); Ben Blue (Mike); Lief Erikson (Bob Hayes); Grace Bradley (Grace Fielding); Rufe Davis (Turnkey); Patricia Wilder (Honey Chile); Lionel Pape (Lord Droopy); Dorothy Howe (Joan Fielding); Russell Hicks (Captain Stafford); Kirsten Flagstad, Tito Guizar, Shep Fields and His Rippling Rhythm Orchestra (Specialties); and: Billy Daniels, Jack Hubbard, Leonid Kinsky, Stanley King, James Craig, Irving Bacon, Wally Maher, Don Marion, Rebecca Wassem, Willy Maher, Bernard Punsley, Rex Moore.

COLLEGE SWING (Par. '38) 86 M.

Producer, Lewis Gensler; director, Raoul Walsh; story, Ted Lesser; adaptation, Frederick Hazlitt Brennan; screenplay, Walter DeLeon, Francis Martin; choreography, LeRoy Prinz; music director, Boris Morros; songs, Frank Loesser, Manning Sherwin, Burton Lane; Frank Loesser and Burton Lane; Frank Loesser and Hoagy Carmichael; Manning Sherwin; camera, Victor Milner; editor, LeRoy Stone.

George Burns (George Jonas); Gracie Allen (Gracie Alden); Martha Raye (Mable); Bob Hope (Bud Brady); Edward Everett Horton (Hubert Dash); Florence George (Ginna Ashburn); Ben Blue (Ben Volt); Betty Grable (Betty); Jackie Coogan (Jackie); John Payne (Martin Bates); Cecil Cunningham (Dean Sleet); Robert Cummings (Radio Announcer); Skinnay Ennis (Skinnay); The Slate Brothers (Themselves); The Playboys (Themselves); Bob Mitchell and St. Brendan's Choristers (Themselves); Jerry Colonna (Professor Yascha Koloski); Jerry Bergen (Professor Jasper Chinn); Tully Marshall (Grandpa Alden); Edward J. LeSaint (Dr. Storm); Alphonse Martel (Head Waiter); Richard Denning, John Hubbard (Students).

GIVE ME A SAILOR (Par. '38) 80 M.

Producer, Jeff Lazarus; associate producer, Paul Jones; director, Elliott Nugent; based on a play by Anne Nichols; screenplay, Doris Anderson, Frank Butler; art directors, Hans Dreier, Earl Hedrick; choregraphy, LeRoy Prinz; music director, Boris Morros; songs, Ralph Rainger and Leo Robin; camera, Victor Milner; editor, William Shea.

Martha Raye (Letty Larkin); Bob Hope (Jim Brewster); Betty Grable (Nancy Larkin); Jack Whiting (Walter Brewster); Clarence Kolb (Captain Tallant); J. C. Nugent (Mr. Larkin); Bonnie Jean Churchill (Ethel May Brewster); Nana Bryant (Mrs. Brewster).

TROPIC HOLIDAY (Par. '38) 75 M.

Producer, Arthur Hornblow Jr.; director, Theodore Reed; story, Don Hartman, Frank Butler; screenplay,

Hartman, Butler, John C. Moffitt, Duke Atteberry; songs, Ned Washington and Augustin Lara; Leo Robin and Ralph Rainger; editor, Archie Marshek.

Bob Burns (Frank Jones); Dorothy Lamour (Manuela); Ray Milland (Ken Warren); Martha Raye (Midge Miller); Binnie Barnes (Marilyn Joyce); Tito Quizar (Ramon); Elvira Rice (Rosa); Roberto Soto (Roberto); Mitchell Visaroff (Felipe); Bobby Meya (Pepito); Fortunio Bona-Nova (Barrera); Matt McHugh (Joe); Pepito (Chico); Sam Cristobal Marimba Band (Themselves); Chris Pin Martin (Pancho); Frank Puglia (Co-Pilot); Duncan Renaldo (Young Blood); Maria and Teresa Olguin (Bullfighters); Victor Romito, Manuel Valencia (Henchmen); Paul Lopez (Young Man); Anna Dematrio (Shopkeeper); Carlos Villarias (Commandante).

NEVER SAY DIE (Par. '39) 80 M.

Producer, Paul Jones; director, Elliott Nugent; story, William H. Post; screenplay, Don Hartman, Frank Butler, Preston Sturges; art director, Hans Dreier, Ernest Fegte; music director, Boris Morros; songs, Ralph Rainger and Leo Robin; camera, Leo Tover; special effects, Farciot Edouart; editor, James Smith.

Martha Raye (Mickey Hawkins); Bob Hope (John Kidley); Andy Devine (Henry Munch); Alan Mowbray (Prince Smirnov); Gale Sondergaard (Juno); Sig Rumann (Poppa Ingleborg); Ernest Cossart (Jeepers); Paul Harvey (Jasper Hawkins); Frances Arms (Momma Ingleborg); Ivan Simpson (Kretsky); Monte Woolley (Dr. Schmidt); Foy Van Dolsen (Kretsky's Bodyguard); Christian Rub (Mayor).

$1,000 A TOUCHDOWN (Par. '39) 71 M.

Associate producer, William C. Thomas; director, James Hogan; screenplay, Delmer Daves; art director, Hans Dreier, William Flannery; songs, Leo Robin and Ralph Rainger; camera, William Mellor; editor, Chandler House.

Joe E. Brown (Marlowe Mansfield Booth); Martha Raye (Martha Madison); Eric Blore (Henry); Susan Hayward (Betty McGlen); John Hartley (Bill Anders); Syd Saylor (Bangs); Joyce Mathews (Lorelie); Tom Dugan (Popcorn Vendor); Matt McHugh (Brick Benson); Hugh Sothern (King Richard); Josef Swickard (Hamilton McGlen Sr.); Adrian Morris (Two Ton Terry); Dewey Robinson (Cab Driver); William Haade (Guard); Jack Perrin (McGlen's First Son); Phil Dunham (McGlen's Second Son); Constantine Romanoff (Duke); Charles Middleton (Stage Manager); Dot Farley (Hysterical Woman); Emmett Vogan (Coach); Fritzie Brunnette, Gertrude Astor (McGlen's Sons' Wives); John Hart (Buck); Wanda McKay (Babe); Cheryl Walker (Blondie); Wayne ("Tiny") Whitt (Big Boy); Bob Layne (Irish).

THE FARMER'S DAUGHTER (Par. '40) 60 M.

Producer, William C. Thomas; director, James Hogan; story, Delmer Daves; screenplay, Lewis R. Foster; assistant director, Roland Asher; song, Frank Loesser and Frederick Hollander; camera, Leo Tover; editor, Archie Marshek.

Martha Raye (Patience Bingham); Charlie Ruggles (Nicksie North); Richard Denning (Dennis Crane); Gertrude Michael (Clarice Sheldon); William Frawley (Scoop Trimble); Inez Courtney (Emily French); William Demarest (Victor Walsh); Jack Norton (Shimmy Conway); William Duncan (Tom Bingham); Ann Shoemaker (Mrs. Bingham); Benny Baker (Monk Gordon); Tom Dugan (Forbes); Lorraine Krueger (Valerie); Betty McLaughlin (Dorinda); Anne Harrison (Rosalie); Pat West (Chuck Stevens); Darryl Hickman (Billy Bingham); John Hartley (Barney Bingham); Etta McDaniel (Anna); Grace Hayle (Torsavitch); Si Jenks (Farmer); Wanda McKay, Jane Webb (Cashiers); John ("Skins") Miller (Carpenter); George McKay (Process Server); Nick Moro (Sound Effects Man); Janet Waldo (Switchboard Operator).

THE BOYS FROM SYRACUSE (Univ. '40) 72 M.

Producer, Jules Levey; director, Edward Sutherland; based on William Shakespeare's *A Comedy of Errors* and the stage play by George Abbott, Richard Rodgers, Lorenz Hart; screenplay, Leonard Spigelgass, Charles Grayson; music director, Charles Previn; choreography, Dave Gould; songs, Rodgers and Hart; camera, Joe Valentine; editor, Milton Carruth.

Allan Jones (Eph/Sy); Irene Hervey (Adrianna); Martha Raye (Luce); Joe Penner (Dro/Mio); Alan Mowbray (Angelo); Charles Butterworth (Duke); Rosemary Lane (Phyllis); Samuel S. Hinds (Angeen); Eric Blore (Pinch); Tom Dugan (Octavius); Spencer Charters (Turnkey); Doris Lloyd (Woman); Larry Blake (Announcer); Eddie Acuff (Taxi Cab Driver); Matt McHugh (Bartender); David Oliver (Messenger); June Wilkins (Secretary); Bess Flowers (Woman); Cyril Ring (Guard); Julie Carter (Girl).

NAVY BLUES (WB '41) 109 M.

Producer, Hal B. Wallis; associate producer, Jerry Wald, Jack Saper; director, Lloyd Bacon; story, Arthur T. Horman; screenplay, Wald, Richard Macauley, Horman; choreography, Seymour Felix; songs, Arthur Schwartz and Johnny Mercer; camera, Tony Gaudio; editor, Rudi Fehr.

Ann Sheridan (Margie Jordan); Jack Oakie (Cake O'Hara); Martha Raye (Lillibelle); Jack Haley (Powerhouse Bolton); Herbert Anderson (Homer Mathews); Jack Carson (Buttons Johnson); Richard Lane (Rocky Anderson); William T. Orr (Mac); Jackie Gleason (Tubby); John Ridgely (Jersey); Howard da Silva (First Petty Officer); Frank Wilcox (Officer); Richard Travis (Tex); William Hopper (Ensign Walters); Hardie Albright (Officer); Marguerite Chapman, Leslie Brooks, Claire James, Katharine Aldridge, Georgia Carroll, Peggy Diggins (Navy Blues Sextette); Ralph Byrd (Lieutenant); Gig Young, Murray Alper, Lane Allen (Sailors); Jean Ames, Maris Wrixon, Lucia Carroll (Girls); Tom Dugan (Hot Dog Stand Proprietor); Gaylord Pendleton, Don Rowan (Marines); Dick Wessel, Victor Zimmerman (Petty Officers); Charles Drake, Emmett Vogan (Officers); Selmer Jackson (Captain Willard); Harry Strang (C.P.O. Lane).

KEEP 'EM FLYING (Univ. '41) 86 M.

Associate producer, Glenn Tryon; director, Arthur Lubin; story, Edmund L. Hartmann; screenplay, True

Boardman, Nat Perrin, John Grant; songs, Don Raye and Dane de Paul; Ned Washington and George Basman; assistant director, Gil Vallee; special effects, John Fulton; camera, Joseph Valentine; editor, Philip Cahn, Arthur Hilton.

Bud Abbott (Blackie Benson); Lou Costello (Heathcliffe); Martha Raye (Barbara/Gloria Phelps); Carol Bruce (Linda Joyce); William Gargan (Craig Morrison); Dick Foran (Jinx Roberts); Truman Bradley (Butch); William Davidson (McGonigal); Charles Lang (Jim Joyce); Frank Penny (Spealer); Loring Smith, Charles King Jr., James Horne Jr., Regis Parton, Scotty Groves (Cadets); Dorothy Darrell, Elaine Morey, Marcia Ralston (USO Girls); Doris Lloyd (Lady with Lipstick); Dick Crane (Cadet Stevens); Virginia Engels (Hat Check Girl); Phil Warren (Pilot); Paul Scott (Doctor); Carleton Young (Orchestra Leader); Harold Daniels (Announcer); Mickey Simpson (Deputy); Gene O'Donnell (Radio Control Operator); James Seay (Lieutenant); Earle Hodgins (Attendant); William Forrest (Captain).

HELLZAPOPPIN (Univ. '41) 84 M.
Producer, Jules Levey; associate producer, Glenn Tryon, Alex Gottlieb; director, H. C. Potter; based on the play by Nat Perrin; screenplay, Perrin, Warren Wilson; songs, Gene DePaul and Don Raye; camera, Woody Bredell; special effects, John Fulton; editor, Milton Carruth.

Ole Olsen (Ole); Chic Johnson (Chic); Robert Paige (Jeff Hunter); Jane Frazee (Kitty Rand); Lewis Howard (Woody Tyler); Martha Raye (Betty Johnson); Clarence Kolb (Mr. Rand); Nella Walker (Mrs. Rand); Mischa Auer (Pepi); Richard Lane (Director); Elisha Cook Jr. (Assistant Director); Hugh Herbert (Detective Quimby); Olive Hatch, Harlem Congeroo Dancers (Specialties); Shemp Howard (Louie); Jody Gilbert (Blonde); Andrew Tombes (Producer); George Davis (Butler); Hal K. Dawson, Frank Darien (Photographers); Eddie Acuff (Drafted Devil); Billy Curtis (Taxi Driver); Harry Monti (Midget); Don Brodie (Theatre Manager); Gil Perkins (Butler in Pool); Dale Van Sickel (Man who Falls into Pool); Gus Schilling (Orchestra Leader); Sig Arno (Cellist); Bert Roach (Man in Audience); The Six Hits, Slim and Sam (Specialties).

FOUR JILLS IN A JEEP (20th, '44) 89
Producer, Irving Starr; director, William A. Seiter; story, Froma Sand, Fred Niblo Jr.; screenplay, Robert Ellis, Helen Logan, Snag Werris; art director, James Baseir, Albert Hogsett; choreography, Don Loper; songs, Harold Adamson and Jimmy McHugh; camera, Peverell Marley; special effects, Fred Sersem; editor, Ray Curtiss.

Kay Francis (Herself); Carole Landis (Herself); Martha Raye (Herself); Mitzi Mayfair (Herself); Jimmy Dorsey and Band (Themselves); John Harvey (Ted Warren); Phil Silvers (Eddie); Dick Haymes (Lt. Dick Ryan); Alice Faye, Betty Grable, Carmen Miranda (Guest Stars); George Jessel (Master of Ceremonies); Glenn Langan (Capt. Stewart); Lester Matthews (Capt. Lloyd); Miles Mander (Col. Hartley); Paul Harvey (General); Mary Servoss (Nurse Captain); Dave Willock, Martin Black, B. S. Pulley, Mike Kilian, Buddy Yarus, Gordon Wynne (Soldiers); Alex Harford (Priest); Mel Schubert, Kirk

Alyn (Pilots); Alex Pollard (Butler); Winifred Harris (Lady Carlton-Smith); Crauford Kent (British Officer); Frances Morris (Surgical Nurse); James Flavin (M.P.); Bernie Sell, Eddie Acuff (Sentries); Mary Field (Maid).

PIN-UP GIRL (20th, '44) 83 M.
Producer, William LeBaron; director, Bruce Humberstone; story, Libbie Block; screenplay, Robbi Ellis, Helen Logan, Earl Baldwin; choreography, Hermes Pan; art director, James Basavi, Joseph C. Wright; music director, Emil Newman, Charles Henderson; songs, Mack Gordon and Jimmy Monaco; camera, Ernest Palmer; special effects, Fred Sersen; editor, Robert Simpson.

Betty Grable (Lorry Jones); John Harvey (Tommy Dooley); Martha Raye (Marion); Joe E. Brown (Eddie); Eugene Pallette (Barney Briggs); Shaley Vanities (Themselves); Dorothea Kent (Kay); Condos Brothers (Specialty); Dave Willock (Dud Miller); Charles Spivak and Orchestra (Themselves); Robert Homans (Stage Doorman); Marcel Dalio (Headwaiter); Roger Clark (George); Leon Belasco (Captain of Waiters); Irving Bacon (Window Cleaner); Walter Tetley (Messenger Boy); Ruth Warren (Scrubwoman); Max Willing (Waiter); Manton Moreland, Charles Moore (Redcaps).

MONSIEUR VERDOUX (UA, '47) 102 M.
Producer-director-screenplay, Charles Chaplin; based on an idea by Orson Welles; associate directors, Robert Florey, Wheeler Dryden; assistant director, Rex Lalley; music, Charles Chaplin; music arrangements, Rudolph Schrager; camera, Roland Totheroh, Wallace Chewing; editor, Willard Nico.

Charles Chaplin (Henri Verdoux, and Narrator); Mady Correll (Mona Verdoux); Allison Roddan (Peter Verdoux); Robert Lewis (Maurice Bottello); Audrey Betz (Martha Bottello); Martha Raye (Annabella Bonheur); Ada-May (Annette); Isobel Elson (Marie Grosnay); Marjorie Bennett (Marie's Maid); Margaret Hoffman (Lydia Floray); Marilyn Nash (Girl); Irving Bacon (Pierre Couvais); Edwin Mills (Jean Couvais); Virginia Brissac (Carlotta Couvais); Almira Sessions (Phoebe Couvais); Bernard J. Nedell (Prefect of Police); Charles Evans (Detective Morrow); Arthur Hohl (Real Estate Agent); John Harmon (Joe Darwin); Vera Marshe (Mrs. Darwin); William Frawley (Jean La Salle); Fritz Leiber (Priest); Barbara Slater (Florist); Fred Karno (Mr. Karno); Barry Norton (Wedding Guest); Edna Purviance (Extra at Wedding Party); Pierre Watkin (Prison Official); Cyril Delevanti (Postman); Charles Wagenheim (Friend); Addison Richards (Bank Manager); James Craven (Annabella's Friend); Franklyn Farnum (Victim of the Crash); Herb Vigran (Reporter); Boyd Irwin (Prison Official); Paul Newlan (Wedding Guest); Joseph Crehan (Broker); Wheaton Chambers (Druggist); Frank Reicher (Doctor).

BILLY ROSE'S JUMBO (MGM '62) 123 M.
Producer, Joe Pasternak, Martin Melcher; associate producer, Roger Eden; director, Charles Walters; based on the musical play by Ben Hecht and Charles MacArthur; screenplay, Sidney Sheldon; songs, Richard Rodgers and Lorenz Hart; art director, George W. Davis, Preston Ames; assistant director, William Shanks; special effects, A. Arnold

Gillespie, Robert R. Hoag, M. C. Millan Johnson; second unit director, Busby Berkeley; camera, William H. Daniels; editor, Richard Farrell.

Doris Day (Kitty Wonder); Stephen Boyd (Sam Rawlins; Jimmy Durante (Pop Wonder); Martha Raye (Lulu); Dean Jagger (John Noble); Joe Waring (Harry); Lynn Wood (Tina); Charles Watts (Ellis); James Chandler (Parsons); Wilson Wood (Hank); Norman Leavitt (Eddie); Grady Sutton (Driver); Robert Burton (Madison); John Hart (Marshal); Roy Engel, Jack Boyle (Reporters); Robert Williams (Deputy); Sue Casey (Dottie); Fred Cob (Andy); William Hines (Roustabout); Michael Kostrick (Michaels); Ralph Lee (Perry); Paul Wexler (Sharpic); Otto Reichow (Hans); Billy Barty (Joey); Chuck Haren (Lennie); J. Lewis Smith (Dick).

THE PHYNX (WB, '70) 91 M.

Producer, Bob Booker; director, Lee H. Katzin; story, Booker; screenplay, Stan Cornyn; assistant director, Les Sheldon; production designer, Stan Jolley; music, Mike Stoller; lyrics, Jerry Leiber; sound, John Kean; camera, Michel Hugo; editor, Dann Cohn.

A. Michael Miller, Ray Chippeway, Dennis Larden, Lonny Stevens (The Phynx); Lou Antonio (Corrigan); Mike Kellin (Bogey); Michael Ansara (Col. Rostinov); George Tobias (Markvitch); Joan Blondell (Ruby); Martha Raye (Foxy); Larry Hankin (Phillaby); Teddy Eccles (Wee Johnny Urlso); Ultra Violet (Herself); Pat McCormack (Father O'Hoolihan); Joseph Gazal (Yakov); Bob Williams (Number One); Barbara Noonan (Bogey's Secretary); Rich Little (Voice in Box); Sue Bernard, Ann Morrell, Sherry Mills (Girls); Patty Andrews, Busby Berkeley, Xavier Cugat, Fritz Feld, John Hart, Ruby Keeler, Joe Louis, Marilyn Maxwell, Maureen O'Sullivan, Harold "Oddjob" Sakata, Ed Sullivan, Rona Barrett, James Brown, Cass Daley, Leo Gorcey, Louis Hayward, Patsy Kelly, Guy Lombardo, Butterfly McQueen, Richard Pryor, Colonel Harland Sanders, Rudy Vallee, Johnny Weismuller, Edgar Bergen, Dick Clark, Andy Devine, Huntz Hall, George Jessel, Dorothy Lamour, Trini Lopez, Pat O'Brien, Jay Silverheels, Clint Walker.

PUFNSTUF (Univ. '70) 105 M.

Executive producer, Sid and Marty Krofft; producer, Si Rose; director, Hollingsworth Morse; screenplay, John Fenton Murray, Rose; art director, Alexander Golitzen; Walter Scott Herndon; music, Charles Fox, Norman Gimbel; assistant director, Chuck Colean; camera, Kenneth Peach; editor, David Rawlins.

Jack Wild (Jimmy); Billie Hayes (Witchipoo); Martha Raye (Boss Witch); Mama Cass (Witch Hazel); Billy Barty (Postman); Johnny Silver (Dr. Blinky/Ludicrous Lion); Angelo Rossitto; Joy Campbell (Orson Vulture/Fireman); Andy Ratoucheff (Fireman); Sharon Baird (Shirley Pufnstuf); and: Jane Dulo, Jan Davis, Buddy Douglas, Ken Creel, Lou Wagner.

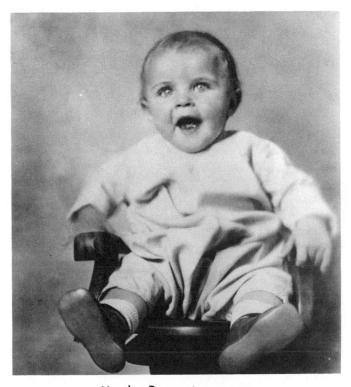

Martha Raye at age one.

With Bob Burns in *Rhythm on the Range* (Paramount, 1936).

With Bing Crosby in *Rhythm on the Range.*

With George Burns and Gracie Allen in *The Big Broadcast of 1937* (Paramount, 1936).

With Gracie Allen, Phil Tead, George Burns in *The Big Broadcast of 1937*.

With Jack Benny in *College Holiday* (Paramount, 1936).

With Ed Brophy in *Hideaway Girl* (Paramount, 1937).

With Bob Burns in *Waikiki Wedding* (Paramount, 1937).

With the Avalon Quartet (Chill Wills is second from left) in *Hideaway Girl*.

Martha Raye, c. 1937.

With Bob Burns, Terry Walker in *Mountain Music* (Paramount, 1937).

With Connee Boswell, Bing Crosby in *Double or Nothing*.

In *Double or Nothing*. (Martha is on the right) (Paramount, 1937).

With Bing Crosby in *Double or Nothing*.

In *Artists and Models* (Paramount, 1937).

With Lynne Overman in *The Big Broadcast of 1938*.

With Ben Blue in *The Big Broadcast of 1938*.

Gracie Allen and George Burns, Martha Raye and Bob
Hope, Florence George and John Payne, Betty Grable
and Ben Blue in *College Swing* (Paramount, 1938).

Publicity pose for *College Swing*.

Martha Raye in 1938.

In *Give Me a Sailor* (Paramount, 1938).

With Bob Hope in *Give Me a Sailor*.

In *Give Me a Sailor.*

With Jesus Topete in *Tropic Holiday*.

In *Tropic Holiday* (Paramount, 1938).

With Bob Burns in *Tropic Holiday*.

With Andy Devine, Bob Hope, Nick Moro in *Never
Say Die* (Paramount, 1939).

With Albert Dekker, Bob Hope, Frank Reicher in
Never Say Die.

With Eric Blore in *$1,000 a Touchdown* (Paramount, 1939).

With Joe E. Brown in *$1,000 a Touchdown*.

In *The Farmer's Daughter* (Paramount, 1940).

Martha Raye shown as she appeared on the witness stand when she was granted a divorce from David Rose in May 1940.

With Richard Denning in *The Farmer's Daughter.*

With Allen Jones in *The Boys from Syracuse* (Universal, 1940).

With Jack Haley, Jack Oakie in *Navy Blues* (Warner Brothers, 1941).

Martha Raye c. 1941.

With Lou Costello in *Keep 'em Flying* (Universal, 1941).

In *Keep 'em Flying.*

In *Hellzapoppin'* (Universal, 1941).

With Ole Olsen, Chic Johnson in *Hellzapoppin'*.

With Kay Francis, Carole Lombard, Mitzi Mayfair in
Four Jills in a Jeep (20th Century-Fox, 1944).

With Phil Silvers in *Four Jills in a Jeep.*

With Joe E. Brown in *Pin-Up Girl* (20th Century-Fox, 1944).

In *Monsieur Verdoux* (UA, 1947).

With Charlie Chaplin in *Monsieur Verdoux.*

With Barry Norton, James Craven, Paul Newlan,
Fred Karno in *Monsieur Verdoux*.

Martha Raye on NBC-TV, 1955.

With Cesar Romero, Irene Dunne, Rocky Graziano,
mid 1950s.

Martha Raye clowns with Dr. Joseph A. Reale, who treated her after she had collapsed. (September 1956).

With Jimmy Durante, Doris Day, Stephen Boyd in Jumbo (MGM, 1962).

With Doris Day, Jimmy Durante, Dean Jagger in
Jumbo.

With Moe Howard, Tim Conway, Danny Thomas, Bill
Cosby, Spike Jones Jr., 1965.

With Bob Hope on NBC-TV, 1966.

Entertaining troops in Vietnam (left) and as the lead
in *Hello, Dolly* (right), 1967.

With guitarist John Carr during 1968 USO tour.

On Red Skelton's CBS-TV show, 1969.

In *Pufnsnuf* (Universal, 1970).

With Mike Kellin in *The Phynx* (WB, 1970).

On TV's *Bugaloos*, 1970.

JOAN DAVIS

5'5"
120 pounds
Green eyes
Reddish brown hair
Birth sign: Cancer

Joan Davis was one of the few comediennes of all time to have appealed both to the intellectuals and the masses. She had the rare ability to combine two opposite poles of comedy to delightful perfection. Joan could execute a pratfall or a double take with the best of them, but she went one step further: with her expertly modulated deep voice and the slightest twisting of a facial gesture, she added highly sophisticated nuances to the broadest of stage slapstick. It made all the difference; she was able to pinpoint the exact nuance she wished to bring out.

In her move from vaudeville to Hollywood, Joan had the good fortune to have been featured in a spate of slickly produced feature films made by Twentieth Century-Fox. Often she would be on screen for just a flash, doing her outrageous bit, singing a wacky little ditty, and then disappearing. But her brief moments of glory stuck in audiences' minds, and she became a star without having had any leading roles in movies. In the 1940s, she moved on to other studios, where she turned out craftsmanlike work in lesser vehicles, which were tossed together to showcase her abundant talent. More importantly, she turned her attention to radio, and conquered that medium with amazing success. With no visuals to distract them, listeners could concentrate on the smart range of inflections that made all the difference in delivering a punch line. In the early 1950s, Joan starred in her own video series, *I Married Joan,* which

has become a classic of the medium, fondly remembered by all viewers of the day.

Joan's stage character was a self-contained individual. She was a man-hungry gal who made no bones about being a well-meaning, gawky female. All of Joan's physical energy was self-directed—she never expended it on others. Rather, she would be so upset with her own clumsiness and stuttering, that she had to slap herself in rebuke or toss herself against an inanimate object in self reproach. If she had critical words to mouth, they were about herself and directed aloud to her own ears.

Only Eve Arden has matched some of the vocal modulation and facial gesticulation that marked Joan's greatness; but Miss Arden was never one to trip and slide across a stage in madcap abandon. Lucille Ball has perfected her own brand of physical comedy and mayhem. However, unlike Joan, Miss Ball's stage character is out for more obvious rewards and glories—Lucy wants to get even with a wrong done her, or show off her own talent.

It is to be deeply regretted that Joan's untimely death robbed the world of a comic star who had many funny moments to share with her audiences.

Joan Davis (nee: Madonna Josephine Davis) was born June 29, 1907, in St. Paul, Minnesota, the only child of LeRoy Davis, a train dispatcher, and Nina Davis.

Although her family had no theatrical background, "Jo" was a born entertainer. At the age of three, she was dancing, singing and reciting at local church gatherings. One of her favorite bits was playing a skinny cupid, using a gilded coat hanger for a bow. When she was six, she audaciously had herself entered at the amateur night contest at a local theatre. Joan bravely recited a serious dramatic selection, and was promptly hooted off the stage, barely missing a barrage of rotten vegetables. Her father advised: "Joan, you lay beautiful eggs. Better be funny not serious. . . . Keep moving! It spoils their aim!" Joan returned to the same theatre the following week with a comedy routine, and song "I Ain't Nobody's Darling" which the low brow audience found much more acceptable.

Spotted by talent scouts, Joan was signed for a vaudeville tour on the then prestigious Pantages Theatre circuit. Billed as the "Toy Comedienne" and "Cyclonic Josephine Davis," she had a fourteen-minute whirlwind act. Her mother went on the road with her, as did a tutor. Whenever the act was laid off, the entourage returned to St. Paul, and Joan attended public school.

When she was no longer a youthful show business novelty, Joan, age sixteen, retired her act and came home. She graduated from St. Paul's Mechanic Arts High School as class valedictorian—an impressive feat for a student with such a helter-skelter education. During her school years, she was an active member of the debating team.

Then Joan took a job at the local Five and Dime, earning $8 weekly. Even there, she could not repress her antic sense of the absurd. She was assigned to the busy goldfish counter. She would frequently tell purchasers: "Yes, ma'am, do you want it wrapped as a gift?" Then she would break into one of her rubbery legs routines, sliding and skipping, and tripping along the floor.

Still bitten by the show business bug, Joan returned to the vaudeville circuit—which, unable to meet the stiff competition of the films, was then already fast declining as a popular art. When no engagement on the circuits materialized, Joan played amusement parks, summer camps, and one-night engagements. By now she had incorporated into her act all her interpretations of the funnier antics of her beloved screen favorite, Charlie Chaplin. Her act consisted of outrageously awkward slapstick antics (such as her famed bit of juggling a huge stack of dishes which seemingly defied the laws of gravity), using her rubbery facial gestures to emphasize her mugging, and pulling out all the stops in her cracked, train dispatcher's voice. She was no longer being billed as the "youthful fit of wit."

Joan had long been considering adding a straight man to her act to boost its class, and provide a stabilized source to bounce her nonsensical humor off at will. On St. Patrick's Day 1931, her manager introduced her to Serenus (Si) Wills. He was already an established vaudeville veteran, who wore bulgy pants, a putty nose, and played the typical hoke comic. Wills later recalled: "When she showed up, I like to died. In her act she wore green ruffled drawers down to her ankles and a hat even a queen wouldn't be seen in." The two teamed up, and were billed professionally as Wills and Davis. They developed their act into a "smart outfit."

On August 13, 1931, they were married in Chicago; they honeymooned on the road, in Cedar Point, Ohio. In mid-1933 their daughter Beverly was born. Wills later reminisced about Joan's compulsive poker-playing in those days, which often left the team in financial straits. She could not resist a good game of cards with the boys, and usually ended up the prize patsy.

By early 1935, Joan and her family had worked their way to the west coast. Joan was determined to break into the movies, which seemed the best medium to showcase her nutty art. Someone advised her that the best way to get into the movies was to offer to do a specialty routine in any film, even if it were performed for free.

Joan attempted to obtain a film assignment at Educational Films, which was then churning out many one and two-reelers as fillers for bills with first run feature films. Many one-time comedy greats of the cinema were working there on the fast professional road down, while other hopefuls, starting a cinema career, were using their efforts there as a stepping stone up (Shirley Temple made her start there in 1932). Joan got no further than the reception desk at Educational. Then she used pull. Through mutual friends, she got Mack Sennett, the king of slapstick, to come to a party she threw. Joan made sure the guest list included plenty of her vaudeville friends who could be counted on to applaud and whistle on cue. During the party, Joan performed one comedy routine after another. Sennett was sufficiently impressed and told her to come by the studio the next day. Joan did, but Sennett's secretary thought Joan was too old for the role. Undaunted, Joan returned the following morning, her hair in curls, with a bow, a short skirt, and her middie blouse starched in adolescent fashion. Recalled Joan: "I had everything but a yo-yo."

About her role in *Way Up Thar,* which was Sennett's last production at Educational, Joan later said: "It ran for a day and a half, including all night. Buster Keaton's mother played my mother in it. I was so worn out before I was through. I told Si: 'If this is the movies, get me out of them, I've aged so since yesterday I won't match in the rushes.' "

Based on a story by Olive Hatch, the Sennett-directed twenty-minute short had Joan as Jenny Kirk. She and her Ozark kinfolk yearn for singing jobs on the radio. Joan sang: "Comin' Round The Mountain," "I'm Gonna Get Married," and "That's Why I Stutter." She repeated her famous falling dishes routine as well.

Others in the cast included The Sons of the Pioneers, a country and western song group of which Roy Rogers was a member. *Way Up Thar* was released to theatres on November 8, 1935. The comedy short was later included in the compilation feature films "Birth of a Star" (1945) and "The Sound Of Laughter" (1963).

As a result of her impressive performance in this short subject, RKO Pictures signed Joan to a stock term contract, probably intending to utilize her in their assorted series of fun shorts. However, for four months, Joan sat around the lot, with scarcely any screen work. Occasionally, she had a zany bit in a feature in production, such as her portrayal of a telephone operator in *Bunker Bean* (1936). This 65-minute programmer was the third remake of the Harry Leon Wilson novel about the cure of a youth's (Owen Davis Jr.) inferiority complex through the suggestion of reincarnation. It opened at Manhattan's Palace Theatre on June 26, 1936, on the bottom half of a double bill with Edward G. Robinson's *Bullets or Ballots,* a racketeer story. By mutual agreement with the studio, Joan's RKO contract was terminated.

Joan was next on screen in a comedy spot in *Millions in the Air,* which debuted at New York's Paramount Theatre, December 11, 1935. Starring Wendy Barrie, John Howard, and Willie Howard, it was a very weak musical satire on the then popular Major Bowles radio amateur hour. The format provided ample opportunity for specialty acts. Dancer Eleanore Whitney, a protege of Bill "Bojangles" Robinson and a rising vaudeville star herself stole the show. Joan sang "You Tell Her Because I Stutter." In her one-star *New York Daily News* review, Wanda Hale termed the movie a ". . . most feeble attempt at burlesquing. . . ." Joan was not even billed in the credits, but she did get a brief mention from *The New York Times* ". . . [she] puts over a comic song extremely well." The *raison d'être* for Joan's appearance in this Paramount effort was that director Ray McCarey had become a friend of the comedienne and as a favor to him she did the bit in his project for free.

When no further film assignments developed, Joan and family returned to the east, finally wangling an engagement at the still potent Palace Theatre on Broadway. Wills and Davis bombed in their big-time stage debut, and the team was demoted quickly to playing an engagement at the Academy of Music on 14th Street in Manhattan, and returning to the grind of playing the lesser vaudeville circuit.

Then, in mid-1936, Joan maneuvered a player's contract option with the newly-merged Twentieth Century-Fox, headed by studio mogul Darryl F. Zanuck. Under Zanuck's aegis, the studio was embarking on a more ambitious musical and comedy film program, and required more specialty acts to bolster and fill out upcoming productions.

Joan's initial role at Twentieth was in *The Holy Terror* (1937). It starred the company's second string moppet star, Jane Withers, who played all the more adventurous and nasty girl roles that prima donna Shirley Temple was not equipped to handle. Joan was fourth billed as Lil, who along with Leah Ray runs the Sailor's Tea Shop. Withers was the mascot of the nearby navy air base, and, in the course of the lightweight entry, succeeded in rounding up a spy ring which wanted the plans for a new bomber. With Tony Martin and Leah Ray handling the bulk of the four song numbers, Joan and veteran studio comic El Brendel supplied occasional Swedish-type comedy relief. *The New York Times*'s review duly noted Joan's standby routine, describing her as a "strange female curtain-climber, with a trick of punching herself in the jaw and a curious resemblance to Olive Oyl in the cartoons."

In *On the Avenue* (1937)—an elaborate Irving Berlin musical starring Alice Faye, Dick Powell and Madelaine Carroll—Joan had a brief role as Miss Katz, secretary to theatrical producer Walter Catlett. Most of her few on-screen moments were devoted to dashing into the producer's office helter-skelter, barking out messages, doing exaggerated double takes, running in place while making frantic exits to carry out her boss's latest orders. She made her short screen time count, and her angular features coupled with her gymnastic entrances and exits stuck in audiences' minds.

Time Out for Romance (1937) concerns heiress Claire Trevor, who has married in leisure and is now repenting in haste by running out on the groom. She joins a car caravan going from New York to California. As Midge Dooley, Joan was one of the very eccentric people heading westward. The critics were fast to single out Joan as a prime source of comedy delight: Kate Cameron in her two-star *New York Daily News* review observed the ". . . newcomer named Joan Davis, whose perfectly natural and breezy brand of comedy gives the picture its chief reason for being noticed. Miss Davis is a comedienne to watch. She and her teammate, Chick Chandler, are the inspirations for most of the laughs heard at the Palace this week." *The New York Times* penned: "Thanks to the presence of that spidery-legged comedienne Joan Davis, who is in the habit of knocking herself out as a form of protest against her human limitations, in one of the forward cars, the film may be classified as endurable second rate."

Wake Up and Live (1937) was a witty spoof on the

radio industry featuring Alice Faye, Walter Winchell, Ben Bernie and Jack Haley. Slapstick personality Patsy Kelly played Winchell's madcap secretary. Joan had a brief, but very telling bit in a stage show sequence, in which she cavorts in a wild Spanish fandango dance with Leah Ray. With legs kicking energetically in all directions, arms flailing in the wind, and her body going through wild contortions, Joan, said *Variety,* "is also a wallop."

Co-billed with *Wake Up and Live,* which opened at the RKO Palace Theatre on May 27, 1937, was *Angel's Holiday.* In this Jane Withers vehicle, Joan played Strivers, a stuttering, jitterbugging character involved with Withers's shenanigans in helping movie queen Sally Blaine to disappear, and then having to find her, when real racketeers step in to kidnap the celebrity. Joan, in her brief bits of mayhem, was forced to compete with Withers's passable imitations of Paramount's own slapstick queen, Martha Raye.

In *You Can't Have Everything* (1937) a minor Alice Faye musical in which the svelte blonde star played a serious playwright lured onto the musical comedy stage of Broadway, Joan had an unbilled assignment. She performed a quick, hectic ballet dance, "The Bells," in between regular featured numbers.

The Great Hospital Mystery (1937) provided Joan with more screen time to build upon her comic antics. She was Flossie, the dumb fledgling nurse, in this tepid adaptation of a Mignon Eberhart murder mystery. Jane Darwell appeared as the all-knowing head nurse. There were ample occasions here for Joan to slide madly down hospital corridors, mangle any medical equipment at hand, and do her best to wreck the patients' chance for recovery. *Variety* commented: "Sole relief from the picture's dullness is provided by Joan Davis, who does her round-heeled slide juggling a bed pan and never spilling a drop."

Sing and Be Happy (1937) was a standard Twentieth musical, outfitted with a bare plot. Tony Martin and Leah Ray are both swing music enthusiasts and performers. Their fathers own competing advertising agencies, both angling for a prize pickle account. In the end, the two rival companies merge. Joan was again teamed with Chick Chandler. This time they played ever-helpful window washers, who cannot resist getting into the swing of things (at one point Joan tumbles backward into a pail). More than one reviewer noted that Joan, "the lady who has collapsible legs," "overdoes her slapstick imitation of Martha Raye," and that she was repeating her favorite bag of stage tricks all too often.

Thin Ice, premiering at the Roxy Theatre September-

ber 3, 1937, headlined skating star Sonja Henie. This time she was in love with prince Tyrone Power at a Swiss village resort. Joan romped through her paces as the leader of the hotel's all-girl orchestra. She had two solo gimmick songs: *My Swiss Hill Billy* and the boisterous *I'm Olga from the Volga.* In the latter, her swing rendition included wild gesticulations of her knees, elbows, and knuckles. *Brooklyn Daily Eagle* reporter Gould Cassal gave tribute to: ". . . the indiscribably funny Joan Davis (who) is at last given a major spot after a series of almost invisible support roles in Grade B flickers. Mere words do not quite catch the quality of Miss Davis' brand of humor. Superficially it is slapstick, but on second consideration it appears rather to be a super-sophisticated distillation of the most elegant type of humor. The comedienne goes directly to the heart of her material in an almost savage manner without once sacrificing method to mugging. You'll have to compare Miss Davis with the obvious Miss [Martha] Raye to see how good she is. Whatever closer analysis will reveal, there's no mistaking Miss Davis' presence in *Thin Ice.* Her songs are not in the front line of comic ditties, but she turns them into howlers."

Life Begins in College (1937) was a middling Fox entry in the campus comedy musical genre. The zany Ritz Brothers were proprietors of Klassy Kampus Klothes and attended Lombardy College; Nat Pendleton was a millionaire Oklahoma Indian football wizard, whom the college must recruit to survive in the athletic endowment competition. Joan was Inez, the gawky lure used by Lombardy to attract the elusive Pendleton to the campus and the football squad. *The New York Herald Tribune*'s Howard Barnes cited Joan for "her bow-legged routines."

Love and Hisses (1937), the tame follow-up to *Wake Up and Live,* had Walter Winchell and Ben Bernie still battling—this time over a supposedly imported singer being promoted by bandleader Bernie. Joan was fourth-billed as Joan, inheriting Patsy Kelly's role as Winchell's frantic Girl Friday. Her vis-a-vis was comedian Bert Lahr. The duo had a running gag of mumbling gobbledygook baby love talk to one another. Joan mugged her way through her song number, "Oh, What a Man." *Variety* noted: ". . . with a pash for Lahr, [Joan] has only her gawks and grimaces to abet her; her lines are lean as bamboo sprouts."

When interviewed during the filming of *Love and Hisses* Joan advised reporters: "Even with 'hokum' comedy, which looks so natural, you need to study and study. One little slip of a finger, one slightly different expression on the face may make all the difference between getting a laugh or a shrug." She estimated that her famous pratfalls required five hundred feet of film each.

Thus Joan ended 1937 with eleven featured appearances in Fox films.

Joan began 1938 auspiciously with a juicy part in *Sally, Irene and Mary,* a generally fun remake of Metro-Goldwyn's 1925 Joan Crawford vehicle. As Irene Keene, she, Alice Faye, and Marjorie Weaver were a manicurist trio seeking their big show business break and looking for Mr. Right. Joan was involved in several song numbers, including a big apple dance, "Who Stole The Jam?", the liveliest of the bunch in the 72-minute picture. Joan also tossed out "Help Wanted—Male" in her by now standard delivery, fortifying her comedienne stage image as a man-chasing virago. With her screen partner, the amorous baron Gregory Ratoff, she performed the energetic song and dance, "I'm A Gypsy." By now, Joan had perfected her art of establishing and carrying out her comedy routines in short order, knowing full well that the camera would quickly pan off her to the established star of the movie. As Joan reflected: "I've always had to sneak in and make good."

Studio head Zanuck, impressed with his rising contract comedy player, informed the press: "Before this year is out, Miss Davis will have won number one ranking as a comedienne." (Joan had already displaced Patsy Kelly's as Fox's leading comedy foil, nipped the competing ascendancy of fellow songstress Leah Ray, and was a leading contender against Paramount's Martha Raye for the cinema capital's crown as top banana of the funnywomen on the silver screen.)

In *Josette* (1938) set in New Orleans, Joan was Mary Morris, chambermaid to ingenue Simone Simon, the girl that both Don Ameche and Robert Young, cast as brothers, wanted. Bert Lahr, as the cabaret operator, was again Joan's screen partner. One Manhattan film critic wrote: ". . . her material is far below the standard she deserves." This lesser musical quickly came and went.

When Paramount's pleasant *College Swing* was released on May 1, 1938, B. R. Crisler in *The New York Times* was prompted to pen a lengthy entertainment editorial on the glaring faults of screen musicals. "Another producer expedient which has always seemed to us fallacious is the trick of trying to cure bad comedy by the addition of supporting acts which are, as a rule, even worse. The occasional Joan Davis, who begins by knocking herself out in a desperate flash of footage and works up to the position of an excellent singing-dancing comedienne, hardly justifies a practice which more often than not encourages people like the Slate Brothers (since the Ritz Brotherhood has ceased to be a beautiful thing on the screen) or the amazing buffoon called Jerry Colonna. . . ."

Joan was back in a top, prestigious vehicle again, when she cavorted in *My Lucky Star,* which debuted at the Roxy Theatre, September 9, 1938. In this Sonja Henie ice musical, Joan was third billed as Mary Boop, a gal at the college where department store worker Henie has been sent to drum up business for her boss. Joan's screen partner here was taxi driver Buddy Ebsen, and they exhibited their gymnastic virtuosity as an acrobatic dance team. With Ebsen, Joan mugged and danced through "Could You Pass In Love?" During the filming of this sequence, Joan took an unexpected pratfall, sailing over lanky Ebsen's shoulder. He landed on her, and she landed in the hospital. It all proved that her screen art contained as many dangers as that of any stuntman or a pro-football player. Eileen Creelman in *The New York Post* found: ". . . the occasional comedy of Joan Davis and Buddy Esben are about all the picture has to offer." Nevertheless, the film did exceptionally well in distribution, finding Henie at the peak of her box-office drawing power.

Hold That Co-Ed (1938) was conceived as just another college football comedy, but it developed into a bright gem. Joan was fourth billed as Lizzie Olsen, an agile tomboy who excels in drop-kicking. The zingy satire had Governor John Barrymore anxious for State University to capture the football championship by winning the big game, which (by some unknown logic) is essential for his bid for a United States senatorial seat. Joan is corralled to play on the football team disguised as a boy and she saves the day. The highlight of the game (and the film) occurs when Joan romps downfield clutching the ball, and trying desperately to cross the goal line. However, there is a stiff wind—almost of hurricane proportions—and it is almost more than she can do to fight the air and make the needed points.

The critics were exceptionally enthusiastic about her rubber-legged wizardry. Howard Barnes in *The New York Herald Tribune* admitted: "Heretofore I have thought her one of the least amusing clowns on the screen. Thanks to the special effects boys, however, she has the major hand in an uproarious climax, when she wins for dear old State in the teeth of a hurricane." *Variety* extolled: "Miss Davis is a near panic all the way, either on or off the football field and her presence, plus that of Barrymore, save the picture. . . . One of the funnier sequences deals with a wrestling match in which the brothers, later recruited for football, are mauling each other but, between grunts, talking the deal over with Miss Davis, seated at ringside. Kyle Crichton, *Collier's* Magazine staff writer praised: "Miss Davis makes flying tackles. . . . She takes off into space in an array of limbs and arms resembling nothing other than an octopus taking a flying test, she ends by falling on her caboose with a crash that not only shakes the stadium, but shakes the inherent faith of man in the frailty of woman."

Her fifth and final 1938 screen performance was in Shirley Temple's *Just around the Corner*. Charles Farrell, as Temple's widowed father, was a once prominent architect who is now unemployed, and living with his daughter in the basement of the same skyscraper in which they used to reside in style. Joan was Kitty, former maid to the Farrell family, and now employed as a confused kennel mistress. Joan's love interest here was saxophonist Bert Lahr, chauffeur to millionaire Claude Gillingwater Sr. Besides her usual clowning, Joan joined with Lahr, Temple, and Bill ("Bojangles") Robinson (the doorman) in a song and dance number.

Since Joan had reached the pinnacle of top featured players, she was assigned to fewer productions, with generally meatier roles. She was now earning more than $50,000 yearly from her film roles. Zanuck carefully calculated her screen time to retain the necessary freshness to keep audiences intrigued and wanting more. While it may have been unsatisfying to her ego to be slapped into any type and quality of Fox picture, for comedy relief, it insured a wide spectrum of filmgoers seeing her perform.

Tailspin (1939) was a hackneyed aviatrix story, costarring Alice Faye, Constance Bennett and Nancy Kelly. Joan was fourth billed as Babe Dugan, grease monkey pal of Faye. The anemic storyline ambled around a woman's air derby from Los Angeles to Cleveland, and pulled every cliche of the genre. Once again, Joan portrayed a man-hungry gal, with no luck in getting herself to the bridal altar. As demanded by the conventions of her part, she could not cry over her bad fate. Rather, with a shrug of the shoulder and a smart quip, she must continue onward. Kate Cameron's *New York Daily News* review mentioned: "Joan Davis has a few amusing lines which she delivers in her expert comedy vein."

In between film appearances, Joan made periodic returns to the stage. *Variety* reviewed her act in Indianapolis on April 14, 1939: "Miss Davis does her eccentric dance and chin-socking (when she reprimands herself for stuttering), familiar to film patrons and sings a medley of songs which she introduced in pictures. Working hard at show caught to overcome a bad cold. Wills doesn't trade on the reputation of his wife, but does all right for himself with a comedy crystal reading bit and as a feeder for Miss Davis." Joan had offers to take her polished act to the British Isles for a tour, but she told reporters: "I waited for them and now they'll have to wait for me. And anyways, I don't see how I can take time off from film work to make the trip now." Because the studio had the contract right to call her back at a given notice, Joan was only able to book her stage act two weeks in advance.

In *Day-Time Wife* (1939) starring the new screen love team of Tyrone Power and Linda Darnell, Joan was featured as Miss Applegate, a cynical, wisecracking reception clerk. Because her boss will not buy any modern mechanical gadgets, she grudgingly must do all the tasks mechanically, such as licking and sealing an endless pile of envelopes and stamps. As always, she milked her comedy routines for all they were worth.

In Fox's long-enduring Jones family series entry *Too Busy to Work* (1939), Joan was Lolly, the orphaned niece who visits the wacky family (headed by Jed Prouty and Spring Byington). To pay for her keep, Joan filled in as the household hired girl, but made chaos out of her cleaning chores. Midst the inspired insanity of this low-keyed production, Joan's effective slapstick made its mark. Wanda Hale in her two and one-half star *New York Daily News* review noted: "Joan Davis is the chief addition to the cast—and what an addition!"

The press was constantly after Joan to explain her success formula. Joan answered: "Most of the good comedians on the screen today started out in vaudeville. And I think that's the only way in which one may learn the important business of timing one's act to get the best laugh return. After you'd been on the vaudeville circuit grind for a couple of years, facing all sorts of audiences, you developed a 'feel' for the comedy situations that carried you through." About funny situations: "Laughs are based on other people's misfortunes—it's awful, isn't it? A good fall always gets a laugh." She pointed out that in movies most directors did not know how to coach comedians for their screen scenes. All they usually told one, Joan said, was "All right, get funny; we'll start the cameras rolling."

Like slapstick queen Judy Canova, Joan enjoyed dressing up off screen, an opportunity her film roles did not afford. She was not upset by the lack of her movie glamor, because "I'll last longer." In fact, she was noted as one of the best-dressed people in Hollywood. She was more than pleased upon going out at night, groomed in ultra high style, to hear the kids on her street yell, "Hello, socko!"

Around Hollywood, Joan was also known as a great sports enthusiast. She rarely missed a Friday evening boxing show at the American Legion Stadium, and she loved to swim and play golf whenever possible.

Meanwhile, her daughter Beverly had been making small beginnings in the entertainment industry. When she was five weeks old, Barbara Stanwyck had carried her onto the stage in a sketch performed at a Boston theatre. Later on, Beverly had a few minor film roles; one was as Irene Dunne's daughter in *Love Affair* (1938).

In late 1939, Joan made headlines. She and friend Virginia White were passengers in seaman Richard H. Gray's car when it sideswiped another vehicle. The 21-year-old sailor informed the police that Joan had advised him to flee the scene of the accident; he later retracted this statement.

In January 1940, when Fox renewed Joan's film contract on a yearly extension, she was then the only major female comedy personality under contract in the cinema capital. Fox had axed Patsy Kelly, and Paramount had let Martha Raye and Marie Wilson go. Later that year, Judy Canova would sign with Republic; and Marjorie Main would blossom as MGM's screen comic queen in *Wyoming* (1940). Joan's endurance was attributed to the fact that she never sought to make her funny comic moments into overextended lead roles, which would have surely worn out her screen welcome long before. By remaining a top featured player, the burden of carrying the film at the box office was never officially on her shoulders.

Free, Blonde and 21 (1940) was a weak follow-up to the somewhat glamorous *Hotel for Women* (1939). It too was a sloshy romantic melodrama of girls in the big city yearning to make good, à la *Stage Door* (1937). This time, the genre was molded to murder mystery. Joan played Nellie, the nosy, impertinent maid at the Sherrington Hotel for Women. Joan's role of the over-helpful domestic called for her to be a determined amateur sleuth as well. As she mutters at one point in the sluggish yarn, while following up a clue: "If Charlie Chan can do it, so can I." (A free publicity plug for Fox's Oriental detective series.) *The New York Herald Tribune* had kind words for Joan's antics: "One must give Miss Joan Davis credit for the few pleasant moments in the picture. Her role of an eccentric, romantically inclined chambermaid harks back to the tradition of the Louise Fazenda school, and makes up in merriment for some of the film's awkwardness."

Her next assignment was another programmer, *Manhattan Heartbeat* (1940), which had the more intriguing working titles of *Marriage in Transit* and then *Rain or Shine*. In this remake of *Bad Girl* (1931), Robert Sterling essayed the woman hater who changes his views on marriage after meeting and falling in love with Virginia Gilmore. Once married, they struggle to make a decent living (he is an aircraft jockey). She gives birth to a child and they find happiness. Joan was

Edna, in love with Edmund MacDonald. To bolster the sagging love yarn, Joan tumbled her nimble-jointed pratfalls at appointed intervals. Kate Cameron's two-star *New York Daily News* review read: "Joan Davis, who can make an old gag look like something brand new in the comedy line, does her best to inject a light and lively tone to a depressing and twice-told film tale."

Sailor's Lady was her final 1940 release. This B picture somehow managed to open at the Roxy Theatre in Manhattan (June 28, 1940). The pointless comedy had Nancy Kelly pretending to be a mother, to test her Navy fiance Jon Hall's love for her. The baby girl in the film was played by infant Bruce Hampton, which said something about the movie's total lack of logic. Joan was Myrtle, a girl always good for a laugh, whose courtship of gob Wally Vernon, said *The New York Times*, ". . . closely resembles mayhem." Her role in this witless programmer was mercifully short. *Sailor's Lady* was cited by film critics as a good reason why attendance at the cinema was declining.

For Beauty's Sake (1941) concerned a college professor who inherited a beauty salon that was a front for blackmailers. *Variety* evaluated: "Joan Davis' comedy material, while somewhat questionable as far as gusty laughs are concerned, may be overlooked to some extent by the comedienne's innate ability. She's one of the cast's lone redeeming features."

Her twenty-fourth and final Fox film under her contract was the A quality *"Sun Valley Serenade"* (1941), which teamed the skating prowess of Sonja Henie with the big band sound of Glenn Miller. Joan was Miss Carstairs, infatuated with dumb Milton Berle, the band's manager. For a change, Joan did not perform any comic slides or falls. Archer Winsten in *The New York Post* remarked: "Joan Davis flits by the camera so fast that you hardly have time to identify her."

Having decided that Twentieth Century-Fox was not about to come through with any good forthcoming comedy (or even dramatic) parts for her, Joan refused to renegotiate her studio contract, preferring to freelance at other lots. She commented about the situation: "In my heart, I feel I am so much more than a screwball."

Meanwhile, in early 1941, Joan had made her radio debut. There have been some doubts on the part of industry executives as to whether her particular brand of visual humor could be properly converted to radio. Listeners could only imagine what her grimaces, pantomime and angularity were all about. On one of her first radio outings, she sang a parody of the then popular song "Hey Daddy," singing the first few lines of the tune as written, then changing the remainder to a monologue. *Variety* approved: "It was a new idea and it was good—and so was she." In August 1941, she appeared on Rudy Vallee's *Sealtest Village Store* program on NBC. She crooned *My Jim* so uniquely that she returned as a guest star frequently and then was made a permanent member of the show.

As Martha Raye would later do in *Keep 'Em Flying* (1941), Joan was contracted by Universal to appear with the ultra-popular slapstick comedy team of Bud Abbott and Lou Costello in *Hold that Ghost* (1941). She was fourth-billed as Camille Brewster, a daffy radio actress who specialized in bloodcurdling screams. She is among the bizarre group joining Abbott and Costello on their trek to Moose Matson's haunted house to retrieve a legacy of hidden cash. When Joan informs her fellow travelers that she is leaving radio and going back to the movies, Costello inquires: "As an actress?"

"No," says Joan, "as an usher."

"When they reach the spooky mansion, the expected routines fall wonderfully into place: candles flicker and glide about by themselves, strange noises and footsteps are heard, apparent ghosts moan, hidden corridors appear and disappear. Joan reacts by promptly collapsing into a state of nervous jitters; falling over buckets, falling into pails and swooning into Costello's plump arms. When she is really scared and attempts to scream, she cannot utter a sound, but faints dead away. Joan and Costello uncover an old Victrola, put on a record (the "Blue Danube" Waltz) and do a marvelous slapstick waltz that concludes in a film-stopping rhumba, with Joan incorporating all her sliding, slipping, tripping, and flipping antics into the scene. Dorothy Masters observed in her three-star *New York Daily News* review: "Joan Davis is on hand to bolster any weak spots in the comedy." The film was a huge box office success. The trio unfortunately were never united again on the screen.

Here final 1941 release was Columbia's *Two Latins from Manhattan,* a quickie production with lots of zest. Joan was Joan Daley, an aggressive press agent who substitutes her two roommates (Jinx Falkenberg and Joan Woodbury) for non-showing Latin American performers as headliners at the nearly defunct Golden Key nightclub. Critics agreed that Joan "tops all comers by sheer vigor and determination." Certainly not as well mounted as even the lowliest of her Fox programmers, this glorified vaudeville show more than made up in pep what it lacked in production values.

When Republic had difficulties with its cornball slapstick star Judy Canova and could not reach an agreement for her to repeat her Broadway role in Lew Brown's *Yokel Boy* (1942), Joan was called in as a replacement. The studio had paid $5000 for screen rights to the Broadway success. Joan's fee now was $50,000 per picture. The zany plot had Eddie Foy Jr. as a local yokel who has seen more movies than anyone else in America. He is brought to Hollywood as a gimmick to help the studio predict boxoffice grosses of its forthcoming films. When Foy suggests the studio hire gangster Albert Dekker to portray a crimeland boss, the racketeer's sister Molly Malone (Joan) charges onto the scene. Joan sings such numbers as "It's Me Again" and "Jim." Unfortunately, Canova's hillbilly expertise was sadly missed and Joan—too sophisticated for the part—received mediocre reviews, a novelty in her film career. *Variety* explained: "Miss Davis sadly overplays for the comedy." Carped another reviewer: "*Yokel Boy* works so hard to be funny, you can see the perspiration standing right out on its brow. And that ain't funny."

Joan's other 1942 release was Columbia's *Sweetheart of the Fleet.* Joan was top-billed as Phoebe Weyms, and was again a press agent. Her chief account was the *Chewy Chums Blind Date with Romance* radio program. She has promised the Navy to produce for a forthcoming Navy recruiting rally the popular, but never seen songstresses who starred on this show. When Joan discovers that the vocalists in question are Brenda and Cobina, two unattractive females, she substitutes two models (Jinx Falkenburg and Joan Woodbury) for the stunt. The truth eventually comes out, despite Joan's hectic maneuvering; but everything ends happily. While fun in its small way, the 65-minute programmer was no more than adequate filler for double-bills at movie theatres.

When Rudy Vallee joined the Coast Guard in early 1943, Joan took his place as co-star of the half-hour *Village Store* program. As one trade paper quipped: "The show not only survived, it developed." Jack Haley was Joan's pleasing vis-a-vis, the store owner. By late 1943, according to the Scripps-Howard newspapers and *The Cleveland Plain Dealer,* Joan was the radio's top comedienne, an impressive feat since initially only 74 NBC radio stations featured her show. Others in the cast included: Vernon Felton (Blossom Blimp); Sharon Douglas (Penny Cartwright); Dave Street (vocalist). Sometimes Eve Arden filled Joan's bill.

About this time Joan explained her pratfall technique to the press: "In simple terms it is this: most people fall too suddenly and too hard. As soon as you trip, stop and think. Say to yourself 'I'm in no hurry. I must be cool and deliberate. I must keep my head down, my eyes on the wall and swing from the hips.' This is the delayed action, or perambulating method, and recommended north of the Tropic of Capricorn. Do I make myself clear?"

"This brings me to the second phase, the 'juste milieu' or 'gentle touch.' This is the matter of stroke. As you near the floor, you should reduce your speed so that, about ten inches away from your destination, you are just gliding. The law of gravity, they tell me, says your speed always increases as you fall, but you can ignore this just as you can any other silly law."

She continued her lecture: ". . . Speaking of mattresses, some people say it's nice to reach for a pillow as you fall. All I can say is, you'd have to have the services of both a valet and a prophet.

"But with my system, you can now walk in the dark unscathed (much), afraid no longer of the kid's toys, your wife's broom or furniture on wheels. Me—I always carry a flashlight—I like to see where I'm falling."

He's My Guy (1943) was one of the countless budget musicals churned out by prolific Universal during World War II. Joan starred as Madge Donovan, a lanky, zany, former hoofer now employed as a riveter in the defense plant. When a morale-building stage show is put on at the plant, Joan helps bring the vaudeville team of Dick Foran and Irene Hervey back together again. *Motion Picture Herald* said: "She lifts this minor musical by its budgetary bootstraps and she stirred its Hollywood preview audience to more laughter than many a production costing a dozen times as much money." Among the specialty acts performing the nine numbers were: Gertrude Neisen, the Mills Brothers, the Diamond Brothers, Louis Da Pron, Lorraine Krueger, and the Dorene Sisters.

Two Senoritas from Chicago (1943) bore a striking similarity to the plot of Columbia's and Joan's earlier *Two Latins from Manhattan*. Herein Joan is Daisy Baker, a maid. While sorting out the trash at the hotel, she finds a play script by a Portuguese playwright. She persuades Jinx Falkenberg and Ann Savage, two other stage struck maids, to pose as Portuguese relatives of the authors, so that the play may be produced and the girls can crash Broadway. *The New York Post* declared: "Joan Davis, a comic figure and not pretty, furnishes the laughs and some relief from all the beauty."

Her third film of the year was RKO's *Around the World* (1943) a hodgepodge minor vehicle for bandleader Kay Kyser. The movie follows Kyser and his group as they entertain troops stationed at bases around the world. The miniscule plot had Joan always on the manhunt, Mischa Auer on a souvenir hunt, and newcomer Marcy McGuire as a vocalist who stows away on Kyser's plane, hoping to find her Dad. (It turns out he died in action.) A brief episode concerns Nazi agents in Cairo. The bulk of the comedy relief was supplied by Joan, who sings "Apple Tree" and by Kyser staff comedian, aardvark performer Ish Kabibble. The critics were rather tolerant of this 81-minute musical long subject. Bosley Crowther of *The New York Times* queried: "How does one say that the humor dished up by Joan Davis and Mischa Auer is straight off the cob, without offending those fellows who will probably think it swell?" *The Christian Science Monitor* informed its readers: "Miss Davis keeps the laughter going in her athletic fashion, diving over the footlights at one point and being bounced out a jeep at another. She can clown with the best of them in a comic song. . . ."

Joan's radio work was fast becoming her most successful show business venture to date. In the Crossley and Hooper radio ratings for January 1944, she was among the top five popular comedy programs. She was still guesting on assorted radio variety shows, often on as many as eight different outings in a week.

When Julia McCarthy of *The New York Daily News* asked Joan to explain some comedy terms for the readers, Joan replied in her usual kidding, double-talk manner: "Skulling, my darling little pupil is simply reactions. For example, someone else in the cast says or does something. I react by making a funny face or gesture—see? It's like the 'double take,' for example. Know what I mean?"

Joan commenced her new radio season on August 31, 1944 (getting a strong beat on her competition), on NBC. Jack Haley continued on as her co-star. For a spell before his death, John Barrymore had graced the show with his comic antics. Besides the regulars and the Fountaineers and Eddie Paul and his Orchestra, her guest stars for the opener included: Eddie Cantor, Rudy Vallee, Johnny Mercer, Arthur Lake, and Kenny Baker. Despite the strong lineup, *Variety* carped: "Timing seems to have gone wrong with this one with tee gee off giving evidence that not enough preparation was given to the first fall show (31). Idea of Miss Davis' Christmas tree and party for overseas G.I.s, while laudable enough, just couldn't carry the running story and the effusive back-from-vacation greeting routine in the village store was overdone."

Typical of one-gag character development jokes abounding on her program was one daughter Beverly contributed for the March 16, 1944, show: A stranger invites Joan to the big St. Patrick's Day dance, stating she certainly is the most appropriate girl he can think of to take to the affair. Intrigued, Joan cannot resist asking why. He blithely replies: "Because,. you're such a greenhorn."

Part of Joan's amazing radio success was due to her deep, well-modulated voice, which could transcend from a low screech to a high-pitched, cracking quiver in no time flat. The timbre of her voice gave substance to her jokes and aided tremendously in her song renditions.

In 1944, Joan signed a two-picture-a-year contract with RKO and Universal, covering the 1944–1946 period. She was given the option of undertaking outside film assignments. Her fee was $75,000 per film, which favorably compared to the approximate $65,000 major stars received at the top studios (computed on a $4000–$5000 weekly salary on a 40-week work year with the star making two or three films annually).

Joan, as Joan Mason, was successfully teamed with Eddie Cantor in *Show Business* (1944), a modestly budgeted black and white vaudeville musical, produced by Cantor for RKO. The film was tapped as Cantor's celebration of thirty-five years in the entertainment field. The story quaintly traces the professional lives of a quartet of performers (Cantor and Murphy, and the sister team of Joan and Constance Moore), from 1912 to 1929. It starts with Cantor's and Murphy's debut at a Bowery amateur night to the group's playing at the Palace Theatre. When not engaged in such intimate production numbers as "Dinah," "Sextette From Lucia," or Cantor's "Making Whoopee" (in the Ziegfeld Follies finale) a modicum of a love story is present. Joan is chasing Cantor, Moore marries and divorces Murphy who is being vamped by burlesque performer Nancy Kelly. One sprightly sequence has Joan and Cantor presenting an amusing, if heavy-handed, burlesque of Antony and Cleopatra. Joan continued to take pushes in the face and kicks in the pants, and also displayed her stock-in-trade—loose-limbed mugging and spewing forth her brand of self-defensive tart comments. *The New York Herald Tribune* commented: "Miss Davis is sometimes a bit too colorful, though, as a foil for Cantor, she is less raucous than usual."

Beautiful but Broke (1944) cast Joan as Lottie, who takes over a talent agency that specializes in booking bands. She forms a girls' orchestra, which is slated for a Cleveland engagement. On the way there, Joan manages to get the group stranded in Nevada, and they end up by appearing in a morale-boosting war bond show at a local defense plant. Jane Frazee supplied most of the musical interludes, when not being romanced by John Hubbard. Doug McClelland in his Jane Frazee career study (*Film Fan Monthly,* November 1970) pays tribute to Joan: "Until it slipped half-way through into redundant slapstickeries, Columbia's *Beautiful but Broke* (1944) was one of Frazee's most enjoyable films. Actually, it was a showcase for that great but neglected clown, Joan Davis, who had one of her best workouts (in every way) in this often screamingly funny, overlooked gem that was the first of two alliterative teamings that year of Davis and Frazee. . . . There was scarcely an early frame that was not used, successfully, for comic effect. When the straight vocalizing of a frumpy female trio threatened to stall things, there was ringside Joanie playing a chicken leg like a harmonica. During Frazee's train solo, a tune protesting war protesters called 'Take the Door to the Left,' an attentive Davis crossed her legs and then couldn't uncross them. While [Judy] Clark tore into 'Mama, I Want to Make Rhythm,' Davis, leading the orchestra, pranced around busily and backed into a Clark kick. Davis' co-players may have been less than amused by all this, but the comedienne was thinking of her audiences. . . ." In the latter part of the "commonplace B entry" (*Variety*) Joan becomes enmeshed in the stage antics of the vaudeville team of Willie, West, and McGinty. At the wrap-up, Joan was left manless, save for the ever-present boy nemesis Danny Mummert, a precocious local child she cannot get rid of to save herself.

Her third 1944 release was *Kansas City Kitty* a brisk, campy 63-minute Columbia comedy showcase for her very effervescent talents. Joan appeared as Polly Jasper, a contortionist and song plugger who opens a learn-the-piano-by-ear-in-six-easy-lessons studio across the street from her dentist boyfriend, Erik Rolf. She and nightclub singer Jane Frazee are conned into buying a declining music publishing firm. As its new owner, Joan soon discovers that the company is in the midst of a big copyright infringement suit with Matt Willis. He claims that the company's one hit tune, "Kansas City Kitty," is a direct steal from his own composition, "Minnesota Minnie." The highlight gag of the film (and a stunt Joan would later use on *I Married Joan*) had her serving dinner to two gentlemen callers at the same time in different rooms of her house. With the stamina of a marathon runner, she trots back and forth trying to be fetching to Rolf and to also woo Willis into dropping his law suit.

Eventually the case comes to trial, and Rolf romps in with a copy of a classical composition, the actual basis of both songs. The suit is dismissed, but not before a final gag. The judge is an amateur songwriter and makes Joan stay behind to hear in full his latest composition. The film ends with Joan's eyes uplifted to heaven and a wry smile on her lips. Few major film critics caught this lightweight entry. Those that did felt obliged to turn sophisticate, and pronounce, as did Archer Winsten in *The New York Post:* "But what can they [the other players in the film] do when Joan Davis is the star and sees a chance to make faces?

She makes some of the worst faces you've ever seen. Oddly enough, at other angles, she reminds you a little of Irene Dunne . . . [but] it's not worth the acute boredom of seeing the rest of the film." Actually, with her pompadour hairdo, and mid-1940s outfits and ankle-strap shoes, Joan bore a closer resemblance to glamor star Joan Crawford.

Joan was now at her popularity peak on radio. In 1945, her ratings were up to 26.0 from the 19.07 of the previous season, and save for Bob Hope and Fibber McGee and Molly, she had the top comedy program on the airwaves.

In September 1945, she moved from the NBC to the CBS network, taking over the Monday evening 8:30–9:00 P.M. spot formerly held by George Burns and Gracie Allen. She signed a $1 million a year radio contract with her sponsor, United Drugs Company, easily making her the top paid comedienne in the medium. Her staff of six top gag writers reflected her affluent status. Wills was still one of her writers, and daughter Beverly had joined the show's cast. Crooner Andy Russell was recruited to give her new program more balance. There was much publicity in the newspapers to the effect that this would be an all-new Joan Davis comedy format. Nevertheless, *The New York World Telegram* reported: "You probably won't even detect any difference. We have Miss Davis . . . running a tearoom instead of a general store. . . . Modes in comedy may come and go but Miss Davis remains the good-humored lass, uneasy about having so much virtue so long. . . . Blessed with a sense of timing that is nothing short of sublime, Joan Davis remains one of the best comediennes in the business."

She Gets Her Man (1945) for Universal, toplined her as Pilky. It was a typical vehicle for the comedy star: thin plot, perfunctory second string lead man or two, and a vocalist and vaudeville comedians tossed in for support—everything allowed for Joan to have free reign to race through her mayhem routines, bat out her wisecracks, and perhaps bounce through a vocal spot of her own.

In this one, she is the unslick hick daughter of a once famous woman detective. She is brought to town by friendly reporter William Gargan to solve a new crime wave. On hand is loose-limbed Leon Errol, the force's dumbest cop, who manages to impede all Joan's amateur attempts to track down the blowgun murderer. Before the finale, in which she arouses the angered townspeople to tackle the culprit, she has run amuck in the local theatre. There nothing is sacred for dumb Joan: she walks into a hot and spicy love scene being performed on stage, later tangles with a sound effects machine, fouls up a bevy of other props lying about the show place, falls through a trap door, and becomes part of a wild car ride and a rough fist fight. Instead of traditional custard pies being heaved about, mustard-covered hamburgers are tossed with deadly accuracy.

Regarding "She Gets Her Man," *The New York Times* complained: "Miss Davis is an able lady comic in brief supporting roles, especially, but she's rather hard to take in large, raw doses." Conversely, the more basic *Motion Picture Herald* reflected the opinion of small town exhibitors who did well with Joan's films: "Murders reach an amazing total in this mystery comedy, but never seem more than another gag routine for the antics of Joan Davis. The comedienne is allowed a bit of everything from smart dialogue to slapstick and manages them all in the frantic, good-humored style which has become her trademark. Old as the gags and situations are, a conscientious objector could hardly escape a couple of laughs. . . . [She] carries the show, whipping herself into a brave stand, driving an idea to its unnatural conclusion and resisting sobriety in favor of speed and wisecracks."

Her other release of the year was *George White's Scandals* (1945) for the more sedate, aristocratic RKO. She was again Joan Mason (as in *Show Business*), an ex-Scandals girl who joins her showmates in the yearly gettogethers. The current time around, Martha Holliday, the daughter of a sister chorine who had married British nobility, is on hand to win a role in the current edition of the Scandals, but mysteriously disappears on opening night. Co-starred with Jack Haley, Joan embarks on a spree of roughhousing, managing such duets with Haley as "Life Is Just a Bowl of Cherries." Their comedy highlight was a lengthy skit entitled "Who Killed Vaudeville?" in which Joan, underplaying her usual horseplay, mimicking instead the mannerisms of several grand dames of the stage. With Haley, she also did a fun takeoff on Salome, with her partner as Bluebeard. Typical of even low budget wartime musicals, there was a host of guest special acts thrown in for good measure. Pushing the black and white film to 95 minutes were such performers as Ethel Smith at the organ, and Gene Krupa at the drums. Joan's daughter Beverly played her mother at age twelve, with Joan supplying the singing while Beverly mouthed the words. There were even clips from other RKO films, including a flash of Ginger Rogers, a quickie scene from *Tall in the Saddle* with John Wayne and Ella Raines.

Joan's radio show was now being broadcast exclusively from Hollywood. To stir up publicity for the new season, she had initiated a lucky buck contest. Her husband was set to travel around the country leaving lucky dollar bills (which would lead to bigger prizes) in an assortment of towns. But the Federal Communications Commission ruled this was a game of chance and not of skill, so Joan reluctantly had to drop the scheme. *Variety* reviewed one of her early October shows, adding background data to their report: "Much of the dark talk about Miss Davis [losing her audience appeal] stems from the well authenticated reports that the Lever Brothers think she's too expensive a package and would like to drop her. That's strictly the bank-roller's business. But showmanwise, Miss Davis is as good as anything on the air. . . . A crack here and there was on the adult side—like the one about 'Miss Weatherby's perfume smelling like a morning in Duffy's Tavern rather than like a night in Madame DuBarry's boudoir.' But the delivery was good, and if a blue nose could take offense that's just too bad—for the blue-nose."

Joan's only 1946 film was *She Wrote the Book* for Universal. Utilizing a favorite film comedy plot, it had Joan as Jane Featherstone, a sedate calculus instructor at a hick Indiana college. Using an alias, the president's wife has written a torrid love novel, *Always Lulu,* which had gained an international reputation and stacked up large royalties. However, she is afraid to confess the truth to her husband, Dean John Litel, and dares not risk the publicity by going to New York to collect her money. She asks Joan, who is heading to Manhattan to give a lecture, to pose as the authoress and accept the royalties. On the way, Joan is involved in a car accident, in which she is bumped on the head. She has a loss of memory and thinks she is the famed blue-line writer, Lulu Winters. Once in New York, Joan is put in the custody of the publisher's unconventional publicist, Jack Oakie, and a new Joan emerges—a glamorous celebrity.

Into the wacky situation comes barkeep Mischa Auer, who later impersonates the hero of Joan's "auto-biographical" novel, and Kirby Grant, the engineer in love with Joan. By the finish, Joan's memory has returned and her ruse has been uncovered. However, Joan saves her job and restores peace at the college by nudging a wealthy philanthropist into giving a large donation to the university. Highlights here include the much publicized sequence in which she is put over Grant's knee and given a sound thrashing, and her energetic carry through of a zany dance. Wearing a sequin-covered gown, white fox furs, and adorned with long cigarette holders, Joan had a rare opportunity to be a clotheshorse onscreen. Otis L. Guernsey, Jr. in *The New York Herald Tribune* remarked: "She departs from her usual energetic face-twisting style and plays this role almost straight, exhibiting within the limits of the material a talent for more subtle comedy performances than she usually gives."

Joan was off the screen in 1947, busy with her radio show, and trying to patch up a marriage run ragged. She would be divorced from Wills on December 8, 1948.

Eddie Cantor engineered Joan's screen return by teaming with her again in *If You Knew Susie* (1948) which Cantor produced in black and white for RKO. Joan was Susie Parker, who with husband, Cantor, renounces a vaudeville career to retire to their New England home town of Brookfield. Arriving on the anniversary of Paul Revere's Ride, the pair find their coming just as unexpected, and certainly less welcomed. The town snobs consider them socially unacceptable. In their old house, they uncover a letter from George Washington bequeathing $50,000 to the heirs of the family's ancestors for past war services. At compound interest, they are the richest family in America. After tangling with kidnappers (Sheldon Leonard and Joe Sawyer) and enduring a slapstick chase which reunites the children and parents, they cancel the government's debt to them—it just is not worth it. They then become their home town's most prominent citizens, renown for their patriotic act.

If You Knew Susie opens with Cantor and Joan performing the title tune and such other songs as "What Do I Want With Money." There are even film clips from *Show Business* showing George Murphy and Constance Moore. Despite tight-lipped reviews (*Times:* ". . . [she] mugs and staggers through a spurious kidnapping sequence. . . ."; *Herald Tribune:* "Their efforts are more conspicuous than effective. . . .") the film proved a neat family package of entertainment. It is one of the most frequently seen of Joan's films on television.

Make Mine Laughs (1949) was a sad finale to Joan's RKO entries. The "feature" was merely a composit of old film from previously released studio shorts and features, tied together by master of ceremonies Gil Lamb, discussing "What Killed Vaudeville?" Naturally this led into the identically titled routine from *George White's Scandals.*

Joan started a new radio show in the summer of 1949. *Leave it to Joan* was heard on Monday evenings at 9 P.M. on CBS, with the American Tobacco Company as the sponsor with Joan receiving an $8,250 weekly salary. Set in a department store, Joan was a man-chasing salesgirl. Tough-to-please critic John Crosby reviewed the program in *The New York Herald Tribune:*

. . . Miss Davis [is] changeless as the tides. She's still a sex-starved, addled and very, very noisy girl. It's been the standard comedy role for women since the days of Mack Sennett and Miss Davis is not a girl to rough up tradition. As a matter of fact, Miss Davis started her film work with Mack Sennett, an experience that left permanent scars.

"Much of her new show . . . smells faintly of lavender and Mack Sennett. As a department store employee, Miss Davis messes up private enterprise with such diligence, she could easily be investigated by a Senate Committee.

"The jokes concerning Miss Davis's difficulties in catching a man have been honed to such a fine thin point it's almost a mathematical exercise thinking up new ones. This has produced what might be described as the inevitable joke. You know what's coming, but you don't know exactly when it's going to get there.

Crosby went on to describe some typical routines:

DEPARTMENT STORE MANAGER: "thought you'd do well in ladies' dresses."
JOAN: "I haven't done too well in them so far."
MGR: "What color is your hair?"
JOAN: "On top, or at the roots?"
MGR: "I'll put you in the exchange department. I can't think what harm you'll do there."
JOAN: "I'll think of something."
MGR: "I've never been so insulted in my life."
JOAN: "Oh, you must have been."

Crosby continued his analysis:

As I recall, the old Joan Davis show once had more plot than *Gone with the Wind* and it seemed a wonder they could work it all in, in half an hour. Being a summer show though—it's picked up a sponsor and will continue through the winter—*Leave it to Joan* seems predicated on the assumption a man might want to drop out to the icebox for a beer without falling hopelessly behind. . . . Somewhere Miss Davis has rounded up the most responsive (studio) audience around.

Joan's other 1949 feature was *Traveling Saleslady,* set at the turn of the century. Topbilled as Mabel King, she decides to peddle her father's soap product so his factory will survive. The west seems a most likely market for the unwanted cleansing product. Following in tow is Joan's chubby, gravel-voiced boyfriend Andy Devine. He cannot bear to be separated from his one true love. Before the closeout, Joan is involved in assorted sagebrush chicanery, Indian uprisings and all. Strangely, there were few physical antics on Joan's part, although the situations were over ripe for them. *The New York Herald Tribune* advised: "Miss Davis is too much of a craftsman not to wring a few bits of humor out of a series of loosely connected situations that would be of dubious value even on radio."

Her sole 1950 film was *Love that Brute,* made at Twentieth Century-Fox. It was a not especially successful remake of *Tall, Dark and Handsome* (1941). As a parody of the Chicago gangster era, circa 1928, Paul Douglas appeared as the syndicate boss who is seemingly ruthless, but is really a softie. Instead of killing his victims, he stashes them away in his jail-cellar. Jean Peters was the nightclub singer who abhors Douglas's way of life, but still falls in love with him. Cesar Romero was the head of the opposition mob. Joan had a small, but fun featured role as Mamie, a songstress pal of Peters.

Joan was only third billed in *The Groom Wore Spurs* (1951), a tepid comedy starring a limp Ginger Rogers and an over ripe Jack Carson. It casts Carson as a famous movie singing cowboy who in real life cannot sing, act, and is afraid of guns and horses. Rogers is a lawyer hired to get Carson out of a Las Vegas jam, when he cannot pay a big gambling debt. Client and attorney romance and then marry. Complications arise when the gambler holding Carson's I.O.U. is murdered, and the cowboy is suspected. The case is solved and Carson cleared. He is given a new movie contract, and his shaky marriage to Rogers is reestablished. Joan had little to do as Alice Dean, Rogers's sympathetic friend. In fact, the movie offered little robust slapstick, save for a frantic airport sequence. The *New York Herald Tribune* sympathized with Joan: "Trying to squeeze a laugh from worn-out material is too tough for the comic."

Harem Girl (1952), at Columbia, was Joan's final feature film and a lacklustre swan song to the medium. She starred in the 70-minute black and white entry as Susie Perkins, secretary-companion to Peggie Castle, a princess whose oil-rich lands have been grabbed by a corrupt sheik. Joan wants to right the situation, but nearly wreaks havoc with the internal politics of the middle eastern country. In trying to outdo the wicked sheik, Joan poses as a harem girl, bounding through a wild impromptu harem dance on a slippery palace floor. She manages to spirit away the key to the villain's arsenal, and leads the sheik's men on a merry chase before being able to help the underdogs carry out the revolt. In the huge castle, Joan went through a bit of inspired pantomime disguised as a palace guard and tangling with a "headless ghost." One reviewer commented: "Miss Davis milks a few laughs and does as best she can with poor material." This was the last of her 44 feature films. She never appeared in a color production.

With the growing popularity of television and the full-scale decline of radio, there was little reason for a comedienne—especially a visual slapstick one like Joan—to continue on in that medium. In early 1952, she appeared in a television pilot of *I Married Joan,* filmed in Hollywood at General Service Studios. NBC bought the series, owned by Joan, and premiered it on Wednesday, October 15, 1952, in the 8–8:30 P.M. time spot. Jim Backus co-starred as her husband, Judge Brad Stevens (of the domestic court). Her ex-husband Wills, wrote for the series. Joan paid herself a weekly salary of $7500. Most of the plots centered on the discrepancy between the Stevens's important community position, and Joan's penchant for continually launching herself and Brad into assorted hairbrained scrapes. Much of Joan's energy—and the plotline—was devoted to keeping her grossly foolish mistakes from her patient, but occasionally exasperated, husband.

Variety reviewed the opening episode of *I Married Joan:*

> Miss Davis mates herself easily to the medium, moves in gracefully as if nothing has changed. The plain fact is that very little has, considering her video baptism is on film. She is no less the fine mugger and cut-up who wastes little motion getting down to brash tacks. She retains her sensitive ear and eye for the ridiculous and is a tongue-in-cheeker of unusual deftness. . . .
> The bow in, partly in flashback, has Backus in his chambers advising an ever-bickering couple. This serves as a solid tool for the judge's narrative on how he met his wife on a plane wherein Miss Davis in her first day as a hostess, virtually breaks up the joint—especially and including him. And so they were married.
> At home, the bride cavorts madly in a long skein of laugh-rigged situations. There's a hilarious bedroom skit and delightful sessions with an amazoneous neighbor (Hope Emerson) who comes into the house plucking a chicken which she brandishes throughout the scene. The main involvement is Miss Davis' purchase of a Persian lamb coat which she tries to secrete from her husband through devious devices and means that, while familiar, never fail at the fun-making objective. For the snapper, the garment comes out shrunken and iced, having been stowed in the freezer. . . .
> . . . whether Miss Davis should solo the end plug (for sponsor General Electric) is something else again.

Early on in the first season, she informed reporter Val Adams of *The New York Times:* "It's the first time I've ever done a domestic comedy. But since I made a reputation as a physical comedienne, I had to continue. We feel that the script is adult, but we don't want to disappoint the children in the audience. There are lots of them from three year olds and up."

The series quickly proved very popular, ranking high among the situation comedies then on television, such as *I Love Lucy* and *My Little Margie.*

Beginning with the November 4, 1953, episode, Joan's daughter Beverly began appearing regularly in the show, playing her sister. No one seemed to mind the slight age discrepancy. Joan quipped: "I always promised Beverly a sister, but neither of us ever imagined it would turn out to be me!"

Joan detailed her hectic professional schedule to Jack Gaver of *The New York Morning Telegraph:* "I've made a lot of movies under all sorts of conditions, but the work was never anything like this. For nine months a year you never stop. . . . I practically live at the Hollywood studio where our shows are filmed. I even sleep there on Thursday nights instead of driving to my home which is only thirty miles away. We have our final rehearsals on Thursday—shoot the program the next day. . . . Part of the week you're working on three programs at the same time, making your first study of the script to be shot next week, looking at the rushes of the film shot yesterday and sitting in on the final cutting of the show before that.

"Every week they have me doing all sorts of things that call for using a tremendous amount of physical energy. But maybe this is good. I don't get all pent up inside, so I avoid the occupational disease of ulcers. If things go wrong occasionally, I just explode for a few minutes and that keeps me in shape." She went on to comment about the burden of starring in the series as well as being its active production head.

In 1954, daughter Beverly had the opportunity to describe Joan's expensive Bel Air home to King Features syndicate writer Cobina Wright: "That lawn is about as safe as a mine field. People keep tripping over the permanent croquet wickets that are cemented into the lawn, or they fall into the pitch-and-putt golf course laid out on the lawn." Reporter Wright continued the description in her own words: "Anywhere in the house a visitor is liable to stumble over fishing gear and the oak-panelled formal dining room could be described as 'gracious' if only it didn't have a billiard table set right smack in the middle of the floor, with a green-shaded light bulb swinging over it, and a business like cue rack that stands against the wall, where any other woman would keep her sideboard full of precious china and silverware."

Joan continued on with *I Married Joan* through April 6, 1955, completing 98 half hour episodes in all. There were rarely any "name" featured players, save for an occasional use of people like El Brendel, her old Fox co-star, who appeared as Joan's Swedish father. Typical plotlines consisted of: Joan substituting as her husband's secretary and then losing a big check; Joan going on a two-day crash diet for a television appearance; Joan filling in for an operatic star at the woman's club annual theatrical; Judge Stevens taking up tropical fishes as a hobby, and Joan pulling wild capers to prove she is more instructive and entertaining; Joan borrowing a rare item from Brad's stamp collection and ignorantly using it for a letter which she mails. The comic situations provided the set-up for Joan to go wild in such places as a laundromat where she ends up in the dryer; climbing in through the upstairs window of her home on a most unsteady ladder; pushing herself through the herculean task of moving the household furniture about to convince her husband he is going crazy. Spotted throughout were Joan's fast one-liners—self-deprecating wisecracks that proved she was well aware of her own frailties.

At the time *I Married Joan* left the air, it had a Thursday night television audience rating of 21.5, compared to 42.4 for the competing show, *Disneyland,* and 32.2 for Arthur Godfrey's program. Joan claimed to be worn out from the energetic workouts the series put her through. She was still under contract to NBC and to sponsor General Electric. *I Married Joan* was nationally re-run in a morning time slot from May 1, 1956 to March 9, 1957. (The syndicate rights were leased to NBC for $1.15 million.) Strangely, it has not had the phenominal rerun history of such contemporary series as *I Love Lucy, My Little Margie* and *Burns and Allen.* However, there are few television watchers of the period who cannot hum a few bars from the theme song of *I Married Joan* (as sung by the Robert Shaw Chorale on the soundtrack, with all the "doo-waas" used to punctuate the lyrics).

In 1956, Joan signed a long term video contract with ABC, and a new comedy series was announced for the fall season. However, nothing materialized. In the spring of 1957, she did settle on the format for a series pilot. It would concern the first woman astronaut, preparing for a moon flight. Joan enthused to the press: "This is it. The first comedy-science fiction show in tv. The humor is based on situations involving me with actual scientific experiments. It may get a little rough on me physically but I'm used to that from my slapstick experience in the past." Beyond the pilot, nothing else happened with this project.

Most of Joan's time now was spent relaxing at her Bel Air and Palm Springs homes. Her Joan Davis Productions was virtually inactive. She began philosophizing to the press: "If show business has been good to me, it has also robbed me of many things. I'd have liked a college education, the chance to travel, and time for friends. Show business cost me my first beaux, and it eventually cost me my marriage.

"And I've been afraid all along that I just wouldn't be funny or pretty enough for the long-time bigtime.

I've kept going on a mixture of gall, guts, and gumption. Faith, too—I've hung onto faith until now I realize every heartbreak has been a stepping stone."

Joan, with her much bleached blonde shingle hairstyle, continued to appear in the press, but usually associated with non-showbusiness topics. In 1954, her twenty-year-old daughter, then divorced from Ed Bambee, had begun dating Alan Crossman, an army lieutenant. They had married in July 1954. The December 12, 1954, issue of *Pictorial Review* carried an article by Crossman, entitled "The Perfect Mother-In-Law"—filled with gratuitous statements of affections about Joan, and her wacky doings. In 1957, Joan, age fifty, was dating Harvey ("Budd") Stock, 33, a safety engineer. She advised reporters: "He's been proposing to me almost since the first day we met. I suppose we're going to be ribbed because of the differences in age, but I don't think that will make any real difference because we're in love."

Long before Barbra Streisand went on to fame in *Funny Girl,* the show's subject, Fanny Brice (in the late 1940s), stated her personal choice of the performer to re-create her life: "There's one dame that could play me, that's Joan Davis."

Joan made only a few guest appearances on the video variety shows, preferring to remain semi-retired from show business. However she was in the news again in 1959 when her romance with Stock hit rock bottom. She filed an assault and battery charge against him, in Palm Springs, claiming he had slugged her. She also returned that year to Honolulu to testify in her $125,000 suit against a local beauty salon there, which had spilled bleach in her eyes back in 1954.

Then on May 24, 1961, at age 54, Joan died of a heart attack. She had complained of pains in her back the night before, and her mother rushed her to the Desert Hospital at Palm Springs. She was wheeled into the emergency room and died at 3 A.M., with her mother and a Roman Catholic priest at her bedside. Following a requiem mass at St. Paul The Apostle Church in Westwood, she was buried at nearby Holy Cross cemetery. She left no will.

In June 1961, her ex-husband Wills, then 57, sued to remove daughter Beverly as special administratrix of Joan's million dollar estate. He argued she lacked the necessary business experience to supervise the extensive holdings. Beverly was then wed to Martin Colbert. A settlement was reached in November 1961, with Wills getting assets worth $52,000 from the estate, and Beverly retaining control of the rest.

Beverly continued her show business career. She had been a regular on the *Barbara Whiting* radio show, appeared in Skirts Ahoy, an MGM feature film of 1952, appeared in the television pilot of *Shape up Sergeant* as part of her ABC-TV contract, and had a small role in *Some Like it Hot* (1959). In 1962, she appeared in *Chips Off the Old Block,* a stage revue presented at the Los Angeles Statler Hilton Hotel.

Then tragedy struck on October 24, 1963. Beverly, age 29, seemingly fell asleep while smoking in her bedroom at her Palm Springs home. The pre-dawn blaze killed her two sons Gray, age 7, and Larry, age 4, as well as her grandmother (Joan's mother), then stated as being age 72. *An instant finis to Joan's lineage.*

FILMOGRAPHY: JOAN DAVIS

Feature Films

MILLIONS IN THE AIR (Par. '35) 71 M.

Producer, Harold Hurley; director, Ray McCarey; screenplay, Sig Herzig, Jane Storm; songs, Ralph Rainger, Frederick Hollander, Leo Robin, Arthur Johnson, Sam Coslow; camera, Harry Fishbeck; editor, Ellsworth Hoagland.

John Howard (Eddie Warren), Wendy Barrie (Marion Keller); Willie Howard (Tony Pagano); George Barbier (Calvin Keller); Benny Baker (Benny); Eleanore Whitney (Bubbles); Robert Cummings (Jimmy); Catherine Doucet (Mrs. Waldo-Walker); Samuel S. Hinds (Colonel Edwards); Halliwell Hobbes (Theodore); Dave Chasen (Dave); Stephen Chase (Gordon Rogers III); Bennie Bartlett (Kid Pianist); Billy Gilbert (Greek Houdini); Ralph Malone (Jason); Marion Ladd (Sally); Irving Bacon (Mr. Perkins); Inez Courtney (Miss Waterbury); Harry C. Bradley (Mr. Waldo-Walker); Russell Hicks (Davis); Harry Tenbrook (Mike); Paul Fix (Drunk); Marion Hargrove (Blonde); Joan Davis (Singer); Adrienne Marden (Girl); Frances Robinson (Blonde Drunk); Paul Newlan—voice of Bing Crosby (Charles Haines, mechanic).

BUNKER BEAN (RKO '36) 65 M.

Producer, William Sistrom; director, William Hamilton, Edward Kelly; based on the novel by Harry Leon Wilson, and the play by Lee Wilson Dodd; screenplay, Edmund North, James Gow, Dorothy Yost; camera, David Abel; editor, Jack Hivley.

Owen Davis Jr. (Bunker Bean); Louise Latimer (Mary Kent); Robert McWade (J. C. Kent); Jessie Ralph (Grandmother); Edward Nugent (Mr. Glab); Lucille Ball (Miss Kelly); Berton Churchill (Prof. Balthazer); Hedda Hopper (Mrs. Kent); Pierre Watkin (Mr. Barnes); Charles Arnt (Mr. Metzger); Russell Hicks (A. C. Jones); Ferdinand Gottschalk (Mr. Meyerhauser); Sibyl Harris (Countess); Joan Davis (Telephone Operator); Edgar Dearing (Cop); Edward LeSaint (Bit).

THE HOLY TERROR (20th, '37) 67.

Associate producer, John Stone; director, James Tinling; screenplay, Lou Breslow, John Patrick; music director, Samuel Kaylin; songs, Sidney Clare, Harry Akst; choreography, Jack Haskell; camera, Daniel B. Clark; editor Nick De Maggio.

Jane Withers (Corky Wallace); Anthony Martin (Danny Walker); Leah Ray (Marjorie Dean); Joan Davis (Lil); El Brendel ("Bugs" Svenson); Joe E. Lewis ("Pelican" Beek); John Eldredge (Lt. Wallace); Gloria Roy (Woman Spy); Andrew Tombes (Commander Otis); Gavin Muir (The Badger); Fred Kohler Jr. (Carson); Victor Adams (Flandro); Raymond Brown (Phelps); Louis Bacigalupi, Oscar Rudolf, William Moore, Allen Fox (Sailors); Henry Otho (Master at Arms); Gaylor Pendleton (Yeoman); Ben Hendricks (Ben); Emmett Vogan (Squadron Commander); Clark and Dexter (Eccentric Dancers); Stanley Taylor, Lew Harvey (Spies).

ON THE AVENUE (20th, '37) 91 M.

Producer, Darryl F. Zanuck; associate producer, Gene Markey; director, Roy Del Ruth; screenplay, Markey, William Conselman; music director, Arthur Lange; songs, Irving Berlin; choreography, Seymour Felix; camera, Lucien Andriot; editor, Allen McNeil.

Dick Powell (Gary Blake); Madeleine Carroll (Mimi Caraway); Alice Faye (Mona Merrick); The Ritz Brothers (Themselves); Alan Mowbray (Frederick Sims); Cora Witherspoon (Aunt Fritz); Walter Catlett (Jake Dibble); George Barbier (Commodore Caraway); Douglas Fowley (Eddie Eads); Joan Davis (Miss Katz); Stepin Fetchit (Herman); Sig Rumann (Herr Hanfstangel); Billy Gilbert (Joe Papaloupas); E. E. Clive (Hansom Cabbie); Douglas Wood (Mr. Trivet); John Sheehan (Stage Manager); Paul Irving (Harry Morris); Harry Stubbs (Kelly); Ricardo Mandia (Luigi); Edward Cooper (Potts); Paul Gerrits (Joe Cherry).

TIME OUT FOR ROMANCE (20th, '37) 72 M.

Associate producer, Milton H. Feld; director, Malcolm St. Clair; story, Eleanore Griffin, William Rankin; screenplay, Lou Breslow, John Patrick; camera, Robert Planck; editor, Al De Gaetrano.

Claire Trevor (Barbara Blanchard); Michael Whalen (Bob Reynolds); Joan Davis (Midge Dooley); Chick Chandler (Ted Dooley); Douglas Fowley (Roy Webster); Bennie Bartlett (Orville Healy); Billy Griffith (Ambrose Healy); William Demarest (Willoughby Sproggs); Lelah Tyler (Cora Sproggs); Andrew Tombes (James Blanchard); Vernon Steele (Count Michael Fontaine); Georgia Caine (Vera Blanchard); Inez Courtney (Mabel); George Chandler (Simpson); Fred Kelsey (Policeman); Pop Byron (Jailer); Guy Usher (Chief of Police); Dick French, Lee

Phelps, George Riley, Franklin Parker (Reporters); Paul McVey (Ship's Officer); Sid Saylor (Truck Driver); Jack Norton, Eddie Kane, Harrison Greene, Larry Wheat (Crapshooters); Grover Liggon, Hal Craig (Motor Cops); Harry Watson (Messenger).

WAKE UP AND LIVE (20th, '37) 91 M.

Producer, Darryl F. Zanuck; associate producer, Kenneth Macgowan; director, Sidney Lanfield; story, Curtis Kenyon, Dorothea Brande; screenplay, Harry Tugend, Jack Yellen; songs, Mack Gordon, Harry Revel; art director, Mark-Lee Kirk; choreography, Jack Haskell; music director, Louis Silvers; camera, Edward Cronjager; editor, Robert Simpson.

Walter Winchell (Himself); Ben Bernie and Band (Themselves); Alice Faye (Alice Huntley); Patsy Kelly (Patsy Kane); Ned Sparks (Steve Cluskey); Jack Haley (Eddie Kane); Grace Bradley (Jean Roberts); Walter Catlett (Gus Avery); Leah Ray (Cafe Singer); Joan Davis (Spanish Dancer); Douglas Fowley (Herman); Miles Mander (James Stratton); The Condos Brothers (Themselves); The Brester Twins (Themselves); Etienne Girardot (Waldo Peebles); Paul Hurst (McCabe); George Givot (Manager); Barnett Parker (Foster); Charles Williams (Alberts); Warren Hymer (Gunman); Ed Gargan (Murphy); William Demarest, John Sheehan (Attendant); Robert Lowery (Chauffeur); George Chandler (Janitor); Gary Breckner (Announcer); Elyse Knox (Nurse); Ellen Prescott (Girl); Harry Tyler (Buick Driver); Andre Beranger (Accompanist).

ANGEL'S HOLIDAY (20th, '37) 71 M.

Producer, Darryl F. Zanuck; associate producer, John Stone; director, James Tipling; screenplay, Frank Fenton, Lynn Root; art director, Bernard Herzbrun; music director, Samuel Kaylin; songs, Harold Howard, Bill Telack; camera, Daniel B. Clark; editor, Nick DeMaggio.

Jane Withers (Angel); Robert Kent (Nick); Joan Davis (Strivers); Sally Blane (Pauline Kaye); Harold Huber (Bob Regan); Frank Jenks (Butch); Ray Walker (Crandall); John Qualen (Waldo); Lon Chaney Jr. (Louie); Al Lydell (Gramp); Russell Hopton (Gus); Paul Hurst (Sgt. Murphy); John Kelly (Maxie); George Taylor (Eddie); Cy Kendall (Chief of Police); Charlie Arnt (Everett); Virginia Sale (Hatchet-Faced Woman); Emmet Vogan (Radio Officer); Irving Bacon (Finger Print Expert); Tom London (Truck Driver); Frank Moran (Tough Man); James Flavin (Detective); Harrison Greene (Fat Man).

YOU CAN'T HAVE EVERYTHING (20th, '37) 99 M.

Producer, Darryl F. Zanuck; associate producer, Laurence Schwab; director, Norman Taurog; story, Gregory Ratoff; screenplay, Harry Tugend, Jack Yellen, Karl Tunberg; songs, Mack Gordon; choreography, Harry Losee; art director, Duncan Cramer; music director, David Buttolph; camera, Lucien Andriot; editor, Hansey Fritch.

Alice Faye (Judith Poe Wells); Ritz Brothers (Themselves); Don Ameche (George Macrea); Charles Winninger (Sam Gordon); Gypsy Rose Lee (Lulu Raley); David Rubinoff (Himself); Tony Martin (Himself); Arthur Treacher (Bevins); Phyllis Brooks (Evelyn Moore);

Louis Prima (Orchestra Leader); Tip, Tap, and Toe (Themselves); George Humbert (Romano); Wally Vernon (Jerry); Jed Prouty (Mr. Whiteman); George Davis (Waiter); Frank Yaconelli (Accordion Player); Frank Puglia (Waiter); Dorothy Christy (Blonde); Bill Elliott (Lulu's Bathing Companion); Margaret Fielding (Miss Barkow); Joan Davis (Dance Bit); Si Jenks (Janitor); Jane Kerr, Mary Gordon, Bonita Weber (Scrubwomen); Clara Blandick (Townswoman); Robert Lowery (Co-Pilot); June Gale (Girl in YMCA); Hank Mann (Cab Driver); Jayne Regan (Stewardess); Lynne Berkeley (Joan); William Mathieson (Bagpiper); Thomas Pogue (Standee); Claudia Coleman (Matron in YWCA); Sam Ash (Publicity Agent); Howard Cantonwine (Tony).

THE GREAT HOSPITAL MYSTERY (20th, '37) 59 M.

Director, James Tinling; based on the story by Mignon Eberhardt; screenplay, Bess Meredyth, William Conselman, Jerry Cady; music director, Samuel Kaylin.

Sally Blane (Ann Smith); Thomas Beck (Dr. David McKerry); Jane Darwell (Miss Keats); Sig Rumann (Dr. Triggert); Joan Davis (Flossie Duff); Wade Boteler (Detective Lt. Mattoon); William Demarest (Mr. Beatty); George Walcott (Allen Tracy); Howard Phillips (Tom Kirby); Ruth Peterson (Desk Nurse); Carl Faulkner, Frank C. Fanning (Policemen); Margaret Brayton (Chart Room Nurse); Lona Andrew (Miss White); Tom Mahoney (Bank Guard).

SING AND BE HAPPY (20th, '37) 67 M.

Producer, Milton H. Feld; director, James Tinling; screenplay, Ben Markson, Lou Breslow, John Patrick; songs, Sidney Clare, Harry Akst; music director, Samuel Kaylin; camera, Daniel Clark.

Leah Ray (Rea Lane); Anthony Martin (Tony Mason); Dixie Dunbar (Della Dunn); Joan Davis (Myrtle); Helen Westley (Mrs. Henty); Allan Lane (Hamilton Howe); Berton Churchill (John Mason); Andrew Tombes (Thomas Lane); Chick Chandler (Mike); Edward Cooper (Mason's Butler); Irving Bacon (Palmer); Luis Alberni (Posini); Bruce Warren (Orchestra Leader); Carroll Nye (Announcer); Cullen Morris (Boy Dancer); Lynn Bari, June Gale (Secretaries); Charles Tannen (Clerk); Arthur Rankin, Paul McVey (Car Passengers).

THIN ICE (20th, '37) 78 M.

Producer, Darryl F. Zanuck; associate producer, Raymond Griffith; director, Sidney Lanfield; based on *Der Komet* by Atilla Orbork; screenplay, Boris Ingster, Milton Sperling; songs, Lew Pollack and Sidney Mitchell; choreography, Harry Losee; music director, Louis Silvers; camera, Robert Planck, Edward Cronjager; editor, Robert Simpson.

Sonja Henie (Lili Heiser); Tyrone Power (Prince Rudolph); Arthur Treacher (Nottingham); Raymond Walburn (Uncle Dornik); Joan Davis (Orchestra Leader); Sig Rumann (Prime Minister); Alan Hale (Baron); Leah Ray (Singer); Melville Cooper (Krantz); Maurice Cass (Count); George Givot (Alex); Torten Meyer (Chauffeur); George Davis (Waiter); Lon Chaney Jr. (American Reporter); Eugene Borden (French Reporter); Nino Bellini (Italian Reporter); Marcelle Corday (Emma);

George Ducount, Jean Perry, Glen Cavender (Secret Service Man); Zoia de Grott (Chambermaid); Greta Mayer (Martha); Egon Brecher (Hans, thc Janitor); Albert Pollet (Waiter); George Renavent, Frank Puglia, Jean De Briac, John Bleifer, Alex Melesh, Adolph Milar (Porters); Joseph De Stefani (Innkeeper); Emil Hoch (Watchmaker); Albert Moriene (Attendant); Iva Stewart, Dorothy Jones, June Storey, June Gale, Clarice Sherry, June Wilkins, Diana Cook, Margaret Lyman, Doris Davenport, Ruth Hart, Wanda Perry, Bonnie Bannon, Monica Bannister, Pauline Craig (Members of Girls Band).

LIFE BEGINS IN COLLEGE (20th, '37) 94 M.

Producer, Darryl F. Zanuck; associate producer, Harold Wilson; director, William B. Seiter; story, Darrell Ware; screenplay, Karl Tunberg, Don Ettlinger; art directors, Hans Peters; music director, Louis Silver; songs, Sidney Mitchell and Lew Pollack; Al Lewis, Charles Tobias, and Murray Mencher; camera, Robert Planck; editor, Louis Loeffler.

Ritz Brothers (Themselves); Joan Davis (Inez); Tony Martin (Band Leader); Gloria Stuart (Janet O'Hara); Fred Stone (Coach O'Hara); Nat Pendleton (George Black); Dick Baldwin (Bob Hayner); Joan Marsh (Cuddles); Dixie Dunbar (Polly); Maurice Cass (Dean Moss); Jed Prouty (Mr. Sterne Sr.); Marjorie Weaver (Miss Murphy), Robert Lowery (Sling); Edward Thorgersen (Radio Announcer); Elisha Cook Jr. (Ollie Stearne); Charles Wilson (Coach); Frank Sully (Acting Captain); Lon Chaney Jr. (Gilks); J. C. Nugent (Ed. Cabot); Dick Klein, Ron Cooley (Cheer Leaders); Jim Pierce, Jeff Cravath (Coaches); Norman Willis (Referee); Hal K. Dawson (Graduate Manager); Edward Arnold Jr. Thomas Kellard, Grant Peters (Huskies); Sarah Edwards (Teacher); Robert Murphy (Rooter); Spec O'Donnell (Ugly Student).

LOVE AND HISSES (20th, '37)

Producer, Darryl F. Zanuck; associate producer, Kenneth Macgowan; director, Sidney Lanfield; story, Art Arthur; screenplay, Curtis Kenyon, Arthur; art directors, Bernard Herzbrun, Mark-Lee Kirk, Thomas Little; choreography, Nick Castle, Geneva Sawyer; songs, Mack Gordon, Harry Revel; camera, Robert Planck; editor, Robert Simpson.

Walter Winchell (Himself); Ben Bernie (Himself); Simone Simon (Yvette Guerin); Bert Lahr (Sugar Boles); Joan Davis (Joan); Dick Baldwin (Steve Nelson); Ruth Terry (Specialty); Douglas Fowley (Webster); Chick Chandler (Hoffman); Charles Williams (Skolsky); George Renavent (Count Guerin); Brewster Twins (Specialty); Chilton and Thomas (Specialty); Peter Sisters (Specialty); Charles Judels (Oscar); Robert Battier (Gangster); Hal K. Dawson (Music Store Clerk); June Storey, Philippa Hilbere, Lynne Berkeley, June Wilkins (Girls); Lon Chaney Jr. (Attendant); Edward McWade (Ticket Seller); Hooper Atchley (Joe Moss); Charles Tannen (Desk Clerk); Fred Kelsey (Officer); George Humbert (Chef); Ben Welden (Bugsy); Pop Byron (Policeman); John Hiestand (Announcer); Donald Haines (Newsboy).

SALLY, IRENE AND MARY (20th, '38) 72 M.

Producer, Gene Markey; director, William A. Seiter; based on the play by Edward Dowling, Cyrus Wood; story, Karl Tunberg, Don Ettlinger; screenplay, Karry Turgend, Jack Yellen; songs, Walter Bullock, Harry Spina; music director, Arthur Lange; choreography, Nick Castle, Geneva Sawyer; camera, Peverell Marley; editor, Walter Thompson.

Alice Faye (Sally Day); Tony Martin (Tommy Reynolds); Fred Allen (Gabriel Green); Jimmy Durante (Jefferson Twitchell); Gregory Ratoff (Baron Zorka); Joan Davis (Irene Keene); Marjorie Weaver (Mary Stevens); Louise Hovick (Joyce Taylor); J. Edward Bromberg (Pawnbroker); Barnett Parker (Oscar); Raymond Scott Quintette (Themselves); Eddie Collins (Captain); Andrew Tombes (Judge); Brian Sisters (Specialty); Mary Treen (Miss Barkow); Charles Wilson (Cafe Manager).

JOSETTE (20th, '38) 73 M.

Producer, Gene Markey; director, Alan Dwan; story, Ladislau Vadnai, Paul Frank George Fraser; screenplay, James Edward Grant; choreography, Nick Castle, Geneva Sawyer; songs, Mack Gordon, Harry Revel; music director, David Buttolph; camera, John Mescall; editor, Robert Simpson.

Don Ameche (David Brossard); Simone Simon (Renee LeBlanc); Robert Young (Pierre Brossard); Bert Lahr (Barney Barnaby); Joan Davis (May Morris); Paul Hurst (A. Adolphus Heyman); William Collier Sr. (David Brossard Sr.); Tale Birell (Mlle. Josette); Lynne Bari (Mrs. Dupree); William Demarest (Bill); Ruth Gillette (Belle); Armand Kaliz (Thomas); Maurice Cass (Furrier); George H. Reed (Butler); Paul McVey (Hotel Manager); Fred Kelsey (Hotel Detective); Robert Kellard (Reporter); Robert Lowery, Lon Chaney Jr. (Boatmen); Slim Martin (Orchestra Leader); June Gale (Cafe Girl).

MY LUCKY STAR (20th, '38) 84 M.

Producer, Darryl F. Zanuck; associate producer, Harry Joe Brown; director, Roy Del Ruth; based on *They Met in Chicago* by Karl Tunberg, Don Ettlinger; screenplay, Harry Tugend, Jack Yellen; songs, Mack Gordon, Harry Revel; camera, John Mescall; editor, Allen McNeil.

Sonja Henie (Kristina Nielson); Richard Greene (Larry Taylor); Joan Davis (Mary Boop); Cesar Romero (George Cabot, Jr.); Buddy Ebsen (Buddy); Arthur Treacher (Whipple); George Barbier (George Cabot, Sr.); Gypsy Rose Lee (Marcelle); Billy Gilbert (Nick); Patricia Wilder (Dorothy); Paul Hurst (Louie); Elisha Cook Jr. (Waldo); Robert Kellard (Pennell); Brewster Twins (June and Jean); Charles Tannen (Saier); Paul Stanton (Dean Reed); Arthur Jarrett, Jr. (Bill); Kay Griffith (Ethel); Frederick Burton (Pillsbury); Frank Jaquet (Burton); Edward J. LeSaint (Executive); Sumner Getchell (Fat Freshman); Cully Richards (Photographer); John Dilson (Department Head); Matt McHugh (Cab Driver); Dora Clement, June Gale (Secretaries); Art Rankin, Harold Goodwin (Cameramen); Fred Kelsey (Detective); Eddy Conrad (Gypsy).

HOLD THAT CO-ED (20th, '38) 80 M.

Producer, Darryl F. Zanuck; associate producer, David Hempstead; director, George Marshall; story, Karl Tunberg, Don Ettinger; screenplay, Tunberg, Ettinger, Jack Yellen; art directors, Bernard Herzbrun, Hans Peters; music director, Arthur Lange; songs, Mack Gordon and Harry Revel; Sidney Clare, Nick Castle, and Jule Styne; Lew Brown and Lew Pollack; choreography, Nick Castle, Geneva Sawyer; camera, Robert Planck.

John Barrymore (Governor); George Murphy (Rusty); Marjorie Weaver (Marjorie); Joan Davis (Lizzie); Jack Haley (Wilbur); George Barbier (Breckenridge); Ruth Terry (Edie); Donald Meek (Dean Thatcher); Johnny Downs (Dink); Paul Hurst (Slapsy); Guinn Williams (Mike); Frank Sully (Steve); Brewster Twins (Themselves); Billy Benedict (Sylvester); Charles C. Wilson (Coach Burke); Glenn Morris (Spencer); Charles Williams (McFinch); John Elliott (Tremont); Fred Kohler Jr. (Daly); Doodles Weaver (Gilks); Carroll Nye (Announcer); Stanley Andrews (Belcher); Paul McVey (Man).

JUST AROUND THE CORNER (20th, '38) 70 M.

Producer, Darryl F. Zanuck; associate producer, David Dempstead; director, Irving Cummings; based on *Lucky Penny* by Paul Gerard Smith; screenplay, Ethel Hill, J. P. McEvoy, Darrell Ware; art director, Bernard Herzbrum, Boris Levin; music director, Louis Silvers; songs, Walter Bullock, Harold Spina; camera, Henry Sharp; editor, Harvey Johnson.

Shirley Temple (Penny); Joan Davis (Kitty); Charles Farrell (Jeff Hale); Amanda Duff (Lola); Bill Robinson (Corp. Jones); Bert Lahr (Gus); Franklin Pangborn (Waters); Cora Witherspoon (Aunt Julia Ramsby); Claude Gillingswater Sr. (S. G. Henshaw); Bennie Bartlett (Milton Ramsby); Hal K. Dawson (Reporter); Charles Williams (Candid Cameraman); Eddy Conrad (French Tutor); Tony Hughes, Orville Caldwell (Henshaw's Assistants); Marilyn Knowlden (Gwendolyn).

TAILSPIN (20th, '39) 84 M.

Producer, Harry Joe Brown; director, Roy Del Ruth; screenplay, Frank Weed; song, Mack Gordon, Harry Revel; music director, Louis Silvers; technical director, Paul Mantz, Cliff Henderson; camera, Karl Freund; editor, Allen McNeil.

Alice Faye (Trixie Lee); Constance Bennett (Gerry Lester); Nancy Kelly (Lois Allen); Joan Davis (Babe Dugan); Charles Farrell (Bud); Jane Wyman (Alabama); Kane Richmond (Dick "Tex" Price); Wally Vernon (Chick); Joan Valerie (Sunny); Edward Norris (Speed Allen); J. Anthony Hughes (Al Moore); Harry Davenport (T. P. Lester); Mary Gordon (Mrs. Lee); Harry Rosenthal (Cafe Manager); Irving Bacon (Storekeeper); Sam Hayes (Announcer).

DAY-TIME WIFE (20th, '39) 71 M.

Producer, Darryl F. Zanuck; associate producer, Raymond Griffith; director, Gregory Ratoff; story, Rex Taylor; screenplay, Art Arthur, Robert Harari; art director, Richard Day, Joseph C. Wright; music director, Cyril J. Mockridge; camera, Peverell Marley; editor, Francis Lyons.

Tyrone Power (Ken Norton); Linda Darnell (Jane); Warren William (Dexter); Binnie Barnes (Blanche); Wendy Barrie (Kitty); Joan Davis (Miss Applegate); Joan Valerie (Mrs. Dexter); Leonid Kinskey (Coco); Mildred Gover (Melbourne) Renie Riano (Mrs. Briggs); Robert Lowery, David Newell (Men); Frank Coghlan (Office Boy); Alex Pollard (Waiter); Mary Gordon (Scrubwoman); Otto Han (House Boy); Marie Blake (Western Union Girl).

TOO BUSY TO WORK (20th, '39) 65 M.

Producer, Darryl F. Zanuck; associate producer, John Stone; director, Otto Brower; screenplay, Robert Ellis, Helen Logan, Stanley Rauh; camera, Edward Cronjager; editor, Fred Allen.

Jed Prouty (Jones); Spring Byington (Mrs. Jones); Kenneth Howell (Jack); George Ernest (Roger); June Carlson (Lucy); Florence Roberts (Granny); William Mahan (Bobby); Joan Davis (Lolly); Chick Chandler (Cracker McGurk); Marjorie Gateson (Mrs. Randolph Russell); Andrew Tombes (Wilbur Wentworth); Marvin Stephens (Tommy McGuire); Irving Bacon (Gilligan); Helen Erickson (Mayor's Secretary); Harold Goodwin (Raymond); Hooper Atchley (Charles Carter); Sherry Hall (Anbruster); George Melford (Dugan); Eddie Acuff (Stage Manager); Edwin Stanley (Frazier); Jack Green (Policeman).

FREE, BLONDE AND 21 (20th, '40) 67 M.

Producer, Sol M. Wurtzel; director, Ricardo Cortez; screenplay, Frances Hyland; camera, George Barnes; editor, Norman Colbert.

Lynn Bari (Carol); Mary Beth Hughes (Jerry); Joan Davis (Nellie); Henry Wilcoxon (Dr. Mayberry); Robert Lowery (Dr. Stephen Craig); Alan Baxter (Mickey); Katharine Aldridge (Adelaide); Helen Ericson (Amy); Chick Chandler (Gus); Joan Valerie (Vicki); Elise Knox (Marjorie); Dorothy Dearing (Linda); Herbert Rawlinson (Mr. Crane); Kay Linaker (Mrs. Crane); Thomas Jackson (Inspector Saunders); Richard Lane (Lt. Luke); Dorothy Moore (Susan); Gwen Kenyon (New Girl); Frank Coghlan Jr. (Bell Boy); Micky Simpson (Cop); Jerry Fletcher (Hotel Clerk); Edward Cooper (Butler).

MANHATTAN HEARTBEAT (20th, '40) 71 M.

Producer, Sol M. Wurtzel; director, David Burton; story, Vina Delmar, Brian Marlow; screenplay, Harold Buchman, Clark Andrews, Jack Jungemeyer Jr., Edith Skowas; music director, Cyril J. Mockridge; camera, Virgil Miller; editor, Alexander Troffey.

Robert Sterling (Johnny Farrell); Virginia Gilmore (Dottie); Joan Davis (Edna); Edmund MacDonald (Spike); Don Beddoe (Preston); Paul Harvey (Dr. Bentley); Irving Bacon (Sweeney); Mary Carr (Lady in Music Store); Ann Doran (Shop Girl's Friend); Joll Bennett (Shop Girl); James Flavin (Truck Driver); Edgar Dearing (Policeman); Jan Duggan (Wife); Harry Tyler (Husband); Gaylord Pendleton (Tony); Edward Earle (Official); Murray Alper (Mechanic); Dick Winslow (Bus Driver); George Reed (Porter); Louise Lorimer, Ruth

Warren (Nurses); Emmett Vogan (Doctor); Lenita Lane (Bentley's Nurse).

SAILOR'S LADY (20th, '40) 66 M.

Executive producer, Sol M. Wurtzel; director, Allan Dwan; story, Frank Wead; screenplay, Frederick Hazlett Brennan; camera, Ernest Palmer; editor, Fred Allen.

Nancy Kelly (Sally Gilroy); Jon Hall Danny Malone); Joan Davis (Myrtle); Dana Andrews (Scrappy Wilson); Mary Nash (Purvis); Larry Crabbe (Rodney); Katherine Aldridge (Georgine); Harry Shannon (Father McGann); Wally Vernon (Goofer); Bruce Hampton ("Skipper"); Charles D. Brown (Capt. Roscoe); Selmer Jackson (Executive Officer); Edgar Dearing (Chief Master-at-Arms); Edmund MacDonald (Barnacle); William B. Davidson (Judge Hinsdale); Kane Richmond (Officer); Lester Dorr (Assistant Paymaster); Don Barry (Paymaster); George O'Hanlon (Sailor); Matt McHugh (Cabby); Peggy Ryan (Ellen); Ward Bond (Shore Patrolman); Barbara Pepper (Maude); Gaylord Pendleton (Information); Eddie Acuff (Guide); Edward Earle (Navigator); Pierre Watkin, Paul Harvey (Captains); Emmett Vogan (Medical Officer).

FOR BEAUTY'S SAKE (20th, '41) 62 M.

Producer, Darryl F. Zanuck; associate producer, Lucien Hubbard; director, Shepard Traube; based on the story by Clarence Buddington Kellard; screenplay, Wanda Tuchock, Ethel Hill, Walter Bullock; camera, Charles Clarke; editor, Nick De Maggio.

Ned Sparks (Mr. Sweet); Marjorie Weaver (Dime Pringle); Ted North (Dillson); Joan Davis (Dottie Nickerson); Pierre Watkin (Middlesex); Lenita Lane (Dorothy Sawter); Richard Lane (Mr. Jackman); Lotus Long (Anna Kuo); Glenn Hunter (Rodney Blynn); Lois Wilson (Mrs. Kenner); John Ellis (Mr. Kenner); Tully Marshall (Pringle); Phyllis Fraser (Julia); Isabel Jewell (Amy DeVore); Nigen DeBruller (Brother); Janet Beecher (Mrs. Merton); Margaret Dumont (Mrs. Evans); Jean Brooks (Operator); Cyril Ring (Hotel Clerk); Ruth Warren (Nurse); Carl Faulkner (Policeman); Matt McHugh (Taxi Driver); Cliff Clark (Lt. Dolman); Ruth Gillette (Fat Woman).

SUN VALLEY SERENADE (20th '41) 86 M.

Producer, Milton Sperling; director, H. Bruce Humberstone; story, Art Arthur, Robert Harasi; screenplay, Robert Ellis, Helen Logan; songs, Mack Gordon, Harry Revel; choreography, Hermes Pans; art director, Richard Day, Lewis Creber; camera, Edward Cronjager; editor, James B. Clark.

Sonja Henie (Karen Benson); John Payne (Ted Scott); Glenn Miller (Phil Carey); Milton Berle (Nifty Allen); Lynn Bari (Vivian Dawn); Joan Davis (Miss Carstairs); Nicholas Bros. (Specialty); William Davidson (Murray); Dorothy Dandridge (Specialty); Almira Sessions (Nurse); Mel Ruick (Band Leader); Forbes Murray (Headwaiter); Ralph Dunn (Customs Officer); Chester Clute (Process Server); Edward Earle, Edward Kane (Men); Lynne Roberts (Receptionist); Ann Doran (Waitress); Walter "Spec" O'Donnell (Western Union Boy); Bruce Edwards (Ski

Instructor); John "Skins" Miller (Sleigh Driver); Fred Toones (Porter); Ernie Alexander (Boy); Shiela Ryan (Telephone Operator); William Forrest (Husband); Dora Clement (Wife); Herbert Gunn, Kenneth Alexander (Ski Patrol Men).

HOLD THAT GHOST (Univ. '41) 86 M.

Associate producer, Burt Kelly, Glenn Tryon; director, Arthur Lubin; screenplay, Robert Lees, Fred Renaldo, John Grant; art director, Jack Otterson; music director, Harry Salter; choreography, Nick Castle; songs, Mort Greene and Lou Singer; Harold Adamson, Mario Logo, and Roberto Roberti; camera, Elwood Bredell; editor Philip Cahn.

Bud Abbott (Chuck Murray); Lou Costello (Ferdinand Jones); Richard Carlson (Dr. Jackson); Evelyn Ankers (Norma Lind); Joan Davis (Camille Brewster); Marc Lawrence (Charlie Smith); Milton Parsons (Harry Hoskins); Frank Penny (Snake-Eyes); Edgar Dearing (Irondome); Don Terry (Strangler); Edward Pawley (High Collar); Nestor Paiva (Glum); Mischa Auer (Gregory); Shemp Howard (Soda Jerk); The Andrews Sisters (Themselves); Ted Lewis (Himself); Russell Hicks (Lawyer); William Davidson (Moose Matson); Howard Hickman (Judge); Mrs. Gardner Crane (Mrs. Giltedge); William Forrest (State Trooper); Joe LaCava (Little Fink); Thurston Hall (Alderman); Janet Shaw (Alderman's Girl); Jeanne Blanche (Pretty Thing); Kay, Kay and Katya (Dancers).

TWO LATINS FROM MANHATTAN (Col. '41) 65 M.

Producer, Wallace MacDonald; director, Charles Barton; screenplay, Albert Duffy; art director, Lionel Banks; songs, Sammy Cahn, Saul Chaplin; camera, John Stunser; editor, Arthur Seid.

Joan Davis (Joan Daley); Jinx Falkenburg (Jinx Terry); Joan Woodbury (Lois Morgan); Fortunio Bonanova (Armando Rivero); Don Beddoe (Don Barlow); Marquita Madero (Marianela); Carmen Morales (Rosita); Lloyd Bridges (Tommy Curtis); Sig Arno (Felipe Rudolfo MacIntyre); Boyd Davis (Charles Miller); Antonio Moreno, Rafael Storm (Latins); John Dilson (Jerome Kittleman); Tim Ryan (Sergeant); Don Brodie (Young Advertising Man); Lester Dorr (Information Attendant); Bruce Bennett, Ralph Dunn (Americans); Stanley Brown (Master of Ceremonies); Eddie Kane (Manager).

YOKEL BOY (Rep. '42) 69 M.

Associate producer, Robert North; director, Joseph Santley; based on the play by Russell Crouse; screenplay, Isabel Dawn; music director, Cy Feuer; songs, Lew Brown, Charles Tobias, and Sammy Stept; Caesar Petrillo, Nelson Shawn, and Edward Ross; camera, Ernest Miller; editor, Edward Mann.

Joan Davis (Molly Malone); Albert Dekker (Bugsie Malone); Eddie Foy Jr. (Joe Ruddy); Alan Mowbray (R. B. Harris); Roscoe Karns (Al Devers); Mikhail Rasumny (Amatoff); Lynne Carver (Vera Valaize); Tom Dugan (Professor); Marc Lawrence (Trigger); Florence Wright (Receptionist); Pierre Watkin (Johnson); Charles Lane (Cynic); Cyril Ril (Reporter); Betty Blythe (Woman Reporter); Lois Collier (Stewardess); Tim Ryan (Waiter); Harry Hayden (Bank President); Anne Jeffreys, Mady

Lawrence (Witnesses at Wedding); Rod Bacon (First Assistant Director); Arthur O'Connell (Second Assistant Director); Emmett Vogan (Doctor); Charles Quigley (Policeman).

SWEETHEART OF THE FLEET (Col. '42) 65 M.

Producer, Jack Fier; director, Charles Barton; story, Albert Duffy; screenplay, Duffy, Maurice Tombragel; music director, M. W. Stoloff; songs, Cliff Friend, Charles Tobias; camera, Philip Tannura; editor, Richard Fantl.

Joan Davis (Photbe Weyms); Jinx Falkenburg (Jerry Gilbert); Joan Woodbury (Kitty Leslie); Blanche Stewart (Brenda); Elvia Allman (Cobina); William Wright (Lt. Philip Blaine); Robert Stevens (Ensign George "Tip" Landers); Tim Ryan (Gordon Creuse); George McKay (Hambone Skelly); Walter Sande (Daffy Bill); Charles Trowbridge (Commander Hawes); Tom Seidel (Bugsy); Dick Elliott (Chumley); Irving Bacon (Standish); Lloyd Bridges (Sailor); Stanley Brown (Call Boy); Boyd Davis (Mayor).

HE'S MY GUY (Univ. '43) 64 M.

Producer, William Cowan; director, Edward F. Cline; story, Kenneth Higgins; screenplay, M. Coates Webster, Grant Garrett; art director, John B. Goodman; music director, Charles Previn; choreography, Carlos Romeros; camera, John Boyle; editor, Fred Feitshans.

Dick Forman (Van Moore); Irene Hervey (Terry Allen); Joan Davis (Madge Donovan); Fuzzy Knight (Sparks); Don Douglas (Kirk); Samuel S. Hinds (Johnson); Bill Halligan (Elwood); Gertrude Niesen (Singer); Mills Brothers (Themselves); Diamond Brothers (Themselves); Beatrice Roberts (Secretary); Louis Da Pron (Specialty); Rex Lease (Office Manager); Lorraine Krueger (Specialty); Eddie Coke (Counter Man); Dorothy Ann Jackson, Gene Skinner (Dorene Sisters); Billy Wayne (Saunders); Harry Strang (Police Officer).

TWO SENORITAS FROM CHICAGO (Col. '43) 68 M.

Producer, Frank MacDonald; director, Frank Woodruff; screenplay, Stanley Rubin, Maurice Tombragel; art director, Lionel Banks; music director, M. W. Stoloff; choreography, Nick Castle; camera, L. W. O'Connell; editor, Jerome Thoms.

Joan Davis (Daisy Baker); Jinx Falkenburg (Gloria); Ann Savage (Maria); Leslie Brooks (Lena); Ramsey Ames (Louise); Bob Haymes (Jeff Kenyon); Emory Parnell (Rupert Shannon); Douglas Leavitt (Sam Grenman); Muni Saroff (Gilberto Garcia); Max Willenz (Armando Silva); Stanley Brown (Mike); Frank Sully (Bruiser); Charles C. Wilson (Chester T. Allgood); Romaine Callender (Miffins); George McKay (Gus); Harry Strang (Electrician); Constance Worth (Sob Sister); Craig Woods, Johnny Mitchell (Reporters); Eddie Laughton (Western Union Clerk); Wilbur Mack (Harry); Anne Loos (Designer); Sam Ash (Jack); Harrison Greene (Sam Gribble).

AROUND THE WORLD (RKO '43) 81 M.

Producer-director, Allan Dwan; screenplay, Ralph Spence; music director, C. Bakaleinikoff; songs, Jimmy McHugh, Harold Adamson; art director, Albert S. D'Agos-

tino, Hal Herman; camera, Russell Metty; editor, Theron Warth.

Kay Kyser (Kay); Mischa Auer (Mischa); Joan Davis (Joan); Marcy McGuire (Marcy); Wally Brown (Pilot); Alan Carney (Joe Gimpus); Georgia Carroll (Georgia); Harry Babbitt (Harry); Ish Kabibble (Ish); Sully Mason (Sully); Julie Conway (Julie); Diana Pendleon (Diane); Kay Kyser's Band (Themselves); Jack and Max (Specialty); Al Norman (Specialty); Lucienne and Ashour (Specialty); Little Fred's Football Dogs (Specialty); Jadine Wong and Li Sun (Specialty); Robert Armstrong (General); Joan Barclay (Barclay); Margie Stewart (Marjorie); Barbara Hale (Barbara); Rosemary La Planche (Rosemary); Barbara Coleman (Coleman); Shirley O'Hara (Shirley); Sherry Hall (Clipper Steward); Joan Valerie (Countess Olga); Frank Puglia (Native Dealer); Peter Chong (Mr. Wong); Duncan Renaldo (Dragoman); Chester Conklin (Waiter); Selmer Jackson (Consul); Louise Currie (WAC); James Westerfield (Bashful Marine); Philip Ahn (Foo).

SHOW BUSINESS (RKO '44) 89 M.

Producer, Eddie Cantor; director, Edwin L. Marin; story, Bert Granet; screenplay, Joseph Quillan, Dorothy Bennett; music director, C. Bakaleinikoff; choreography, Nick Castle; songs, George Jessell and Ben Oakland; Jack Brooks; Sammy Stept; Gus Kahn and Isham Jones; art director, Albert S. D'Agostino, Jack Okey; camera, Robert DeGrasse; editor, Theron Warth.

Eddie Cantor (Eddie Martin); George Murphy (George Doane); Joan Davis (Joan Mason); Nancy Kelly (Nancy Gaye); Constance Moore (Constance Ford); Don Douglas (Charles Lucas); Bert Gordon, Gene Sheldon, Pat Rooney, Jesse and James, George Jessel (Themselves); Forbes Murray (Director); Bert Moorhouse (Desk Clerk); Shirley O'Hara, Dorothy Malone, Daun Kennedy, Elaine Riley (Girls); Jerry Maren (Midget); Joseph Vitale (Caesar); Claire Carleton (Nurse); Russ Clark (Army Doctor); Chef Milani (Head Waiter); Ralph Dunn (Taxi Driver); Myrna Dell, Mary Meade, Ruth Valmy, Gloria Anderson, Dorothy Garner, Shelby Payne, Barbara Coleman, Kay Morley, Doris Sheehan, Alice Wallace (Show Girls); Stymie Beard (Harold); Harry Harvey Jr. (Page Boy); Billy Bester (Call Boy).

BEAUTIFUL BUT BROKE (Col. '44) 72 M.

Producer, Irving Briskin; director, Charles Barton; story, Arthur Housman; screenplay, Monte Brice; art director, Lionel Banks; music director, M. W. Stoloff; songs, L. Wolfe Gilbert and Ben Oakland; James Cavanaugh and Walter G. Samuels; Jimmy Paul, Dick Charles and Larry Markes; Mort Greene and Walter Donahue; camera, L. W. O'Connell; editor, Richard Fantl.

Joan Davis (Dottie); John Hubbard (Bill Drake); Jane Frazee (Sally Richards); Judy Clark (Sue Ford); Bob Haymes (Jack Foster); Danny Mummert (Rollo); Byron Foulger (Maxwell McKay); George McKay (Station Master); Ferris Taylor (Mayor); Isabel Withers (Mrs. Grayson); John Eldredge (Waldo Main); Grace Hayle (Birdie Benson); John Tilson (Putnam); Willie West and McGinty (Specialty); Emmett Vogan (Hotel Manager);

Ben Taggart (Pullman Conductor); Helen Ireland, Gloria Chappell, Janice Simmons (Saxophone Players); Marguerite Campbell, Laura Gruver, Genevieve Durah (Trumpet Players); Dorothy Prons (Trombone Player); Lorraine Paige (Drums); Gerald Pierce (Elevator Boy); Joseph Palma, Brian O'Hara, Kernan Gripps (Defense Workers); George Bronson (Shy Soldier); John Tyrrell (Sergeant).

KANSAS CITY KITTY (Col. '44) 72 M.

Producer, Ted Richmond; director, Del Lord; screenplay, Manny Self; art director, Lionel Banks; music director, Martin Skiles; songs, Walter Donaldson; Ervin Drake and Zequinta Abrau; Mann Curtis and Vic Mizzy; Saul Chaplin; camera, Burnett Guffey; editor, Gene Havlick.

Joan Davis (Polly Jasper); Bob Crosby (Jimmy); Jane Frazee (Eileen Hasbrook); Erik Rolf (Dr. Henry Talbot); Tim Ryan (Dave Clark); Robert Emmett Keane (Joe Lathim); Matt Willis (Oscar Lee); John Bond (Chaps Wiliker); Charles Wilson (Mr. Hugo); Lee Gotch (Ali Ben Ali); Charles Williams (George W. Pivet); William Newell (Gas Man); The Williams Brothers (Specialty); Edward Earle (Mr. Burgess); Vivian Mason (Check Room Girl); Doodles Weaver (Joe); Vic Potel (Painter); Ed Allen (Cop).

SHE GETS HER MAN (Univ. '45) 73 M.

Producer, Warren Wilson; director, Erle C. Kenton; screenplay, Wilson, Clyde Bruckman; art director, John B. Goodman, Robert Clatsworthy; camera, Jerry Ash; editor, Paul Landres.

Joan Davis (Pilky); William Gargan (Breezy); Leon Errol (Mulligan); Vivian Austin (Maybelle); Milburn Stone (Tommy Gun); Russell Hicks (Mayor); Emmett Vogan (Hatch); Virginia Sale (Phoebe); Eddie Acuff (Boze); Ian Keith (McQuestion); Maurice Cass (Mr. Pudge); Chester Clute (Charlie); Leslie Denison (Barnsdale); Bob Allen (Specialty); Vernon Dent (Doorman); Pierre Watkin (Johnson); Syd Saylor (Waiter); Ruth Roman (Glamor Girl); Hank Bell (Clem); Olin Howlin (Hank); Harold Goodwin (Companion); Heine Conklin (Cigar Gag); Kit Guard (Boot Black Gag).

GEORGE WHITE'S SCANDALS (RKO '45) 95 M.

Producer, Jack J. Gross, Nat Holt, George White; director, Felix E. Feist; story, Hugh Wedlock, Howard Snyder; screenplay, Wedlock, Parker Levy, Howard Green; choreography, Ernest Matray; music director, C. Bakaleinikoff; songs, Jack Yellen and Sammy Fain; B. G. DaSylva; Lew Brown and Ray Henderson; Tommy Peterson and Gene Krupa; camera, Robert De Grasse; special effects, Vernon Walker; editor, Joseph Noriega.

Joan Davis (Joan Mason); Jack Haley (Jack Williams); Phillip Terry (Tom McGrath); Martha Holliday (Jill Martin); Ethel Smith (Swing Organist); Margaret Hamilton (Clarabell); Glenn Tryon (George White); Jane Greer (Billie Randall); Audrey Young (Maxine Manner); Rose Murphy (Hilda); Fritz Feld (Montescu); Beverly Wills (Joan—As a Child); Rufe Davis (Impersonations); Wesley Brent, Grace Young, Lorraine Clark, Diana Mumby, Linda Claire, Susanne Rosser, Marilyn Buford, Marie McCardle, Vivian Mason, Vivian McCoy, June Frazer (Showgirls);

Betty Farrington (Buxom Woman); Larry Wheat (Pop); Tom Noonan (Joe); Carmel Myers (Leslie); Holmes Herbert (Lord Asbury); Dorothy Christy (Lady Asbury); Sid Melton (Song Writer); Forence Lake (Mother); Minerva Urecal (Teacher); Crane Whitley (Father); Effie Laird, Hope Landin (Scrubwomen); Neely Edwards (Lord Quimby).

SHE WROTE THE BOOK (Univ. '46) 74 M.

Executive producer, Joe Gershenson; producer, Warren Wilson; director, Charles Lamont; screenplay, Wilson, Oscar Brodney; music director, Edgar Fairchild; art director, Jack Oilerson, Richard H. Reidel; special camera, D. S. Horsley; camera, George Robinson; editor, Fred R. Feitchaus Jr.

Joan Davis (Jane Featherstone); Jack Oakie (Jerry Marlowe); Mischa Auer (Boris/Joe); Kirby Grant (Eddie Caldwell); Jacqueline DeWitt (Millicent); John Litel (Fowler); Thurston Hall (Van Cleve); Lewis L. Russell (George Dixon); Raymond Largay (Governor Kilgour); Verna Felton (Mrs. Kilgour); Jack J. Ford (Orchestra Leader); Phil Garris (Elevator Boy); Edgar Dearing (Motorcycle Cop); Selmer Jackson (Fielding); Cora Witherspoon (Carrothers); Olin Howlin (Baggage Master); Walden Boyle, Frank Dae (Professors); Marie Harmon (Blonde); Milton Charleston, Pat Lane (Reporters); Chester Conklin (Man at Bar); George Bunny (Gardner); Wilbur Mack (Man on Train).

IF YOU KNEW SUSIE (RKO '48) 90 M.

Producer, Eddie Cantor; director, Gordon M. Douglas; screenplay, Warren Wilson, Oscar Brodney; music director, C. Bakaleinikoff; songs, Harold Adamson, Jimmy McHugh; art director, Albert D'Agostino, Ralph Berger; camera, Frank Redman; editor, Philip Martin.

Eddie Cantor (Sam Parker); Joan Davis (Susie Parker); Allyn Joslyn (Mike Garrett); Charles Dingle (Mr. Whitley); Phil Brown (Joe Collins); Sheldon Leonard (Steve Garland); Joe Sawyer (Zero Zantini); Douglas Fowley (Marty); Margaret Kerry (Marjorie Parker); Dick Humphreys (Clinton); Howard Freeman (Mr. Clinton); Mabel Paige (Grandma); Sig Ruman (Count Alexis); Fritz Feld (Chez Henri); Isabel Randolph (Mrs. Clinton); Bobby Driscoll (Junior); Earle Hodgins (Auctioneer); Charles Halton (Pringle); Jason Robards Sr. (Ogleby); Harry Harvey (Sedley); George Chandler (Reporter); Don Beddoe (Editor); Addison Richards (Senator); Ellen Corby (Woman); Syd Saylor (Proprietor of Pet Shop); Robert Clarke (Orchestra Leader); Tom Keene (Graham); J. Farrell MacDonald (Policeman); Mary Field (Telephone Operator); Donald Kerr (Window Washer); Eddy Hart (Burly Man).

MAKE MINE LAUGHS (RKO '49) 65 M.

Producer, George Bilson; director, Richard O. Fleischer; art director, Feild Gray; music, C. Bakaleinikoff; camera, Jack Mackenzie; editors, Robert Swing, Edward W. Williams.

Gil Lamb (Master of Ceremonies);
Program: Jack Haley, Joan Davis, "Who Killed Vaudeville?" (from *George White's Scandals* [1945]); Frances

Langford, "Moonlight Over the Islands" (from *Bamboo Blonde* [1946]); Leon Erroll, Dorothy Granger, Myrna Dell (from *Beware of Redheads* [1945]); Freddie Fisher and Band (from *Seven Days' Leave* [1942]); Frankie Carle and Orchestra, "The Turkish Rondo" (from *Carle Comes Calling* [1947]); Ray Bolger, "Prizefight Sketch" (from *Four Jacks and a Jill* [1941]); Dennis Day, "If You Happen to Find a Heart" (from *Music in Manhattan* [1944]); Rosario and Antonio; Robert Lamouret; The Titans; Manuel and Marita Viera and Orchestra (Specialties).

TRAVELING SALESWOMAN (Col. '50) 75 M.

Producer, Tony Owen; director, Charles F. Riesner; screenplay, Howard Dimsdale; art director, Carl Anderson; music director, Mischa Bakaleinikoff; songs, Allan Roberts, Lester Lee; camera, George B. Diskant; editor, Viola Lawrence.

Joan Davis (Mabel King); Andy Devine (Waldo); Adele Jergens (Lilly); Joe Sawyer (Cactus Jack); Dean Riesner (Tom); John Cason (Fred); Chief Thundercloud (Running Deer); Harry Hayden (J. L. King); Charles Halton (Clumhill); Minerva Urecal (Mrs. Owen); Eddy Waller (Mr. Owen); Teddy Infuhr (Homer); Robert Cherry (Simon); William Newell (Bartender); Harry Woods (Jenkins); Ethan Laidlaw (Mike); Harry Tyler (Jasper North); Alan Bridge (P. Carter); Gertrude Charre (Squaw); Emmett Lynn (Desert Rat); Stanley Andrews (Banker); George Chesebro (Horseman); Heine Conklin (Man); Chief Yowlachie (Sam); Bill Wilkerson (Tony); Nick Thompson (Indian Itch); George McDonald (Bob); Fred Aldrich (Cow Puncher); Louis Mason (Livery Stable Man); Jessie Arnold (Lady Customer); Bob Wilke (Loser).

LOVE THAT BRUTE (20th '50) 86 M.

Producer, Fred Kohlmar; director, Alexander Hall; screenplay, Karl Tunberg, Darrell Ware, John Lee Mahin; art director, Lyle Wheeler, Richard Irvine; music director, Lionel Newman; camera, Lloyd Ahern; editor, Nick De Maggio.

Paul Douglas (Big Ed Hanley); Jean Peters (Ruth Manning); Cesar Romero (Pretty Willie); Keenan Wynn (Bugs); Joan Davis (Mamie); Arthur Treacher (Quentin); Peter Price (Harry); Jay C. Flippen (Biff); Barry Kelley (Burly Detective); Leon Belasco (Ducray); Edwin Max (Puggy); Sid Tomack (Louie); Clara Blandick (Landlady); Charles Lane (Joe); Marion Marshall (Dawn O'Day); Leif Erickson (Commandant); Dick Wessel, John Doucette, Frank Richards, Joe Gray (Gangsters); Kenneth Tobey, Jack Elam (Gangsters); Arthur O'Connell, Eugene Gericke (Reporters); Lester Allen (Agent).

THE GROOM WORE SPURS (Univ. '51) 81 M.

Producer, Howard Welch; director, Richard Whorf; story, Robert Carson; screenplay, Carson, Robert Libbott, Frank Burt; art director, Perry Ferguson; music director Emil Newman, Arthur Lange; camera, Peverell Marley; editor, Otto Ludwig.

Ginger Rogers (Abigail Furnival); Jack Carson (Ben Castle); Joan Davis (Alice Dean); Stanley Ridges (Harry Kallen); James Brown (Steve Hall); John Litel (District Attorney); Victor Sen Yung (Ignacio); Mira McKinney (Mrs. Forbes); George Meader (Bellboy); Kemp Niver (Killer); Gordon Nelson (Ricky); Robert B. Williams (Jake Harris); Richard Whorf (Richard Whorf).

HAREM GIRL (Col. '52) 70 M.

Producer, Wallace MacDonald; director, Edward Bernds; screenplay, Bernds, Elwood Ullman; art director, Paul Palmenlota; music director, Mischa Bakaleinikoff; camera, Lester White; editor, Richard Fantl.

Joan Davis (Susie Perkins); Peggie Castle (Princess Shareen); Arthur Blake (Abdul Nassib); Paul Marion (Majeed); Donald Randolph (Jamal); Henry Brandon (Hassan); Minerva Urecal (Aniseh); Peter Mamoks (Sarab); John Dehner (Khalil); Peter Brocco (Ameen); Russ Conklin (Sami); Wilson Miller (Habib); Ric Roman (Hamad); Nick Thompson (Ben Ahmed); Alan Foster (Suleman); Robert Tafur (Captain LeBlanc); Shepard Menken (Major Blanchard); Pat Walter, Vivian Mason, Helen Reichman (Harem Girls); Guy Teague (Messenger); Peter Virgo (Maleen); George Khoury (Ben Gali).

With Fred Kohler Jr., Joan Davis, El Brendel (at piano), Jane Withers, Joe E. Lewis, Leah Ray in *The Holy Terror* (20th Century-Fox, 1937).

In *Time Out For Romance* (20th Century-Fox, 1937).

With Michael Whalen, Claire Trevor, Chick Chandler
in *Time Out for Romance*.

In *Wake Up and Live* (20th Century-Fox, 1937).

With Ben Bernie in *Wake Up and Live.*

With Frank Jenks in *Angel's Holiday* (20th Century-Fox, 1937).

With Chick Chandler, Helen Westley in *Sing and Be Happy* (20th Century-Fox, 1937).

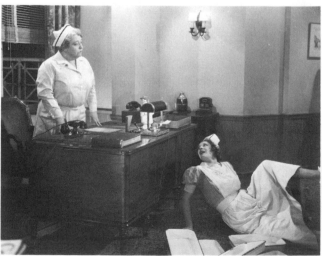

With Jane Darwell in *The Great Hospital Mystery* (20th Century-Fox, 1937).

With June Gale (violin), Leah Ray, June Storey (flute)
in *Thin Ice* (20th Century-Fox, 1937).

With Nat Pendleton in *Life Begins at College* (20th
Century-Fox, 1937).

With Ben Bernie, Bert Lahr, Walter Winchell in *Love and Hisses* (20th Century-Fox, 1937).

In *Sally, Irene and Mary* (20th Century-Fox, 1938).

With Gregory Ratoff in *Sally, Irene and Mary.*

With Barnett Parker, Alice Faye, Marjorie Weaver in
Sally, Irene and Mary.

With Robert Young, Simone Simon, Don Ameche in
Josette (20th Century-Fox, 1938).

With Sonja Henie (back seat), Buddy Ebsen in *My Lucky Star* (20th Century-Fox, 1938).

With Richard Greene, Sonja Henie in *My Lucky Star*.

With Bert Lahr in *Just Around the Corner* (20th Century-Fox, 1938).

With George Murphy in *Hold that Co-Ed* (20th Century-Fox, 1938).

With Jane Wyman, Nancy Kelly, Alice Faye in *Tail Spin* (20th Century-Fox, 1939).

With Linda Darnell in *Daytime Wife* (20th Century-Fox, 1939).

With Irving Bacon in *Too Busy to Work* (20th Century-Fox, 1939).

With Buster Keaton in the late 1930s.

With Chick Chandler in *Free, Blonde and 21* (20th Century-Fox, 1940).

With Pierre Watkin, Cliff Clark, Lotus Long, Ned Sparks, Ted (Michael) North, Marjorie Weaver (seated) in *For Beauty's Sake* (20th Century-Fox 1940).

With Cliff Clark, Lotus Long, Ned Sparks in *For Beauty's Sake.*

With Virginia Gilmore (at piano) in *Manhattan Heartbeat* (20th Century-Fox, 1940).

With Robert Sterling in *Manhattan Heartbeat.*

With Wally Vernon in *Sailor's Lady* (20th Century-Fox, 1940).

With Milton Berle in *Sun Valley Serenade* (20th Century-Fox, 1941).

With Lou Costello in *Hold That Ghost* (Universal, 1941).

With Jack Cheatham in *Two Latins from Manhattan* (Columbia, 1941).

In *Yokel Boy* (Republic, 1942).

With Tim Ryan in *Sweetheart of the Fleet* (Columbia, 1942).

With Jinx Falkenburg, Joan Woodbury, Irving Bacon
in *Sweetheart of the Fleet.*

With Fuzzy Knight, Dick Foran in *He's My Guy* (Universal, 1943).

With Douglas Leavitt, Frank O'Connor, Emory Parnell in *Two Senoritas from Chicago* (Columbia, 1943).

With Jinx Falkenburg, Ann Savage in *Two Senoritas from Chicago.*

With Emory Parnell, Harry Strang in *Two Senoritas from Chicago.*

With Eddie Cantor in *Show Business* (RKO, 1944).

With Eddie Cantor, Constance Moore, George Murphy in *Show Business.*

With Tim Ryan, Robert Emmett Keane in *Kansas City Kitty* (Columbia, 1944).

With William Gargan in *She Gets Her Man* (Universal, 1945).

With Jack Haley in *George White's Scandals* (RKO, 1945).

With John Eldredge, Grace Hayle in *Beautiful But Broke* (Columbia, 1944).

With Jack Oakie in *She Wrote the Book* (Universal, 1946).

With Jack Oakie in *She Wrote the Book*.

With Eddie Cantor, Allyn Joslyn, Harry Harvey in
If You Knew Susie (RKO, 1948).

In *Make Mine Laughs* (RKO, 1949).

With Hank Mann, Emmett Lynn, Fred Aldrich in
Traveling Saleswoman (Columbia, 1949).

With Paul Douglas, Arthur Treacher, Peter Price in
Love That Brute (20th Century-Fox, 1950).

With Arthur Blake in *Harem Girl* (Columbia, 1951).

With Jack Carson, Ginger Rogers in *The Groom Wore
Spurs* (Universal, 1951).

Joan Davis in 1957.

JUDY CANOVA

5'6"
127 pounds
Gray eyes
Reddish brown hair
Birth sign: Scorpio

Judy Canova and family introduced their novel hill-billy song and dance act to America in the early 1930s. The public immediately cottoned to the frenetic mixture of good vocalizing and country bumpkin humor. As time went by and Judy became a solo act, she more fully developed her ingratiating characterization of the rural miss, a little addled, but a delightfully honest creature. No matter that her manners might need a little polishing or that her guileless nature might embarrass one with its forthright honesty. Here was a fun person, who represented the basic stock of American culture. All she asked was to be accepted as one's friend; to be helpful whenever possible; and if lady luck smiled on her, to land a man of her own.

Conquering Broadway and the motion pictures, Judy found her greatest success in radio during the 1940s. Each week millions tuned in to little Miss Judy's show, starring the not so pretty girl, who had a most pleasing voice that could sing swing, ballads, or opera. One minute her crystal clear voice was wrapped around a lilting tune; the next, she was her hickish self, pushing her acquired nasal twang and yodeling for all it was worth. It did not require much imagination to picture the farm-bred hoyden—clad in gingham and pigtails—sliding along the street of life, goodnaturedly slapping an acquaintance on the back, and yelling out a raucous greeting. That most listeners (sub)consciously considered themselves superior to this gal certainly enhanced her audience appeal. Her primitive style—jokes that played havoc with the King's English and man's pretentions—required no cultivation. It was of the very essence of life. Later, such shows as *Beverly Hillbillies, Green Acres,* and *Petticoat Junction* would adapt Judy's folksy humor style to the less critical demands of television.

Judy Canova (nee: Juliette Canova) was born November 20, 1916, in Starke, Florida, seat of Bradford County, about thirty miles south of Georgia's Okefenokee Swamp. She was the youngest of eight children born to Joe and Henrietta (Perry) Canova. Her father was a cotton broker, who later went into the construction business. Her mother had been a concert singer before marrying. She was a descendant of Antonio Canova, the famous eighteenth-century Venetian sculptor. On her mother's side, she was related to Commodore Matthew C. Perry, who carried a letter from President Fillmore to the Emperor of Japan in the 1850s and opened up that country to western trade.

As a child, Judy and her brothers and sister—who had survived infancy—Anne (real name Diane, born in 1909), Zeke (real name Leon, born in 1902) and Pete (real name Harry, born in 1900) were all musically inclined and studied voice, piano, and other instruments. Judy was a born ham, and was performing song stints at family affairs and elsewhere at the age of three.

When a traveling show played Starke in 1928, Judy made her "professional" debut, portraying an old lady in their production. Then Judy teamed up with a classmate and made the rounds of local amateur show contests, winning the majority of them. When Judy's partner dropped out, Mrs. Canova substituted Anne and Zeke in the lineup, and helped the Canova Cracker Trio get some air time on station WJAX in Jacksonville with the troupe singing, tap dancing and improvising comedy routines. By now, the Canova children were playing around with the hillbilly accents that would later bring them fame. According to Judy, the youths had acquired the style when they were vacationing with their parents in North Carolina some years back.

By the time Judy had reached high school, she had come to grips with her rather plain physical appearance: ". . . I thought it was terrible that I didn't look like Clara Bow or Evelyn Brent. But no matter how I tried, I didn't. So one day, I got smart and not only accepted my lack of glamor, but made the most of it." It led to her becoming an extroverted teenager, always ready to perform and amuse her friends.

Judy had serious intentions of becoming a concert singer, preferably opera, when she grew up. One of her favorite performance numbers over the years would be "The Bell Song" from Leo Delibes's *Lakme*. She hoped to attend the Cincinnati Conservatory of Music, as Anne and Zeke had done in the late 1920s. However, Mr. Canova died (circa 1930) and Judy had to give up plans on further musical schooling. She persuaded her mother to take her to New York. She studied tap dancing with Tommy Nip, who thought she was a promising rhythmic contortion performer. When no definite career opportunities developed, mother and daughter returned to Florida. For a while, Judy had a part time job teaching contortion dancing at the Ebsen School in Orlando (Ebsen was the father of performers Buddy and Velma).

Then in 1932, Judy, Anne and Zeke arrived in New York again, determined to make a dent in show business. According to some accounts, it was only with much persuasion that Judy got her brother and sister to include her in their loosely formed act, as they thought she was not high-tone enough for them. They had just about enough money to share a four-flight walkup room on West 65th Street. Their landlord was Mrs. Gimmi. "She gave nothing," recalled Judy. "The room was so small if you ate a square meal you couldn't get in. She allowed no rehearsals so we used to go to Central Park to practice. There and the Bond Building, where we tried to get bookings. Our yodels, grunts and hog-calls opened windows to see what jungle animals were now invading Broadway."

The trio had discovered the hard way that their serious pop and semi-classical harmonizing was not in demand, but that their corny back country vocalizing was at least different. Judy remembers ". . . the hillbilly gags went over and we grabbed a $50 job and dinner at Jimmie Kelly's (Club). I just wanted the dinner."

The trio then landed a paying job at the Village Barn, a free and easy Greenwich Village club noted for showcasing new talent. They remained there for 22 months, doing their popular yokel act. (Thus Judy was able to bypass her promise to return home to Florida if she did not make good within a year.) Zeke would play the ukelele or guitar and harmonize with his two sisters— known as the Happiness Girls—as they sang up a storm. Sometimes in mid act, the girls would scoot over to the piano, and dash off a lively tune before continuing on to their next song.

By now, Judy had adopted her standard stage costume, which was to become traditional over the years: oversized ankle boots with sloppy sox, a formless short skirt and checkered colored blouse (to give her an overgrown hick youth look), and her dark hair braided in pigtails.

The group performed on the Rudy Vallee radio show and later was spotted by veteran bandleader Paul Whiteman. He signed them to appear in a featured spot on his weekly radio show. They remained with his program for a year. It was clear to all that Judy was by now the bread and butter of the act, and that her relatives were just support. It was she who performed most of the solo song numbers, with her nasal-twanged singing, yodeling, shouting, and cawing. This brand of presentation was a distinct novelty to urban audiences, generally unfamiliar with the "Grand Ole Opry" brand of performance, later to be made famous through radio, television, and recordings.

Between radio broadcasts, the trio went on the vaudeville circuit, solidifying their growing reputation as the topnotch barnyard threesome.

Then Judy, Anne, Zeke, and Pete (who had rejoined his family in New York) won roles in Lew Brown's musical revue, *Calling All Stars*. The show had songs by Brown and Harry Akst. After a tryout engagement in Boston, it opened at the Hollywood Theatre on Broadway December 13, 1934. The versatile cast included: Lou Holtz, Phil Baker, Jack Whiting, Gertrude Niesen, Mitzie Mayfair, Martha Raye, and Ella Logan. The production was financed by Warner Brothers Pictures, and coincidentally the Canovas obtained term contracts with the studio the following year.

Judy's highlight in the potpourri show was a sketch entitled "Last of the Hill Billies," in which she broadly burlesqued the song "If it's Love." She performed the ballad in an exaggerated country and western style. Said one New York play reviewer: "The sketch launches a quaint and enormously self-possessed girl named Judy Canova, apparently a Hill Billie herself, judging from the bland manner in which she sings from the bridge of her nose. She has a talent." *Calling All*

Stars only lasted 36 performances.

The Canovas packed and went to Hollywood to fulfill their Warners' agreement. The studio was producing a widely successful cycle of musicals, starting off with *Forty-Second Street* (1932) and pushing onward with *The Gold Diggers of 1933* (1933) and *Dames* (1934). Thus the Canovas had plenty of chances to do their stints in the song and dance films being churned out.

In Caliente, released in mid-1935, was a not-so-elaborate Lloyd Bacon production, with dance numbers staged by Busby Berkeley. The tinsel story had flighty magazine publisher Edward Everett Horton shipping his ace editor off to Agua Caliente to avoid the clutches of gold digger Glenda Farrell. Horton hires dancer Dolores Del Rio to attract O'Brien and keep him occupied, not realizing that O'Brien had once reviewed her Broadway show and had unfairly panned her performance. Leo Carrillo was Del Rio's bizarre business manager. In an elaborate production number performed at the local hotel, "The Lady In Red" (by Mort Dixon and Allie Wrubel), Judy made her unique motion picture debut.

As the song progressed, Berkeley indulged in his penchant for expanding the song story line from the single lead singer (Wini Shaw) to a chorus of dancing girls, herein dressed in Spanish outfits with large brimmed hats. As the girls weaved in and out on the stage in precise geometric designs, the dance leaders lit candles at the ringside tables. Meanwhile, the film cut back and forth to Shaw vocalizing the hot ballad. Suddenly in the midst of all this, the camera focused on a pillar, and out popped Judy dressed in Mexican hillbilly attire with her hair in braids. Wearing the straightest of innocent faces, she did a few swirls and gestures and sang a few bars of the song—all in a sharp parody of Shaw's torchy rendition. Then the camera moved away, and back to the chorus. It was enough to gain Judy instant notice, even if, as *Variety* termed it, her bit had been "dragged in." It fractured audiences then and still does when shown on television and at revival screenings. Later on in the movie, the four Canovas performed one of their standard hillbilly routines, sandwiched in with other acts such as the DeMarco Sisters, et al. "The Lady in Red" number was definitely the highlight of a rather ordinary musical.

Broadway Gondolier (1935) also directed by Lloyd Bacon—but without the bazazz of Busby Berkeley—opened at Brooklyn's Strand Theatre on July 17, 1935. In this film, Dick Powell is a Bronx taxi driver who aspires to a singing career. After muffing his big chance as a radio crooner, he departs for Italy, where he is later discovered by Louise Fazenda, owner of a New Jersey cheese factory and sponsor of the Flangenheim Cheese Radio Show at the station where Joan Blondell is production secretary to the president. Adolphe Menjou was woven into the plot as a broken-down music teacher. In this production line movie, the Canovas were briefly spotted as a radio variety act.

Going Highbrow (1935) also opened at the Strand Theatre, a month later (August 22, 1935). It featured ZaSu Pitts as a noveau riche woman, crashing New York society. Guy Kibbee was her befuddled Kansas farmer husband, with Edward Everett Horton as their crafty but dumbfounded business manager who is engineering their debut into Long Island society. Judy appeared in this programmer without her family, and she had an actual characterization to portray. She was seventh billed as Annie, a not so bright waitress. This passable 67-minute entry was directed by Robert Florey. *Variety* noted: "Judy Canova adds a simple-minded character to round out some of the goofy atmosphere of the film." Judy regrets that her one chance at dramatics while at Warners was in a "not so hot" role.

With this film, the Canovas concluded their Warners' contract.

Judy was then signed—without her sister or brothers —for the Broadway show *Ziegfeld Follies of 1936,* which debuted at the Winter Garden Theatre on January 30, 1936. Produced by Lee Shubert, directed by John Murray Anderson and Edward Clark Lilley, it had sketches by David Freedman and lyrics by Ira Gershwin. The musical revue had a fine cast: Fannie Brice, Josephine Baker, Bob Hope, Gertrude Niesen, Eve Arden, Cherry and June Preisser, the Nicholas Brothers, and Ben Yost Varsity 8. *The New York Sun* thought "Judy Canova endangers the stability of the Winter Garden with her parodies." In one sketch, as the hillbilly Elvira Mackintosh, she sang "The Music Goes Round and Round." *Women's Wear Daily* reported: ". . . [her] imitation of a hill billy singer is one of the comedy treats of the evening. It even made the critics, most of whom are theatre tired, laugh." Among the other skits she was featured in were "The Gazooka," a spoof on Warner Brothers musical films, "Amateur Night," and "The Petrified Elevator." The show ran for 115 performances, and then closed for the summer season. When it reopened September 14, 1936, Judy, busy elsewhere, was not in the cast.

Judy had met Robert Burns, a New York State insurance man, and they were married in Maryland at this time. The wedding went unnoticed by the columnists. Any who thought about Judy's personal life assumed she was still single.

Then Judy reteamed with her family and was heard on the Woodbury *Rippling Rhythm Revue* Sunday evenings at 9:15 over WJZ and NBC radio network. Other regulars on this variety show included Shep Fields' Orchestra and Frank Parker. *Variety*'s on-the-spot review read: "Judy Canova in being called on for three turns, not only risks the novelty of her hillbilly narrations, but on this program had to step partly out of character to make the script stretch. This particular sketch had her perching in a penthouse with a butler, some no-good friends, a couple of animals, and an assortment of amorous chasers. Climax was a dud. Bit should have been omitted." The show lasted through the 1936–1937 season, with the Canovas receiving a $1700 weekly salary.

Paramount Pictures contracted three of the Canovas (Pete had entered the business management field) for a series of appearances in their musical films. In the studio's important release *Artists and Models,* which played the New York Paramount Theatre as of August 4, 1937, Judy was seventh-billed as Toots, with Anne and Zeke cast as themselves. The elaborate black-and-white musical featured Jack Benny as the head of a posh Manhattan advertising agency, whose chief account is Richard Arlen's Townsend Silverware. Benny's girl, Ida Lupino, a tough professional model, wants the job herself; while Benny is drawn toward socialite Gail Patrick as the model for the advertising campaign.

Judy played Lupino's drab but enthusiastic roommate, and she is first seen in the film in an amusing bubble bath song number, "Pop Goes the Bubble" (reminiscent in flavor to Winnie Lightner's broad mugging of "Singing in the Bathtub" from the 1929 *The Show of Shows*). The incongruity of nasal-singing, and her pigtail-bedecked, ultra feminine (in a tomboy way) acting, provided a good showcase for both her vocalizing and her comic ability. When she steps out of the tub and the bubbles burst away, she is revealed wearing a one-piece bathing suit. Then Judy broke into her "straight" acting, which became her standard poise over the years. Sympathizing with the distraught Lupino, she exuded an earnest, sincere air—with those soulful eyes opened wide, her chin jutting forward, and her feet shuffling like a perplexed horse pawing the ground—that she projected tremendous believability. One could not be that gullible, gauche, and naive without being sincere. The running gag in the Florida hotel segment of the film had Judy pursuing a snails-pace romance with stuttering, fumbling double-take Ben Blue, erstwhile rainmaker. During their evening courtship, the two mangle "Stop, You're Breaking my Heart," a fast-paced Ted Koehler and Burton Lane comedy tune. Later on, the Canovas performed a specialty number, which is often cut from prints shown

on television. Howard Barnes in *The New York Herald Tribune* evaluated: "Ben Blue and Judy Canova are intermittently funny and the latter does her familiar hill-billy chanting." One of the other specialty performers in "Artists and Models" was Martha Raye, Judy's "Calling All Stars" fellow player.

At the time, Judy was having a well-publicized "feud" with ventriloquist Edgar Bergen, then a big vaudeville and radio star. The public became aware of the so-called romance when Judy broke her "engagement" to Bergen in September 1937, claiming that Bergen's stage partner, puppet Charlie McCarthy, was the cause of it. Said Judy "It's an obsession with Eddie. He thinks and talks of nothing but Charlie. Eddie can stuff his old dummy in his trunk and get in with him." The strange romantic triangle received tremendous publicity, and was even the subject of a coy entertainment editorial in the September 6, 1937, issue of *The New York Times*. That same day, in Chicago, Bergen told the press: "It was a terrible blow to me that Judy Canova should break our engagement without me being informed of the engagement or even becoming acquainted with her." What Judy's then husband, Robert Burns, thought of the situation is not known. She and Burns would soon divorce.

Judy's other Paramount film, *Thrill of a Lifetime,* opened at the Paramount Theatre, December 8, 1937. It starred the Yacht Club Boys (Bing Crosby was a former member) and Judy was second billed. The harmless yarn was set at Camp Romance, owned by playwright Leif Erikson, who has decided to try out his Broadway-bound musical there. Eleanore Whitney and Johnny Downs played professional show business folks at the camp, seeking a man for their love-starved sister Judy. They finally pair her up with fumbling Ben Blue. Others in the cast included studio contract players Buster Crabbe (a swimming instructor), Betty Grable (Erikson's lovelorn secretary), and Dorothy Lamour (show business performer). Archer Winsten in the then-conservative *New York Post* appraised: "Another eye-opening false dawn occurred when the Canova trio started out to make sweet harmony but fell into the noisy Martha Raye error." The critic was referring to the Canova style, which was to take a pop tune, begin their presentation in a conventional way, and when the audience had been lulled into thinking them standard performers, suddenly changing tempo and interpretation midway through, moving into an accelerated country and western style. Naturally, the more often they performed, the less of a surprise the routine became.

Paramount did not renew the Canovas' film option; they had been drawing a $6000 weekly paycheck. Judy recalled: "I would have done better getting eighteen bucks a week and a good part." However, the notorious soft-touch Judy had had annuity fund set up for her, which by then had built up to a sizable amount. Judy was philosophical about her good-hearted weakness: "I'm Annie the apple woman in reverse. Twenty times a day I'm plucked."

The Canovas returned to vaudeville, then they traveled to England for a two-week engagement at the Cafe de Paris in London, opening February 21, 1938. A local reviewer there noted that despite a sparse attendance, the Canovas' hillbilly act was warmly received. Returning to Hollywood, they signed a 13-week contract to appear on the Edgar Bergen–Charlie McCarthy *Chase and Sanborn Hour* (Sundays, 8–9 P.M., NBC). *Variety* was of the opinion: ". . . there was a noticeable absence of mugging by Judy and quicker delivery by her two co-workers (Anne and Zeke). Initial appearance found them exchanging quips with Charlie McCarthy, official welcomer on the show, which ingratiated them instantly with listeners. Looks like comedy banter with the Edgar Bergen character could be developed into a regular virile asset."

Joking about her squabble with Bergen (and McCarthy) the previous year, Judy told the press: "Charlie must have been mad at me, too. I never got to talk to him but once."

The Canovas took home a $4300 weekly paycheck from the radio show.

In March 1939, news leaked out of Judy's marriage to Burns, while she was in Florida seeking a divorce. Judy reasoned: "It is almost impossible to maintain a marriage when you are in the limelight and separated from your husband because of a career."

The Canovas were playing vaudeville in Philadelphia at the Fox Theatre on April 12, 1939, when *Variety* caught their act: "Judy Canova with Anne and Zeke repeat the sock they registered at the Earle here a short space back. Trio is tops on both sight and sound the hillbilly stuff, and tosses in an extra flash with the fine keyboard solo work of Anne. Only hitch of the act this time is in the dress of the two femmes. A hillbilly gal in fine silk stockings is incongruous and it detracts. Funny colored hose they wore previously was better. Another weakener is the lengthy patter with Charley Barnett (the orchestra leader) for the sake of a couple of laughs. It slows up proceedings and should be sliced. The 'Jesse James' number is sockeroo, as is Judy's short hoofing bit for an encore."

Back in New York, Judy, Anne, and Zeke appeared on experimental NBC-TV on May 3, 1939, along with Nick Lucas and Hanya Holmes. They had the distinction of being the first hillbilly act videocast on American commercial television.

Les Brown, producer of *Calling All Stars,* lured Judy back to Broadway to star in *Yokel Boy,* which opened July 6, 1939, at the Majestic Theatre. With a book by Brown and songs by Brown, Charles Tobias, and Sam Stept, the cast included Phil Silvers, Buddy Ebsen, Dixie Dunbar, Mark Plant, Lois January, as well as Anne and Zeke Canova.

The premise had Judy, a hillbilly from Lexington, Massachusetts, accompany Miss January to Hollywood, when the latter is discovered by a movie talent scout. January's loyal boyfriend, Ebsen, also tags along to the coast, where he becomes a successful film dancer. To her surprise, Judy is transformed into a novelty cinema star. A highlight of the comedy occurs when Phil Silvers, in his Broadway debut, enacts the impatient music teacher, giving the confused Judy a most brutal voice lesson. (According to Judy: "It was an old burlesque bit that Phil Silvers asked me if I wanted to try—we started with four minutes and ad libbed it up to nine minutes.")

Judy pranced through her parade of performing tricks: yodeling, mugging, shouting, and singing with a voice which "constantly gets away from her and goes shooting madly off by itself." She wore a variety of her typical costumes, such as her first act garb, which found her adorned in strange, fancy underwear, oversized brown buttoned shoes, topped by her tight pigtails beneath her Buster Brown hat. Many critics were surprised to discover that the new radio favorite had great versatility and a strong stage presence. Her standout number in the show was "A Boy Named Lem." *The New York Times* wrote: "A rowdy mixture of Beatrice Lillie and other comediennes along parallel lines in the general direction of Fanny Brice, this one pretty much puts the summer in its place. As 'Catherine The Great' she tells the legend of that Lady of the Russians, in 'Jukin',' she interprets the south, with 'Comes Love' she shows that she can look at an honest sentiment, face to face. Quite a girl on the whole." Another Gotham aisle-sitter carped: "She is, however, a specialist more suitable for toning up a show here and there rather than carrying the major burden as she was forced to do last night." *Yokel Boy* ran a solid 208 performances.

Having conquered Broadway, Judy was now in demand in Hollywood. She was offered contracts by many of the major studios, but Judy decided to accept Herbert J. Yates's deal at Republic Pictures. She was starred in *Scatterbrain* (1940). She reasoned she would rather be the star of lower-budgeted films than a specialty act in major productions. She did not reckon with the all-powerful influence of Yates, who took more than a personal interest in her. When Judy did not reciprocate his approaches, he got even by cutting her film production budgets.

On paper *Scatterbrain* had a more complicated plot than its breezy 72 minutes of screentime revealed. Alan Mowbray, producer-director at Perfection Pictures, agrees with press agent Eddie Foy Jr.'s plot to have his girlfriend Isabel Jewell "planted" with an Ozark family, so she can be "discovered" and play a hillbilly heroine, Ruthybelle, in *Thunder over the Ozarks*. Jewell is packed off to live with Judy and her cantankerous pappy, Emmett Lynn. By error, Judy is signed for the film; she and pappy arrive in Hollywood, raring to go. The only out for the studio is to get her married, which would violate Judy's film contract. Foy is chosen as the stooge to romance and marry the cornbelt ingenue. To help him along, Professor Luis Alberni, a specialist in mind transference, is hired to perculate Judy's desire to marry and return to her farm and the pigs. After assorted complications, Judy makes her screen test and proves to be a real sensation. Then she becomes a genuine star under the tutelage of Foy and Mowbray.

Highlights of the film reveal Judy housecleaning in her own illogical way. She scrubs the kitchen floor by attaching brushes to roller skates and zooming back and forth over the expanse. In a repeat variation of her *Yokel Boy* music lesson, Judy is instructed in the finer art of vocalizing by a tongue-twisting, exasperated music teacher, Billy Gilbert. As expected, Judy was dressed in calicos and wore pigtails. The "cavemouthed yodeler" sang—at full volume—"Benny the Beaver (You Better Be Like That, Yeah, Yeah)."

Scatterbrain opened in August 1940 to amazingly good reviews and exceptionally strong box office receipts. *Variety* evaluated: "Judy Canova displays sufficient personality and ability in her backwoods character to indicate sticking around for several pictures and possible box office rating for the rural and family houses as time goes on." Reported *The New York Daily News* in its three-star review: "The gags are good, the situations funny, and Judy Canova herself a riot in her first starring role for the screen." Abroad, the *British Monthly Film Bulletin* noted with approval: ". . . [she] booms through her part like a strident, energetic and infectious fog-horn."

Herbert J. Yates, realizing he had suddenly unearthed a goldmine, showed foresight in signing Judy to a five-year contract. It called for three starring pictures yearly. Next to Gene Autry, Roy Rogers, and John Wayne, Judy was touted as the studio's hottest property.

She was scheduled to appear in *The Hit Parade of 1941* (1940), but Republic instead dusted off the old Rose Melville Broadway evergreen *Sis Hopkins*. It had already been filmed in 1919 with Mabel Normand in the lead. The plot had not improved over the years, despite Republic's efforts to update the screenplay.

Judy reads a newspaper item about her uncle, Charles Butterworth, stating he is "Jobless after 30 years." She is too naive to realize the caption refers to his retirement as wealthy ex-plumbing executive. Judy graciously invites him to visit at her farm. He arrives to learn that she has been burned out. Tired of his wife's social over-ambitions and the preening of his self-centered daughter (Susan Hayward), Butterworth brings the refreshingly frank Judy home with him. Expectedly, she is snubbed by her relatives. But Butterworth remains firm in his desire to do right by his bumpkin niece. He enrolls her in college, which annoys classmate Hayward to no end. Later wacky Professor Jerry Colonna persuades Judy to participate in the college musical. When her talents prove impressive, her role is enlarged at the expense of Hayward's To get even, Hayward dupes Judy into appearing in a burlesque show, telling the innocent girl that it is all part of a sorority initiation. Judy barely escapes from a police raid on the theatre. For her involvement with these doings, Judy is expelled from college. At the last moment, her uncle explains all to the college dean; Judy is reinstated, and rejoins the big show, just in time to be its sensation.

Here, as usual, Judy was playing the underdog: the wholesome, if ignorant, country girl competing against class snobbery in the big sophisticated city. This was an obvious factor in Judy's success, as her awkward gaucheries proved extremely poignant. Who could not adore a gawking hick who enters a big lavish mansion and exclaims "Why it couldn't be purtier if it were a gas station." Then noting the extensive expanse of marble floor, she cannot resist sliding along its surface like an overgrown kid on imaginary roller skates. Later on, while traveling to college, she gives Bob Crosby and his "hep" collegiate friends a poignant lesson in the value of the plain old American farmer by singing "It Ain't Hay (It's The U.S.A.)"

Much of the movie's crackerbarrel fun derived from Judy's interaction with Colonna, who proved an admirable foil for her dumb actions. Colonna has his own solo highlight when he takes a bubble bath, and then decorously rises from the tub. The camera reveals him wearing a bathing suit. With poop-eyed modesty, he apologizes to the camera eye: "The Hayes office made me do it."

Judy displayed a very impressive array of vocal talent, ranging from excerpts of "La Traviata" to such Frank Loesser–Jule Styne songs as "It Ain't Hay (It's The U.S.A.)" and "Cracker Barrel County." For the film's finale, she is first dressed as Cleopatra, then Marie Antoinette, and finally is decked out in a sequinned evening dress. She proved she could put over a swing number as well as any. Bob Crosby and his band were along in the story to provide bland musical interludes.

The movie premiered at the Fox Theatre in St. Louis, April 4, 1941, and opened in New York at Loew's Criterion on April 30. Republic found it had invested its $750,000 wisely, for Sis Hopkins did well all over the country. (It would be reissued four times in the years to come.) Gilbert Kanour in *The Baltimore Evening Sun* wrote: "Judy Canova is the current Sis, and she ploughs into the role with all the subtlety of a steam shovel. Yet she has unbounded animation, and when she sings, either in a whinny or an operatic soprano, flashes her toothy smile . . ., sets her agile dogs in motion and otherwise disports herself as a loud and lusty comedienne, she has her points as an attraction." *The British Monthly Film Bulletin* confirmed: ". . . [she] dominates the film with her keen sense of burlesque comedy combined with a voice that is perfectly equal to the well-blended score as it varies between swing and opera."

Throughout the film, Judy constantly replies to statements with: "You're Telling I"—an expression that soon became her trademark.

When asked by the press her feelings about kissing a leading man in her movies, Judy replied: "I'll bide my time. One of these days they'll deliver me a leadin' man and then watch this kiddie show them how to really pitch woo for the movies."

Judy saw to it that she constantly reinforced her scatterbrained screen image via public shenanigans. In 1941, Republic sent its top stars, Judy and Gene Autry, on a personal appearance tour. They stopped in Washington, and were among celebrities invited to the White House. When Judy was introduced to President Roosevelt, she went cold with fear and forgot his name, mumbling "How do you do, Sir." When the President passed around a box of cigars after the luncheon, Judy took one. Autry inquired: "What did he say when you took a cigar?" Judy replied: "He asked me if I wanted a light."

Judy made headlines in June 1941 when she vacationed in Honolulu. On June 10, she and army corporal James H. Ripley, a hometown friend from Florida, became engaged; on June 14, they married. That same night, Ripley was arrested by the military police and jailed for being A.W.O.L. Judy at first denied the marriage, thinking she might get her new husband in more trouble. Then, in a widely printed press statement, she claimed: "I don't know what hit me on the head the hardest, that uniform of Ripley or that soft Hawaiian moon. Anyhow, we upped and got married, and now my poor groom is in the jail house. And I love him so."

Judy returned to the mainland and her career. On October 8, 1941, she won an annulment in Los Angeles, stating Ripley had ". . . deceived me and told me lies; his being a soldier didn't have anything to do with it."

With brother Pete as her business manager, Judy expanded her blossoming career. In September 1941, she was in New York, performing at the Paramount Theatre on the same bill with Ken Murray. *Variety* reported: "His skit with Canova in which he plays a teacher showing her how to sing 'Short'nin Bread' is extremely funny. Miss Canova also presents several songs in her hillbilly style."

Judy proved to be demanding at Republic. She wanted script, cast, and director approval for each of her films, and she got it. Under a revised agreement with the studio, she became co-owner of her movies. Nevertheless, contractual differences led to Judy dropping out of the movie version of *Yokel Boy* (1942) for which Republic had paid $5000 for stage rights. Joan Davis was hired to replace Judy, and the resulting film was one of the few times Miss Davis—not being suited to bucolic style humor—received unfavorable screen reviews.

Puddin'head, nationally released June 25, 1941, had many similarities to previous Judy films. She was Judy Goober, who, along with uncle Slim Summerville, owns a farm that happens to be situated on Manhattan's Fifth Avenue. A gigantic new radio station is being constructed on adjacent property, and the owners discover that the rising edifice extends one foot onto Judy's property. Sharp talkers Raymond Walburn and Eddie Foy Jr. and suave fake prince Francis Lederer are employed to get hayseed Judy to sell out, when a plot to scare her off the land by "haunting" the house fails. Judy is eventually wooed by a fake radio contract, which supposedly will make her a singing hit. Purely by accident everything works out well, as Judy becomes the station's songbird.

Judy proved to be up to her expected stock in trade. At home, she mows the kitchen floor, because grass has grown through the cracks. When she is confronted by an assortment of ghostly apparitions, it is a tossup as to who mugs more or ends up more frightened. Judy and co-star Foy have a field day when he gives her boxing lessons. A running gag in *Puddin'head* has glass shattering every time Judy vocalizes. In one scene, as she walks down a New York street and breaks out into a hearty yodel, a window on the 25th floor of a nearby skyscraper cracks. To prove that she isn't always a slouch, Judy gets to wear some fancy duds in the proceedings. Her songs include: "Minnie Hotcha," "Hey, Junior!", "Manhattan Holiday," and "You're Telling I" (dueting with Foy).

The Dallas Morning News said about *Puddin'head:* "Miss Canova, like Martha Raye, doesn't take to the glamourizing process. Both ladies are better when they stick to their original conception. There are songs in case you like Judy's wide-mouthed raucous vocalizing, but don't listen for the tunes on the Hit Parade. Corn is okay and so is glamour, but the two just don't mix." *Variety* termed Judy "the bucolic Myrna Loy" and admonished: ". . . there should be a limit to off-the-cob celluloid."

MGM offered Judy a lucrative acting contract, but she turned it down. "I don't want any more big studios for a while. You get lost."

Her busiest screen year was 1942, with three pictures opening. *Sleepytime Gal,* released by Republic in March 1942, had Judy working in the kitchen of a Miami hotel as the cake decorator. The three screwball chefs there—Billy Gilbert, Fritz Feld, and Jay Novello—think Judy is quite musically talented, and plot with bell captain Tom Brown to enter her in a radio singing contest. The prize is a singing stint at the hotel with Skinnay Ennis and His Orchestra, as well as a recording contract. Ennis has been informed by a big shot gambler that he had better award the prize to Ruth Terry or else. Brown secretly replaces Terry's audition record with Judy's. Then, when Terry arrives in Miami, the chefs kidnap her to an Everglades spot, and Judy goes on in her place. Before long, the crooks kidnap Judy and stuff her in a deep freeze. She is found in time, defrosted, and makes her entrance for the finale.

In the course of the helterskelter plot, Judy eats five creampuffs filled with soap, falls off a fire escape, is nearly frozen solid in the refrigerator, takes a dozen spills during a comedy dance, is knocked over by a line of waiters, used as a rug, and suffers an attempted poisoning when the gangsters try to rub her out by piping deadly gas through her microphone. Commented Judy about the tribulations of being a slapstick performer: "The world today needs a laugh. If a couple of broken bones and a flock of bruises will give it to them—well, here we go." Her songs included: "Barrelhouse Bessie," "I Don't Want Anybody At All," "When The Cat's Away," and the title tune. *The Hollywood Reporter* observed that Judy does ". . . anything for a laugh . . . [but] the script doesn't do right by its strong array of talent."

Judy was originally scheduled to perform in *Showboat Sally* for Paramount under a one-picture loanout agreement, but instead, she starred in *True to the Army,* released in June 1942. It was a broad remake of the studio's 1934 Bing Crosby–Miriam Hopkins comedy, *She Loves Me Not.* Judy was Daisy Hawkins, a circus tightrope walker who witnesses a murder, and runs away to Ft. Bragg army camp where her boyfriend Jerry Colonna is serving. (He is in charge of the carrier pigeons and is experimenting by breeding the pigeons with parrots, hoping to evolve a talking message bird.) With the racketeers hot on her trail, Judy has to stay at the camp, so she masquerades as a soldier, moustache and all. Private Allan Jones is producing the camp's morale-building show and induces the leary Judy to perform in it. Ann Miller as the colonel's tap dancing daughter and William Demarest as the top sergeant round out the supporting cast. At the variety show, Judy proves a winner, and the gangsters, who are in the audience, are captured by the police—aided no little by Judy's abilities as an expert marksman.

Judy barrelhoused through all the expected bits of army humor, from the physical examination to the rigors of the mess hall, the rifle range, and the training arena. She even had a tricky bit in the camp's musical revue in which, playing a man, she had to pretend to be a woman. In her military getup, Judy bore a remarkable likeness to Charles Chaplin in *Shoulder Arms* (1918). Between Judy's hillbilly renditions, Jones's crooning, and Miller's footwork, the musical numbers got quite a workout: "Need I Speak?", "Jitterbug's Lullaby," "Spangle on My Tights," "In the Army," "Wacky for Khaki," "Swing in Line," "Love in Bloom," and "I Can't Give You Anything but Love."

Variety penned: "Miss Canova is handicapped by the poor material provided, while Jones and Calonna seem to strain in attempting to overcome the deficiencies of their respective assignments." In her 2½-star review, Kate Cameron of *The New York Daily News* complained: ". . . both she and Jerry Colonna overwork their farcical routines until there is little or no spontaniety left in them."

Joan of Ozark was her other Republic film of the year, released in August 1942. Wide-mouth funster Joe E. Brown, who had made the dismal "$1,000 Touchdown" 1939) with slapstick queen Martha Raye, was utilized by Republic to play opposite Judy. While out hunting one day, Ozark thrush Judy shoots a carrier pigeon, which has a Nazi spy message attached to it. Her accidental patriotic act makes her a nationwide heroine. Talent agents Brown and Eddie Foy Jr. are commissioned to hire Judy for Manhattan's Club 76, because the club's owner is a Nazi and he has been ordered by the Gestapo to dispose of Judy as an object lesson to Americans. Brown has to pretend he is a G-man and that he needs Judy to pose as a vocalist at the Club in order to investigate alleged Axis activities there. Judy jumps at the opportunity to be a G-woman and dashes off to New York. She stumbles into the real spy nest at the club, and after much confusion and bungling on her part, she is responsible for the roundup of the enemy and the destruction of a Japanese submarine in American waters. In the midst of her hog calling and yodeling, Judy sings "Backwoods Barbecue," "The Lady at Lockheed," and "Wabash Blues."

Archer Winsten of *The New York Post* was not enthralled. "The type of humor offered by Judy Canova and Joe E. Brown needs no introduction and cannot precipitate an argument. Either you like it or you don't." Evidently enough of the country's filmgoers did, because Judy's pictures performed admirably at the box office. She was known as "the Beatrice Lillie and the Jenny Lind of the Ozarks." Judy and Joe E. Brown would repeat their roles in *Joan of Ozarks* on radio's "Screen Guild Playhouse" in February 1945.

On March 14, 1943, Judy married private Chester B. England in the First Presbyterian Church at Newton, New Jersey. (She had been dating Los Angeles attorney Warren McKinney at the time of her divorce from Ripley in 1941.) Judy had met England while doing her Cafe de Paree engagement in London back in 1938.

Having guested on most major radio shows, Judy, on July 6, 1943, began *The Judy Canova Show* Tuesdays at 8:30 P.M. on CBS, replacing Al Jolson's program. As the advertisements ballyhooed: "she portrays a country cousin come to the big city for adventure. She finds it a-plenty and so do her sophisticated urban friends showing her the sights." *Variety* reported on her debut broadcast: "The program's humor, which was uniformly of the bell-ringing species, remained well within the precincts of radio's well-guarded parlor manners. Most of it was a hybrid of the stuff that tickles the tall-pine folk and hot-off-the-cob witticisms from Hollywood and Vine. Topics cracks about the OPA and CC's marriage mingled with jokes about Miss Canova's quaint relatives. 'Is this a room with bath?' 'Hoo,' Judy replies, 'The only thing we got here is a room with a path?' . . . Miss Canova, when given to songs, spreads her style from scat to rhythm to plain hog calling, but it was all entertaining." The show's cast of regulars included: Elvira Allman, Mel Blanc, Ken Niles, Gordon Jenkins and his Orchestra.

Judy's brand of jokes—good, bad, and indifferent—became standard fillers in newspapers throughout the country. "My new synthetic stockings are made out of a mixture of coal, wood and rubber. When I get a run in my stockings, I don't know whether I've got a clinker, a splinter or a blowout." "Judy Canova's counsel to big heads: "Remember more people have been flattened by a right to the back than a left to the jaw." Hogwash or not, these items helped increase Judy's fame.

Republic's *Chatterbox,* which opened at the Brooklyn Strand Theatre April 29, 1943, had Judy second billed to screen partner Joe E. Brown. She was Judy Boggs, a slavey at the Victory Dude Ranch. Brown was a bogus radio cowboy signed to a new film contract by Majestic Pictures. When the cameras start rolling at the dude ranch, Brown mounts his horse, but is quickly tossed off when the horse bucks at the sound of Judy's nearby singing. Judy rescues Brown and is hired by the studio. However, reporter Rosemary Lane and others are on hand, Brown's horse opry career appears ruined. The studio publicity boys devise a stunt that might restore his he-man popularity. Judy is planted in a mountaintop shack, with a nearby charge of dynamite set to explode; Brown is scheduled to rescue her. The scene turns into a reality, and Brown proves a true hero.

Chatterbox's premise bore great similarities to several other movie satires of the radio industry and western movies, not to mention the Broadway musical *Hold on to Your Hats* (1940), which starred Martha Raye and Al Jolson. The teetering cabin sequence was a direct steal from Charles Chaplin's *The Gold Rush* (1925) and suffered by comparison.

Judy's best number was "Why Can't I Sing A Love Song?" The Mills Brothers and Spade Cooley were present for additional musical flavor. A typical line of dialogue in *Chatterbox* had film director John Hubbard asking naive Judy to show him her profile. She indignantly replies: "If it ain't a-showin', you're not a-goin' to see it."

Variety appraised: "This one strings together a series of moth-eaten episodes for unfunny conclusion. Brown and Miss Canova are directed to mug broadly and generally over-act, which does not help the proceedings."

Sleepy Lagoon, released by Republic in September 1943, featured Judy as Judy Joyner—an agile young radio personality who sings nightly over the local station. She is elected mayor of burgeoning Sleepy Lagoon by the women's reform party headed by Ruth Donnelly. Their platform is to throw out the town's saloons and build an amusement park instead—to provide clean fun for the hordes of defense workers who have moved to the once moribund community. Unknown to Judy, gangsters establish an illegal gambling house in the tunnel of love at the park. With her beau Dennis Day, and the members of the women's reform party, she has mopped up the gang by the fadeout. Even her timorous uncle, Ernest Truex, comes out of the potential scandal clean, for it proves he had been coerced by the hoods to keep silent about Judy's innocence in the amusement park corruption plan.

Along the way, much screen time is devoted to Judy's combatting the unknown elements in the park's fun house. She falls through trap doors, gets snarled in the wind tunnel, etc. She sang "I'm Not Myself Anymore" and with punk Joe Sawyer dueted "You're the Fondest Thing I Am Of."

The Hollywood Reporter pointed up the weaknesses of this 65-minute black-and-white programmer: "There is little opportunity for her to do her cavorting and grimaces and sing her stylized songs." Even the usually lenient *Motion Picture Herald* criticized: "An attempt to create a running vein of frivolity in 'Sleepy Lagoon' fails despite the cast strength. . . . The innocuous story web gives the quartet little opportunity to promote their talents."

Judy remained active in her tours of Army camps and embarked on war-bond selling trips. But in 1944, she remained close to home, as she was expecting a baby. In August, she gave birth to Juliette, her first child. Two weeks later, her husband was shipped overseas for active military duty.

That same month *Louisiana Hayride* (1944), her first film away from Republic, went into release for Columbia. Judy had been dissatisfied with the production setup at Republic and hoped to improve the situation by agreeing to a revised loanout contract at Columbia. Unfortunately, her new employer was not noted for spending money freely even on their A products. Her three Columbia movies were uniformly shoddy backstopping, which only served to make Judy's screen presence wear mighty thin.

Louisiana Hayride had Judy as Judy Crocker, a hillbilly debutante who is thought to own oil-rich lands. Crooks Richard Lane and George McKay fleece Judy out of $3000 to invest in a phony film, *Louisiana Hayride,* which they promise will star the rich miss. In Hollywood, Judy's benefactor proves to be bellhop Ross Hunter who forces the conmen to actually make the movie. At the crucial moment, her money runs out, and production is shut down. However, after a potentially fatal plagiarism suit is averted and Judy auditions for a pro film director, the shooting continues. All ends satisfactorily for everyone, save the wrongdoers.

With a threadbare script to work from, Judy was far from her best. She tried to instill pep into her cavorting, but it just was not there. When not punctuating every other sentence with her "hey hey," she managed to sing "You Gotta Go Where the Train Goes," "Put Your Arms around Me Honey," "Rainbow Road," "I'm a Woman of the World," and a bit of "Short'nin Bread."

Judy returned to the airways with a new radio show on Saturday nights, beginning January 6, 1945, on NBC. She had been off the air since June 1944 when her previous half-hour program had ended, after garnering none-too-spectacular ratings. Verna Felton replaced Isabelle Randolph as wealthy aunt Agatha Frost, Joe Kerns was Mrs. Frost's butler, Ruby Dandridge was the maid Geranium and Mel Blanc was Pedro the gardener (and also Roscoe Wortle).

By now, radio audiences were well acquainted with Judy's basic format. She supposedly came from Unadella, Georgia (Judy had once passed through the town and had been fascinated by the sound of its name); she, had relatives in Cactus Junction out west; she made periodic visits to the big city to visit her rich aunt. The jokes ran as follows:

JUDY: "Your kisses sure send me."
STRANGER: "Shucks. Some people don't care how they travel."

Or:

JUDY: "I'm goin' to sing the Miseries from Il Trovatore."
MR. CIVIC (of the Opera Association): "Miss Canova, that's the *Miserere*—not the Miseries."
JUDY: "You ain't heard me sing it yet."

In most every show, the gardener Pedro could be counted on to say: "Pardon me, for talking in your face, senorita." Then there was cousin Ureenus who happened to like chopped liver ice cream. Judy would close each show by singing "Good Night Sweetheart."

By the fall of 1945, 128 NBC radio stations were carrying Judy's program. As with her motion pictures, Judy's production company had a firm percentage of the property's profits.

Hit the Hay was Judy's only 1945 film release. It was 72 minutes of silliness, exploiting Judy's ability to sing operatic selections. One day while lunching at the Market Place, Ross Hunter, who runs the Civic Opera Company with his father, hears Judy singing while she is milking the cows. He quickly hires her for the coming season, and he and girl friend Doris Merrick promote Judy as the company's big new discovery. Only it turns out that Judy is just an untutored lass, who cannot perform according to a script or libretto. In desperation, Hunter hires an actress (also played by Judy) to double for his star. Thus on opening night, Judy is hidden in the fly galleries, while the actress mouths the words from the stage. As expected this does not work out, and it is only when the Civic Company presents a swing version of *William Tell,* entitled *Tillie Tell,* that songstress Judy gets into the groove. Fortunately the opera group's backer is pleased, and everyone is happy.

More important than her undemanding dual role

assignment was Judy's singing of arias from *Rigoletto, La Traviata,* and *The Barber of Seville.* For those who expected barnyard melodies, Judy also screamed out "Old MacDonald Had a Farm" and "No Other Love."

The advertisements for *Hit the Hay* really stretched a point. They read: "She sings; she clowns; she makes love. And you'll get a barrow full of laughs as the pride of the Ozarks goes in for fancy costumes and funny business." At least actor Ross Hunter went on to become the very successful producer of such films as *Imitation of Life* (1958) and *Airport* (1970).

Singin' in the Corn was released in late December 1946, and was a very slim Christmas gift from Columbia Pictures to theatre patrons. As Judy McCoy, a carnival fortune teller, she inherits $250,000 on condition that she return a ghost town to its rightful Indian owners within one day of her arrival there. In McCoy's Gulch, gambler Alan Bridge and his gang scheme to prevent Judy and her carnival spieler pal Allen Jenkins from making good—they want to turn the town into another Reno gambling spot. Guinn ("Big Boy") Williams is converted into an ally, because of his love for Judy, and he helps her convince the suspicious redskins that McCoy's Gulch is not really haunted. It does take an unexplained visit from Judy's deceased uncle to make everything work out right.

The wild west settings, mostly backlot studio shots, were decorative at best, with Judy reacting and combatting the fake ghosts in expected manner. She did pepper viewers with such tunes as "Pepita Chiquita," "An Old Love Is a True Love," "I'm a Gal of Property," "Ma, He's Making Eyes at Me." Before the film —then called *Ghost Town*—went into its quickie production in early 1946, Judy told the press she hoped Boris Karloff and Peter Lorre would be her co-stars. *Variety* quipped: "It's a tossup as to what comprises the majority of footage; stock shots or those turned out for the film. Quality-wise the stock shots win in a walk. . . ."

Judy was reported to be compiling a book of reminiscences in 1946, entitled *There Is Punch in Judy,* but the volume was not published.

Judy was faring much better on radio. A trade paper report stated: "There's something peculiar to Miss Canova's show. . . . [Her personality] somehow lifts the piece off a nether shelf, projecting it into a thirty-minute segment of amusing stuff.

"When she breaks into song—and this is one show where no bones are made about the music, no effort to integrate unintegratable material—she's sock. Her comedy arrangement of 'Three Blind Mice' on the teeoff was, except for its unintellectual lyric-content, as good as some of the better satire by a master like Danny Kaye."

A follow-up review by *Variety* of the Saturday 10–10:30 P.M. show revealed: "Pig-tailed mimic is becoming more big-citified in her mannerisms and quips and seems to be acquiring some of the tricks of her male contemporaries. Her timing and line-punching are rarely off beat and zesty asides are ad-libbed over the rough spots. Given solid support . . . it develops upon the chief aggressor of the comedy foray to keep on her toes lest a subordinate subordinate her. The Canova lass is singing better than ever and her tonal qualities have an insouciant lilt. . . ." Judy's rating improved under the new Hooper "diary" system of checking the listening habits of small town residents. From a 11.6 rating in the 1945 season, she moved up to a 15.6 high point, putting her in the top ten radio shows.

The format of the show had now solidified, with Judy alternating the program's locale from Crescent City, where her uncle had a mine, to Cactus Junction, and to the big city where Aunt Aggie resided.

There was always a steady stream of man-hungry, love-starved jokes:

JUDY: "My Aunt Aggie says nice girls don't kiss."
SUITOR: "Do you really believe that nice girls shrink from kissing?"
JUDY: "Shucks, no. If that was true, I'd be nothing but skin and bones."

A constant theme on the program was Judy's effort to crash into society.

MRS. PROOTWHISTLE: "Most of the families in the Saddle and Hunt Club have been riding to the hounds for thirty years."
JUDY: "Shucks. My family went to the dogs long before that."

Judy's singing was still getting its share of ribbing from the scriptwriters, who often had her jokingly referred to as the "world's greatest coloraturo."

STRANGER: "Do you sing 'Faust'?"
JUDY: "Sure, I sing 'Faust' or slow."

With the penchant of Judy and the rest of the cast to mangle the language, puns were constantly tossed into the script.

HE: "I've got a lot of poise and personality."
JUDY: "That's you—poison personality."

The Judy Canova Show cost $10,000 weekly for talent, in contrast to such other standards as *Lux Radio*

Theatre ($16,000) and the highly popular *Mr. District Attorney* ($4500). In 1946, Judy got 250,000 fan letters, and sent out over 150,000 photographs.

Judy's last film appearances for Columbia were in two 1946 Screen Snapshot short subjects. In "Famous Hollywood Mothers" she is seen at home with her daughter Julietta. Other celebrities appearing in the two-reeler were: Rosalind Russell, Eleanor Powell, Brenda Marshall, Eve Arden, Ginny Simms, and Constance Moore. In "Radio Characters of 1946," Judy was shown in an eleven-minute excerpt from her radio broadcast. Said *Variety* of this short: ". . . [she] stooges in action and a couple of cameras look at audience—cargo of corn."

The pride of the farm folks took her see-sawing cinema career philosophically. When Judy was apprised by one columnist that she had won a magazine title as "the corniest actress in the movies," she retorted, with a straight face: "I'm deeply flattered to be called an actress."

Judy's biggest ambition was to do the lead in the film version of *Annie Get Your Gun,* which was the sensation of post-World War II Broadway. She would campaign for the role in the next years, but to no avail. MGM purchased it for Judy Garland, and when the actress became too ill to go on with the shooting, the studio replaced her with Betty Hutton, borrowed from Paramount Pictures.

Pete Canova died June 11, 1947, in Hollywood, of a heart attack at the age of 43. Later that month, Judy embarked on a nightclub tour of Latin America. She received a $10,000 weekly salary for her performing.

Radio would continue to be her mainstay in the coming years. Acerbic John Crosby in *The New York Herald Tribune* reviewed Judy's opening show on October 2, 1948: "Miss Canova represents an almost vanishing type of American humor once immortalized by Mack Sennett. She is the girl who is always chasing and never quite catching a man. In her headlong pursuit she scatters gags with the profligacy of Bob Hope, whose style she appears to have studied closely.

"In other respects, she sounds quite a lot like feminine version of Bob Burns—raucous, twangy, and incurably hayseed. Now and then for the purposes of comedy, she mingles with the gentry, spitting puns in all directions."

Variety detailed that Judy's Saturday evening show which paid her $8,500 weekly had a listening audience of about eighteen million per segment. It approved of her new format: "No longer are characters dragged in by the heels to parry a pun with Canova and be gone. The partitions have been knocked down. Now it's just one big happy family living in one big house. Situation

replaced slapstick and the thread of continuity is not snapped just for the sake of a big joke. Judy has come out of [the] mountains and is now resident of Beverly Hills."

Variety went on to describe Judy's unique method of pre-testing her weekly live shows: "After the broadcast, the ushers shoo the audience for a fresh intake of auditors. Half hour later Canova and the cast are previewing next week's show, which gives scripters [Henry] Hopple, [Fred] Fox, and [Artie] Phillips, a week to work over the rough spots and flit the bugs."

Typical of the radio ads for her show was: "You'll laugh till your sides ache when joyful Judy Canova falls asleep in . . . of all places . . . the dentist's chair; in the next hilarious episode in the laughable, lovable life of the merry one. . . . It's the treat of the week that can't be beat."

On February 24, 1950, Judy divorced Chester B. England, then a cosmetic manufacturer. Although she had been dating Dr. Robert Thompson since her separation from England in 1949, she married Philip Rivero, a wealthy Cuban importer. The wedding occurred a few weeks after her divorce from England.

Meanwhile, Judy was making a series of personal appearances at the bigger fairs throughout the southwest. *Variety* caught her act at the Dallas State Fair on April 6, 1950: "The gal Judy Canova, who parlayed a couple of high c's, a 3-octave range and inimitable flair for comedy into national fame, is every inch a trouper. One of those rare entertainers who can walk on a stage and gather the audience into the palm of her hand by the time she reaches center stage. . . ."

For the record, *Variety* reported on the opening show of the 1950 season (October 7) of Judy's radio outing. ". . . Miss Canova and the rest of the cast drawing some yocks via a situation where the uppity aunt of one of Miss Canova's boy friends tried to dissuade her nephew from taking an interest in the gal via an attempt to establish her illiterate background. This paved the way for a fairly funny backwoods scene. Windup had the aunt, to her dismay, learning one of her cousins was a mountain boy himself.

". . . Miss Canova herself gets in a few laughs, in addition to showing up nicely in the vocal department. Among tunes offered by gal on the initialer were 'Goodnight Irene' and 'Shortnin' Bread.' Latter was given a comic rendition with both numbers coming over for good results."

Judy was lured back to the screen in 1951. Herbert J. Yates, president of Republic Pictures, was in the need of a star to headline his low budget productions, which still found booking in the rural markets. Gene Autry had left the studio in 1947, and Roy Rogers departed in 1951. Judy was the logical choice to fill the gap for Yates's quickie features shot in three or four weeks' time.

Honeychile (1951), in the studio's new improved trucolor process, was her first multi-hued motion picture. Judy, an amateur song composer, has sent one of her tunes to music publisher Walter Catlett, who has published it under another composer's name; the song becomes a hit. Catlett sends Eddie Foy Jr. to Cactus Junction, Wyoming, to win a release from Judy. Since Judy wrote the melody for her boyfriend Alan Hale Jr., Foy must show up Hale as the crook he really is. Claire Carleton is used as a vamp for this purpose. Before the finale, Hale is out in the cold, Foy has participated in a chuck wagon race with Judy (the townfolk have all bet on her to win), and it seems Judy and Foy just might marry.

Not to disappoint her song-loving fans, Judy sang an operatic version of "Rag Mop," as well as pop versions of "Tutti Frutti," "More Than I Care to Remember," and the title tune. *Variety* decided: ". . . [it] figures as okay top-of-the-bill material for the smaller runs, particularly rural or small-town trade. . . . Miss Canova gives an energetic portrayal to her familiar character as well as singing four numbers in her specialized style. . . . Sidney Picker's production supervision supplies a bucolic look to the picture that fits the comedy pitch."

Judy was still going strong on radio, despite the onslaught of the competing television medium, which had caused the cancellation of many other radio stars' contracts. In the 1951–1952 season, she moved to the 9:00–9:30 P.M. Saturday night spot. Her cast now included Mel Blanc, Verna Felton, Joe Kearns, Hans Conried, Sheldon Leonard. *Variety* evaluated: "Miss Canova presents a harmless little show. There's little folk quality in her tunes, it's straight hillbilly fodder which has a mass following.

"Her chatter seems a bit inane at times. The writing is several notches short of adequacy, and the cast of characters impress as being caricatures of rural types.

"The item with major appeal is Miss Canova's singing. She can yodel picturesquely and can even handle a tune in a straight forward manner."

Judy's jokes may have belonged back on the farm, but audiences adored them.

Judy, the self-debaser
JUDY: "When I was four years old, my father took me to the zoo."
HE: "What happened?"
JUDY: "They rejected me."

Or:

JUDY: "I'm only human."
STRANGER: "You're exaggerating!"

And:
JUDY: "I've got a lot of get-up-and-go."
STRANGER: "Really."
JUDY: "Yeah, but it got up and went in the wrong direction."

The man-hungry Judy
AUNT AGGIE: "Being denied the companionship of men is sometimes a healthy thing."
JUDY: "Take a look at the healthiest girl in California."

Or:

JUDY: "Ours is a football marriage."
HE: "A football marriage!"
JUDY: "Yeah, we're both waitin' for the other to kick off."

Judy the philosopher
GERANIUM: "I sure wish I had money."
JUDY: "Geranium—you ought to know that money doesn't always bring happiness."
GERANIUM: "No ma'am. But if you've got the money, you can pick out the kind of misery you enjoy the most."

Or:

JUDY: "Pedro, you've got your shoes on the wrong feet."
PEDRO: "Senorita, dese are de only feet I hev."

Judy, the hillbilly
STRANGER: "You will ride in a carriage with four horses."
JUDY: "With four horses? Won't that be a little crowded?"

Or:

STRANGER: "Have you ever been to Cannes?"
JUDY: "No, but I had an uncle who was in the jury."

Judy, the (un)talented performer
STRANGER: "If you're an actress, I'm a monkey's uncle."

JUDY: "Well, I'm an actress. Let's see you hang by your tail."

Judy's first 1952 release was *Oklahoma Annie* an 89-minute entry filmed in trucolor. If the title gives any indication, someone in the script department had the ambitious notion of combining the charm of *Oklahoma* with the salty characterization of "Annie Get Your Gun"—it did not work. Judy, billed as "Queen of the Cowgirls," owns a shop in Coffin Creek. As soon as handsome new sheriff John Russell comes to town, Judy tells him of the crooked gambling saloon run by Grant Withers. To get Judy off his back, the sheriff promises her she can be a deputy if she captures bank robber Roy Barcroft. Through pure mischance and a lot of gumption, she corrals Barcroft in her general store. Now she can both live up to her grandmother's reputation (as a marvelous gun-toting sheriff) and be near the man she hankers for, Russell. With the help of the sheriff and the county's militant females, Judy rids the town of the gang. Judy is appointed the new sheriff when Russell takes over the county's supervisory job from convicted politico Frank Ferguson.

The entire film could have been condensed to a half hour television episode; in fact, the limited production values were on a par with that expended for the video show. Once again, the best segments of this film were her vocalizing. The opening tune, "Blow The Whistle," starts out imaginatively, with the camera panning in on an electric train set up in Judy's shop. Her smooth vocalizing and obvious enjoyment make her immature hand gesturing more than pardonable. Her other tunes included: "Have You Ever Been Lonely," "Never Never Never," "Oh Dear What Can The Matter Be," and "Billy Boy." As *Variety* saw it: "Miss Canova is an asset, selling the corn in her familiar, gallus-snapping manner and giving the country touch to . . . tunes. . . ."

During the summer of 1952 Judy toured eastern towns, playing one-night engagements and recording those sessions for use on her forthcoming radio season.

The Wac from Walla Walla, released in October 1952, returned Judy to the service comedy genre, à la her *True to the Army* of a decade before. She plays a backwoods western girl whose family has been in the military for generations. Judy is in love with Stephen Dunne, which upsets both her and his families, since the two households have been feuding for generations. Since Dunne is a lieutenant in the army, he suggests that Judy join the WACs, which she does. Judy is not too familiar with the ways of service life, and conniving blonde June Vincent—also out to get Dunne—makes things worse by pulling some fast ones here and there.

Meanwhile, Judy happens on a spy plot to steal missile secrets from the base. Her resourcefulness and dumb luck manage to save the day. After a wild chase in which Judy uses the guided missile homing devices to dumbfound the heavies, she captures them and hands them over to Dunne.

Judy is at her best in a scene which finds her mixed up with a platoon plowing through an obstacle course. Irene Ryan as the eccentric WAC sergeant and George Cleveland as her hot-tempered grandpa offer the best cast support. A running gag through the film has Judy continually destroying the ancestral statue of Judson Canova, her great grand-father, who fought and died a hero's death at Bull Run. Every time Cleveland gathers together the bits of rubble and puts the statue together—which takes him seven years—somehow Calamity Judy accidentally causes its destruction. Judy croons four tunes: "Boy, Oh Boy," "If Only Dreams Came True," "Lovely" and "Song of the Women's Army Corps."

Judy finally made her major television debut on November 2, 1952, as guest star of *The Colgate Comedy Hour* (Sunday at 8:00 P.M., NBC). She had appeared on the network's *Cavalcade of Stars* September 26, 1952, to ballyhoo her forthcoming show). As a solo Judy sang "I Ain't Got Nobody" and "He's Making Eyes at Me"; she reteamed with brother Zeke and sister Anne for "Jesse James." With Liberace supplying piano accompaniment Judy vocalized "Dark Eyes." Cesar Romero and Zsa Zsa Gabor were on hand as her special guests. Besides re-creating a typical Ma and Pa routine from her radio show days, Judy was featured in a screen test sequence. In a protracted skit with Gabor, the two women were seen on a train fighting over a pullman birth. Gabor was garbed in a lush negligee, and Judy wore a flannel nightgown. Gabor states she is wearing "Spring Night in Venice" perfume; Judy proudly informs her bunkmate: "I'm wearin' 'Hot Night on a Chicken Farm.'"

Later in the train sketch, Judy encounters the porter.

PORTER: "What kind of chicken you got in that cage?"

JUDY: "That's a Rhode Island purple."

PORTER: "You mean Rhode Island Red."

JUDY: "I don't neither. After layin' thirty-seven eggs, she's purple."

The critics did not cotton to her humors. Jack Gould of *The New York Times* reported: ". . . her maiden presentation was a sadly misguided effort . . . Miss Canova's talents are specialized. She can yodel; she can grimace; she can twist her mouth into astonishing shapes. She can scream, and she can roughhouse. These assignments are executed in a costume designed to suggest that she is a little mountain girl; who lives away off the main road. There are the long pigtails, the straw hat, the checkered jacket and the battered suitcase."

Variety concluded: "Miss Canova has television potentialities if the yokel characterization is developed along less zany lines and if she's integrated into a stronger story."

Due to the birth of her daughter Diane, born June 2, 1953 in West Palm Beach, Florida, Judy was off the screen in 1953. Late in the year she did plan a *Judy Canova Show,* with Paul Jones producing, but it did not materialize as a video series entry. She guested on Milton Berle's variety show and on Danny Thomas's *Make Room for Daddy.*

Judy starred in *Untamed Heiress* for Republic in 1954, a modest black and white rehash of her old skits. She was the orphaned daughter of an opera-singing ma, once loved by now wealthy George Cleveland. Cleveland hires two detectives to locate Judy's ma, and they return with Judy. Meanwhile, Cleveland has been declared incompetent to manage his large holdings, and villain Hugh Sanders has taken possession of the old gent's desert castle. Aided by gangsters Donald Barry and Jack Kruschen, Judy storms the castle and fights off the crooks successfully. She then adopts Cleveland as her grandfather.

Judy parlayed her haunted house gambit for another outing. Here she runs amuck in the spooky castle, with armor striking out, trap doors, beds that close up into the wall, secret panels, etc. She sings: "Welcome," "A Dream for Sale," and "Sugar Daddy." Judy's daughter Julietta (nicknamed Tweeny) played Judy as a child, and her five month old baby Diana even had a bit in the movie. *Variety* concluded: "Judy Canova is about the only excuse for this two-reel comedy idea that has been stretched out to 69 minutes. However, her presence may be excuse enough for the rural and small-town trade where she rates. Elsewhere, it has nothing to offer. . . . The gal can growl a good blue note."

With no more radio show and only a few television appearances, Judy found time to play the Hotel Sahara nightclub in Las Vegas for a three-week engagement in April 1954.

Judy had two 1955 releases. *Carolina Cannonball* cast Judy and her grandpa Andy Clyde as the sole residents of Roaring Gulch. In the hope that someday the town will come alive, they maintain the community's only connection with the outside world, a steam-driven trolley called the "Carolina Cannonball." Enemy agents Sig Ruman, Leon Askin, and Jack Kruschen sidetrack an American guided missile, which lands near Roaring Gulch. Judy finds the missile and innocently uses it as a replacement for the trolley's burned-out boiler. The finale finds the villains, Judy, grandpa, and government agent Ross Elliott having a frenzied free-for-all aboard the revitalized trolley. Her songs included: "The Carolina Cannonball," "Wishin' and Waitin' " and "Busy as a Beaver.'

Her final Republic movie was *Lay that Rifle Down* (1955). She works at a small town hotel run by her greedy aunt, Jacqueline de Wit. Despite a heavy load of chores, Judy finds time to take a correspondence school charm course, and even invents an imaginary suitor to impress her dour relative. When she has to produce him, she corrals stranger Robert Lowery for the task. He is a con man who thinks he an turn a tidy profit by using Judy's farmland as bait. She has been using the property to house a group of orphans. Lowery's confederate convinces the bank that the land is now valuable and almost forces Judy to sell it to him. However, Lowery becomes conscience-stricken and tries to make amends. Judy does her duty, corners the crooks, and discovers that she is rich, because oil deposits have been located on her property. Judy vocalizes: "I'm Glad I Was Born on My Birthday," "Sleepy Serenade," and "The Continental Correspondence Charm School."

With Republic Pictures phasing out of theatrical filmmaking, Judy concluded her film contract with the studio.

Occasionally, Judy would appear on a television show, such as *The Danny Thomas Show* (March 17, 1958—CBS) in which she was Elsie Hoople, Thomas's protege from the West Virginia Hills. Her video production company, Carvan Inc., in which she was partnered with Albert C. Gannaway, remained virtually inactive. In July 1958, Coronet Records released "Judy Canova—Country Cousin—Sings," consisting of reissues of such singles as "Wabash Blues," "Butcher Boy," and "Blow Whistle Blow."

Judy's mother died August 30, 1958, in Burbank, California, of a heart attack at the age of 70.

On May 29, 1960, Judy returned to the public eye. She made her dramatic television debut on *Alfred Hitchcock Presents* (CBS) in the episode "Party Line." She was Helen Parch, who had been tricked into hanging up on a party line by her neighbor. The next time he tries to get her off the phone she refuses, even though he says his wife is dying.

Interviewed by the press, Judy was described as looking like a blonde country Dinah Shore. Judy announced plans to make another foray into television. For Four Star Productions she prepared a pilot episode, which deemphasized the hillbilly humor she was so long noted for. Said Judy: "It's hard trying to get something like a country act started these days over the objections of the Madison Avenue boys. They'd say it was too corny. . . . Some folks may have thought my stuff was corny in the beginning, but the public bought it. After I got started doing country stuff with my brother and sister, I couldn't get out of it. . . . A lot of my act was tongue in cheek. But I guess I did it so well, that people took me seriously." The project, scripted by Charles Stewart and Jack Elenson, received no network sponsor bids; nor did a *Lil' Abner* pilot made about this time.

Then Judy was hired for a cameo role in Samuel Goldwyn Jr.'s new version of *The Adventures of Huckleberry Finn.* Judy advised the press: "I've only done one other straight dramatic role and I want to do more. It's the same old story, every comedienne wants to become a tragedian and visa versa. . . . People told me my first dramatic part came off pretty good. It made my lawyer cry, and that's pretty hard to do." When asked if money necessitated her film comeback, Judy answered: "I don't have to work. Fortunately I put the money away when it was coming in." (She had invested in Florida and California real estate.) About retirement. "This has happened to me again and again. I get times when I just like being lazy. Then I get started working again and I get going like crazy."

The Adventures of Huckleberry Finn was released in July 1960. Directed by Michael Curtiz, Judy was seventh billed in a cast that included Tony Randall, Eddie Hodges, Patty McCormack, Neville Brand, and Archie Moore. She had the role of the sheriff's wife. *Variety* felt: ". . . [she] does not do all she might have in her single scene with 'Huck,' potentially a memorable one."

After that, no more "suitable" movie offers came her way. Occasionally she would appear on television, mostly on game shows. Camden Records released "Judy Canova: Comedy! In Person!" in late 1960, composed of taped skits from her radio shows.

She and Philip Romero were divorced in 1964.

Judy was next in the news in May 1968, when she was released from La Vina Hospital in Hollywood, where she had spent 46 days for treatment of a respiratory ailment.

In early 1970, Judy filmed another television pilot at Paramount, *The Murdocks and McClays,* portraying a trombone-playing hillbilly, Ida Murdock. The project co-starred Dub Taylor, Kathy Davis, Noah Beery Jr., and Nydia Westman. It was an Ozarkian variation of the Romeo and Juliet theme, with the generation gap motif tossed in. The badly conceived series did not sell, and ABC-TV utilized it on a summer package of fill-in programs, airing the segment on September 2, 1970.

After that last pilot fiasco, Judy retired to her San Fernando Valley home, where she resides with her daughters on a rather elegant spread. Now and then she would bring her famed bumpkin stage character out of retirement to adorn some company's television commercial, such as the Shake and Bake ad a few seasons back. But Judy is not very fond of the new medium. As she told this author: "I do think it has been a very bad influence on the youth of our country and has been a great detriment to education generally—a means of escape for youngsters and grownups—therefore they're not using their *own* thinking."

Since it was announced in mid 1971 that the road company for the smash Broadway revival of *No, No, Nanette* would require a new battery of nostalgia names to bolster the musical's cast, there had been speculation that Judy would assume the Patsy Kelly role of the overworked housemaid Pauline. And sure enough, when the national touring company of the "new 1925 revue" opened in Cleveland in late December 1971, Judy was among the players, which included June Allyson and Dennis Day. The Pauline role allows Judy to mug ferociously with a recalcitrant vacuum cleaner and to bless the audience with assorted exaggerated double takes, as well as strumming the ukelele and joining in the chorus of the title song. More importantly, it offers a new generation of theatre-goers an opportunity to watch Judy in action.

It can only be hoped that *No, No, Nanette* will be the stepping stone to bringing Judy back to where she belongs—front and center on a stage, whooping it up for a delighted audience. With so many other less talented country and western performers attracting wide fanship today, there is no earthly reason why Judy should not be in the limelight.

FILMOGRAPHY: JUDY CANOVA

Feature Films

IN CALIENTE (WB '35) 84 M.
Director, Lloyd Bacon; story, Ralph Block, Warren Duff; screenplay, Jerry Wald, Jules Epstein; songs, Harry War-ren, Al Dubin, Mort Dixon, Allie Wrubel; dance numbers staged by Busby Berkeley; camera, Sol Polito; editor, Jimmy Gibbons.

Dolores Del Rio (Rita Gomez); Pat O'Brien (Larry MacArthur); Leo Carrillo (Jose Gomez); Glenda Farrell

(Clara); Edward Everett Horton (Harold Brandon); Phil Regan (Pat Casey); Winifred Shaw ("Woman in Red"); Dorothy Dare (Baby Blonde); Harry Holman (Biggs); Herman Bing (Mexican Florist); William B. Davidson (Man); Luis Alberni (Magistrate); Olive Jones, The Canova Family, The DeMarcos (Singers); John Hyams (Reporter); Henry De Silva (Waiter); Milton Kibbee, Sam Appel (Drivers); Chris Pin Martin, C. I. Dafau, Carlos Salazer, L. R. Felix (Mexican Quartet).

BROADWAY GONDOLIER (WB '35) 98 M.
Director, Lloyd Bacon; story, Sig Herzig, Hans Kraly, E. Y. Harburg; screenplay, Herzig, Warren Duff, Jerry Wald, Julius J. Epstein; songs, Al Dubin, Harry Warren; camera, George Barnes; editor, George Amy.

Dick Powell (Richard Purcell); Joan Blondell (Alice Hughes); Adolphe Menjou (Professor De Vinci); Louise Fazenda (Mrs. Twitchell); William Gargan (Cliff); George Barbier (Hayward); Grant Mitchell (Richards); Hobart Cavanaugh (Gilmore); James Burke (Uncle Andy); Bob Murphy (Irish Cop); Ted Fio Rito and Band (Specialty); Mills Brothers (Specialty); The Canova Family (Specialty); June Travis (Check Girl); Joe Sawyer (Red); Mary Treen (Woman); Jack Norton, Bill Elliot (Reporters); Selmer Jackson (Director); Sam Ash (Singer); Ernie Wood (Clerk); George Chandler (Photographer).

GOING HIGHBROW (WB '35) 87 M.
Director, Robert Flory; based on the play *Social Pirates* by Ralph Spence; screenplay, Edward Kaufman, Sy Bartlett; songs, Louis Allen, John School; camera, William Rees; editor, Harold McLernon.

Guy Kibbee (Matt Upshore); ZaSu Pitts (Caro Upshore); Edward Everett Horton (Augie); Ross Alexander (Harley Marsh); June Martel (Sandy); Gordon Westcott (Samuel Long); Judy Canova (Annie); Nella Walker (Mrs. Marsh); Jack Norton (Sinclair); Arthur Treacher (Waiter); Milton Kibbee (Acme Press Man); Frank Dufrane (Officer); Walter Clyde (Captain); Christine Gess (French Actress); Sherry Hall (United Newsman); Joseph E. Bernard, Jack H. Richardson (Stewards); Olaf Hytten (Butler); Irving Back (Clerk); William Jeffrey (Proprietor); Maude Turner Gordon (Mrs. Vandergrift).

ARTISTS AND MODELS (Par. '37) 97 M.
Producer, Lewis Gensler; director, Raoul Walsh; story, Sig Herzig, Gene Thackery; screenplay, Walter DeLeon, Francis Martin; songs, Ted Koehler and Burton Lane; Leo Robin and Frederick Hollander; Robin and Ralph Rainger; Koehler and Victor Young; camera, Victor Milner; editor, Ellsworth Hoagland.

Jack Benny (Mac Brewster); Ida Lupino (Paula); Richard Arlen (Alan Townsend); Gail Patrick (Cynthia); Ben Blue (Jupiter Pluvius); Judy Canova (Toots); The Yacht Club Boys (Themselves); Cecil Cunningham (Stella); Donald Meek (Dr. Zinner); Hedda Hopper (Mrs. Townsend); Martha Raye (Specialty); Andre Kostelanetz and Orchestra (Specialty); Louis Armstrong and Band (Specialty); The Canova Family (Specialty); Connie Boswell (Specialty); Peter Arno, McClelland Barclay, Arthur William Brown, Rube Goldberg, John La Gotta, Russell

Patterson (Artists); Sandra Storme (Model); Dell Henderson (Lord); Harry Hayden (Early); Virginia Brissac (Seamstress); Pat Moran (Tumbler); Ethel Clayton (Woman); David Newell (Romeo); Edward Earle (Flunkey); Jane Weir (Miss Gordon).

THRILL OF A LIFETIME (Par. '37) 75 M.
Producer, Fanchon; director, George Archainbaud; story, Seena Owen, Grant Garrett; screenplay, Owen, Garrett, Paul Gerard Smith; music director, Boris Morros; music arrangements, Victor Young, Arthur Franklin; choreography, LeRoy Printz, Carlos Romero; songs, Frederick Hollander, Sam Coslow, Carmen Lombardo, Yacht Club Boys; camera, William C. Nellor; editor, Doane Harrison.

Jimmy, Charlie, Kelly, Red (The Yacht Club Boys); Judy Canova (Judy); Ben Blue (Skipper); Eleanore Whitney (Betty Jane); Johnny Downs (Stanley); Betty Grable (Gwen); Leif Erikson (Howdy Nelson); Larry Crabbe (Don); Zeke Canova (Himself); Anne Canova (Herself); Tommy Wonder (Billy); Franklin Pangborn (Mr. Williams); Dorothy Lamour (Specialty); Si Jenks (Messenger Boy); Howard Mitchell (Business Man); June Shafter (Receptionist); Tommy Wonder (Billy).

SCATTERBRAIN (Rep. '40) 73 M.
Associate producer-director, Gus Meins; screenplay, Jack Townley, Val Burton; additional dialogue, Paul Conlon; music director, Cy Feuer; art director, John Victor Mackay; songs, Hy Heath, Johnny Lange, and Lew Porter; camera, Ernest Miller; editor, Ernest Nims.

Judy Canova (Judy Hall); Alan Mowbray (J. R. Russell); Ruth Donnelly (Miss Stevens); Eddie Foy Jr. (Eddie MacIntyre); Joseph Cawthorn (Nicolas Raptis); Wallace Ford (Sam Maxwell); Isabel Jewell (Esther Harrington); Luis Alberni (Professor DeLemma); Billy Gilbert (Hoffman); Emmett Lynn (Pappy Hull); Jimmy Starr (Joe Kelton); Cal Shrum's Gang (Themselves); Matty Malneck and Orchestra (Themselves).

SIS HOPKINS (Rep. '41) 99 M.
Associate producer, Robert North; director, Joseph Santley; based on the play by F. McGrew Willis; screenplay, Jack Townley, Milt Gross, Ed Eliscu; art director, John Victor Mackay; music director, Cy Feuer; songs, Frank Loesser, Jule Styne; camera, Jack Marta; editor, Ernest Nims.

Judy Canova (Sis Hopkins); Bob Crosby (Jeff Farnsworth); Charles Butterworth (Horace Hopkins); Jerry Colonna (Professor); Susan Hayward (Carol Hopkins); Katherine Alexander (Clara Hopkins); Elvia Allam (Ripple); Carol Adams (Cynthia); Lynn Merrick (Phyllis); Mary Ainslee (Vera de Vere); Charles Coleman (Butler); Andrew Tombes (Mayor); Charles Lane (Rollo); Byron Foulger (Joe); Betty Blythe (Mrs. Farnsworth); Frank Darren (Jud).

PUDDIN' HEAD (Rep. '41) 80 M.
Associate producer, Albert J. Cohen; director, Joseph Santley; story, Jack Townley; screenplay, Townley, Milt Gross; additional dialogue, Howard Snyder, Hugh Wedlocks Jr.; art director, John Victor Mackay; music director,

Cy Feuer; songs, Jule Styne, Eddie Cherkose and Sol Meyer, Jule Styne and Eddie Cherkose, Walter Scharf; camera, Jack Marta; editor, Ernest Nims.

Judy Canova (Judy Goober); Francis Lederer (Prince Karl); Raymond Walburn (Harold Montgomery Sr.); Slim Summerville (Uncle Lem); Astrid Allyn (Yvonne); Eddie Foy Jr. (Harold Montgomery Jr.); Alma Kruger (Matilda Montgomery); Hugh O'Connell (Kincaid); Chick Chandler (Herman); Paul Harvey (Mr. Harvey); Nora Lane (Miss Jenkins); The Sportsmen (Specialty); Vince Barnett (Otis Tarbell); Wendell Niles (Randall).

SLEEPYTIME GAL (Rep. '42) 84 M.

Associate producer, Albert J. Cohen; director, Albert S. Rogell; story, Mauri Grashin, Robert T. Shannon; screenplay, Art Arthur, Albert Duffy, Max Lief; art director, Russell Kimball; music director, Cy Feuer; songs, Jule Styne and Herb Magidson, Anze Lorenzo, R. A. Whiting, J. R. Alden, and R. B. Egan; camera, Jack Marta; editor, Ernest Nims.

Judy Canova (Bessie Cobb); Tom Brown (Chick Patterson); Ruth Terry (Sugar Caston); Mildred Coles (Connie); Billy Gilbert (Chef Acropolis); Harold Huber (Honest Joe); Fritz Feld (Chef Petrovich); Jay Novello (Chef Gonzales); Skinnay Ennis (Danny Marlowe); Jerry Lester (Downbeat); Jimmy Ames (Gus); Elisha Cook Jr. (Ernie); Frank Sully (Dimples); Thurston Hall (Mr. Adams); Paul Fix (Johnny Gatto); Vicki Lester (Blonde); Lester Dorr, Walter Merrill, Pat Gleason, Fred Santley, Mady Laurence (Reporters); Edward Earle (Dr. Bell); Hillary Brooke (Railroad Station Blonde); Ric Vallin, Cyril Ring (Clerks); William Forrest (Hotel Manager); Carl Leviness (Husband); Gertrude Astor (Wife); Marguerite Whitten (Maid); Dwight Frye, Eddie Acuff (Muggs); Eugene Borden (Maitre D'Hotel).

TRUE TO THE ARMY (Par. '42) 76 M.

Producer, Sol C. Siegel; associate producer, Jules Scherman; director, Al Rogell; based on *She Loves Me Not* by Edward Hope, Howard Lindsay; screenplay, Art Arthur, Bradford Ropes; songs, Frank Loesser and Harold Spina; Loesser and Joseph J. Lilley; Leo Robin and Ralph Rainger; Dorothy Fields and Jimmy McHugh; camera, Daniel Fapp; editor, Alma Macrorie.

Judy Canova (Daisy Hawkins); Allan Jones (Private Bill Chandler); Ann Miller (Vicki Marlow); Jerry Colonna (Private J. Wethersby "Pinky" Bates); Clarence Kolb (Colonel Marlow); Edward Pawley (Junior); William Wright (Lt. Danvers); William Demarest (Sgt. Bates); Edwin Miller (Ice); Arthur Loft (Ray); Gordon Jones (Private Dugan); Rod Cameron (Private O'Toole); Eddie Acuff (Sgt. Riggs); Edgar Dearing (Target Sergeant); Mary Treen (Mae); Selmer Jackson (Congressman); Harry Barris (Piano Player); Frank Sully (Mugg); Ralph Dunn (Officer); Stanley Blystone (Police Officer); Syd Saylor (Private); Joseph Crehan (Police Chief); George Turner (Military Policeman); Dorothy Sebastian (Gloria); Donald Kerr (Soldier).

JOAN OF OZARK (Rep. '42) 82 M.

Associate producer, Harriet Parsons; director, Joseph Santley; screenplay, Robert Harari, Eve Greene, Jack Townley; additional dialogue, Monte Brice, Bradford Ropes; choreography, Nick Castle; music director, Cy Feuer; songs, Mort Greene and Harry Revel; Dave Ringel and Fred Meinken; art director, Russell Kimball; camera, Ernest Miller; editor, Charles Craft.

Judy Canova (Judy Hull); Joe E. Brown (Cliff Little); Eddie Foy Jr. (Eddie McCabe); Jerome Cowan (Philip Munson); Wolfgang Zilzer (Kurt); Alexander Granach (Guido); Anne Jeffreys (Marie Lamont); Otto Reichow (Otto); R. H. Van Twardowski (Hans); William Dean (Karl); Paul Fung (Yamatako); Donald Curtis (Jones); George Eldredge (Chandler); Olin Howlin (Game Warden); Ralph Peters (Window Cleaner); Chester Clute (Salesman); Emmett Lynn (Hillbilly Driver); Kam Tong (Japanese Commander); Cyril Ring, Eric Alden, Ralph McCullough (Reporters); Lloyd Whitlock (Colonel Ashley); Horace B. Carpenter (Mountaineer); Bobby Stone (Newsboy); Bud Jamison (Cop).

CHATTERBOX (Rep. '43) 77 M.

Associate producer, Albert J. Cohen; director, Joseph Santley; screenplay, George Carleton Brown, Frank Gill Jr.; music director, Walter Scharf; songs, Harry Akst and Sol Meyer; art director, Russell Kimball; camera, Ernest Miller; special effect, Howard Lydecker; editor, Ernest Nims.

Judy Canova (Judy Boggs); Joe E. Brown (Rex Vane); John Hubbard (Sebastian Smart); Rosemary Lane (Carol Forest); Chester Clute (Wilfred Peckinpaugh); Emmett Vogan (Roger Grant); Gus Schilling (Gillie); Anne Jeffreys (Vivian Gale); George Byron (Joe); Art Whitney (Assistant Director); Frank Melton, Gary Bruce, Matty Kemp, Ray Parsons (Reporters); Mary Armstrong (Guest at Dude Ranch); Mills Brothers (Specialty); Roy Barcroft (Laborer); Earle Hodgins (Wrangler); Nora Lane (Secretary); Joe Phillips (Producer); Edward Earle, Herbert Heyes, Sam Flint, Gordon DeMain (Production Assistants); Spade Cooley (Singing Musicians); Marie Windsor (Hostess); Ruth Robinson (Wardrobe Woman); Robert Conway (Announcer on Train); Pierce Lyden (Wrangler); Billy Bletcher (Black Jake); Ben Taggart (Foreman); Dickie Dillon (Indian Boy).

SLEEPY LAGOON (Rep. '43) 65 M.

Associate producer, Albert J. Cohen; director, Joseph Santley; story, Prescott Chaplin; screenplay, Frank Gill Jr., George Carleton Brown; art director, Russell Kimball; music director, Walter Scharf; songs, Ned Washington and Phil Obman, Eric Coates and Jack Lawrence; camera, Bud Thackery; editor, Richard Van Enger.

Judy Canova (Judy Joyner); Dennis Day (Lancelot Hillie); Ruth Donnelly (Sarah Rogers); Joseph Sawyer (Lumpy); Ernest Truex (Dudley Joyner); Douglas Fowley (J "The Brain" Lucarno); Will Wright (Cyrus Coates); Herbert Corthell (Sheriff Bates); Forrest Taylor (Samuel); Eddy Chandler (Ticket Seller); Kitty McHugh (Mrs. Small); Ellen Lowe (Mrs. Simms); Margaret Reid (Mrs. Crumm—Chief of Police); Sammy Stein, Jack Kenney, Jay Novello, Eddie Gribbon (Lugs); Jack Raymond (Joe the Clown); Mike Riley and Band (Themselves); Larry

Stewart (Man); Emil Van Horn (Gorilla); Rondo Hatton (Hunchback); Frank Austin (Wolf Man); Johnny Walsh (Boy); James Farley (Bailiff); Frank Graham (Narrator).

LOUISIANA HAYRIDE (Col. '44) 67 M.

Director, Charles Barton; story, Paul Yawitz, Manny Self; screenplay, Yawitz; art director, Lionel Banks, Walter Holschier; music director, M. R. Bakalienikoff; songs, Kim Gannon and Walter Kent; Jerry Seelen and Saul Chaplin; Junie McCree and Albert Von Tilzer; camera, L. W. O'Connell; editor, Otto Meyer.

Judy Canova (Judy Crocker); Ross Hunter (Gordon Pearson); Richard Lane (J. Huntington McMasters); Lloyd Bridges (Montague Price); Matt Willis (Jeb Crocker); George McKay (Canada Brown); Minerva Urecal (Maw Crocker); Robert Cavanaugh (Malcolm Cartwright); Eddie Kane (Warburton); Nelson Leigh (Wiffle); Arthur Loft (Director); Robert Homans (Officer Conlon); Russell Hicks (Ferbes); Harry Wilson (Listener on Train); Eddie Bruce, Syd Saylor, Pat West (Men); Ben Taggart (Conductor); Ernie Adams (Pawnbroker); Charles Sullivan, Jack Gardner, Brian O'Hara (Cab Drivers); Jack Rice (Hotel Clerk); Walter Baldwin (Lem); Earl Dewey (Governor); George Magrill, George Frod (Troopers); Bud Jamison (Doorman); Lane Chandler, Eddie Chandler (Plainclothesmen); Constance Purdy (Mrs. Vanderguft); Frank Hagney (Bartender); Christine McIntyre (Female Star).

HIT THE HAY (Col. '45)

Producer, Ted Richmond; director, Del Lord; screenplay, Richard Weil, Charles R. Marion; art director, Perry Smith; camera, James Van Trees; editor, Viola Lawrence.

Judy Canova (Judy Stevens); Ross Hunter (Ted Barton); Fortunio Bonanova (Mario Alvini); Doris Merrick (Sally); Gloria Holden (Mimi Valdez); Francis Pierlot (Roger Barton); Grady Sutton (Wilbur Whittlesey); Louis Mason (Frisby); Paul Stanton (J. Bellingham Parks); Clyde Pillmore (Mayor Blackburn); Maurice Cass (Prompter); Luis Alberni (French Professor); Cosmo Sardo (Makeup Man); Charles Marsh, Billy Snyder (Reporters); Victor Travers (Stage Hand); Buster Brodie (Bald Man); Jack Frack (Camera Man); William Newell (Cab Driver).

SINGIN' IN THE CORN (Col. '46) 65 M.

Producer, Ted Richmond; director, Del Lord; story, Richard Weil; screenplay, Isabel Dawn, Monte Brice; art director, Sturges Caine; songs, Doris Fisher and Allan Roberts, Sidney Clare and Con Conrad; camera, George B. Meihan; editor, Aaron Stell.

Judy Canova (Judy McCoy); Allen Jenkins (Glen Cummings); Guinn "Big Boy" Williams (Hank); Alan Bridge (Honest John Richards); Charles Halton (Obediah Davis); Robert Dudley (Gramp McCoy); Nick Thompson (Indian Chief); Frances Rel (Ramona); George Chesbro (Texas); Ethan Laidlaw (Silk Stevens); Frank Lackteen (Medicine Man); The Singing Indian Braves (Themselves); Guy Beach (Judge); Jay Silverheels, Rod Redwing (Braves); Dick Stanley, Charles Randolph (Indians); Si Jenks (Old Man); Pat O'Malley (O'Rourke); Chester Conklin (Austin Driver); Mary Gordon (Mrs. O'Rourke).

HONEYCHILE (Rep. '51) 89 M.

Associate producer, Sidney Picker; director, R. G. Springsteen; screenplay, Jack Townley, Charles E. Roberts; additional dialogue, Barry Trivers; art director, Frank Hotaling; music, Victor Young; songs, Jack Elliott and Harold Spina, Johnnie Wills and Deacon Anderson, Ted Johnson and Matt Terry; camera, Jack Marta; special effects, Howard and Theodore Lydecker; editor, Richard L. Van Enger.

Judy Canova (Judy); Eddie Foy Jr. (Eddie Price); Alan Hale Jr. (Joe Boyd); Walter Catlett (Al Moore); Claire Carleton (Betty Loring); Karclyn Grimes (Effie); Brad Morrow (Larry); Roy Barcroft (Walter Judson); Leonid Kinskey (Chick Lester); Gus Schilling (Window Washer); Irving Bacon (Abner); Fuzzy Knight (Ice Cream Vendor); Roscoe Ates (Bob); Ida Moore (Harriet); Sarah Edwards (Sarah); Emory Parnell (Mayor); Dick Elliott (Sheriff); Dick Wessel (Bartender); William Fawcett (Ben Todd); Robin Winans (Boy); Stanley Blystone (Mr. Olson); Donia Bussey (Mrs. Olson); John Crawford (Martin McKay); Cecile Elliott, Cecil Weston (Women).

OKLAHOMA ANNIE (Rep. '52) 90 M.

Associate producer, Sidney Picker; director, R. G. Springsteen; story, Jack Townley, Charles E. Roberts; screenplay, Townley; art director, Frank Arrigo; music director, Nathan Scott; songs, Jack Elliott and Sonny Burke, George Brown and Peter De Rose, S. Sherwin and Harry McClintock; camera, Jack Marta; special effects, Howard and Theodore Lydecker; editor, Richard L. Van Enger.

Judy Canova (Judy); John Russell (Dan Fraser); Grant Withers (Bull McCready); Roy Barcroft (Curt Walker); Emmett Lynn (Paydirt); Frank Ferguson (Eldridge Haskell); Minerva Urecal (Mrs. Fling); Houseley Stevenson (Blinky); Almira Sessions (Mrs. Fudge); Allen Jenkins (Bartender); Maxine Gates (Tillie); Emory Parnell (Judge Byrnes); Denver Pyle (Skip); House Peters Jr. (Tullett); Andrew Tombes (Mayor); Fuzzy Knight (Larry); Si Jenks (Old Man); Marian Martin (Le Belle La Tour); Herb Vigran (Croupier); Hal Price (Sheriff); Fred Hoose (Bookkeeper); Lee Phelps (Taylor); Bobby Taylor (Bobby); William Fawcett (Painter).

THE WAC FROM WALLA WALLA (Rep. '52) 83 M.

Associate producer, Sidney Picker; director, William Witney; screenplay, Arthur T. Hortman; art director, Fred A. Ritter; music, R. Dale Butt; songs, Jack Elliott and Harold Spina; camera, Jack Marta, special effects, Howard and Theodore Lydecker; editor, Tony Martinelli.

Judy Canova (Judy); Stephen Dunne (Lt. Tom Mayfield); George Cleveland (Gramps Canova); June Vincent (Doris Vail); Irene Ryan (WAC Sgt. Kearns); Roy Barcroft (Mr. Prentiss); Allen Jenkins (Mr. Redington); George Chandler (Jud Canova); Elizabeth Slifer (Betty Canova); Thurston Hall (Col. Mayfield); Sarah Spencer (Recruiting Sgt.); Dick Wessell (Sgt. Malone); Pattee Chapman (Lizzie); Republic Rhythm Riders (Themselves); Dick Elliott (Sheriff); Carl Switzer (Private Cronkheit); Tom Powers (General); Jarma Lewis, Emlen Davies, Virginia Carroll (Specialists); Evelynne Smith (Judo Instructor); Phyllis Kennedy (WAC Tex. Sgt.).

UNTAMED HEIRESS (Rep. '54) 70 M.

Associate producer, Sidney Picker; director, Charles Lamont; story, Jack Townley; screenplay, Barry Shipman; art director, Frank Arrigo; assistant director, Roy Webb; music, Stanley White; songs, Jack Elliott, Donald Kahn; camera, Reggie Lamont; special effects, Howard and Theodore Lydecker; editor, Arthur Roberts.

Judy Canova (Judy); Donald Barry (Spiker Mike); George Cleveland (Andrew "Cactus" Clayton); Taylor Holmes (Walter Martin); Chick Chandler (Eddie Taylor); Jack Kruschen (Louie); Hugh Sanders (Williams); Douglas Fowley (Pal); William Haade (Friend); Ellen Corby (Mrs. Flanny); Richard Wessel (Cruncher); James Flavin (Cop); Tweeny Canova (Tweeny).

CAROLINA CANNONBALL (Rep. '55) 70 M.

Associate producer, Sidney Picker; director, Charles Lamont; story, Frank Gill Jr.; screenplay, Barry Shipman; art director, Frank Hotaling; assistant director, A. J. Vitarelli; music, R. Dale Butts; songs, Donald Kahn, Jack Elliott; camera, Reggie Lanning; special effects, Howard and Theodore Lydecker; editor, Tony Martinelli.

Judy Canova (Judy); Andy Clyde (Grandpa Canova); Ross Elliott (Don Mack); Sig Ruman (Stefan); Leon Askin (Otto); Jack Kruschen (Hogar); Frank Wilcox (Professor).

LAY THAT RIFLE DOWN (Rep. '55) 71 M.

Associate producer, Sidney Picker; director, Charles Lamont; story, Barry Shipman; assistant director, A. J. Vitarelli; art director, Carroll Clark; music, R. Dale Butts; songs, Donald Kahn, Jack Elliott; camera, John I. Russell; special effects, Howard and Theodore Lydecker; editor, Arthur E. Roberts.

Judy Canova (Judy); Robert Lowery (Nick Stokes); Jil Jarmyn (Betty); Jacqueline de Wit (Aunt Sarah); Richard Deacon (Glover Speckleton); Robert Burton (Professor); James Bell (Mr. Fetcher); Leon Tyler (Horace Speckleton); Tweeny Canova (Tweeny); Pierre Watkin (Mr. Coswell); Marjorie Bennett (Mrs. Speckleton); William Fawcett (Wurpie); Paul E. Burns (Mr. Gribble); Edmund Cobb (Sheriff Cushing); Donald MacDonald (Johnny); Mimi Gibson (Terry); Rudy Lee (Billy).

THE ADVENTURES OF HUCKLEBERRY FINN
(MGM '60) 107 M.

Producer, Samuel Goldwyn Jr.; director, Michael Curtiz; based on the novel by Mark Twain; screenplay, James Lee; music, Jerome Moross; art director, George W. Davis, McClure Capp; songs, Burton Lane, Alan Jay Lerner; assistant director, L. C. McCardle Jr.; special effects, A. Arnold Gillespie; camera, Ted McCord; editor, Frederic Steinkamp.

Tony Randall (The King); Eddie Hodges (Huckleberry Finn); Archie Moore (Jim); Patty McCormack (Joanna); Neville Brand (Pap); Mickey Shaughnessy (The Duke); Judy Canova (Sheriff's Wife); Andy Devine (Mr. Carmody); Sherry Jackson (Mary Jane); Buster Keaton (Lion Tamer); Josephine Hutchinson (Widow Douglas); Parley Baer (Grangerford Man); John Carradine (Slave Catcher); Royal Dano (Sheriff); Dolores Hawkins (River Boat Singer); Sterling Holloway (Barber); Dean Stanton (Slave Catcher); Minerva Urecal (Miss Watson); Roy Glenn (Drayman); Rickey Murray (Cabin Boy); Fred Kohler Jr. (Mate); Eddie Fetherston (Townsman); Sam McDaniel (Servant); Virginia Rose (Woman at Circus); Fred Coby (Sheriff); Henry Corden (Mate); Haldane Zajic (Percy); Patric Whyte (Uncle Harvey).

With Anne, Zeke, and Pete Canova in *In Caliente*
(WB, 1935).

With Gordon Westcott in *Going Highbrow* (WB, 1935).

Judy Canova in 1936.

With Hugh O'Connell on Broadway in *Ziegfeld Follies of 1936.*

With Ben Blue, Ida Lupino in *Artists and Models* (Paramount, 1937).

With Ben Blue in *Artists and Models.*

With Johnny Downs, Eleanore Whitney in *Thrill of a Lifetime* (Paramount, 1937).

With Ben Blue in *Thrill of a Lifetime*.

A Fred Fox caricature, c. 1940.

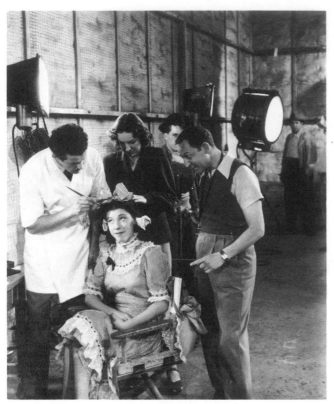

With Eddie Foy Jr. in *Scatterbrain* (Republic, 1940).

In *Scatterbrain.*

With Charles Butterworth, Charles Coleman in *Sis Hopkins* (Republic, 1941).

Judy Canova and her husband James Ripley, 1941.

In *Puddin'head.*

In *Puddin'head* (Republic, 1941).

With Eddie Foy Jr. in *Puddin'head.*

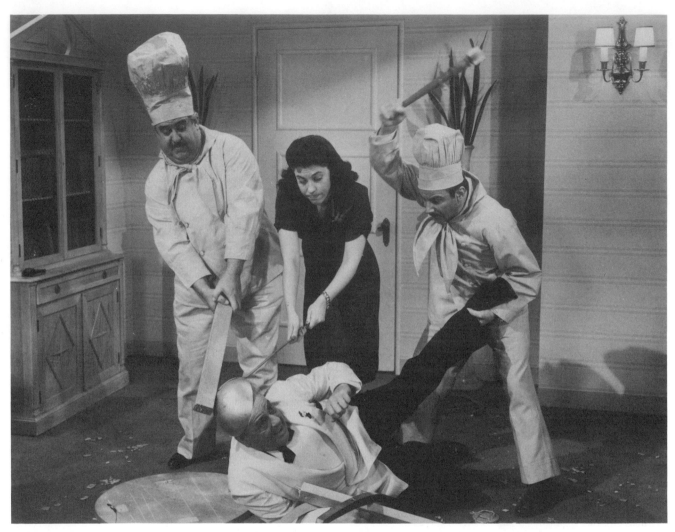

With Billy Gilbert, Thurston Hall, Fritz Feld in *Sleepy-time Gal* (Republic, 1942).

With Jerry Lester in *Sleepytime Gal.*

With Mary Treen, Gordon Jones, Charlotte Sullivan
in *True to the Army*.

With Allan Jones, Jerry Colonna in *True to the Army* (Paramount, 1942).

With George Eldredge, Donald Curtis in *Joan of Ozark* (Republic, 1942).

With Jerry Colonna in *True to the Army*.

With Donald Curtis in *Joan of Ozark*.

With Alexander Granach, William Dean, Wolfgang Zilzer, George Eldredge, Hans von Twardowski, Donald Curtis, Jerome Cowan in *Joan of Ozark*.

With John Hubbard, Joe E. Brown, Gus Schilling in
Chatterbox (Republic, 1943).

With Dennis Day in *Sleepy Lagoon* (Republic, 1943).

With Ernest Truex, Ruth Donnelly, Dennis Day in
Sleepy Lagoon.

With Jessie Arnold, Walter Baldwin in *Louisiana Hay-ride* (Columbia, 1944).

With Matt Willis in *Louisiana Hayride*.

In *Hit the Hay* (Columbia, 1945).

In *Louisiana Hayride*.

With Allen Jenkins in *Singin' in the Corn* (Columbia, 1946).

With Guinn "Big Boy" Williams in *Singin' in the Corn.*

Judy Canova in 1947.

Judy Canova in the late 1940s.

With Eddie Foy Jr. in *Honeychile* (Republic, 1951).

In *Honeychile.*

With Si Jenks, Frank Ferguson in *Oklahoma Annie* (Republic, 1952).

With John Russell, Si Jenks, Frank Ferguson in *Oklahoma Annie.*

In *Oklahoma Annie.*

In *Wac from Walla Walla* (Republic, 1952).

With Stephen Dunne in *Wac from Walla Walla*.

With James Flavin in *Untamed Heiress* (Republic, 1954).

With Jack Kruschen, Chick Chandler, George Cleveland, Taylor Holmes, Donald Barry in *Untamed Heiress.*

With Ross Elliott, Andy Clyde in *Carolina Cannonball*
(Republic, 1955).

With Andy Clyde in *Carolina Cannonball.*

In *Lay that Rifle Down* (Republic, 1955).

With Chick Chandler on CBS TV's *Danny Thomas Show* (March 17, 1958).

 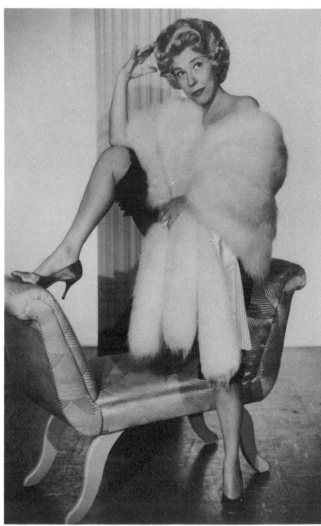

Judy Canova on "Party Line" (*Alfred Hitchcock Presents*, CBS-TV, 1960), and, at right, in spoof of glamor photos.

Judy Canova today.

PHYLLIS DILLER

5'4"
120 pounds
Hazel eyes
Brown hair
Birth sign: Cancer

Phyllis Diller is indisputably show business's dean of self-deprecation and the queen of the one-liner jokes. Regarded as the female Bob Hope, she is perhaps the most successful practitioner of the quipster's art in any media.

Phyllis at work is an amazing sight to behold—and she thrives on it. She has the grace of a crippled stork, emphasized by her skinny legs and arms, her long nose, shaved eyebrows and topped by her ashen mop of fantastically wild hair. There is hardly a feature of her well-known stringy anatomy that she has not criticized for good, clean belly laughs. When she has exhausted all avenues of verbally tearing herself to shreds, she turns with a quick fierceness on the vanities and foibles of the middle class American housewife.

Her barbs bite deep, but audiences always know that she is including herself among the targets. With her throaty cackle of a laugh, she can make most any stone-faced watcher turn into a puddle of guffaws. To make sure everyone gets her funny points, she punctuates each laugh line with her famed mobile cigarette holder, and caps this with staggers of dismay and horrible grimaces. Often she ends up a quickie satirical routine with her tongue hanging out and her wide eyes popped in true gargoyle fashion.

From being an unknown plain-Jane housewife in 1955, Phyllis has evolved into an international institution with a $1 million yearly income. She has made energetic forays into filmmaking, television, and stage acting. However, she is at her best performing in nightclubs, where she does not have to submerge her professional image into a pre-written characterizations. There is no one today who can puncture mankind's pretenses and frivolities with the speed and punch of madcap Phyllis. As her raucous self, she has no peers in the ranks of the stand-up comics.

Phyllis Diller (nee Driver) was born in Lima, Ohio, on July 17, 1917, the only child of Perry Marcus Driver, an insurance sales manager, and Frances Ada (Romshe) Driver.

Phyllis's middle-aged parents were convinced that their freckled-faced, plain, shy daughter was musically talented and overdosed the youth with voice, violin, saxophone, and piano lessons. More interested in the opposite sex than musical scales, Phyllis recalls that she was definitely not "the type that boys had to lash themselves to masts to stay away from." She remembers her mother advising her that she would never be really attractive and that she should take advantage of any asset she had.

Phyllis attended Franklin Grammar School and the local Central High School. She participated in dramatics, wrote for the school newspaper, and played tennis. In her spare moments, she sang in the school and church choirs.

After graduating from high school in 1935, Phyllis's parents entered her at Sherwood Music Conservatory in Chicago, determined that their daughter was destined for a concert career of some sort. Music students were required to supplement their studies with courses in other fields. Phyllis enrolled at Northwestern University where she obtained high grades in psychology, but received a D in German and dropped the language course immediately.

Phyllis much preferred pop tunes to the highbrow studies at the Conservatory. She secretly began making the rounds of Chicago clubs, hoping for at least an audition. Talent agents were equally unimpressed by her gawky looks and her unformed singing style.

According to Phyllis: "It suddenly dawned on me that music is a discipline . . . if you're going to be a musician, you're going to blow everything else, like marriage." Since she was convinced she was never going to be good enough for the concert stage, Phyllis quit Sherwood. She returned to Lima, planning to sharpen her practical abilities and secretarial skills at a local business college. But her parents insisted she put her expensive music training to some use, and enrolled her at nearby Bluffton College. There, they reasoned, she could at least earn a degree as a music teacher.

At Bluffton, Phyllis soon became noted as the wacky class clown. It was the typical case of the ugly duckling seeking consoling attention, no matter how she earned it. One of her more outrageous pranks occurred the night she pranced out of the dormitory shower room, naked save for curlers in her hair, a belt around her waist, and a rose clenched in her teeth. She then paraded down the hall doing a wild imitation of Gypsy Rose Lee.

In her senior year, Phyllis met Sherwood Anderson Diller, age 26, the son of a well-to-do Bluffton family. The couple eloped to Kentucky and were married November 4, 1939. They returned to Bluffton, where Phyllis continued her college courses. However, she dropped out two months before she would have received her B.A. degree.

The Dillers then moved to Ypsilanti, Michigan, for a spell. Their first child, Peter, was born September 22, 1940. Phyllis later confided: "I was an only child and it was pretty lonely at times. I suppose that was why I always wanted a big family of my own. I was sorry I had to quit with just five. If we could've afforded 'em, I would've had twenty. I was like the Easter bunny, ready to lay 'em like eggs." (Her other children: Sally, November 17, 1944; Suzanne, March 8, 1946; Stephanie, October 9, 1949; and Perry, February 3, 1950.)

Thinking life might be more rewarding out west, the Dillers moved to California in 1941, and settled in a housing project in Alameda, a suburb of San Francisco. Sherwood Diller first worked in real estate, then landed a modest post as civilian inspector at the Alameda Naval Air Station.

Phyllis recalls that there was never enough money at this point in their lives, and that as a housewife and mother, she worked "as hard as I think it is possible for a woman to work. I scrubbed, washed, ironed, mended, cooked and had babies." Nevertheless, she did find time to conduct the children's choir at the Alameda Presbyterian Church.

When her father died, Phyllis's mother moved to California, and with the insurance money from the estate, she purchased an old house. The Dillers moved in with her, and to supplement their income they took in boarders. The added income helped, but the additional burden on Phyllis was immense. Said Phyllis: "They wanted the kids kept quiet. I'd be scrubbing their halls and toilets and have to dash downstairs to answer their calls."

When the family budget reached the breaking point, Phyllis was forced to go job-hunting. Since she possessed no professional experience, she met constant refusals at employment agencies. She finally convinced the editor of the *News-Observer* in nearby San Leandro that his newspaper required a society column, and that Phyllis was the girl to do it. She was hired at $50 weekly. The new family maid, Mabel Bess, claimed $20 of her new paycheck.

Domestic life still did not run particularly smooth, with financial problems top on the list of fight-provoking subjects. After one particularly fierce argument with her husband, Phyllis stalked out of the house. She happened to pass a strange church, and on an impulse walked in. She later informed *Saturday Evening Post* interviewer Alex Haley: "I heard the minister reading and I've never forgotten the words: 'Whatsoever things are true . . . whatsoever things are pure . . . think on these things. . . .' They seemed to be addressed directly to me, as if God himself were giving me a message. . . . I didn't change my life overnight, but at least I glimpsed what I had to do. I had to stop wallowing in negative thoughts."

Meanwhile, Phyllis was developing into a laundromat comedian. ("To hide our awful mess from the neighborhood, I acted as if I didn't have a care. I think I began being funny almost unconsciously.") She would entertain the housewives at the local cleaning establishment with jokes about family life and its constant woes: "I used to be eight years behind in my ironing. Now it's nine. But I've worked out a system. I bury a lot of it in the backyard." To punctuate her growing repertoire of self-tested quips, Phyllis would garb herself in outlandish outfits, often carrying a pot and pan with her, to make perfectly clear to her audience when a punch line in her stream of one-liners had arrived. As she grew more confident in her new role as the local housewife-jester, more and more of her excess energy vented itself in her impromptu joke telling sessions. She was trying very hard to make light of those years, which she later described as: "Strictly pablum, diapers, Drano, and no money."

Professionally, Phyllis soon obtained a better paying position writing advertising copy for Kahn's Department Store in Oakland. For a spell, she had a cooking show, then she became a continuity writer for radio station KROW in Oakland, and eventually headed the merchandising and press relations office at radio station KSFO in San Francisco. In this capacity, she had a private office, medium-sized car, and a healthy expense account.

Phyllis continued experimenting and expanding her off-the-cuff performing. Said Phyllis: "It was fun for me now that I wasn't hiding something. I was really just being myself." She appeared at PTA shows, Women's Club affairs, and took to entertaining at Red Cross shows at the Alameda Naval Air Station. For the latter "benefits," she was paid $17 and a live turkey per performance. Her son Peter would often accompany her on the banjo.

The turning point in Phillis's professional life occurred when she chanced to read Claude Bristol's *The Magic of Believing*. Said Phyllis "It expressed things I had known in my mind but couldn't translate into living. It opened up a whole new world."

Increasingly impressed by Phyllis's innate comedy abilities, Sherwood Diller was convinced his wife should try her hobby professionally. Phyllis later confirmed: "He insisted that I become a comic. There were times when I felt he almost whipped me mentally. When I was working in a little club, he'd say 'why aren't you working the hotels?' He was always thinking about the next thing. He did a lot of great things for me. He put me in the business, mentored me, pushed me, encouraged me."

Phyllis practiced writing comedy routines for herself, and studied the television performances of such comics as Bob Hope ("That's my idol, Rapid Robert"), Joan Davis, Milton Berle, Lucille Ball, et al. She studied with a dramatics coach to smooth out her faltering delivery.

After ten months of preparation, she obtained an audition with Keith Rockwell, manager of the Purple Onion in San Francisco. The small, popular nightclub was noted for encouraging new talent. ("I came out of a group of comics that were at the time, in the beginning, called off-beat, Mort Sahl, Elaine May, Mike Nichols, Milt Kamen, the Smothers Brothers. . . . All those people were called 'off-beat.' It's just that we were always ahead, baby.") The club's regular comic was about to take two weeks' vacation, and Phyllis was hired as a substitute. She quit her job at KSFO.

On March 7, 1955, Phyllis made her club debut, with a weekly salary of $60. For her premiere act, she spoofed Eartha Kitt's popular song, "Monotonous," with her version "Ridiculous." She satirized Yma Sumac's soprano singing, played the zither, and told some topical jokes hurriedly culled from newspaper stories. Audiences were polite but not enthralled.

Phyllis remembers: "I wasn't good enough. I still had a thousand things to learn."

When the regular comic returned, Phyllis was told by the Purple Onion's manager that he would book her again soon. Two weeks later, he kept his promise, and she rang up a total of 89 weeks at the club.

As the weeks passed, Phyllis refined her routines, which still smacked of the amateur trying all possible avenues, hoping to hit on a socko presentation. Typically, her act included a segment devoted to ludicrous advertisements culled from magazines, which she had pasted onto huge cardboards. She was still borrowing jokes from wherever or whomever she could, jotting down the successful ones in huge notebooks to reuse in the future. She later recalled: "It took me a long time to stop singing and to stop using props. I had funny glasses, I had funny stoles, I had funny furs—I borrowed furs from the audiences and did bits. I couldn't do a thing without a funny prop."

Billed as the "homely friendmaker," Phyllis soon became a San Francisco favorite—the pride of the town. She wrote a feature column for *The San Francisco Examiner* humorously commenting on goings on about town. Other columnists began quoting her outrageous wisecracks: "You know what keeps me humble? Mirrors! I considered changing my name when I entered show business—but with a face like this, who cares!" Or: "I wore one of those topless swimsuits to the beach the other day. It took me twenty minutes to get arrested—and then it was because I was parked by a fire hydrant. That night I had a phone call from a Peeping Tom. He asked me to pull my window shades down!"

By this time, Sherwood Diller had quit his job (his positions ran from being a taxi driver to a refrigerator salesman at Sears Roebuck, to a night watchman) and worked full time as Phyllis's business manager. Their five children were sent to a relative in St. Louis for the duration. The Dillers hit the road, playing engagements across the country.

George Clark in *The Boston Daily Record* reviewed her 1958 engagement at Phil Bayon's Number 12 Carver Street, where she was performing three times nightly. "To begin with she's a mugger. . . . Miss Diller's grimaces are priceless, and frequently take the place of words. Secondly, she has a holler's laughter, one who throws back her head and really lets go. Who can resist it? And third, her material is slick, sanguine, and frequently macabre."

One of the meaningful high points of her career occurred in 1959, when Bob Hope caught her act while she was appearing in a not-so-swank Washington, D.C., club. "It was the wrong place and me competing with a chorus of breastworks. . . . I was sandwiched between a line of girls whose job it was to mingle, and the starring act, Betty Riley, the Irish Senorita." Phyllis recalled to this author: "I knew he [Hope] was in the room and in my total embarrassment I tried to sneak out while Riley was on. He popped up from his table, caught me behind a pillar and told me I was great. You wouldn't possibly know what that meant to me. From then on when times are rough I'd think: 'If Bob Hope likes my work, I must have something.' "

Phyllis's initial LP comedy record album appeared in September 1959 entitled: "Wet Toe In A Hot Socket," it contained runthroughs of her best routines to date. In the years to come, there would be such comedy albums as "Laughs" (August 1961), "Are You Ready?" (March 1962), "Great Moments" (January 1965), "Best of Phyllis Diller" (December 1966), "What's Left" (February 1968), "Beautiful" (February 1969). Turning away from the comedy, she made "Born to Sing" (December 1968) which gave her the opportunity to show her own vocal styling. In "Harold Arlen Revisited" (June 1970) and in "Arthur Schwartz Revisited" (December 1970), she joined Cab Calloway, Blossom Dearie, Gloria DeHaven, and others in these campy Ben Bagley musical disc productions.

On the way to success, Phyllis had several professional setbacks. As her first engagement with General Artists Corporation, she was hired to play the Fontainebleu Hotel in Miami Beach (previously, she had been without agent, writer, or press for the first four years of her career). Phyllis recalls: "I opened the bill for Don Cornell. My thinking was that when you work a large, plush supper club in a hotel, a lady would wear a long gown. I truly believe this was my major error. I have never been able to be funny before or since with a gown that goes to the floor. The second show I switched to my Chanel suit (knee length) and was very funny. However, the powers that were did not see the second show and they had already made up their minds." As a result of this fiasco, she became "poison" in the industry for a spell, and had trouble obtaining bookings.

One performer who helped her immensely was Jack Paar. By early 1961 she had appeared on his national television program over thirty times. Phyllis remembers how she broke the solid ice to get on the prestigious show: "My pianist at #1 Fifth Avenue (Club), Harold Fonville, called the Paar Show staff daily until in complete desperation and to be rid of him forever, they said 'bring her down this afternoon and we'll audition her in the office.' We did that. I was on the show that night —the old Hudson Theatre next to the Luxor Baths [which became an inside Paar Show joke], and the rest

was history. At the end of my bit there was one of those moments that is electric. It was felt by everyone. The people on the show that night were Peggy Cass and Paul Henreid."

Phyllis found it emotionally tough to adjust to the demands of her profession: "For my first five years in the business, I was petrified every time I went on. . . . The toughest battle I ever faced was to get self-confidence and I couldn't manage until Liberace helped me realize that my nervousness was just a bad habit. If you're conscious of a bad habit, you can best it. I bested it, but it was agony." About shyness: "It was like a disease, and I conquered it. But talk about childish fears! I had a trembling dread of the San Francisco Bridge, because I knew it was waiting for me—just me —to fall into the water."

Also in 1959, Phyllis engineered a screen test for herself at Paramount Studios. She was up for the lead in a television series dealing with female Navy personnel, *Permanent Waves*. The show never jelled. Phyllis wrote recently to this author: "My screen test was lousy. I didn't know how to prepare for a scripted test and didn't have the skill to handle as many props as required. I had to shave a man while doing the lines. It was abominable! A couple of months ago (late 1970) Jerry Lewis and Patti invited my husband, Warde Donovan, [she had divorced Diller in 1965] and me to dinner and he spent hours looking for the test, as he was going to show it to me to spoil my appetite. He couldn't find it—God is good!"

At any rate, as a result of her constant television exposure, Phyllis solidified her stage performance: ". . . one day I envisioned how it would be if I stepped out of the curtain without anything but my makeup and cigarette holder. I made myself do it. Believe me, it was hard, after leaning on a piano for years. But I did it on the Paar show and have been doing it ever since." In 1965, Phyllis offered another rationale: "I was always camping it up as a kid. I loved Bette Davis. Maybe because of her I have reduced my once numerous props to only a cigarette holder. I used it to set the mood, to punctuate, to say, 'I'm the Queen.' "

In March 1961, Phyllis played the Bon Soir Club in New York. Having eliminated the battery of songs and impersonations from her act, she now relied strictly on jokes, rapidly pushing them across to the audience. She focused on subjects she knew best: marriage, sex, automobiles, American morality: "Nowadays, insecurity explains everything. If your kids dynamite the house, it's because they're insecure. It's all muzzie's and dadsie's fault. Honey, let me tell you about a real childhood shakeup. When I was three, my folks sent me out for bubble gum. While I was out, they moved!"

Phyllis became renown for her one-liners, which were gaining her the reputation as being one of the best stand-up comedians in the business, and one of the few females to ply this precarious trade. ("The field of comedy has been as open as the cave door in Adam and Eve's day. There has never been anything to keep women out of this field, except their lack of ability.") As Phyllis explains her comedy style: "I've always had the knack of building one [liners]. . . . I'd lay something out and then top it . . . because silence makes me so nervous. . . . You wouldn't believe it. Therefore, I always have these little phrases—one word, three words, four words—that at the end of each line is a laugh. Now, I'm building to a big punch or maybe I've given 'em a big punch and I add, add, add, add— topper, topper, topper, topper, topper. . . . That's one of my big things. It makes me different." Phyllis claims: ". . . I have a great sense of timing and a sense of when to speak, when not to speak, so it was a professional attitude toward comedy right from the start."

In the summer of 1961, Phyllis reached her dream goal—headlining at the Hungry i Club in San Francisco. Her tightly honed act clicked. It was at this time that *San Francisco Chronicle* writer Jim Walls made his famous observation about Phyllis: "It was difficult to decide whether it was the performer talking, or the person, or both."

When she returned to New York for her Blue Angel club engagement in October 1961, Justin Gilbert of *The New York Mirror* penned: "She's a sterling example of womankind at its worst—which makes her the shrewdest and most mouthful miss on the nightclub circuit today. . . . Then she mugs. And believe me, the Rubber-Faced Men never had the versatility of this rolling-eyed rooster.

Time magazine appropriately described the now established Phyllis Diller: "Onstage comes something that, by its own description, looks like a sackful of doorknobs. With hair dyed by Alcoa, pipe-cleaner limbs, and knees just missing one another when the feet are wide apart, this is not Princess Volupine. It is Phyllis Diller, the poor man's Auntie Mame. . . . [she] is not just a buffooning grotesque. Her form of comedy is even older than she is, and it runs counter to the trend of modern, story-like comedians, but her hard, calculatedly frenzied style goes over brilliantly in a nightclub atmosphere."

Although she was now playing the swankier clubs, her format was still geared to the middle-class housewife. ("When I open my mouth, they know I'm one of them and from that second we both can feel the two-way radar going between us. We girls are compatriots with 10,000 things in common. I'm just the one onstage talking for us.") Her advice to this segment of Americana was still bizarre: "Stay in bed until 4:30 P.M. and then put furniture polish behind your ears. It makes you smell tired when your husband comes home." For her joke-telling, she was now earning $4000 weekly.

Phyllis had also perfected her array of stage outfits. Typically, she would appear in such ensembles as a cellophane dress, pink gloves, pink ankle boots (size 8AAAA), pink cigarette holder, and wild fright wig. A favorite prop was a ratty fur piece. ("My stole. Isn't that pitiful! How unsuccessful can a girl look? People think I'm wearing anchovies. The worst of it is I trapped these under my sink!") When she changed to a different colored outfit, she snapped on a matching pair of tinted contact lens. To accentuate her angular facial features, she wore extra long false eyelashes. On the road, she carried two dozen pieces of luggage, containing an assortment of elaborate gowns deliberately styled to be baggy and to accentuate her unique figure, which she claims qualified her as a Slenderella reject. By the mid 1960s, Phyllis would have five hundred outfits catalogued for personal and professional use.

When asked why she has adopted an extensive use of hand gestures, Phyllis theorized: "The reason for the cigarette holder is to portray a certain type woman, plus it gives me an excuse to hold up one hand. It is an attention getter. When you flag a train, you raise your hand. When you get attention from the teacher to leave the room, you raise your hand. Over the years I have found very descriptive uses for the cigarette holder. It projects and is continually used for hostility moves and punctuation marks. These gestures that I use are natural for me." (Since Phyllis does not smoke, she has a wooden stick painted to resemble a cigarette inserted in her holder.)

Along with the large shrugs of her bony shoulders, staggers of dismay and horrible grimaces, Phyllis's most famous trademark became her deep, throaty guffaw "aah ha ha haa." As she told Larry Wilde in *"Great Comedians Talk about Comedy"* (1968): "That's my own laugh. When I laughed at first in my act, I'll bet anything I was laughing because they weren't and I was trying to prime the pump and it worked. Then, later, a lot of people would criticize and say 'Oh, she laughs too much. I don't like that silly laugh.' But I then became absolutely famous for that laugh and I've gotten big rich commercials out of it—cause all they wanted was the laugh, so you don't listen to anybody. You listen to the small voice within you. You know what you're doing and if you don't, get out."

In her act, Phyllis is always pointing her long, bejewelled cigarette holder, telling innumerable jokes about Fang, her imaginary husband ("What else are you going to call a man with only one tooth?—two inches long?). As she explained: "Fang is Dagwood. He's an archetype, a husband when you're not getting along or when he's lazy, and won't fix the door. Everything I say on stage is a cartoon. I really don't hate anybody."

Typical of the legendary Fang jokes: "Fang cut himself and lost so much blood his eyes cleared up." Or: "I realized on our first wedding anniversary that our marriage was in trouble. Fang gave me luggage. It was packed. My mother damn near suffocated in there."

Also in line for fierce stage ribbing are her imaginary mother-in-law, Moby Dick, and her sister-in-law, Captain Bligh. Then there is her neighbor, Mrs. Clean, whose mania for tidiness and sanitation has provided Phyllis with countless oneliners.

Having eschewed the areas of politics, religion, and race, Phyllis has most often poked fun at herself: "My legs are so skinny, I have to have my hosiery altered." "The year I finally lost my baby fat, I got middle-aged spread." About her famous hair (actually wigs designed to dart in all sorts of directions simultaneously): "You think this is my hair. It's nerve ends. A ha ha, ha ha."

Clearly and deliberately, Phyllis made herself the representative of millions of homely housewives, showing that one of them could make good. Not only did she put herself on the firing line, but any type of unlovely creature: "I also know a lady who is so fat that when she wears a white dress they show movies on it. And her idea of a sandwich is a roast between two pizzas."

In 1961, when Ed Sullivan and Jack Paar were having their famous television feud, Phyllis was one of the few major performers to appear on both shows, due to prior contractual agreements. She received $3,500 for her Sullivan appearance. She told the press that her career dream was to have "my own television show . . . something wild and creative . . . something out of the ordinary groove." Phyllis already was receiving special treatment on the tube. As she told the author: "I have always had poetic license of a certain sort. In the old days I was the only person allowed to use the word 'broad' as a substitute for woman or lady." Her video material differed very little from what she utilized on the stage, which she still terms: "adult, sophisticated—yes; dirty—no."

Phyllis began expanding her career to cover stock work. She appeared in *Dark at the Top of the Stairs* (1961) as the sister-in-law Lottie. The rapid-fire comedienne made the difficult transition to a pre-written theatrical role. Said Phyllis: "I sincerely feel that I did the role well. I have said many times if Eileen Heckert plays a role it is for me. Another way to put it is "if

the woman wears a lot of jewelry and is a kind of nut, it is for me. . . . *Dark at the Top of the Stairs* . . . was at the beginning of my career and was non-comedy. I wrote a line to cover it—'People came expecting to see a play about bulb snatching.'" Other shows followed: *Wonderful Town* (1962), *Happy Birthday* (1963). She was offered the Beatrice Lillie role of Madame Arcati in the national tour of *High Spirits,* but declined the offer.

Also in 1961, Phyllis made her inauspicious motion picture debut in *Splendor in the Grass,* starring Natalie Wood and Warren Beatty. In the 1920s tale of frustrated young love, Phyllis had the bit assignment of nightclub hostess Texas Guinan. She had a quickie scene emceeing the floor show at the club visited by Beatty and his father, Pat Hingle. The film was shot in Manhattan and on Long Island. It did extremely well at the box office.

In 1962, Phyllis purchased a house in St. Louis and was finally able to reunite her family in her own home. She figured that Ohio, besides being home to her, was also midway between club engagements on either coast.

When in 1963, she appeared at the plush Royal Box club in Manhattan Eugene Boe of *Cue* magazine noted: "In her 'quieter' costumes, she looks like a drag queen at Mardi Gras; letting go, she became a new species born of science fiction. . . . The distance between quality quips can be quite a stretch, as the best of stand-up comics. She is brave to venture into an area so dangerous for women, and she is clever to be even intermittently successful in this elusive craft."

By now (1963), Phyllis was guesting on the major television variety shows from Bob Hope to Perry Como and Andy Williams, and was appearing on such game shows as *First Impression, Picture This,* and *Play Your Hunch.* On November 28, 1963, Thanksgiving Day evening (11:20 P.M.), she hosted a ninety-minute special entitled *The Phyllis Diller Show* (ABC), directed by Linwood Kingman. Among her guests were Joe Harnell, singer Warde Donovan, and Pete Diller playing the banjo. The magic that she created in person seemed to elude the tube. On radio she could be heard doing such commercials as the big Snow-Crop vegetable and vegetable casserole campaign, which had the catchy opener: "Ladies, when you're as beautiful as I am, who needs to cook?"

Phyllis returned to the Royal Box in July 1964. Leonard Harris of *The New York Times* described the star: "Picture in ascending order, a set of gold booties, a pair of skinny calves, a tinkly gold dress and a sparkling silver choker she insists is made of kidney stones taken from King Farouk. . . . Atop it all, is an incredulous face and a mass of blonde hair that seems to have been arranged by a runaway harvester. At the end of one hand waves a red cigarette holder. . . ." And Phyllis's routines still dealt with domestic problems such as household tips on how to stuff a turkey (spoon fed through the mouth), plastic surgery, airlines, and hostesses.

She was awarded the Golden Dill Award at the Pump Room at the Ambassador Hotel in Chicago, sponsored by the ancient and honorable order of the gilded dill. (It made good press copy for her.) She was still lampooning herself: "The older I get, the funnier I get. Think what I'll save in not having my face lifted."

Phyllis once theorized on the male-dominated field she worked in: ". . . right away you walk out to almost total rejection. Almost nobody wants you to be a female comic and they give you a lot of static just because of your sex. . . . Now it's not necessary so. It frequently is true, but then I still had to go through the onus of that even though I was never unfeminine—cause I'm a feminine person."

On why there are not more female comics: "One thing is they don't have the motivation I had. My big motivation was making money for my kids. And, baby, I'd do anything to get out of Alameda."

On stage personality: "All top flight comics have a basic premise on which they build their humor and characterization. I operated on the premise that I used to be quite lovely until I went to a supermarket and got my face caught in an automatic door. In my comedy, I make cracks about young, pretty girls, and I'm always advising other housewives on life and love."

About audience disturbers: "I don't have hecklers. My timing is so precise, a heckler would have to make an appointment to get a word in."

On success: ". . . guts. It takes so much to make it. Once you've made it, you're the queen and life is beautiful and everybody wants your body and they want to give you gifts. But man, before you make it, *you're* nothin'! You're negative nothin'! You're below zero and you know it, you feel it. However, the secret is don't accept it. It's there, but you never accept it."

Phyllis made her entry as a television series star, with the low-keyed, low-budgeted *Show Street,* a half-hour local ABC-TV originated project from New York, which debuted on September 19, 1964. It was created as a fill-in prelude to the network's fancy Saturday night variety showcase, *The Hollywood Palace.* Phyllis served as emcee for the program, which introduced new and rising talent. Lainie Kazan was the featured guest on the initial show. Phyllis stated recently: "I was very anxious to have a television series. I loved that show. I was offered a second season. However, since I had to fly from wherever I was working on my day off, re-

hearse two shows, tape two shows and then rush back, it was a physical grind. I doubled the price and they dropped the show. I do feel, however, that it paved the way for my next series—*The Pruitts of Southampton* on ABC. *Show Street* claimed Phyllis's presence for thirteen segments.

In 1965, Phyllis made her second venture into feature filmmaking. It was little more than a dry run. *The Fat Spy* had scant release in the United States, and is dubious fodder even for the television market. Phyllis appeared as Camille, a cosmetic manufacturer, seeking the fountain-of-youth beauty formula controlled by rival businessman Brian Donlevy. She tramps off to the Florida Island owned by Donlevy hoping to uncover his secret process. Meanwhile, a group of youths come to the island searching for buried treasure. Donlevy sends his daughter, Jayne Mansfield, to assist the paid caretaker-private detective Jack E. Leonard (who plays a dual role) to keep a wary eye on the invading youths.

Phyllis had relatively few scenes in the film, which was more a showcase for the musical talents of Jordan Christopher and The Wild Ones. The plotline was so haphazard that part way through the script, the story suddenly shifts to Cypress Gardens, Florida, and the almost nonexistent finale is a hasty wrap-up using a series of title cards. *Variety,* in panning the film, did note that Phyllis handled her brief role "credibly." Phyllis reasoned: "I was very anxious to make movies. My agency came up with it. It was unbelievably bad. (A word of advice: "Don't ever work in a tropical swamp during the rainy season among mosquitoes!") About her performance in *The Fat Spy,* she groans "ugh!"

Phyllis continued wowing them in clubs and to a lesser extent on television. She still made zany personal appearances, such as her gimmick presence at the hot line booth for the National Tennis Championship, which found her holding court at Grand Central Station (August 24, 1965).

In her personal life, a reasonable degree of domestic bliss was noticeably absent. She and Sherwood Diller were divorced September 3, 1965. She received custody of the children, with Diller paying a token $1 monthly child support. She claimed general indignities. After the divorce, she and her family spent less time at their suburban Webster Grove, Missouri home. On October 7, 1965, Phyllis married singer Warde Donovan, 49. It was the second marriage for each. He already had two sons, Shane (born 1948), and Toddy (born 1953). Things did not run smoothly for the newlyweds, and they were soon separated. Phyllis did not hesitate to amusingly air her grievances to the press about this post-haste disaster. However, the couple later reunited.

In early 1966, Phyllis filed a legal claim in St. Louis federal court against Sherwood Diller's mother, and his sister, Dr. Jeanne Diller, an osteopath. The comedienne alleged that on October 6, 1965, Diller and his relatives had demanded the television networks forbid Phyllis to make any reference to them, à la Captain Bligh and Moby Dick. Phyllis's suit demanded $50,000, stating that the format and "names" were an "integral and component part of a unique style of humor developed over a number of years at a great cost." The suit was settled out of court.

Under a five-picture movie contract with Bob Hope, Phyllis co-starred with the comedian in his modestly budgeted, color comedy, *Boy, Did I Get a Wrong Number* (1966). The slender plot concerned bubble bath cinema star Elke Sommer who fled the horrors of Hollywood, for a quiet retreat in a small Oregon town. Hope, a local real estate dealer there, accidentally uncovers her identity when trying to place a call through to his wife, Marjorie Lord. Sommer hides out in one of Hope's isolated cabin properties, of which Phyllis, Hope's busybody maid, owns a share. The police eventually locate Sommer, mistakenly think Hope has murdered her, and when he manages to escape their clutches, the cops ride in hot pursuit. Phyllis athletically comes to the rescue on her motorcycle, and is almost successful in impeding the police so her boss can make his getaway. By the finale, Hope is cleared, reconciled with his jealous wife, and Sommer returns to Hollywood and her cheesecake filmmaking. Phyllis is left with the pots and pans, and housecleaning.

Phyllis had little opportunity in this anemic feature to expand on her wacky stage personality. As the frenetic, nosey maid, who eavesdrops on Hope's phone calls and misinterprets his talks with Sommer, she was more eccentric than humorous. Only occasionally did her unique way-outness shine through, as in the kitchen sequence in which she peers into a polished frying pan and exclaims: "Mirror, mirror on the wall—who is the fairest of them all? Okay, shuddup."

Her wild gymnastics in the chase finale were largely the work of stuntmen. She had few chances to display her famed series of exaggerated double takes and broad mugging. Said *Variety:* ". . . [she] is a little nuttier than usual with her wild hair standing every-which way and her humor the kind that hits spectators right in the paunch." Wanda Hale in her two-star *New York Daily News* Review noted: *"And in case you tv fans are interested in the outcome of Phyllis Diller's film debut [sic], it can be dismissed in haste—with a shudder."*

Nevertheless, the effervescent spark of Phyllis's presence worked wonders to bolster Hope's sagging box office record. *Boy Did I Get A Wrong Number* did

extremely well, grossing $4.01 million in domestic rentals. It proved to the industry that Phyllis was able to boost a film's receipts.

In 1966, Phyllis bought the $250,000 twenty-two room Brentwood mansion of Mrs. Merriweather Post. She quickly remodeled and renamed the various rooms of the lush house. There was the Edith Head (bathroom), the Edwin Booth (phone room), etc. A big painting of Bob Hope was on prominent display.

Her *An Evening with Phyllis Diller,* a half-hour color special, was syndicated by Chicago's WGN in 1966. Then she got her own series, *The Pruitts of Southampton,* an ABC video show that Beatrice Lillie had rejected. Inheriting Mr. Ed's dressing room at the Los Angeles filming studio, Phyllis set to work filming segments for the half-hour show. The series premiered September 6, 1966. Its premise cast Phyllis as Phyllis Poindexter Pruitt, a once-wealthy Long Island socialite matron, now an impoverished, but madcap widow. Among the supporting cast were Gypsy Rose Lee as her neighbor Regina, Grady Sutton as the stuffy butler Sturgess, Reginald Gardner as her dottering old uncle Ned, and dour Richard Deacon as Baldwin, the hard-pressing internal revenue agent hounding Phyllis for back taxes. Most episodes pointed up the reality of poverty in contrast to the illusion of wealth.

The critics were not kind. Jack Gould of *The New York Times* complained: "Last night's introduction was totally inept slapstick that only made one appreciate all over again the artistry of Lucille Ball. Miss Diller is just contributing her familiar monologue and patented laugh in new trappings and the show never rises above a personal appearance for its star." Besides cavorting through the less than humorous shenanigans, Phyllis even sang the title tune weekly. But it did not please the powers to be. Cleveland Amory in *TV Guide* commented: ". . . Phyllis still has to work too hard. It's too bad someone hasn't told her that everything in the world is not as broad as it is long, and one important thing that it isn't is—pardon the expression—drawing room comedy."

By January 1967, Phyllis was telling the press: "They tried everything they can think of and fouled it up pretty good. All that mess is over, now we go back to my way." The series moved to a new time slot on January 13, 1967. The program was changed to the *Phyllis Diller Show* and had the elegant Pruitt Mansion turned into a deluxe boarding house with a range of peculiar tenants. It did not help. The series floundered and went off the air on September 11, 1967.

Phyllis joined Bob Hope, James Stewart, Carolyn Jones, Herb Alpert and the Tijuana Brass and others in Warner Brothers "Hollywood Star Spangled Revue," a charity-appeal theatrical short subject released in September 1966. She was among those who went with Hope on his December, 1966 tour of Vietnam and far east Army bases, scoring heavily with the military audiences.

Phyllis was involved in the animated feature film, *Mad Monster Party,* made by Japanese creative talent and American-based performers in 1967. Along with Boris Karloff and others, Phyllis was among those providing the voices for the animated puppets. The story had Baron Frankenstein (Karloff), the master of the secret of destruction, suddenly deciding to name a successor. He invites all the leading monsters of the world to his Isle of Evil. Among those who come there are: Dracula, Werewolf, The Invisible Man, Dr. Jekyll-Mr. Hyde, The Hunchback of Notre Dame, "It," the Monster and his mate (Phyllis), and the Baron's human nephew, Felix Flagin.

Each puppet was designed much as the monster had appeared in feature films. Phyllis's puppet was a miniature of her stage character, mini skirt, ankle boots, cigarette holder, fright wig and all. Phyllis had a song: "You're Different," which demonstrated her interesting if flat singing style.

Once at the island, the Baron reveals to the assembled group his plans to name a successor, indicating that it will most likely be his nephew. This sets the monsters against each other, fighting to gain control and win the throne as the new chief. Phyllis has her series of quips for each occasion: To Dracula: "Don't kiss, you always leave marks." When shaking Wolfman's hand: "Ouch. You need a manicure, baby." About the Mummy: "I wonder how he got his invitation. He has an unlisted tomb." About the werewolf: "Didn't I see him at the Transylvanian Gardens in the main event?" Phyllis refers to Frankenstein's monster as Fang, constantly berating him for his lack of couth. Her puppet's appearance is aptly summed up by Dracula who says: "You look the creature of decadence."

At the finale, "It" proves to be King Kong, and in the mad fighting between the contenders, the Baron's magical new destructive explosive is ignited, and the island is destroyed. Felix escapes with the Baron's secretary, a put-together robot.

Mad Monster Party did not see extensive kiddie matinee release until 1969, a year before it showed up on television. Howard Thompson in *The New York Times* enthused: "In this peppery and contagiously droll little color package, a collection of animated puppets scamper across some clever miniature sets, exchanging sass and barbs and occasionally warbling some sprightly tunes. . . . And the voices applied to the animal figures —Boris Karloff and Phyllis Diller are credited with their own—are a riot."

Eight on the Lam released in mid-1967, provided Phyllis with a more active role. Bank teller Bob Hope is a widower with seven children, and not much money to raise them properly. One night he finds $10,000 on the street, and he is urged by his family and the baby-sitter-housekeeper Goldie (Phyllis) to keep it. When his bank discovers $50,000 is missing, Hope is immediately suspected. Hope thinks his game is truly up, when bumbling pudgy detective Jonathan Winters shows up at the house. In fact, he has come to court his girlfriend Goldie. Phyllis delays Winters, while Hope and his kids escape. They eventually settle at a Nevada dude ranch, with Winters hot on their trail, despite Phyllis's fumbling delaying tactics. After much ado, it is discovered Hope's bank employer, Austin Willis, also at the ranch, is the real culprit. Hope marries his girl, Shirley Eaton, and at the same ceremony Phyllis and Winters are hitched. For once, she gets a man at the story's end.

Highlights of this feeble color comedy include a freeway traffic jam outside Los Angeles, with Phyllis bounding over car tops in an effort to get on her way. The finale chase has the energetic participants tinkering with golf carts and horses, ending with Phyllis and hapless Winters plunked into a swimming pool. Her delayed double take is a gem of careful reaction.

Phyllis received some good reviews. Howard Thompson in *The New York Times* championed: "But the woman of the day is Miss Diller, as a raucous baby-sitter, streaking through the picture like a berserk comet, every hair standing on end." Said *Time* magazine: ". . . Phyllis Diller attacks her customary fright wig role with the comic appeal of a black widow spider putting away a fly."

The lacklustre production did gross $3 million in domestic rentals.

Since stuntman Von Deming doubled for Phyllis in the gymnastics of the traffic jam and finale sequence, only the close-up reaction shots can be credited to Phyllis's talent. She had a few zingy remarks; such as "You point 'em out, and I'll sit on 'em."

About her subdued physical slapstick antics as compared to those of Martha Raye or Carol Burnett, Phyllis has said: "I wish I could do it. One of my main problems is when a writer has written in physical things for me to do that I find impossible to carry off. I am physically delicate to the point of being fragile."

Of her *Eight on the Lam* co-star Jonathan Winters, Phyllis commented: "I have been a fan of his from the time before I was in the business. I love him personally and professionally. However, when we work together I never feel that he relates to me. There is some kind of gap between us."

Phyllis also invaded the world of book-writing full scale, with the publication of *Phyllis Diller's House-*

keeping Hints on October 6, 1966. (She had earlier authored "Phyllis Diller Tells All About Fang" in 1963.) The humor volume, with an introduction by Bob Hope and drawings by Susan Perl, ". . . is filled with such helpful half-truths, quarter-truths, even 1/64 truths. Just like I'm going to say, 'This book was recommended by a marriage counselor,' and I won't add, 'who wanted some business.' " The book was quite successful, going through five printings before it went into a paperback edition in 1968. In 1967, *Phyllis Diller's Marriage Manual* appeared, which was "dedicated to my darling husband, Warde Donovan, the Richard Burton of the Geritol set." The short humor-advice book, also with drawings by Susan Perl, "deals with reality and teaches the kinds of truth not available in other so-called marriage manuals." It was filled with such timely advice as: ". . . get married with the feeling it is going to last. Not like the bride I knew who doubled the wedding cake recipe and froze one." The book concludes with a tongue-in-cheek "happy marriage test which is certain to clear up any remaining problems." Her most recent excursion into the literary world was *Phyllis Diller's Complete Mother* (1969). Phyllis has carefully eschewed utilizing any of the material from her books and record albums in her later stage appearances.

As the first of her four-picture contract with Universal Studios, Phyllis in 1967 starred in *Did You Hear the One about the Traveling Saleslady?* Like the studio's Don Knotts comedies, the movie had limited theatrical release in urban areas, milking instead the rural and kiddie markets.

From its unfunny, sagging opening, the color-Technirama film went downhill fast. The title credits are interspersed between a pantomime of Phyllis whispering a joke to another of the movie's characters, and it being passed on from actor to actor, until, when it is finally retold to her, she smacks the last story-teller.

She is Agatha Knabenshu, descendant of a long line of salesmen. She arrives in Primrose Junction, Missouri, one day in July 1910, raring to peddle her player pianos. After an array of male sellers emerge from the train, Phyllis comes scrambling into view, yelling "Hey fellas, wait for me!" She is bedecked in a grotesque lined chamise, topped by a wild feathered hat. She tosses off one-line jokes to anyone in sight: "Did you hear about the midget why played the tuba and got sucked in?" When the conductor inquires if she is a traveling saleswoman, Phyllis replies: "Let's not bring sex into it." A running joke throughout the film has Phyllis hoisting her skirts à la Claudette Colbert in *It Happened One Night.* The sight so frightens a nearby horse that it scampers off. When she picks on a young male passerby to help her unload her piano, he pleads he must go home to milk the cow. Phyllis shrugs her

spindly shoulders and remarks: "That's the first time I've ever been stood up for a cow." With that, she trudges into the local men's bar and causes a near riot. She attempts to sell a piano to the saloon owner. Sitting herself down at the keyboard, kicking out her zebra colored boots, and sporting her long cigarette holder, she screeches through "In The Good Old Summertime." The sheriff saddles into sight, determined to rid the town of this public nuisance. He intends to arrest her for entertaining without a license. She chirps back: "I guess you didn't hear me sing."

What there is to the meagre plot gets underway, when the local (mis)inventor, and Mr. Fixit, Bob Denver, cannot repair Phyllis's piano, which he has mutilated. To pay for a new demonstration model, they go into partnership. They scheme to enter his automatic milking machine in a competition. However, their trial run causes a cattle stampede. To pay for this latest fiasco, they enter Denver's wood-burning automobile in the Fair's car race. When Denver is arrested, Phyllis drives the makeshift vehicle and manages to win. Then, with the timely aid of Denver's kissing machine, she patches up the problems created by her hurricane-arrival in town.

Phyllis had a wide variety of costume changes in this period piece, including a striped bathing suit number for her modeling chores for amateur photographer Denver. (Phyllis remarks: "I once sent a photograph to a beauty contest. They sent it back. Said they don't accept x-rays.") In the auto race, she has to disguise herself as a man, because she is also wanted by the law. Garbed in a long riding coat, checkered cap, goggles, and a big moustache, she charges off to do her worst. At one point Denver's Pa thinks the only fit use for Phyllis is as a scarecrow, and he plants her on a stake for a spell.

For a geared-for-children picture, there was a surprising number of double entendres and sex-oriented material. When Phyllis's boss telephones her from St. Louis to inquire of her progress, he exhorts his employee: "Remember, you are in virgin territory." Phyllis blushes and cups her hand over the mouthpiece. Later, a crusty old Civil War veteran takes a shine to Phyllis, and in one scene she finds herself in his lap. He tries to kiss her, and she runs off, wondering aloud: "Why do I always get there fifty years too late?" During the hectic car race, one competitor tells her: "I'm going to beat the pants off of you." The indignant Phyllis replies: "If you do, you're in for a big surprise." Later on in the race, another driver inquires: "What happened to your voice." (She has forgotten to maintain her deep-pitched tone.) Phyllis quickly retorts with: "You try riding in this position and see what happens to your voice." At the fadeout, in which everyone is kissing everyone, sneaker-clad Phyllis turns toward the camera, and exclaims: "Welcome to Shangri-la" and partakes in the fraternizing.

One of the few major newspapers to catch, let alone review, this low-budget antic production was *Variety:* ". . . Miss Diller, an excellent comedienne; though in her pictures her one-liner forte must be complemented by other adroit comedy elements generally missing here."

Did You Hear the One about the Traveling Saleslady was filmed in six weeks. Phyllis recalls: "Most of the film was shot out of doors on a very old, very elaborate outdoor set on the back lot of Columbia. The day after we completed outdoor filming that lot burned to the ground." Phyllis states she was uninvolved with the screen image used in this film: "Many people who direct and write for me emphasize the 'always on the make' side of my work. Since I had nothing to do with the writing of the film, I don't really know [why Agatha was such a sex-oriented creature]."

Another luckless film venture, was Phyllis's guest role in *The Silent Treatment,* made in the fall of 1967, and yet to be released. The producers capitalized on the idea of having well-known comics perform cameo parts in a story that would be filmed without dialogue. The slim plot had Marty Engels winning a contest sponsored by an advertising agency. To collect the $10,000 prize, he must first live for two weeks on a lavish scale, without spending a penny. Sherry Jackson portrayed the girl from the agency, who falls in love with him; Paul Lynde was his boss. Among others in this $150,000 production filmed in Los Angeles were Rowan and Martin, Jerry Lewis, Wally Cox, Jackie Coogan, Rudy Vallee, Gene Autry, Barry Sullivan, George Raft, and Godfrey Cambridge. Phyllis had two scenes in this helter-skelter project: in one, she and Engels are at a cage type counter procuring a marriage license. In her other sequence, she is a lady of the evening who accepts credit cards."

On October 25, 1967, Phyllis starred in another television special, *The Phyllis Diller Happening* (NBC). Among her guests were Bob Hope, Sonny and Cher, Mike Douglas, and trumpeter Hugh Masakela. One prolonged skit found her and Hope as the last surviving hippies on earth. Said *The New York Times:* "The show was Miss Diller's and, while she's an engaging hostess, she doesn't seem strong enough as a comedienne or as a personality to carry a program without a Bob Hope to bring it alive."

And then she was given another series, *The Beautiful Phyllis Diller Show,* which debuted on NBC on September 15, 1968. The Sunday evening hour program was videotaped in Hollywood. Guests on the first outing were Johnny Carson, Ed MacMahon, Rowan and Martin, Sonny and Cher, Norm Crosby and the Pearce Sisters Juvenile jazz band. There was little to distinguish this program from the myriad of other variety shows populating the tube.

The New York Times criticized: "A little more of Miss Diller as a gracious human being might handily add to the effectiveness of her flight into extreme horseplay." On the other hand, *Variety* thought: ". . . the gawky comedienne is a novel and strangely appealing femcee for an hour variety show. . . . Rivved up regular Rip Taylor appeared in a hair-dresser sketch with Miss Diller which was that deep in the television groove a viewer felt he could write it himself."

After many false starts, the show died a quiet death and left the air December 22, 1968. Phyllis bemoaned: "My show really didn't have much of an image, it was just another show. . . . Everything around me should have been a caricature when I was mixed up with it. Gee whiz, I guess they wanted to make an actress out of me, or something . . . it was played so straight. . . . You can't mix up the public. They've got to know exactly what you're about. I made a mistake going along with the serious part of the show. Never again. For one thing, I found out I'm a rotten interviewer."

Meanwhile, her third and last film to date with Bob Hope, *The Private Navy of Sergeant O'Farrel,* had a quiet saturation release around the country throughout the latter part of 1968. The hodgepodge plot presented Hope as an overripe master sergeant on a small Pacific island base, Funapee, during World War II. To boost the morale of his men, Hope arranges for a huge shipment of beer to be sent to the desolate foothold; but the ship carrying it is torpedoed by a Japanese submarine. To make up for this loss, Hope persuades his superior officer to have a bevy of beautiful nurses commandeered to Funapee from stateside. However, teetotaler Lt. Commander John Myhers sabotages Hope's plot again, and the nurse corps consists of one sole scarecrow female, Phyllis. She is overjoyed to be trapped on an island with all these woman-hungry men.

Daffy Phyllis joins forces with Hope, a Japanese-American deserter, and Navy lieutenant Jeffrey Hunter to track down the sunken cargo of beer. By the closeout, Hope has shot down a Japanese Zero, captured an enemy sub, been reunited with his prewar fiancee Gina Lollobrigida, and been proclaimed a hero.

Variety penned: "Bob Hope and Phyllis Diller will constitute the prime draw for *The Private Navy of Sergeant O'Farrel,* an okay but crudely plotted comedy set in World War II. . . . Hope is engaging a boxoffice resurgence, particularly with Miss Diller his frequent television comedy partner, so a certain amount of box office action must be expected." The color production garnered $2.4 million in domestic rentals.

Phyllis had less opportunity to exert her exuberance in this film, hemmed in by the overly-involved plot, and having to share the limelight with so many other top-featured performers. She had an amusing sequence in which she tracked down Hope's jungle-hidden liquor still, sniffing it out like a St. Bernard. She reports the find to Hope's commander, who immediately orders the still blown up. Sent into the bush for protection, she encounters the friendly Japanese-American. Wild with fear, she shrieks: "They've landed!", and in her panic runs out into the open, falling down near the burning fuse of the explosives. Hope rushes in to save her. Another brief episode had Jeffrey Hunter dreaming of Phyllis as a tempting Eve and a devastating Cleopatra, which allowed Phyllis to cavort in costume à la Imogene Coca. Throughout, she was tossing off self-deprecating wisecracks about her failure to attract men.

When queried about her three Bob Hope movies, Phyllis informed the author that she had no part in writing her screen characterizations: "I did every word exactly as it was written in the script. Mr. Hope doesn't allow anyone to mess with the script. Sometimes he changes a little something or asks the writers of the script to give him something stronger." Phyllis stated that none of her performed scenes from Hope movies were cut at all.

By now, Phyllis was earning $1 million a year, an impressive feat for a fifty-year-old former housewife. She had a large staff: three scriptwriters, an executive housekeeper, secretary, five gardeners, two car mechanics (she has eight cars) three maids and a butler, four assistant secretaries. No longer did Phyllis gather and collect all her stage material herself. In the early 1960s, she had relied heavily on jokes sent from the public through the mails. As the volume got heavier, she hired two editors to process the material. If she bought the joke, she had a copy of the joke typed out and returned with the payment check. Phyllis found that the best jokes came from housewives, the same audience she was always projecting to in her act. "The closer [the joke] is based to absolute solid truth, the funnier it is because you bring out a funny attitude in a great truth."

Now Phyllis was constantly being quoted as an expert jokester, one in the same league as her idol Bob Hope. When asked about her delivery and its content of jokes: "Bob Hope goes for six huge boffs a minute and he says that his writers have clocked my work and he claims I get twelve. Course, I talk faster and my material is geared differently. I work more frantically than he does. I work wild—like a woman would. He lays it right out and then looks at you."

About the media: "I find it's the same problem no matter where you are. You either make 'em laugh or you don't. I love to play tents, I love radio, I love television, I love club work, I love theatre, I love it all."

Re agents: "Your act sells you. Your agents don't sell you. It's not possible to sell things like that. You create the demands—you must create the demand. You have to do all the work. You do it out on stage in the lights. That's where all the work happens."

About her following: "The first group that supported me insanely were faggots. They were my maddest fans. The next group that I rolled up into a nice little ball were housewives . . . when my material stopped being chi chi and music and talk . . . when it became more talk and it became more center-based in my world—home, children, family, sex, automobiles. Then I had picked up all the women. Then through the women I got the men. Then through my Snowy Bleach commercials and my 'Pruitts' series, I got the kids; you would not believe the kids—what fans they are."

Phyllis was in great demand as the subject of magazine articles, wanted for charity guest appearances, and all the other obvious indices of top stardom. Like many other upper echelon performers, she went the merchandizing route, forming BAM (Believe All Magic) Corporation. Then there was Oma of Omaha, her dressmaker, which created a line of patch-work pillows and quilts.

In 1968, Phyllis was announced by Universal as a star in a movie version of Elmer Rice's famed play *The Adding Machine*. Art Carney was at first scheduled to play opposite her, but later dropped out, and was replaced by Milo O'Shea. Producer-director-scripter Jerome Epstein thought Phyllis was just the type the playwright had in mind for the part. When she went to England for the lensing, she quipped to the press: "I wanted to help Lady Bird Johnson's program to keep America beautiful, so I left the country." While filming the movie at London's Shepperton Studio, Phyllis made several appearances on British television.

The Adding Machine (1969) is her last theatrical motion picture to date. In this pessimistic fantasy, O'Shea was Mr. Zero, a downtrodden bookkeeper in a big store. To compensate for his nagging wife (Phyllis), he dreams of an affair with Billie Whitelaw, a coworker. When he is replaced by a newly invented adding machine he murders his boss. Later, he is convicted, condemned, executed and goes to heaven, only to be put in charge of an adding machine in the hodge-podge world there, with the bleak knowledge that he will be reincarnated on earth and must endure the same hellish routine all over again. Phyllis played the shrewish wife, wearing no makeup, no false eyelashes, no contact lenses, no crazy laughter; with her straight dark hair tied back in a bun.

The Adding Machine was not released until September 23, 1969, when it had a limited art house release at the Kips Bay Theatre in Manhattan, and disappeared from distribution soon thereafter. *The New York Times* was generally unimpressed: "Although Phyllis Diller, because of name value draws first star billing, as a shrewish New York wife who has nagged her bookkeeper husband for twenty-five years, Milo O'Shea in this role cops top interest . . . Miss Diller socks over her nagging with a vengeance." Barry Glasser of *Motion Picture Daily* was more enthusiastic about her offbeat characterization: "Miss Diller is in command of what she is doing all the way, exemplified by a five-minute scene midway through the film and the last she appears in. O'Shea, on the morning of his execution, is visited by his wife eagerly anticipating the martyrdom of notorious widowhood. It's a difficult posture to bring off comically and she does it adroitly. That short sequence highlights an otherwise listless enterprise." The British *Films and Filming* in reviewing this production, set in Manhattan of the 1930s, thought she ". . . proves herself an able dramatic actress."

That same month, Phyllis was hospitalized for acute gastritis and over-exhaustion. Her jokes to the press got better coverage and reviews than her solo attempt at serious filmmaking. Phyllis snapped: "I've been eating my own cooking. My hair isn't in such great shape either."

Slowly, but surely, the public was becoming accustomed to the tremendous surprise of viewing Phyllis in her off-stage garb, when she was well-dressed. In October 1969, she told a *New York Morning Telegraph* reporter: "I have convinced the public through the tube that I'm a monster. They don't believe I'm elegant until they see me in person. Then their first reaction is: 'My God, she's pretty.'"

When she returned to the Royal Box club in Manhattan in late 1969, reviewers recorded: "Her references to her husband are still the main prop of her act. This time in, her material is far better than it has been previously." Regarding husband Warde Donovan, who usually appeared on her bill: "He seems to have the knack of taking highly interesting material and making in mundane."

Like her mentor Bob Hope, Phyllis continued to be all over the tube, appearing on such shows as NBC's *Laugh-In* and *Hollywood Squares* and ABC's *Love American Style*.

No one in the entertainment world was prepared for producer David Merrick's announcement in late 1969 that Phyllis Diller would take over the lead role in the ultra-long-running Broadway musical, *Hello, Dolly!* which had already starred Carol Channing, Ginger Rogers, Martha Raye, Betty Grable and Pearl Bailey. Phyllis told reporters that she would closely study and follow the script. After all, she reasoned: "Dolly is a nice woman and my standup character is an idiot."

By early January 1970, Phyllis was ensconced on the Main Stem as Dolly Levi. In reviewing her performance, Clive Barnes of *The New York Times* concluded: "Miss Diller, making what I presume is her Broadway debut, is, I suspect, something of an acquired taste that, clearly unlike most of the audience, I have never acquired. But she sings a lot better than I feared a cabaret artist might, she mugs affectionately to her audience and keeps the thing going. Even so, when Dolly comes down that staircase, call it charisma, call it chutzpah, call it what you like, but she either has it or she hasn't. For me, Miss Diller hasn't."

At the end of March 1970, Ethel Merman replaced Phyllis. The comedienne admitted that performing in the show had cost her $200,000 in delayed club dates. Merrick had given her a guaranteed salary plus a percentage of the weekly profit. However, the filmed version of the comedy starring Barbra Streisand opened on Broadway in early 1970 and cut deeply into the potential audience for the stage version. Phyllis does admit: "It was one of the most glorious things I ever did as far as my satisfaction goes."

Recuperating from her show run, Phyllis prepared for another world tour of nightclubs. Before embarking, she made sure the American public would not forget her during her brief absence. She prepared a batch of television commercials, such as the one she made for In-Sink-Erator, which she pitched as a "Successor to Fang as the world's finest garbage disposer." Then on June 17, 1970, she opened the first Phyllis Diller Exotic Plant Store in the New York area at 1320 Third Avenue. When asked what had prompted her venture into this particular arena of commerce, Phyllis answered: "In my very first apartment in Ohio I bought twenty ivy plants. They all died. They got that white stuff all over them." (And she has never outgrown her love of greens.) On the road, she always buys plants for her suite, and then at the end of her stay, she gives them as gifts to the hotel employees. She mentioned that her husband, Warde Donovan, ". . . has such a thing about plastic plants. He kicks them and sometimes he even spits on them in hotel lobbies."

Reporting on Phyllis's engagement at London's Toast of the Town theatre-restaurant, the October 29, 1970, *Village Voice* carried a bylined review by Charles Marowitz:

Diller is a mugger and a mouthpiece. I believe she shares some of Hope's writers; I guessed as much because behind her endless stream of abuse against ugly women, fat women, horrid in-laws, there is something mechanistically routine. Like some oddly chosen go-between, she conveys what the committee intellect has conceived. She has all the traditional equipment: timing, a sense of comic delivery, the ability to milk and to mug, and yet one feels, after 40 minutes in her company, she is a stranger. A stranger albeit, with some marvelously wrought comedy material to dispense. . . . There is more to stand-up comedy than a manic committment to anatomical derision. I suppose she would say that's her 'thing.' She is an odd-looking lady making capital out of being unlovely. But she pushes unloveliness so far it almost conjures up a need for its opposite. We want her to say something funny about being pretty or wanted or sympathetic. . . .
. . . She is a true pro, and her professionalism is clearly seen. But I felt all through the evening her material was preventing me from touching her, from knowing her, and I grew to dislike it the way one does a host who elongates introductions when you're anxious to shake somebody by the hand.

Back in the States, Phyllis continued her round of television guesting. When she appears on a talk show, according to Phyllis, "I dress normally as I would for a social engagement. In other words, when I wear the fright wig, the dog collar, gloves, cigarette holder and boots, I am the onstage 'comic' Phyllis Diller. The cigarette holder is really the difference between me on stage and me for real." Gradually, Phyllis is introducing more music into her act, but she hesitates to reintroduce singing into her own performance, preferring to be teamed with such singers as Barbara McNair, the Establishments, or Jack Jones.

In November 1970, newspapers carried a big feature story on Phyllis's non-smoking cruise. She had been hired by a New York group, the Institute for New Motivations, to be the guest performer on a luxury liner, going from Manhattan to the Caribbean, carrying 250 "nicotine fiends." And Phyllis was up to her own brand of publicity-getting wisecracks. According to her this was not the first non-smoking cruise. "There was a similar one on a ship called the *Titanic*. No one ever smoked after that cruise." Or: "Isn't it marvelous that when you've finished this cruise and given up smoking you can look forward to another cruise right away? This one will be so you can take the cure for alcoholism you've picked up while giving up cigarettes."

On January 13, 1971, Phyllis made—at least according to publicity releases—her television dramatic debut on *Night Gallery* (NBC). In the Rod Serling episode, "Pamela's Voice," she was co-starred with John Astin in a two-character yarn about a haunting with a weird twist. It dealt with a magpie wife, murdered by her husband who wreaks her own ironic revenge. Save for being better garbed, her monologue bore a striking resemblance to her shrewish wife character from *The Adding Machine*.

Phyllis is deeply committed to personal appearances in order to keep her timing sharp. She was performing at the Now Grove, Los Angeles, when *Variety* reviewed her January 12, 1971, opening: "Miss Diller, sticking to format that put her up there, appears in silver outfit and cigaret holder, whips her one-liners across with customary zeal and timing. Hubby Fang, the neighborhood, plastic surgery, Mrs. Kleen, the kids —all get their lumps. If material is familiar, comedienne still manages to flash brightly and turns on audience." Since then, she has returned to the Las Vegas nitery scene and other spots across America.

The legend of Phyllis grows and grows, as she continues to mop up the arenas of past victories and waits for new fields to conquer. She is eager to appear in more movies, especially one with friend Ruth Gordon. She only regrets not having been offered the role of the madam in *The Cheyenne Social Club* (1970) because she would have adored working with James Stewart and Henry Fonda. Bob Hope has further plans for her. According to Phyllis: "I have noticed that Bob always uses me in a service role (maid, baby sitter, nurse). He is currently working on a [television] series for me where I would be a waitress. Somehow he always sees me in uniform—and you know how fond he is of people in uniform!"

On February 26, 1971, Phyllis was the subject of Ralph Edwards's *This Is Your Life* (ABC-TV), with Bob Hope as the chief celebrity guest (courtesy of videotape). The synthetic and saccharine quality of the program was fortuitously softened by the genuine warmth that Phyllis radiated and the patience she demonstrated when confronted by syrupy Edwards who seemed to have not the least idea of what Phyllis did for a living or what her brand of humor might be about.

In August, 1971, a pilot for *Phyllis Diller, Kitchen Kween* was scheduled to be shot by Tomorrow Entertainment, Inc., the General Electric subsidiary, with plans to syndicate the program for fall release. The project came to naught.

Obviously, Phyllis has a very good press agent ready to get her coverage on every conceivable occasion.

When the show business world was agog over the obvious restraints clamped down on the shooting of Paramount's *The Godfather,* a release quietly appeared in the trade paper stating Clair Huffaker had prepared an original screenplay for a new film entitled *The Godmother* and that none other than Phyllis would have the lead role in this Norman Baer production. Needless to say, nothing further developed on this way out project.

Recently, Phyllis has cut down on the number of television guest appearances she makes, but she was among the eighteen female personalities on *The Bob Hope Special* (September 20, 1971, NBC-TV), which finally united her with another slapstick queen, Martha Raye, as well as such other divergent types as Dr. Joyce Brothers, Imogene Coca, Sue Lyon, Jacqueline Susann, and Barbara McNair. *Variety* reported: "Only Martha Raye, Phyllis Diller and Jo Anne Worley—knockabout comics to a girl—put any extra effort into their characterizations."

Just to end the old year on a new note, Phyllis made her debut as a serious concert pianist December 31, 1971, at the Apparel Mart Showtime in Dallas. With the 85-piece Dallas Symphony Orchestra backing her, she performed Beethoven's First Piano Concerto. She ended the evening on a familiar strain, by reverting to comedy routines from her club act.

Phyllis is now a grandmother. Her daughter Suzanne, married and since divorced, gave birth to a child Paul Mills on November 7, 1969. Phyllis's oldest son Peter, a county assessor for Los Angeles, has written four film scripts of the *Dr. Strangelove* variety.

Not to be outdone, the multi-talented Phyllis has even penned her own prayer, a sentiment which gives insight into her *raison d'être.* "On this happy day we are thankful for our blessings and we pray for renewed belief in ourselves and each other, and hope this bond of love will expand to envelop the entire universe."

FILMOGRAPHY: PHYLLIS DILLER

Feature Films

SPLENDOR IN THE GRASS (Warner Brothers, 1961) 124 M.
Producer-director, Elia Kazan; associate producer, William Inge, Charles H. Maguire; screenplay, Inge; assistant director, Don Kranze; choreography, George Tapps; music, David Amram; production designer, Richard Sylbert; camera, Boris Kaufman; editor, Gene Milford.

Natalie Wood (Wilma Dean Loomis); Warren Beatty (Bud Stamper); Pat Hingle (Ace Stamper); Audrey Christie (Mrs. Loomis); Barbara Loden (Ginny Stamper); Zohra Lampert (Angelina); Fred Stewart (Del Loomis); Joanna Roos (Mrs. Stamper); Jan Norris (Juanita Howard); Gary Lockwood (Toots); Sandy Dennis (Kay); Crystal Field (Hazel); Marla Adams (June); Lynn Loring (Carolyn); John McGovern (Doc Smiley); Martine Bartlett (Miss Metcalf); Sean Garrison (Glenn); William Inge (Minister); Charles Robinson (Johnny Masterson); Phyllis Diller (Texas Guinan); Phoebe MacKay (Maid).

THE FAT SPY (Magna, 1965) 75 M.
Producer, Everett Rosenthal; director, Joseph Cates; screenplay, Matthew Andrews; music, Al Kasha, Joel Hirshhorn, Hans Hunter; assistant director, George Goodman; camera, Joseph Brun; editor, Barry Malkin.

Phyllis Diller (Camille); Jack E. Leonard (Irving/Herman); Brian Donlevy (Wellington); Jayne Mansfield (Junior); Jordan Christopher (Frankie); The Wild Ones (Themselves); Johnny Tillotsin (Dodo); Lauree Berger (Nanette); Lou Nelson (The Sikh); Toni Lee Shelly (Mermaid); Penny Roman (Herself); Adam Keefe (Special Voice).

BOY, DID I GET A WRONG NUMBER! (United Artists, 1966) 99 M.
Producer, Edward Small; associate producer, George Beck; director, George Marshall; story, George Beck; screenplay, Burt Styler; Albert E. Lewin, George Kennett; assistant director, Herbert S. Greene; art director, Frank Sylos; music, Richard Lasalle; camera, Lionel Lindon; editor, Grant Whytock.

Bob Hope (Tom Meade); Elke Sommer (Didi); Phyllis Diller (Lily); Cesar Danova (Pepe); Marjorie Lord (Martha Meade); Kelly Thordson (Schwartz); Benny Baker (Regan); Terry Burnham (Doris Meade); Joyce Jameson (Telephone Operator); Harry Von Zell (Newscaster); Kevin Burchett (Larry Meade); Keith Taylor (Plympton); John Tod Roberts (Newsboy).

MAD MONSTER PARTY (Embassy, 1966) 94 M.
Executive producer, Joseph E. Levine; producer, Arthur Rankin Jr.; director, Jules Bass; screenplay, Lee Korobkin, Harvey Kurtzman; songs, Maury Laws, Jules Bass.

Voices of: Boris Karloff, Ethel Ennis, Gale Garnett, Phyllis Diller.

THE SILENT TREATMENT—Unreleased—Filmed, October '67
Producer-director, Ralph Andrews; associate producer, Frank Worth.

Marty Engels, Phyllis Diller, Rowan and Martin, Jerry Lewis, Wally Cox, Jackie Coogan, Rudy Vallee, Gene Autry, John Forsyte, Maureen Arthur, Sherry Jackson, Pat Carroll, Rose Marie, Barry Sullivan, George Raft, Paul Lynde, Godfrey Cambridge, Aldo Ray, Forrest Tucker.

EIGHT ON THE LAM (United Artists, 1967) 107 M.

Associate producer, Bill Lawrence; director, George Marshall; story, Bob Fisher, Arthur Marx; screenplay, Albert E. Lewin, Burt Styler, Fisher, Marx; assistant director, Frank Baur; art director, Walter Simonds; music, George Romanis; camera, Alan Stenvold; editor, Grant Whytlock.

Bob Hope (Henry Dimsdale); Phyllis Diller (Golda); Jonathan Winters (Jasper Lynch); Shirley Eaton (Ellie Barton); Jill St. John (Monica Day); Kevin Brodie (Steve); Stacy Maxwell (Linda); Robert Hope (Mike); Glenn Gilger (Andy); Avis Hope (Dana); Debi Storm (Lois); Michael Freeman (Mark); Austin Willis (Mr. Pomeroy); Peter Leeds (Marty).

DID YOU HEAR THE ONE ABOUT THE TRAVELING SALESLADY? (Universal, 1968) 96 M.

Executive producer, Edward J. Montagne; producer, Si Rose; director, Don Weis; story, Jim Fritzell, Everett Greenbaum; screenplay, John Fenton Murray; assistant director, Phil Bowles, Robin Clark; art director, Alexander Golitzen, Robert C. MacKichan; music, Vic Mizzy; camera, Bud Thackery; editor, Edward Haire, Dale Johnson.

Phyllis Diller (Agatha Knabenshu); Joe Flynn (Hubert Shelton); Bob Denver (Bertram Webb); Eileen Wesson (Jeanine Morse); Paul Reed (Pa Webb); Jeanette Nolan (Ma Webb); Bob Hastings (Lyle Chatterton); George Neise (Ben Milford); Anita Eubank (Young Girl); David Hartman (Frank Jennings); Kelly Thordsen (Enoch Scraggs) and: Jane Dulo, Charles Lane, Dallas McKennon, Herb Vigran, Lloyd Kino, Warde Donovan, Eddie Quillan, Eddie Ness.

THE PRIVATE NAVY OF SGT. O'FARRELL (United Artists, 1968) 92 M.

Producer, John Beck; director, Frank Tashlin; story, John L. Greene, Robert M. Fresco; screenplay, Tashlin; art director, Bob Knoshita; music, Harry Suskman; assistant director, Kurt Neuman; special effects, Charles Spurgeon; camera, Alan Stensvold; editor, Eda Warren.

Bob Hope (M/Sgt. Dan O'Farrell); Phyllis Diller (Nurse Nellie Krause); Jeffrey Hunter (Lt. Lyman P. Jones); Gina Lollabrigida (Maria); Mylene Demongeot (Gaby); John Mhyers (Lt. Comdr. Roger Snavely); Mako (Calvin Coolidge Ishimuna); Henry Wilcoxon (Rear Adm. Arthur L. Stokes); Dick Sargent (Capt. Elwood Prohaska); Christopher Dark (Pvt. George Strongbow); Michael Burns (Pvt. Johnny Bannon); William Wellman, Jr. (Cpl. Kennedy); Robert Donner (Marine Pvt. Ogg); Jack Grinnage (Pvt. Roberts); William Christopher (Pvt. Jack Schultz); John Spina (Cpl. Miller).

THE ADDING MACHINE (Universal, 1969) 99 M.

Producer-director, Jerome Epstein; based on the play by Elmer Rice; screenplay, Epstein; assistant director, Ray Corbett; art director, Jack Shampan, John Lagen; music, Mike Leander, Lambert Williamson; camera, Walter Lassally; editor, Gerry Hambling.

Phyllis Diller (Mrs. Zero); Milo O'Shea (Zero); Billie Whitelaw (Daisy); Sidney Chaplin (Lt. Charles); Julian Glover (Shrdlu); Raymond Huntley (Smithers); Phil Brown (Ben); Libby Morris (Ethel); Hugh McDermott (Harry); Paddie O'Neil (Mabel); Carol Cleveland (July); Bruce Boa (Detective); John Brandon (First Cell Jailer); Kenny Damon (Joe); Hal Galili (Second Cell Jailer); Tony Caunter (Third Cell Jailer); Bill Hutchinson (Judy's Lover); Helen Elliott (Second Apartment Girl); C. Denier Warren (Jury Foreman); Tommy Duggan (Judge); John Bloomfield, Helena Stevens, Alan Surtees, Christine Pryor, Cal McCord, Shirley Cooklin, Anthony Harwood (Apartment Tenants); Bill Nagy (Lawyer); Nicholas Stuart (District Attorney); Gordon Sterne, Mike Reed (Exercise Yard Guards); Lola Lloyd (Coffee Girl); George Margo (Gateman in Arcade); George Roderick (Hot Dog Vendor); Janet Brown (Fat Woman); Janie Baron (Thin Woman); John Cook (Husband).

Phyllis Diller as a baby, 1917.

Phyllis Diller in Chicago, 1937.

With Peter, Sally, Sue, Stephanie and Perry, c. 1953.

With Jack E. Leonard in *The Fat Spy* (Magna Pictures, 1965).

In *Boy, Did I Get a Wrong Number!* (UA, 1966).

With Bob Hope in *Boy, Did I Get a Wrong Number!*

In *Boy, Did I Get a Wrong Number!*

With Bob Hope, Elke Sommer in *Boy, Did I Get a Wrong Number!*

Caricature, publicising Phyllis's ABC-TV show, *The Pruitts of Southampton* (1964).

From *The Pruitts of Southampton.*

From *The Pruitts of Southampton.*

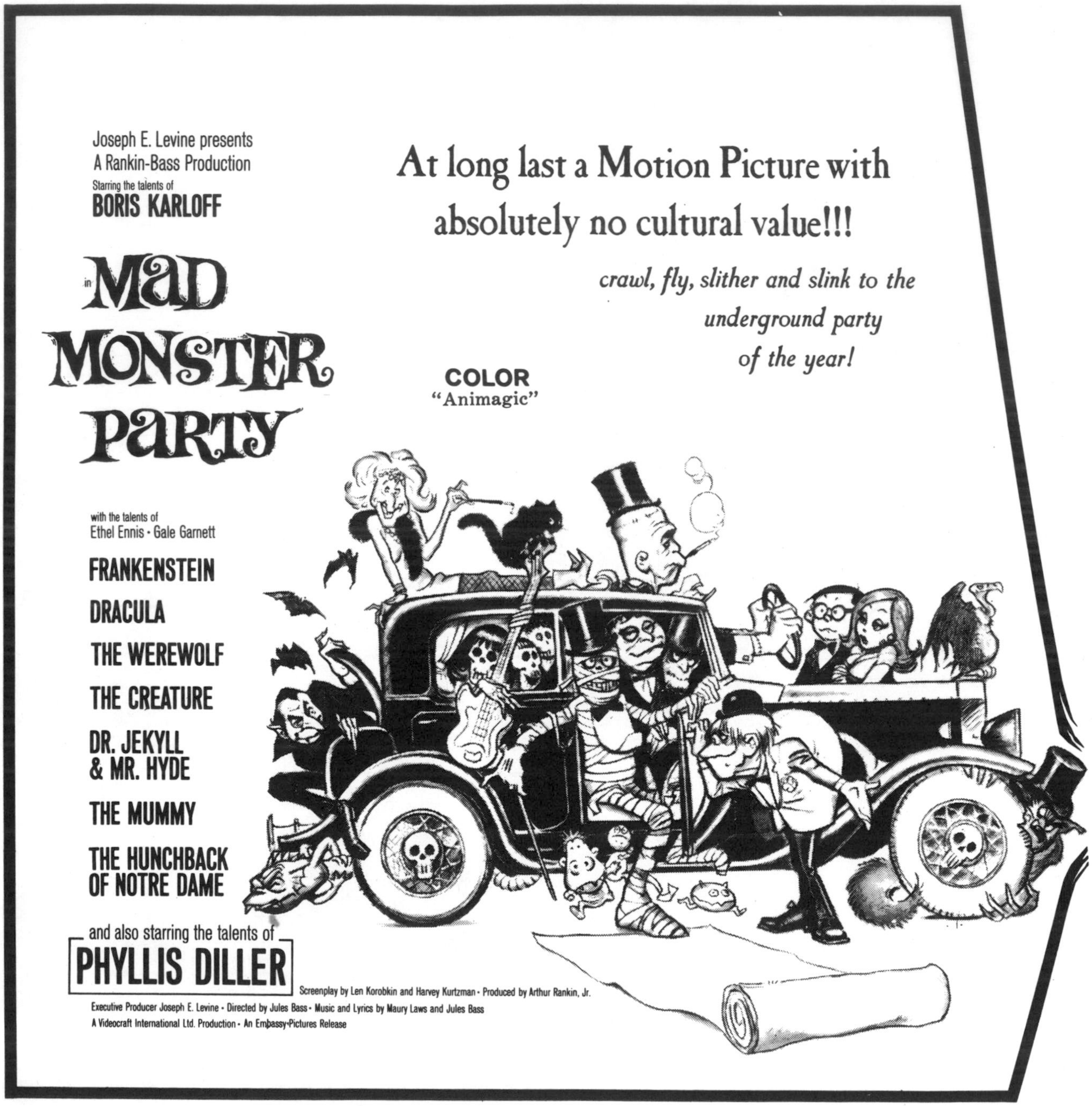

Advertisement for *Mad Monster Party* (Embassy, 1967).

With Bob Hope on his TV special, 1967.

With Paul Lynde on ABC-TV.

In *8 on the Lam* (UA, 1967).

In *8 on the Lam.*

With Jonathan Winters in *8 on the Lam.*

With Bob Denver in *Did You Hear The One About
The Traveling Saleslady?* (Universal, 1964).

Phyllis's husband, Warde Donovan, is at the far left in this pose.

In *Traveling Saleslady.*

With Kate Smith on NBC-TV (1968).

As Eve in *The Private Navy of Sgt. O'Farrell* (UA, 1968).

With Mylene Demongeot in *The Private Navy of Sgt. O'Farrell.*

With Phil Brown, Libby Morris, Paddie O'Neil, Hugh
McDermott in *The Adding Machine* (Universal, 1969).

In *The Adding Machine.*

With Milo O'Shea in *The Adding Machine.*

In *The Adding Machine.*

In *Hello, Dolly!* on Broadway (1970).

Backstage with Bob Hope in *Hello, Dolly!*

On the Tom Jones ABC-TV special, 1970.

On NBC-TV's *Night Gallery*.

Phyllis Diller in 1971.

The New Phyllis Diller.